ENGAGING LEVITICUS

ENGAGING LEVITICUS

Reading Leviticus Theologically
with Its Past Interpreters

Mark W. Elliott

CASCADE *Books* • Eugene, Oregon

ENGAGING LEVITICUS
Reading Leviticus Theologically with Its Past Interpreters

Copyright © 2012 Mark W. Elliott. All rights reserved. Except for brief quotations in critical publications or reviews, no part of this book may be reproduced in any manner without prior written permission from the publisher. Write: Permissions, Wipf and Stock Publishers, 199 W. 8th Ave., Suite 3, Eugene, OR 97401.

Cascade Books
A Division of Wipf and Stock Publishers
199 W. 8th Ave., Suite 3
Eugene, OR 97401

www.wipfandstock.com

ISBN 13: 978-61097-411-0

Cataloging-in-Publication data:

Elliott, M. W. (Mark W.)

Engaging Leviticus : reading Leviticus theologically with its past interpreters / Mark W. Elliott.

xliv + 332 p. ; 25.4 cm. Includes bibliographical references.

ISBN 13: 978-1-61097-411-0

1. Bible. O.T. Leviticus—Commentaries. 2. Bible—Reader-response criticism. 3. Bible—History. I. Title.

BS1255.53 E45 2012

Manufactured in the U.S.A.

To Chris Seitz

Contents

Acknowledgements · ix
Introduction · xi
Abbreviations · xxii
Gallery of Major Interpreters of Leviticus · xxiii

COMMENTARY
Leviticus 1 · 1
Leviticus 2 · 13
Leviticus 3 · 22
Leviticus 4 · 28
Leviticus 5 · 39
Leviticus 6 · 49
Leviticus 7 · 58
Leviticus 8 · 67
Leviticus 9 · 82
Leviticus 10 · 90
Leviticus 11 · 98
Leviticus 12 · 113
Leviticus 13 · 126
Leviticus 14 · 139
Leviticus 15 · 147
Leviticus 16 · 157
Leviticus 17 · 174
Leviticus 18 · 182
Leviticus 19 · 196
Leviticus 20 · 210
Leviticus 21 · 223

Leviticus 22 · 235
Leviticus 23 · 243
Leviticus 24 · 255
Leviticus 25 · 268
Leviticus 26 · 288
Leviticus 27 · 301

Bibliography · 313

Acknowledgments

THE FIRST SKETCHES FOR this commentary were done in 2005 then followed up by research during a leave semester in 2008 spent at *L'Ecole Biblique*, Jerusalem, Wycliffe College, Toronto, and the University of Regensburg. I would like to thank all I met at these places, but for intellectual and spiritual hospitality I would like to single out Donald Rappé, Pavel Trzopek, Justin Taylor, Jerome Murphy-O'Connor, Gregory Tatum, and Terence Crotty in Jerusalem; Chris Seitz and Ephraim Radner in Toronto (also for their continuing interest); and Andreas Merkt, Tobias Nicklas, Christoph Dohmen, and Rev. Rhona Dunphy at Regensburg. Around this time papers at SBL meetings, both Annual and International, the Biblical Colloquium at Louvain, the Geneva Calvin Conference, and other such *fora* enabled me to try out some ideas.

The following year (2009) further progress was made through reading Leviticus 1–12 and its reception with a master's class, here in St. Andrews. 2010, however, was the year in which most of the hard work of writing was done. I am particularly appreciative of the space I found in New College Library, Edinburgh, away from interruptions. I am indebted to other libraries and their special collections—at St. Andrews, Edinburgh, Glasgow, Cambridge, Oxford, Manchester, and the British Library as well as the *Bibliothèque Nationale*, Paris, and the theology library at Munich. The Institute for Bible, Theology, and Hermeneutics in the Divinity School here at St. Andrews has given me some context in which to carry out such research. I have especially appreciated the interest, expertise, and friendship of Dr. Bill Tooman, Dr. Alison Jack, and Prof. Alan Torrance over the last two years or so. Profs. Chris Rowland and Markus Bockmuehl of Oxford have offered constant encouragement from a long way back, and Profs. Gary Anderson and Donald Collett more recently. My parents, Ian and Ann, have continued unflaggingly in their support, for which I am unreservedly grateful.

Acknowledgments

In early 2011 I found a publisher and an editor who believed in the project enough to take it largely as it was, with all its idiosyncrasies. As one who felt that the story of the Jewish reception of Leviticus required specialized treatment and that any impressionistic account could do more harm than good, the openness of Wipf and Stock and Robin Parry to something quite one-sidedly Christian has been welcome, where other publishers and editors had proved to be less sympathetic. I have appreciated the cheerful efficiency of Heather Carraher in preparing the manuscript for publication.

These kinds of "experimental" commentaries in whatever series have been going now for barely a decade and so I hope that this offering will contribute to a maturing of the genre, even while it serves its primary purpose of showing how the history of interpretation helps to cast light on the texts of the Bible and even through them.

Chris Seitz ran a Scripture and Theology seminar at St. Andrews where not only I but also a generation of St. Andrews postgraduates learned to do exegesis, hermeneutics, and theology at the one sitting, on a weekly basis, in a congenial atmosphere. Since then Chris has gone on to do even more in this area, principally with students and colleagues on the other side of the Atlantic. It is with gratitude and affectionate respect that I dedicate this volume to him.

Mark W. Elliott
St Mary's College
St Andrews University
June 1, 2011

Introduction

"There may be many things there, chiefly in the booke of Leviticus, touching ceremonies that will make a man wonder wherefore they did serve. But thou, O man of God, what ever thou reads into that booke, reade it with reverence & saye, *the mouth of the Lord* hat said it [Isa 40:5]. All the prophets armed them selves with thus, saith the Lord."
(ZACHARY BOYD, SERMON ON HEBREWS 1:1.)

"The study of the Jewish ceremonial law can be of no benefit to anyone, but least of all to a young lady . . . for there are many of the injunctions as disgusting, that they cannot be read even by men."
(JAMES HOGG, "SERMON FOR YOUNG WOMEN." IN *A SERIES OF LAY SERMONS ON GOOD PRINCIPLES AND GOOD BREEDING*, EDITED BY GILLIAN HUGHES. 1834. REPRINT. EDINBURGH: EDINBURGH UNIVERSITY PRESS, 1997, 26.)

"Why do young children commence with the Priests' manual [i.e., Leviticus] and not with Genesis?—Surely, it is because young children are pure and sacrifices are pure; so let the pure come and engage in the study of the pure." (*Midr. Lev. Rab.* 7:2)
(JACOB MILGROM, LEVITICUS 2004, 3.)

WHAT FOLLOWS THIS INTRODUCTION is a history of interpretations, chapter by chapter, not a history of interpreters. Historical information about the lives and times of the authors mentioned will be confined a preliminary chapter, except where some contextual explanation is absolutely necessary. It might appear that this book takes too seriously the by now largely dismissed notion of Gerhard Ebeling, that church history can be (best) done as the history of biblical interpretation. Leppin (2005) queries Ebeling's eschewing of J. Semler's distinction between Bible and Word of

God, as well as his confining his interest to more elite genres, rather than religious art and other expressions of "spirituality." (See also Steiger-Heinen 2006, VI–VIII.) Yet that is every bit just as much a dogmatic position. Nevertheless the point remains: who is going to be interested in pre-critical exegesis at all except cultural historians looking for confirmation of their theories? Well, possibly those who are interested in the message of biblical texts as they speak in all their particularity to particular people. And, as Gadamer reminded us, this includes a dialogue with the tradition of interpretation as with the text itself. However some attempts to show influence and trace the ebb and flow of different schools has sometimes got in the way of simply observing the dialogue between text and interpreter. The Word is not abstract but shuttles between the text and those interpreting it, like a lace tying up a shoe.

In what follows this preface there might seem something of a bias towards the pre-modern. In part this is because our contemporary commentaries do a good job of reporting on other commentaries from the mid-nineteenth century onwards, and it is the period before that that has been comparatively neglected. (Hartley's commentary includes a very worthwhile sketch of the history of interpretation, but very little chapter by chapter.) As soon as one leaves behind the world of Latin commentary, at a point somewhere between Leclerc and Calmet, i.e., 1700, one moves to biblical scholarship that is beginning to be about the composition of the books and ancient historical geography, with dissertations on the whereabouts of Ophir and the origins of money: that in itself is a kind of interpretation, but what the text meant or means seems gradually to become of less importance than its role in furnishing "encyclopedic" evidence for ancient geography and culture, historical reconstruction, then literary habits. It is a generalization, but perhaps one worth venturing, that with some honorable exceptions (Keil and Delitzsch, Bertholet) this tendency developed in the modern history of Christian biblical interpretation to its apogee in the commentaries of Noth and of the 150-year quest to determine the *Grundschrift* (C. Nihan, E. Otto). It has taken the Jewish commentators to put theology back on the agenda to which some Christian scholars have responded positively (e.g., Zenger, Rendtorff, and Kiuchi).

Also patent in what follows is a preponderance of texts drawn from *commentaries* on Leviticus. In part this is because Leviticus compares weakly with even other parts of the Pentateuch in the amount of inspiration it has given to music, fine art, and literature. There is some consideration of its effect on church practice, in liturgy and lifestyle as reflected in canon law, and other such non-commentary works. However, put boldly, Leviticus is itself "art enough" for it to have made its mark on the people of God and hence "society" without requiring the mediation of less obviously churchy-scholarly forms of discourse. Biblical commentary is a genre that always, at least to some extent, bends itself to the shape and concerns of the biblical texts well as to the hearers or readers of the exegete. In that sense it is a mediatory genre in which hearing the text can be observed, and in attempts to apply it clear signs of influence are on view. Commentaries were so often written and edited reproductions of sermons; hence the commentary is that halfway house between what one might call the genres of theology and spirituality. Commentaries do reflect their cultures of origin and are arguably less prone to misinterpretation than art, architecture, etc. One may, of course, surmise and even infer conclusions from non-literary sources, e.g., the shape of church buildings resembles that of the Tabernacle, until we remember that more is owed to Exodus and Kings here. More can be gained from looking a little at the evidence we have of liturgy from missals and commentaries thereon (from Amalarius through Durandus and Biel and beyond). But even then it become apparent that the use of Leviticus for informing the liturgy is only occasional and that rather than copying the house, as it were, the commentators on the liturgy, as on Leviticus, mine the biblical text for gems to enhance rather than hold up the liturgical edifice.

The intention to read the text closely is not always to the fore in modern critical scholarship. Take for example Calum Carmichael's *Illuminating Leviticus*: Leviticus responds not to historical contexts but to a collection of stories. The Babylonian exile was a time of looking for identity and origins; annals of stories as well as corpora of laws lay before the author. Carmichael sees such stories lying behind Leviticus 12. Leviticus 9 can be related as a story: the priests and people congregate to experience the divine presence, but this expectation is spoiled in Leviticus 10 by the first infraction; this is a response to 1 Samuel 1–6. Likewise in Leviticus 25, Jubilee seems impossible to take seriously as a social program, especially given the chaos that would result from returning land. The announcement is made on Day of Atonement; as when Joseph made reconciliation with his brothers in Genesis 45. "The lawgiver's intent was to give sharper definition to an Israelite's identity by having him recall his nation's experience when living in a foreign land" (Carmichael 2006, 136). The law offers a corrective to what was bad in the stories. The law of Leviticus, according to Carmichael, hangs on stories that can be seen as traces in the book even today. On the other hand, Ithmar Gruenwald's *Rituals and Ritual Theory in Leviticus* (2003) tells us that stories are tertiary links in a chain that starts with ethos and moves to ritual. The stories deal with problems needing to be solved or with damage needing repair in a community (105–17). Impurity is simply that: it is a surd that cannot be explained on grounds of physical unhealthiness or morality. Theology is relevant to setting the context of religious rituals but not to structuring them in terms of performative essence (201). "One cannot leave it to theology to fight the demonic. Proving the un-truth, even the non-existence, of the demonic, or declaring it idolatrous, has had little effect" (220). One has to annihilate it, concludes Gruenwald. Leviticus is again reduced to a recipe for the easing of tender consciences.

These two recent accounts conflict as to the priority of story and ritual, but are agreed that the point is "ethics." They are also more interested in what gave rise to the text than in the text itself. In some sense these attempts to make sense of Leviticus seems just as far fetched and speculative as what we find in the tradition, which also believes in fulfillment.

So right away it needs to be said that before the Enlightenment very few thought in terms of a biblical text as something to be examined and explained, but rather as something to be fulfilled, and from that starting point onwards be to some extent understood. Early Christians could not get into the minds of ancient Israelites, but the text-related ancient experience resonated with theirs. Therefore the history of the reception of Scripture is reception as cheerful and creative obedience, even where it includes misunderstanding of, or indifference towards, the details of the Old Testament text. It is a history of spirituality-driven praxis, and a spirituality that is conceptually formed as a consequence of such "resonances," not some free-floating "participation" in signed metaphysical "realities." The pre-moderns (obviously some much more convincingly than others) tend to have no issue between seeing Leviticus as a book that speaks of a divinely ordered reality and holding that it summons people to see creation as reflecting the compassion and also the judgment of God. Before a Christian commentator linked the text to Christ and the church there was usually an attempt to speak of realities common to both testaments, and even to both faiths, Jewish and Christian. For example, Irenaeus had a positive evaluation of the OT cult and the usefulness of sacrifice as something God wills for the sake of his children. The Lord was recalling people from idols to serve God and moving them from the temporal to the eternal. The OT cult gave humans a way to show their love to God. This "friendship" theme is taken up by Augustine in *City of God* XI—sacrifice is a species of worship in which people are drawing near to God, as the sacramental summons a contrite heart.

As things stood, Leviticus could not be given a literal interpretation, except *in spe*. "Perhaps that is why Sifra was written, as it were, 'in the optative mood' (Wilken 1995, 88). Before long, however, the Rabbis (in Sifra) understood this command (Lev 11:45; 19:3) to teach separation from evil as well as commitment to ethical goodness" (Harrington 203, 399). However by the time of *Leviticus Rabbah*, a century or two later, moral discourse became quite detached from any reference to the cult, which is not going to be restored any time (Wilken 1995, 89) The medieval Jewish interpretation of Leviticus tended towards the "praeterist"/historicist, as when Rashi's observed that the instruction to "wait outside pending clearing from suspicion of leprosy" referred to the Gate of Nicanor of the Second Temple. All through this era, from Origen (see Wilken 1995) through the Victorines and Lyra, then Tostado and Abranavel, the influence of Jews and Christians was markedly a mutual one (Gaon 1993). Both Jews and Christians were interested in reading the text closely. In Catholic circles the literal translation from the Hebrew of Sanctes Pagnini inspired a literal commentary with a moral message at the end of each chapter in, for example, the work of Jerome Oleaster (1557). There needs to be commentary because some Hebrew idiom cannot be translated, no matter how skilled the translator (Rodrigues 1990, 233).

However, pre-modern interpretation, Jewish or Christian, does not conform to the semantic units of the text as one might expect it to. The text does not have its way as it does more for modern commentaries—where sequence is very important. The "gist" or *dianoia* is what matters, such that when Luther spoke of the Word being preached, it was not something unfamiliar to medieval exegesis. The interpreters spot repetitions in chapters and hence comment on the two verses at the same time. When we take the one example of medieval interpretation of Leviticus: the church altar is like the altar of burnt offerings; the bishop's dress recalls that of Aaron; the deacons are the successors of the Levites whose name they moreover took during the Carolingian period; the eucharistic bread is the unleavened bread; and the prayer on the offerings refers back to Exodus and Leviticus (Cf. Riché-Lobrichon 1984, 616). Or, "Petrus Cellensis judges that Leviticus is par excellence the book of the monk, because he finds described in it all the sacrifices of purification to which he ought to commit himself in his cell" (De Lubac II, 147).

In an important article Adrian Schenker has indicated how a Jewish-Christian rapprochement in interpretation could be found, one that did not have to lose the distinctive differences of either faith's interpretation. Thomas Aquinas' treatment of the Old Law in Q102 of *Summa Theologiae* I–II is dense in citations from Maimonides' *Guide for the Perplexed*, but more importantly it borrowed a hermeneutical key—that all laws were meaningful, with their purpose always discernible. The purpose of Levitical legislation then is that the people might know, love, and worship God. It both sets out a vision of communal harmonious life and also forms characteristics in people to make this vision a possible reality. Maimonides had given the cultic laws pedagogical but not formative function; they are introductions to the spiritual worship. Thomas thought they were both. In directing worship in a careful outward way, spiritual sense could follow, rather than vice versa (Schenker 1993). I think this reflects Thomas's Aristotelianism rather than a Dionysian influence as Schenker thinks, but in any case a model of the hidden God and the hidden responding soul is given in Leviticus. So for Thomas the Levitical cult was not so much to be left behind, as it was for Maimonides, but to provide a model for the incarnation *and* for Christian worship (Aquinas *ST* Ia–IIae, 102, 2).

The idea of a two-fold reference and sense operation in language sounds like, but ultimately is opposed to, Gilbert Dahan's suggestion (2002, 220) that, as well as there being a sense which was literal and informed by the history of God's economy, there was also a "pure reference" in which language pointed towards God without containing conceptual meaning as such. It is my opinion that any rapprochement or ecumenical reading is found at the level of meaning and not just of a common referent. Having said all that, I regret not having had time, space, or (most of all) competence to do full justice to the Jewish history of interpretation, and that most of it appears in this commentary only as received by the Christian writers, especially from the High Middle Ages onwards. It is, I think, significant that for all the repetition of liturgy, from Leviticus to the Roman rite, it is the lection which is variable and fresh, and so the influence of preaching on the laity should not be downplayed.

Yet was the church's appropriation pure supersessionism, or rather could it be that the church identified itself exactly and closely with the religion of the First Testament, albeit in a new mode? At least as early as Cyril of Alexandria's *De Adoratione* and all the way through the Middle Ages and beyond in Catholic-Orthodox circles the liturgy promoted the importance of sacred space and Leviticus' part in conception and implementation of that. And yet as has been noticed in recent studies of medieval cathedrals (e.g., Recht 2008) the liturgy is never self-serving but promotes an ethical remembrance of God, as though one trains for the obvious forms of obedience (holy living) through obeying curious liturgical commands. The glory of God is the point at all stages, whether BC or AD, whether Jewish or Christian. True, Leviticus has very little about the *kabod* (glory) theology that is picked up again in Ephesians 1; one could say that Leviticus deals with the human side, the response required to God's presence. This may come as a surprise to canonical readers of the Pentateuch who have left Exodus with the cloud above or on the tent and the glory within the tabernacle. Milgrom summarizes: "Exodus contains the story of the construction of the cultic implements, the Tabernacle and the priestly vestments, whereas Leviticus converts this static picture into scenes from the living cult" (Milgrom 1971, 147). We have moved from the mountain and what holiness is is less "obvious." Even if

Mary Douglas is right to see Exodus as the basis for what Leviticus works out, the *Shekhina* as "God as experienced," this happens in ways that are in the context of everyday-yet-graced life as a means of its interruption (Ego-Lange-Pilhofer, 1999). The Sabbath ordinance was given in the context of *pausing* from *"künstlich"* creativity in imitation of God. Leviticus as part of institution in creation of gifted grace: not just about sin offering (Luciani 2005). One does not have to go as far as to say there is no sin in Leviticus, simply that it is not the first or last word in the book. It is a book about the enabling of a graced response to God's glory and salvation. The delivery from Egypt is not a deliverance from sin as much as from darkness and it is unbelief ending in the exile, yet forecast in the children of Israel's wandering in the desert that Leviticus presupposes in as much as it sees the tabernacle as the only hope for errant people. So God wants his people to acknowledge him and also to deal with their sins in front of him. In offering for sin, forces of impurity are also removed. Leviticus has a subtle and variegated view of what the cult achieves and how it achieves it.

There is of course the matter of what the text might be saying today (and "forever") as in Ephraim Radner's Brazos commentary where he looks at the tradition of interpretation as a means to saying what the book has always been saying to the church and would still say today. It would be unfortunate either to ignore or to overemphasize a reading of Leviticus that foregrounds the ethical part of Leviticus, as perhaps did Joseph A. Seiss, pastor of St. John's Lutheran, when he wrote on the High Priest of Leviticus 8: "A public man is like a town clock; upon which much more depends than upon private time-pieces" (1860, 89). Thomas Staubli claims that a liberating christological and trinitarian lecture of Leviticus can sharpen our eyes to see oppression in the church and the world (1996, 36). Of course, Leviticus might well be composite in its formation. The P (priestly) section might run to chapter 16 and H (Holiness Code) take over as from another pen. Yet in the final form we can see how the ethical proceeds from the ritual, but never leaves it behind. Holiness is where spirituality becomes ethics. The moral theology/spiritual theology divide which has operated since early modern times is lamentable (Aumann 1980). These are things to ponder.

Holiness can be viewed as having to do with a way of coping with death and disorder, involving classification and separation. It is not clear from Mary Douglas whether Christianity completely overcame any such separation (Douglas 1975, 283), for she seems to say that Christianity's Jewishness would not allow for that (*pace* Crossan 1982, 33). Jesus lived within the world of Leviticus; he expands this holiness to the church, such that Matthew 15:17–20 is about what makes one unclean in addition to or in tandem with cultic holiness. The cult (and by extension Jesus' own remaking of that in his own death) is what provides a remedy to, not a further cause of, human moral uncleanness, as the liturgy is transformed into something life-giving as participants in the liturgy come to understand the symbolism. (See also Cortese-Kaswalder 1996, 25.)

According to Douglas's later book *Leviticus as Literature* (Oxford, 1999), the fruit of a lifetime of anthropological and biblical research, Leviticus is not about general pollution theory, but rather compassion for creatures, including lepers who are not kept at too far a distance: it has to do with God, persons, animals. "It is hard to realize how completely their strict monolatry separated the religion of Israel from the others in the region" (*Leviticus as Literature*, 3). It is a humanitarian document in disguise, with an emphasis on protecting the dignity of the weak. While applauding Douglas's insistence on the Israelite way as different and distinctive and on her keynote that the religion of the cult and its worship provides for the human sense of unholiness, there is in her interpretation a bit of a loss of the holy otherness of God. She has at least taken the apparent illogic of the Hebrew Bible here to be just as logical according to their presuppositions. But for all her helpful provocation, the moral and the cultic are divided, as though to say: What they did made sense for *them*, but it doesn't make a universal or timeless sense, and certainly doesn't speak to *our* world. However, Radner (2008) helpfully uses De Maistre to propose a universal and constructive notion of sacrifice, which was ready for Christ to come and inhabit, not an "annihilating" and nihilistic one (i.e., not a notion of sacrifice that is life-denying). Even though everyday things such as menstruation, even death, are, as such, profane and that is why they are to be kept away from the world of the cult or at least to be regulated, nevertheless in doing so the world of the universal and everyday (food, sex, death) is not ignored but put in its place and paid respect in both its beauty and its corrupt state. Jacques Cazeaux has recently (2007, 292) emphasized that with tents and tabernacles, as in Exodus 25–40, there are not the dangerous limitations of a fixed temple. "Leviticus thinks of itself as being super-temporal." The history of Israel in the Pentateuch, as Jewish voices have suggested, is interrupted and joined to a trans-temporal law of worship.

For a world obsessed with blame and compensation, the psychological and social aspect of regaining cleanliness in one's relationship to the Holy found in the words and messages of Leviticus are well worth reflecting on. The church's job is not only to hold out to the world forgiveness (John 20:21), but by modeling how to ask for it, to enable others to seek forgiveness together. It might be no coincidence that it has been post-Shoah German biblical theologians who have kept interest in the question alive: Janowski and Breytenbach in particular.

Symbolism is not the same as magic. Offerings are not just about dealing with sin, but also communing and giving thanks, as well as recognizing of weakness and personal responsibility: blood is a sign of God's readiness to forgive, not a means of salvation (Utzschneider 1996, 119). The "anti-Tübingen" thesis insisted that, according to the NT, gift and symbolic identification operate with no fixed price, offering good and bad rather than paying off or expiating. A communicative ritual in Hebrews 9:22—blood symbolizes death—is not something that really washes away sin, although it deals with the bad relationship. Any violence is "accidental," i.e., not part of the essence of the thing, but reflects the hunting past of ancient societies (Burkert 1983); what is essential is the admitting of fault by the gift and the bringing of rightly ordered life out of death. In this way it might be possible to see the Eucharist as continuing to offer up Christ's death, without believing that blood is involved, but that a debt is being repaid (Track 1996).

Track's useful article relates how Grotius in his *Defensus fidei catholicæ de satisfactione Christi* (Leiden 1617) echoed Duns Scotus's *acceptilatio* thesis that God demands an "arbitrary" price to be paid for the sake of moral order, which was not that different from Anselm in the sense of how God's honor is appeased (not God himself). The Reformation subjectivized things: there was a reality of death to escape and life to step into. Yet in the duty to bear one's own responsibility, sacrifice becomes an ambivalent quality. In truth, Jesus' sacrifice was not literally a cultic action, but makes use of that metaphor while disarming it before our eyes—and *that* is the necessary usefulness of the cultic metaphor. Unfortunately medieval cross-devotion that appropriated the model of scapegoat and atonement ritual to pinpoint "our" guilt and to suggest that God wanted Jesus to die—and Jesus had such a death-wish—meant that we too needed to annihilate ourselves (as Nietzsche and feminist critiques—e.g., that of Mary Daly—would point out). For Track—with Dalferth (1994), Girard (1989), and Schwager (1978)—in Jesus God shows another way: that of liberation that bypasses the cult and deals with ingrained, attitudinal human opposition to God (1996, 164). Likewise Friederike Nüssel (Nüssel 2005) relates how the Enlightenment had problems with loading any salvific freight on the active obedience of Jesus' life—how could a virtue of another person atone for each of us? If the cross had value it was something worked out by God himself in his Son for his own sake, his own reconciliation. Nüssel's account sees Kant as the point of no return, by his criticism of the satisfaction theory as one in which people are allowed to offload at least some of their moral responsibility; Schleiermacher then allowed Jesus to be only a "representative" (*stellevertretend*), as a foundational example for human beings. The further Hegelian contribution is outlined and reaffirmed in Ingolf Dalferth (1994): sacrifice is not activity directed to God but is that which comes from God and is in turn recognized in the light of God's love. So that what God can make happen in Jesus is limited to some *symbolic* arrangement with thereby revelatory force, rather than anything that operates out at an *ontological* level. Furthermore, Jesus sacrifice should be seen as the end of all sacrifice, such that we should not be prolonging Jesus' sacrifice any more in the sphere of ethics than in the Eucharist. According to Stoellger, in the same volume as Nüssel (2005), Jesus' death does not so much symbolize as it reduces meaning to itself so that our personal interpretations of it (and not of the associated doctrines) are what matters.

This seems not only to ignore certain parts of the canon, and arrogantly deprecate the past religious heritage, it also ignores the fact that anxiety and violence are part of who we are, and they need to be dealt with. The cult, whether Levitical or eucharistic, is at very least an essential reminder of this possibility of pardon (cf. Luciani 2005, 51). More than that, it can be viewed as the divinely appointed means for forgiveness in and through community: one is taught about "forgiveness . . . as . . ." (cf. Boda 2008, 75; *contra* Gane 2005). The redressing of moral order is what Jesus came to achieve, but Colossians suggests that sacrifice is not at an end, especially where it benefits others. Gary Anderson has reminded us that the message of Ephraim and Augustine is to render impurity as indebtedness, following a trajectory already in the earlier Jewish tradition, and arguably within Leviticus itself. The corollary is that in lending one is trusting that God will repay—one gives to him through the poor. There is a move from "cleansing" to "debt" as the key metaphor. Leviticus 26 describes Israel in debt, as she needs redeeming at national level. In return she is to show favor out of being shown favor. In the NT Colossians 2:14 with its "IOU" image is central. Working with this debt metaphor—*rāsâah* in Leviticus 7:18 and 19:5, 7 means "credited"—Anderson can conclude: "The divine Father was not so much collecting the punishment due on his bond as he was rewarding the self-donation Christ made out of his love for humanity (Anselm, *Cur Deus Homo* 1.8). The Isaac-centered approach to atonement found in *Lev. Rabbah* 2.11 means to remind God of Akedah, where the pain of punishment is experienced as satisfaction" (Anderson 2009, 197–200).

However there remains an important place for the image of the cleansing of the conscience (Heb 9:14; 10:2), which only the cross can achieve. Irenaeus saw this as real enough (*Haer.* IV, 18, 1), the spiritualizing of the offering requiring something to be spiritualized, namely Christ's body (Grässer 1993, 163f.). Christ posits his salvific work anew in the liturgy of the church (Casel 1960); Christ as pneuma is then able to penetrate all parts of our soul (Balthasar 1993, 195, following Casel) and institute a "right relationship with God" which is the meaning of the "cleansing of the conscience." Blood is thus a metaphor for life flowing between God and humanity (Backhaus 2009, 138). *Hilasterion* is mentioned five times in Leviticus 16, which takes the pressure off seeing Isaiah 53 alone as the background to Romans 3:25. Even C. Breytenbach in his study, which plays down to a minimum the importance of the cult as the background of Pauline "reconciliation," admits that the expiating death might be the foundation for the establishment of "eschatological" reconciliation (1989, 215). In a survey of the Johannine material Knöppler admits that *Sühne* and *Versöhung* are connected. Fulfillment of "atonement" does not mean the category is redundant, for Jews or for Christians. Smoke is that which all Levitical offerings had in common (Eberhart 2002), and this symbolizes an attempt to reach God, to be in his presence. But that does not mean that the cost of the offering is secondary in significance in relation to the gift.

Lastly, some words of a formal nature. There is more paraphrase than quotation and I have not given exact page numbers, but have contented myself that the reader who wants to go to the commentaries themselves should be able to locate the page by looking for the biblical lemma in question. The editions of the commentaries used can be found in the next "chapter": Gallery of Major Interpreters. Unless stated, "Calvin says" refers to his commentary, etc. As for non-commentary works, it sometimes is simpler just to mention them in the text (Augustine, *On the Trinity* 8.5.3) especially if they only appear once or twice. In this case, editions used can be found in the first part of the bibliography. Where a claim is made, e.g., by Lyra that Rashi says: . . . I have not chased it to check its accuracy, since that is not the point of the commentary. I have given preference to the present text when relating what is in these commentaries: in some sense they are living, present texts. When it comes to medieval Jewish commentary, my default guide has been the JPS *Miqra Gedalot*, edited by M. Carasik (JPS 2009), for which I have had reason at many times to be grateful.

Abbreviations

BA	*Bibliothèque Augustinienne*
CCCM	*Corpus Christianorum Coninuatio Medievalis*
CCSL	*Corpus Christianorum Series Latina*
CIC	*Corpus Iuris Canonici*
CO	*Calvini Opera*
CR	*Corpus Reformatorum*
CSCO	*Corpus Scriptorum Christianorum Orientalium*
CSEL	*Corpus Scriptorum Ecclesiasticorum Latinorum*
FC	*Fathers of the Church*
FChr	*Fontes Christiani*
GCS	*Griechischen Christlichen Schriftsteller*
LW	*Luther's Works*
MHG	*Monumenta Germaniae Historica*
OED	*Oxford English Dictionary*
PG	*Patrologia Graeca*
PL	*Patrologia Latina*
PO	*Patrologia Orientalis*
SC	*Sources Chrétiennes*
ST	*Summa Theologiae*
WA	*Weimarer Ausgabe*

Gallery of Major Interpreters of Leviticus

MOST OF THE PEOPLE below are those who wrote commentaries on the book of Leviticus and hence made a major contribution to its interpretation. Others who are mentioned in the text are those who have commented on a few verses in a work other than a commentary, although these cases are exceptional, since I have tried to limit myself to work that is exegetical in purpose. In those cases the work will be referred to in the text and bibliography. In what follows the commentators will be listed in chronological order. The name and date will be followed by the source used.

CLEMENT OF ALEXANDRIA (D. 211)

The *Paidagogos* (Clément d'Alexandrie, *Le pedagogue*. Paris: Cerf, 1960–70) and the more ambitious work *Stromateis* (Clément d'Alexandrie, *Les stromates*, Tom. 1. Paris: Cerf, 1951) both show less a systematic approach to Scripture than a magpie-like approach to shiny biblical texts. The influence of the Hellenistic Jewish exegete-philosopher Philo (d. 50 CE) is huge (Runia 1993) and in his exegesis of passages on priests and temples often seems like a Christian version of Philo on these Levitical texts.

ORIGEN (C. 185–254)

His upbringing at Alexandria equipped him with an awareness that great texts contained truth that needed a spiritual or intellectual vision to be discerned. An additional factor was his residing for the last and exegetically most productive period of his life (from 231 onwards) at Caesarea where he could learn from Jewish scholars methods of reading the text in a closer way that paid attention to variants According to P. Nautin, the sermons on Leviticus were given between 239 and 242, possibly as part of a Sun-Wed-Fri three year cycle, yet H. Buchinger (2005) would date them later, after his return from Athens, hence 245. We have them only in the Latin translation made by Rufinus around 400, in the modern edition: *Origène: Homélies sur le Lévitique*, edited by M. Borret. Sources Chrétiennes 286–87 (Paris: Cerf; 1981). Origen prefers to see the sacrifices as representing Christ, reserving to the Aaronic priesthood an ecclesiological (not christological) interpretation.

HESYCHIUS OF JERUSALEM (D. 455)

Hesychius of Jerusalem (monk then presbyter there from 412), on the basis of admittedly patchy evidence, moved in an increasingly mia- or mono-physite direction at the time of the Council of Chalcedon (451 AD), expressed in his opposition to Leo's Tome. (Perrone 1980, 60–79.) However, he was later recognized for his saintliness by the Eastern Church. His complete commentary remains only in Latin translation (*Patrologia Graeca* 787–1180), which is not always comprehensible (Wenger 1956, 466) and at some point in its transmission the Vulgate text got superimposed as *lemmata*, even though the text of the commentary clearly did not use that biblical text. The commentary was hugely significant in this Latin translation as the foundation of the *Glossa Ordinaria*, which was, in turn, the foundation of almost all medieval Western Latin interpretation of Leviticus.

CYRIL OF ALEXANDRIA (376–444)

De adoratione (*On Adoration and Worship in Spirit and in Truth*; Patrologia Graeca 68) is commonly held to be one of the earliest of Cyril's works, and the earliest of his exegetical publications. It is a treatise on various questions that then find their answers by a quotation from Scripture or three, and then a following interpretation. The relatively large amount of attention to Leviticus which is present is given a strong christological reference. His slightly later *Glaphyra* ("Elegant Comments" PG 69, 539–90) are also well informed by a consideration of the meaning of Leviticus.

THEODORET OF CYRRHUS (393–458)

Although Theodoret (bishop of Cyrrhus from 423) was anathematized in 553 at the Second Council of Constantinople for Nestorian tendencies, this did not stop the Eastern Church appreciating his work, though it might have done damage to his reputation in the West. The *Questions on the Octateuch* in the early 450s represent the maturity of his exegetical work. (Guinot 1995, 63). The modern edition is Theodoretus, *Quaestiones in Octateuchum* 181, edited by N. Fernández Marcos and A. Saenz-Badillos. Madrid: CSIC, 1979; translation: *Theodoret of Cyrus: The Questions on the "Octateuch": On Leviticus, Numbers, Deuteronomy, Joshua, Judges, and Ruth*, vol. 2. Translated by Robert C. Hill. Library of Early Christianity. Washington DC: Catholic University of America Press, 2008.)

AUGUSTINE OF HIPPO (354–430)

Although no doubt drawing often on exegetical sketches made beforehand, the work *Quaestiones in Heptateuchum* (*Sancti Aurelii Augustini quaestionum in Heptateuchum libri VII, Locutionum in Heptateuchum libri VII, De octo quaestionibus ex Veteri Testamento*. Turnholt, Belgium: Brepols, 1958) is to be dated sometime in 419 (with the writing of *De gratia Christi* and *De anima et eius origine* as *termini a quo* and *ad quem*, respectively). Augustine is clear that to be worthy of treatment a text has to offer a real difficulty.

PROCOPIUS OF GAZA (C. 465–528)

Procopius was known as a compiler of the interpretations of others. It appears that the short commentaries (*scholia*) on the historical books of the OT are in part his own, even if they are very much dependent on sources read but unacknowledged. What he has done is provide a synthesis or epitome of a much larger work that was a collection of all the fathers' thoughts on the first eight books of the Bible. As a result, what we have then is similar to the *Glossa Ordinaria* in Latin yet with all attribution suppressed.

EASTERN ANTIOCHENE EXEGETES

In the Nestorian exegetical tradition of the Syriac Nestorian churches, for which Theodore of Mopusestia remained "the interpreter," Iso bar Nun, in his *Questions and Answers* (*The Selected Questions of Ishō bar nūn on the Pentateuch*, Edited and translated from MS. Cambridge Add. 2017: With a Study of the Relationship of Ishōʾdādh of Merv, Theodore bar Kōni, and Ishō bar Nūn on Genesis. Edited by Ernest George Clarke. Leiden: Brill, 1962), and Theodore bar Koni, in his *Scholia*, simplified, modified, and popularized Theodore's exegesis. The bishop of Hedatha, Ishodad of Merv in his commentary (*Commentaire d'Išoʾdadh de Merv sur l'Ancien Testament*. Edited by J-M. Vosté and C. van den Ende. Louvain: Durbecq, 1950–63), in the middle of the ninth century, adopted a freer stance and used Theodore to provide some amount of answers to questions, yet he turned question and answer into indirect question: "and it is being asked why, etc." (Leonhard 2001, 25.) The "question and answer" method and *scholia* (short, contained exegetical pieces on a verse or two) became popular alongside the running commentary genres and had a monastic dialogic origin, although going back further to Plato. The Palestinian Theodore bar Koni's *Scholia* are much more theological and philosophical than Ishodad's *Questions and Answers*.

GREGORY THE GREAT (C. 540–604)

R. Wasselynck (1965) shows us how the commentary extracted by Paterius from other writings of Gregory (PL 79: 685–1136) had considerable influence. Also, the written epistolary responses of Gregory (ET: *Letters of Gregory the Great*. Translated by John R. C. Martyn. Toronto: PIMS, 2004), including some interpretation of the ceremonial law, are probably genuine or at least "Gregorian." Since they undermined his ecclesiology, Boniface attempted in 736 to show them to be a forgery.

THEODORE OF CANTERBURY (602–90)

The commentaries from the Canterbury School of Theodore and Hadrian (*Biblical Commentaries from the Canterbury School of Theodore and Hadrian*. Edited by Bernhard Bischoff and Michael Lapidge. Cambridge: Cambridge University Press, 1994) are, in form simple, glosses of phrases from the biblical text, done largely out of philological interest.

BEDE (C. 672/3–735)

According to Gorman (1996), Bede (in PL 91:189–394) is rather a product of the late Middle Ages. There is, however, some use of Leviticus 24:1–9 in his liturgical-mystical work *De tabernaculo* (Bede. *De tabernaculo*. Edited by D. Hurst, 1–139. CCSL 119A. Turnhout, Belgium: Brepols, 1969; ET: *Bede: On the Tabernacle*. Translated Texts for Historians 18. Translated by Arthur G. Holder. Liverpool: Liverpool University Press, 1994.)

RABANUS MAURUS (C. 780–856)

Rabanus Maurus was in some sense the spiritual successor to Charlemagne's favorite scholar, Alcuin, having been taught in Tours. He was by 822 abbot of Fulda, before becoming bishop of Mainz from 847–56. To him, the ultimate source of all *iudicia* remained the *lex divina*, by which he usually did not mean the whole of Scripture, but the Old Testament. Rabanus Maurus's work on Leviticus (as available in PL 108: 245–586) is not much more than a patchwork of Hesychius and Origen. What can be said is that he helped establish a commentary-based theology. When they privileged the authoritative commentaries of the Fathers, Carolingian biblical scholars also established the Western hermeneutical tradition. Study of the Bible became study of *interpretations* of the Bible. The biblical verses themselves served only to organize the exposition. (Contreni 1996, 9—following Silvia Cantelli, *Angelomo e la scuola esegetica di Luxeuil*.) There is more useful application in his *De institutione clericorum* (edited by D. Zimpel. Bern: Lang, 1996.)

GLOSSA ORDINARIA

The *Glossa Ordinaria*, which presented each verse of the Bible with a comment immediately below ("interlinear") and then more in the margins, is almost completely drawn from exegetes who roughly could be called "patristic." It was originally (and influentially in Migne's *Patrologia*) attributed to Walafrid Strabo. (See Smalley 1983, 56–60.) However, the only connection Walafrid has to the gloss is that the Laonian Glossators used bits of his *Collectanea*—but only for Genesis and Exodus. The Laonian Glossator of much of OT including the Pentateuch was Gilbertus Universalis (of Auxerre) around 1120. Adolph Rusch of Strassburg's 1480/81 edition is that from which "all later editions . . . derive their basic text" and "it represents the standard text which scholars from the late twelfth century to the late fifteenth would have recognized" (Gibson & Froehlich, *Biblia Latina cum Glossa Ordinaria, Facsimile Reprint of the Editio Princeps Adolph Rusch of Strassburg 1480/81*. Edited by Karlfried Froehlich and Margaret T. Gibson. Brepols, Belgium: Turnhout, 1992, v.)

MEDIEVAL JEWISH COMMENTARY

Rashi (1040–1105) in Northern France, Ibn Ezra (1089–1164) and Nahmanides (1195–1270) in Spain and the wider Mediterranean, and Gersonides (1288–1344) in Provence represent the strengths of literal, grammatical, mystical, and philosophical exegesis, which, along with Maimonides (1134–1205) in his *Guide for the Perplexed*, would permeate much Christian exegesis, not least in early modern times. The Portuguese commentator Isaac Abravanel (d.1508) is often referred to by early modern Christian scholars.

LAWS AND LEVITICUS

The Penitential books of Irish and Carolingian Christianity will be introduced individually in this commentary. However, 214 out of 300 biblical texts in the Penitential book known as the *Hibernensis* were from the Old Testament. An attempt is made to systematize some of these responses in *Pauca Problesmata** (Edited by G. MacGinty.

CCCM 173. Turnhout, Belgium: Brepols, 2000). The Laws of the Wessex king, Alfred the Great (849–99) in the *Liber ex Moysi* supported his attempt to unite his kingdom. In this work we have eleven extracts from Leviticus (Larès 1971, 83) but also Irish nonreligious laws that claimed Moses as master legislator, even if these were not always internally consistent. The Pentateuch was the supreme authority. Another place where Pentateuchal texts are found is in the *De oratione Moysi* of Aelric a century later, although with a preference for narrative rather than law. The "success" of Leviticus is shown in its being the second most often cited OT book (after Genesis and the Psalms) in Gratian I's *Decretals* (*Distinctiones et Causae*. Gaudemet 1984, 368.)

ANDREW OF ST. VICTOR (D. 1175),

Andrew was possibly the most famous Christian Hebraist of the early Middle Ages and his comments, although pithy to the point of sparse, are significant for trying to make sense of the plain sense of the text. The exegetical fruit of a philological approach to Leviticus (*Andreae de Sancto Victore opera. 1, Expositionem super Heptateuchum*. Edited by Charles Lohr and Rainer Berndt. CCCM 53. Turnholt, Belgium: Brepols, 1986) is rather sparse. Paying little attention to the possibility of *pesher* as part of the literal sense, he cleaved to the rule that allegory was an affront to Scripture. Andrew's colleague, Hugh, had a less radical approach to the OT, with more place for its application, as seen in his *On the Sacraments of the Christian Faith* (*De sacramentis*). Translated by Roy J. Deferrari. Cambridge, MA: The Medieval Academy of America, 1951.

RUPERT OF DEUTZ (C. 1075–1129)

For Rupert, in his commentary on the Pentateuch (c. 1114; PL 167: 743–836), the Law of Moses was only perpetual where it was consistent with the prophets. (Van Engen 1983, 263ff.) Independence as spiritual commentator was of chief importance to him (Maier, 2006, 262). Consequently, Rupert became suspect for his new hermeneutical approach. In his emphasis on the forward-looking aspect in the Law, he missed out "the Holiness Code," skipping over chapters 17 to 23.

RALPH OF FLAIX (FL. 1157)

At a meeting at his abbey in Flaix, sixty miles north of Paris, Ralph became aware of how Jews were winning the battle for the OT in the understanding of Christian leaders (Van Engen 2001). The Leviticus commentary was written sometime in the

1140s. Like Rupert, Ralph uses the prophets to prove how "shadowy" the Law was. They did not really know Moses' intention as "they do not look into the brightness of the face of Moses" (Ralph, *Lev*, 48). As religious orders became more educated they started to read the texts of Scripture. Ralph needed to lead them from the literal to the mysterious sense. Ralph's commentary (*Radulphi Flauiacensis, In mysticum illum Moysi Leuiticum libri XX*: 1536. Facsimile printed at Marburg) was preferred during the in the scholastic period to the inadequate *Glossa Ordinaria*.

BRUNO OF SENGI (C. 1049–1123)

Bruno studied canon law in Bologna, possibly disputed in Rome with Berengar (at Gregory VII's invitation in 1079), preaching faith, theological authorities (i.e., the fathers), and love against his opponent's "rationalism" and suggesting that the faithful receive Christ's effect by osmosis (PG 174, 956D), although remembering Christ daily on the altar of one's heart is also vital. After opposing Pope Pascal II (in 1111) on his compromise on investiture, he had to resign from the abbey, allegedly calling the Pope a heretic as a parting shot. In the Leviticus commentary (PL 164.377–464) he used Isidore's *Questions on Pentateuch*, and did not follow the Gregorian-Origenian threefold sense, for the literal sense predominates (Spicq 1944, 199ff) with a space for moral signification.

PETER CANTOR (1130–97)

Peter Cantor taught in Paris and glossed the whole Bible. He also wrote a widely-loved manual for preachers, the *Verbum abbreviatum*, known for its moralizing approach to the Bible. He relies a lot on his two principal sources, the *Glossa Ordinaria* and Ralph of Flaix; his own contribution is really a summarizing one. His few comments on Leviticus are to be found in his *Verbum Abbreviatum* (*Petri Cantoris Parisiensis Verbum adbreviatum: textus conflatus*. Edited by Monique Boutry. CCCM 196. Turnhout, Belgum: Brepols, 2004), whose content is a string of exhortations to clergy, through mysteries found in material things. A byproduct of the moralizing tendency in exegesis by the school of Peter Cantor, *La Bible Moralisée* was produced for a French lay audience and a royal one at that, between 1215 and 1250. Lipton (1999) argues there is an independence of the Parisian moral school, at least on the issue of social egalitarianism.

STEPHEN LANGTON (1155–1228)

Stephen Langton, pupil of Peters Comestor and Cantor, whose aim to comment on the whole Bible inspired him such that most of his work was done before he left Paris for Canterbury in 1205. He was a great synthesizer of those before with meditative style appreciated by Cistercians (Quinto 1994, 32). He developed Peter Cantor's approach, weaving in his own original contribution. Stephen took sin seriously: evangelism should lead the way from the church militant to the church triumphant. This led to his being named *Lingua-Tonante* (thundering tongue). In his Leviticus commentary (*Commentarium in Leviticum*: Paris MS lat 255) Stephen included questions from Peter Lombard, but they were mostly to do with practical morality and he found biblical theological answers for the penitent (Quinto 2004, 214).

WILLIAM OF AUVERGNE (C. 1180–1249)

William of Auvergne, bishop of Paris, practiced an applied or "sermonic" exegesis on Leviticus (*Guilielmi Alverni Opera omnia*. Frankfurt: Minerva, 1963). What he had learned from his Parisian schooling was used as bishop in service of practical (not mystical) preaching with plenty of examples or illustrations (Dahan 2005, 239). There was a liking for the thematic which took the form of drawing in other Scriptures by catchword. For William, the Mosaic Law formed at least *part* of the eternal law of the gospel and should be held to be *honesta* (worthy, decorous) (Smalley 1974). Spiritually immature children "today" need instruction in detail and also the study of many laws would occupy their minds and keep them from distractions. Nothing that God has given in the Law can be absurd or ridiculous: nothing can be ignored even if the outward details, accommodated to the Jews, have to be "seen through."

ROBERT GROSSETESTE (1175–1273)

When Leviticus was cited by William's near-contemporary, Robert Grossteste, in his *De Cessatione Legalium* (Edited by R. C. Dales and E. King. London: Oxford University Press for the British Academy, 1986), it is not with reference to ceremonies (which have passed) but to moral laws such as the Sabbath law, which is expressly called a "*legitimum sempiternum*" (Lev 23:21; ibid., I, ii, 8; 10f), The ceremonial law to abstain from blood can only mean that we should abstain from delighting in sin (ibid., I, x, 14; 56f), and was originally imposed because God's command can make binding law, which he can as easily rescind. We might compare the view of Roger Marston, the English Franciscan provincial in the 1290s, that the "man of God" who prophesied to Eli about the future fall of his house in 1 Kings 2:27–36 was really talking about the fall of the entire line of Aaron (Klepper 2007, 68)

HUGH OF ST. CHER (C. 1200–1263)

Hugh stood at the moment when exegesis passed from schools to universities. Dahan (2004, 66) calls him the founder of Dominican exegesis. His contribution was scholarly, not least in his Bible concordance and the corrected version of the Vulgate, but also his *Postilla in totam bibliam* (*Biblie cum postilla domini Hugonis Cardinalis*. Basel: Johann Amerbach for Anton Koberger, 1498–1502). A novelty was providing a resume of the history of exegesis of Leviticus, especially the line: Origen-Hesychius-Rabanus (with a much longer list for Exodus). He loved to draw "distinctions" in the meanings of words to aid the preacher as he tried to develop the spiritual interpretations. For Hugh, exegesis was not an end in itself (Bataillon 1986) and there were no scholastic questions, although there is a methodical approach to the what, why, and where of "offerings." Along with Peter Comestor, he commented that while the Greeks call it "Leviticus," Latins call it "*Offertorius/Sacrificaticus*." This might well reflect a Western interest in the action rather than the actors of Leviticus.

DOMINIQUE GRIMA (1274–1347)

Grima, of the Order of Preachers, was a "Thomist exegete" (Morin 2000, 325), a Paris-trained Dominican who then taught in his native Toulouse (1310–21) before becoming papal theologian to John XXII at Avignon (to whom he dedicated his Pentateuch commentary). He strove to show how Aquinas was a great teacher because he was a great exegete, and argued against those who preferred to see the Bible as a repository of prophecies and their fulfillment. Thomas, against Joachim, had insisted that these laws could not and should not be kept but the Ten Commandments must be (Schachten 1980, 214).

NICHOLAS OF LYRA (1270–1349)

Lyra was best known for his *Postilla super totam bibliam*, which had two parts, a literal (*Opus Biblie una cum postillis . . . Nicolai de Lyra cumque additionibus per Paulum Burgensem editis; ac replicis magistri Mathie Dorinck*. Nuremberg: Koberger, 1485) and a moral exposition (*Postille morales seu mistice super omnes libros Sacrae Scripturae*. Coloniae: Johann Koelhoff, the Elder, 1478). There was also a strong theological influence from Duns Scotus on Nicholas, who had studied in the Franciscan house in Paris and from 1319 was the order's provincial in northern France. On

Nicholas's reading, the spiritual sense can be the moral sense for "today" since the literal sense is a double one, containing the figurative and spiritual meaning. Within his work there is a scholastic or Aristotelian concern to divide the texts properly and a huge debt to Rashi's exegesis (L. Smith 2007). Nicolas viewed Rashi as a sort of Jewish *Glossa Ordinaria* (see esp. Michalski 1915–16). Strangely, his *Postilla* was popular without being influential in its approach. Lyra resisted the idea that to be spiritual was to look forward to the Age of the Spirit: rather it was about looking back to biblical values, to seeing the Franciscan Rule as summoning the friar to a place of biblical simplicity.

DENYS THE CARTHUSIAN (*DENIS RYCKEL*) (1402–71)

Denys was a Carthusian monk who trained at Deventer and Köln and entered the Carthusian House at Roermond in 1424, thus no longer having no ties to a university system. Denys was quite possibly the most prolific writer of the Middle Ages, for no better reason than that he agreed with Jerome that, if prayer was speaking to God, then studying (*Scriptura et item "Catholicorum volumina"*) was when God spoke. Denys believed in a tripartite theology: symbolic, intelligible (scholastic), and mystical. The first is formed by meditative commentary on Scripture, and it provides the foundation for the other two. In the Prologue to Leviticus (*D. Dionysii Carthusiani Enarrationes piae ac eruditae, in quinque Mosaicae legis libros, hoc est, Genesim, Exodum, Leviticum, Numeros, Deuteronomium* Coloniae: ex officina Joannis Quentel, 1548), Denys tells us that the key principle in Leviticus is "honor the Lord with your substance."

ALONSO TOSTADO ("ABULENSIA") (1400–1455)

Although his work is not directly used, the influence of the polymathic bishop of Avila on early modern commentators was large.

CONRAD PELLICAN (OR *KÜRSCHERER*) (1478–1556)

Pellican was self-taught in Hebrew but helped by the Hebraist Reuchlin. He worked as a printer in Zürich, having been brought from Basel (where he had worked with Oecolampadius) by Zwingli to join "the *Prophezei*" thirty years earlier when he was already almost fifty years old, finally shaking off his Franciscan Minorite affiliation with that move. He did not have contact with unconverted Jews and even warned his colleague Capito of "dangers" in rabbinic exegesis (Zürcher 1975, 193). Pellican spent a large share of his time from 1530 onwards in the Grossmünster library on his whole-Bible commentary, "*Commentaria Bibliorum*," starting with *In explanationem sacrorum librorum Veteris Testamenti Praefatio* (Zurich: Froschauer, 1533). He saw his calling in writing commentaries to equip students and pastors with a fresh understanding for the sake of the *edificatio* of churches (Zürcher 1975, 87). As his *curriculum vitae* might suggest, Pellican's treatment of the Law is not only humanist, it could be even called "humanitarian."

CAJETAN (*THOMAS DE VIO*) (1469–1534)

Self-consciously following Aquinas in insisting on the literal sense since arriving in Rome in 1501 onwards, Cajetan turned to biblical exegesis after finishing his commentary on the *Summa Theologiae*, and after his encounter with Luther. His scholarship could be exact and exacting and there seems to be a sharing in Scripture's wonder at creation and saving history rather than a rush to allegorize it. In his preface to *Omnes Authenticos Veteris Testam. Historiales Libros* (Rome 1533)—dedicated to the Pope Clement VI—he claimed that Deuterocanonical books can be read for edification but have no authority for doctrine. The corollary of this is that the other OT books *did* possess that "dogmatic" authority.

JOHANNES BRENZ (1499–1570)

The Bible commentaries of the Schwäbisch reformer seem to have been written in tandem with his preaching. After NT exegesis such as Romans (*Explicatio Epistola Pauli Ad Romanos*. Edited by S. Strohm. Tübingen: Mohr 1986), in his 14th Homily on Penance (1528) he speaks of the Levitical feast days as reminding us to pay attention to Christ and his Word every day, but especially in celebrating the Lord's Supper, when we should bring prayer, thanksgiving, obedience, and contrite hearts. Brenz published his Leviticus commentary (*In Leuiticum librum Mosi commentarius* Frankfurt: ex officina Petri Brubachii, 1542) in the same year as his response on the Eucharist to Bullinger and Vermigli. The controlling lens appears on the frontispiece: "Hebrae ix" (Heb 9). The NT Epistle to the Hebrews is like a commentary on Leviticus, and that means the NT church paid Leviticus much attention, the better to understand the sacrifice of Christ. Pagans like Lucian ridiculed sacrifices; but the Holy Spirit laughs back.

MARTIN BORRHAUS (*CELLARIUS*) (1499–1564)

Borrhaus was one who seemed to regain respectability as Karlstadt's replacement at Basel in 1544, something he had lost after drifting away from Wittenberg in favor of Anabaptist ideas, coming under much suspicion by Zwingli. He had once rated Luther as higher than apostolic in a sort of dispensationalist account of covenantally-driven salvation history. The OT was more than just typological in its value. Carnal things would not be altogether be replaced by spiritual things in the *eschaton*, and for that reason the OT Law retains its worth. He predicted a pre-eschaton return of Israel to city and temple. The Second Helvetic Confesion (11) would condemn such "Jewish dreams." In the Leviticus commentary (*In Leviticum*. Basel: Ex Officina Ioannis Oporini, 1555) he is intent on finding rather mystical-sounding references to Christ.

JOHN CALVIN (1509–64)

For Calvin, there is no intrinsic superiority of Christianity over the religion of Moses and the Law, even if Christ brought a new covenant that dispensed with the old. It is all "word" (Cottret 2003, 62ff). More technically, the Mosaic covenant is spiritual in substance but legal in form or administration (*Institutes* II, 11,3). According to *Institutes* I, 3, it would be a perverse error to say that the perfection of the evangelical law is much greater than that of the old Law. Christ was no Second Moses; he *purged and restored* the Law, but he did not add to it. When it comes to his late *Harmony on the Pentateuch* (Geneva: Estienne, 1563; French translation, 1564), his first attempt at this is recorded in the notes taken of Calvin's comments before the congregation in 1559. There he opines that the ceremonies were instituted to keep people on their obedient toes. However in the preface to the commentary itself, written three to four years later, as E. de Boer has noted (2003, 209), Calvin seems to go much further: "Ceremonies are but accessories, . . . to keep the faithful in the service of God . . . and to call on him with praises which show one is not ungrateful toward him and to humble oneself in order to bear all afflictions with patience" (*Calvini Opera* 24:7–8).

DAVID CHYTRAEUS (OR *KOCKHAFE*) (1530–1600)

David Chytraeus was a protegé of Melanchthon at Wittenberg, whose studies were interrupted by the Schmalkaldic War and the Interim (1547–52). In time he received at Rostock a doctorate (1551) and then a chair in theology (1563). As part of preparation for his contribution to the Formula of Concord, he wrote *De sacrificio novi testamenti* translated as *Chytraeus on Sacrifice: A Reformation Treatise in Biblical Theology*. His Leviticus commentary dates from 1575 (*Tertius liber Moyais, qui inscribitur Leviticus*, addita enarratione. Wittenberg, 1575.) Of course, these offerings did not placate God's anger. One best sees them as types of the spiritual worship, or as forms or every good work and virtue kindled by the Holy Spirit (cf. 1 Pet 2 and

Heb 13), including gospel preaching and consecrating one's whole self. The main point is that one cannot apply a sacrament to someone else, for application happens by personal faith and use of the sacrament.

CYRIACUS SPANGENBERG (1528–1604)

Spangenberg was trained at Wittenberg where he was among the last of Luther's students, although he was more guided by Melanchthon. He was minister at Eisleben then Mansfeld in 1553 as the Duke's preacher where he wrote a large history of that part of Saxony (*Chronica*). His career was troubled by his insistence on sin's corruption reaching to the essence of human beings. This was found too extreme even for Lutherans like Jacob Andreae and he was forced out from Mansfeld in 1575. In his *Pentateuchus: sive Mosis libri quincque* (Aristorf-Basel, 1618), rather than write a standard commentary, he set out the Pentateuch text in the form of tables, with the aim of representing the sublime sanctity of the content to serve as aids to memory; one was not to expect "Ciceronian eloquence" in such notes. Jerome, Hesychius, and Brenz were his sources, but Christ and celestial mysteries were what were to be sought in the text of Leviticus. Never a Hebraist, he used the S. Pagnini Latin translation, as amended by Vatable and others.

HENRY AINSWORTH (1571–1622)

Trained at Caius, Cambridge, Ainsworth was pastor of the English Separatist congregation that had fled in 1593 from London and reassembled in Amsterdam until his death (Sprunger 1982, 57). For Ainsworth, holiness meant separation from sin, the Anglican Prayer Book, and Dutch Reformed spouses. He published his *Pentateuch Observations* between 1616 and 1619 (Amsterdam). These *Annotations* were recommended as a foundation for the marginal notes that were intended to accompany the revision of the Authorized Version, planned by the Cromwellian Council of State in 1652. Ainsworth was best known for his *Apologie or Defence of Such True Christians as Are Commonly (but Unjustly) Called Brownists* (n.p., 1604). Crucial to his approach to Scripture is the repudiation of any sort of nationally binding covenant. Likewise the teaching of the Pentateuch was for the church, and did not give the magistrate any authority, which belonged to Christ alone as the antitype of Moses and Aaron (Selement 1973, 69). He tried to give precise renderings of Hebrew words (Muller 2003, 163). There is also a "tendency to gravitate towards rabbinic sources" (Muller 2003, 169–73).

ANDREW WILLET (1562–1621)

Willet became a Cambridge fellow and ordained into Anglican ministry in the mid 1580s. From the mid 1590s, although a doctor of divinity of Cambridge, he was Rector at Barley on the Hertfordshire-Essex border. Willet argued that the true identity of Melchizedek (Gen 14/Heb 7:3) was Shem and argued that the NT text demythologized the OT one so that he should be understood as an earthly-royal not heavenly priest figure (Muller 2003, 197). In his commentary on Leviticus (*Hexapla, that is, a six-fold commentary on the Pentateuch*. London: printed by Aug. Matthewes for Robert Milbourne, 1631), each chapter had treatment: "1.of the contents; 2. Divers readings; 3. the questions discussed; 4. places of doctrine; 5. errors confuted; 6. Moral observations." The word "ceremony" does not come from *Ceres* or *cereis* (wax candles) but from *cherem* (ban)! (ibid., 5.) Allegories were, for Willet, "Popish" "whom Lorinus followeth, but Tostatus widely declineth." He observes with Hesychius that the Pentateuch is one perpetual history, divided "as the traveller divideth his journeys in the way" (ibid., 2). He often says he will not stay on "mystical applications" but he always likes to mention those of Hesychius and sometimes Ralph, although Thomas Aquinas is more appreciated for his sobriety as an interpreter.

JESUIT SCHOLARSHIP

Jesuits, such as Menochius (1575–1655) from Padua, wrote much on the history and political and economic institutions of the Israelites in turn, but was best known for the *Brevis explicatio sensûs litteralis totius Scripturae*, first published at Cologne in 1630, which was built on these earlier scholarly foundations. It is technical and concise, yet widely relied on and soon translated into French, and re-issued well into the nineteenth century. Johannes Lorinus (1559–1634), one of Galileo's outspoken critics, was also active in the mission to the Jews in France. He taught in Paris (at first philosophy as well as exegesis), Milan, and Rome and was theologian to the general of the Jesuits. His commentaries were known for their employment of patristic exegesis, and no less on Leviticus is this erudition made to serve polemical ends: *Ioannis Lorini Societatis Iesu Commentarii in Leuiticum*. 2nd ed. Antwerp: Petrum & Belleros, 1620. Cornelius a Lapide was the outstanding early modern Jesuit exegete. Hailing from present-day Belgium, Lapide, after a long spell as Professor of Exegesis in Leuven, starting in 1596, then moved to Rome in 1616 at the Collegium Romanum in Rome where he remained. He focused on the historical sense on which he superimposed the distilled riches of spiritual interpretation from the Patristic and Middle Ages (Armogathe 1989). With his *Commentaria in Pentateuchum Mosis* (Antwerp: Nutium, 1630) Lapide became very popular in Jesuit circles at a time when the order considered the Bible's interpretation as its jurisdiction in defense of doctrines such as "created grace." His lack of precise knowledge of Protestant theology might well reveal a preference for biblical over controversial theology (Boss 1962, 89).

JOHANNES PISCATOR (1546–1625)

Piscator came from Strasbourg, then taught at Neustadt for a few years before finding his place at the true Reformed seminary of Herborn in Nassau. He published his *In Leviticum* in November 1614 (*Commentarius in Leviticum*. Herborn in Nassau, 1615), using the Tremellius-Junius translation as a guide, rather than his own German translation, although in many places he would use his own. Piscator considered juridical laws still to be valid. This connects with his rejection of any imputation of Christ's obedience to believers which would leave them with nothing to do (see Mühling 2009). In his approach to Scripture, the rule was: "First the general then the particular; first the original then the derived" (Bos 1932, 58). In practice this meant "argument" and "textual observations" before exegesis. He was most of all concerned with implications for Christian practice. Piscator had been the editor of Ramus's *Logic* after the latter's untimely death. In the introduction to *Leviticus* he promises: (1) logical analysis of individual chapters; (2) *scholia*; (3) observations of a topical (commonplace) sort. He ends the introduction by telling us what the book is all about. In his attempt to grasp the Hebrew truth through the language, Piscator's way is to write *scholia* on the Hebrew text before giving us his observations. It is not clear that these are always very enlightening.

HUGO GROTIUS (1583–1645)

The Dutch Remonstrant lawyer and polymath believed in apostolic tradition and patristic exegesis as important for interpretation of Scripture (Reventlow 1997, 224). The "charismatic" transparency of the written text gave way in later Israelite writing to something more institutional (Laplanche 2006, 54), but Leviticus was an early expression of natural religion, yet with lessons for magistrates. Some things in the OT that look like prophecies are better understood as types; so one can speak of a higher sense, but not a proper sense of their foreseeing the NT. Grotius followed the style of L. Valla's *Annotations* (cf. later examples by Erasmus, Beza, and Johann Camerarius). According to the *Preface to the Reader* in his *Annotata ad Vetus Testamentum: Tomus I* (Paris: Cramoisy, Architypographi, Cramoisy, 1644, though written twenty years earlier) he has gladly "drawn from extra-biblical sources whatever pertained to the confirming or explaining of the sacred history." Grotius used the Targums, with help from Tremellius, but also the Christian exegesis by those familiar with the

Jewish tradition: Jerome and Chrysostom, and more recently, Vatable, Junius, and Menochius.

ABRAHAM CALOV (1612–86)

Abraham Calov was at first a professor at Königsberg and pastor in Danzig (1643–50), then a professor at Wittenberg where he failed to win the Jena faculty over to condemn the "syncretist" Calixt. Calov asked the question, "What matters more than biblical theology?" Foundational for this approach was his *Criticus sacer biblicus* (1643/1672) and he argued against the Roman Catholic view that the LXX was higher, and against much of what Bellarmine had represented. Much of Calov's commentary (*Biblia Testam. Veteris [et Novi] illustrata. insertis etiam ex voto eruditorum annotatis Grotii vniversis.* (Frankfurt: Christoph Wust, 1672) was written in extended adversarial dialogue with Grotius. The main purpose of Leviticus was as a visible and real sermon to foreshadow the propitiating sacrifice of Christ which, as Hebrews 11:3 reminds us, were laid down from the sacrifices in Adam's family after the proclamation of the gospel. The secondary purpose is to promote God's honor and worship, providing images of the true internal worship and signs of spiritual sacrifices.

LOUIS CAPPEL (1585–1658)

Educated at Sedan and then Saumur, as well as two years studying Arabic at Oxford, Cappel became best known for his controversial thesis in his *Arcanum punctuationis revelatum* (Leiden: Apud Iohannem Maire, 1624) that the vowel points of the Hebrew Bible originated no earlier than with the Massoretes halfway through the first Christian millennium. This gave him the confidence to offer textual emendations to the Hebrew text, and, accordingly, new interpretations (*Critica Sacra.* Paris, 1650). His biblical commentaries were published posthumously by his son in 1689 in *Commentarii et notae criticae in Vetus Testamentum*. The Hebrew Bible was the oldest of all religious texts and that gave it authority or at least to be the battleground for controversy. (Laplanche 1994, 14; Klauber 1993).

JOHANNES COCCEIUS (1603–69)

Professor at Leiden in the mid-seventeenth century in his *Summa doctrina de foedere et testamento Dei* (Leiden: Voorn, 1648), Cocceius discovered the same subject everywhere in the Bible, and especially in the prophecies: Christ and his kingdom. "The Bible became a prolonged prophecy of the history of the Christian Church" (Van den

Wall 2003, 201). The OT legal precepts, however, belong to the covenant of works, and all they could have given was *aphesis* but not full *paresis* (Van Asselt 2001, 282f). Therein a five-step abrogation or implosion of the covenant of works is described. "Friendship with God," which was the content of the new covenant (Van Asselt 2001, 256), seems something much more internal and individual than the public religion of Israel. His introductory remarks to Leviticus (*Opera Omnia*. Amsterdam: Blaeu, 1701, I, 158) state that these precepts were heavy and not life-giving.

AUGUSTIN CALMET (1672–1757)

In 1704, Augustine Calmet became Professor of Exegesis in Münster then in 1715 took on a series of positions as head of priories in eastern France. His *Commentaire littéral sur tous les livres de l'ancien et du nouveau testament* (Paris: Emery, 1709) shows that, as with his Reformed counterparts at Saumur, to Calmet the OT seemed ethically inferior. For Calmet the OT was at best simply preparatory for NT, and in fact all its rites and laws were meant to humble the Israelites and provide a foil for the graciousness of the NT (Laplanche, 1994, 66, with reference to Calmet's Preface, 22). For an enlightened scholar he is still very interested in the religion of the OT as having much to commend it, and was a firm believer in Mosaic authorship. The logical conclusion from Calmet's devaluation of much of the Pentateuch was drawn by Voltaire in his discussion of the Pentateuch, *La Bible enfin expliquée: par plusieurs aumoniers de S.M.L.R.D.P.* (1776), which devoted barely seven pages (156–63) to the whole Pentateuch, omitting discussion of any section that is "purely ceremonial."

JEAN LECLERC (1657–1736)

Leclerc was educated in a still-orthodox Geneva, from 1676–78, and although taught by the Cartesian J.-R. Chouet, his work under Lockean influence was empiricist rather than rationalist (Reventlow 1988, 1–19). In his *De Institutionis theologiae ordine ac methodo* he attacks scholastics for thinking Scripture was not clear enough and for making things complicated, which leads to conflicts. One must keep Christian metaphysics out of "Moses" and for Christian dogmatics NT texts alone should be used. For him there were two types of commentary—a grammatical one and a theological-exegetical one, and he preferred the former. For Leclerc, God gave the Jews the cult to inoculate them against worse pagan practices. There is a strong influence in the commentary (*Mosis Prophetae Liber Tertus*. Amsteloami: De Lorme, 1693) of J. Spencer's *De legibus hebraeorum ritualibus et earum rationibus*. Then in 1693 Leclerc reversed his view (*Dissertatio de Scriptore pentateuchi Mose*) and affirmed Mosaic authorship (Woodbridge 1989, 71). There did, however, remain a disparagement of the OT in general, and the Levitical laws in particular.

SIMON PATRICK (1626–1707)

Simon Patrick was an Anglican bishop who came from a Presbyterian family. As bishop at Chichester (1689) and then Ely (from 1691) he was Latitudinarian, and a promoter of the "Society for the Propagation of Christian Knowledge." In his *Commentary upon the Historical Books of the OT* (5th ed. London: printed for D. Midwinter, 1738; 1st ed. 1694), he says he has heard of Leclerc but had no time to read him due to "public business." In the preface he writes that Moses has taught us more than any other author about the beginning of the world, as the inventor of arts, laws, and kingdoms. Maimonides and Procopius seem to feature, with Pellikan being his favorite among the more recent. He sees the OT as a purely practical religion. God does not tell his people to find strange animals to sacrifice, but rather those that lay to hand.

MATTHEW HENRY (1662–1714)

Matthew Henry was born to a Puritan manse, which meant that, as a nonconformist, by 1685 he was forbidden to attend university by the 1661 Act of Uniformity. However, he learned enough theology to become pastor of Chester Presbyterian Church, then latterly that of Hackney. In his *An exposition of all the books of the Old and New Testament* (London: printed for J. Clark and R. Hett, et al., 1721–25) he turns at times to Patrick for historical details but is largely unconcerned with historical details or textual problems, such is his interest in the spiritual-typological sense, received through prayer, resulting in occasional "brilliant insights" (Old 2007, 523f).

CARL KEIL (1807–88)

After basic training and conversion in Dorpat (Tartu), Keil wrote his dissertation under E. W. Hengstenberg in Berlin, although he would be a more careful scholar while subscribing to a model that saw the testaments linked "organically" by salvation-history rather than by prophecy fulfillment (Siemens 1994, 212). Professor at Dorpat from 1839, he combated rationalism in theology and was in close contact with systematicians like Havernick. *The Biblischen Kommentar über das Alte Testament* (BC) was his answer to the *Kurzgefaßten Exegetischen Handbuch über das Alte Testament*, as contributed to by Knobel. His Leviticus commentary was issued in 1862 (rev. 1870), and translated as *Biblical Commentary: Pentateuch* (Edinburgh:

T. & T. Clark, 1864–66). It reflects a decade of debate with J. H. Kurtz, his successor at Dorpat, over the need to accord with Lutheran confessional view, e.g., on biblical authorship. In any case Leviticus was "the codex of the spiritual ordering of life of the community of Jehovah."

AUGUST KNOBEL (1807–63)

Knobel studied from 1826 at Breslau. He always seemed to have a wide-ranging intellectual interest, having researched in historical and practical theology. He wrote commentaries on Qohelet and the book *Der Prophetismus der Hebräer* (1837). After moving to Giessen, a battle with Ewald—who had attacked his Isaiah commentary in the 1840s—displayed him as a rationalist in his writing. On the Pentateuch, his source-critical observations were on the way to the new documentary hypothesis, although his own can be described as *"Ergänzungshypothese,"* i.e., that the Pentateuch as it stands represents an original from the time of Moses to which much has been added. His *Bücher Exodus und Leviticus* was published at Leipzig in 1857 as part of the *Kurzgefaßten exegetischen Handbuches zum Alten Testament*, whose proclaimed goal was to *describe* as much of the detail of grammar and historical insight as could be squeezed into such a series (Kraus 1982, 169).

AUGUST DILLMANN (1823–94)

August Dillmann was a student of Ewald at Tübingen in 1840s. After being professor there in 1854, he took the Chair of Oriental Languages at Kiel. A decade later he went to Giessen as Professor of OT Exegesis, then finally (1869) to Berlin as a successor to Hengstenberg. His strength in Ethiopic makes it not surprising that his Pentateuchal treatments, not least in his reworking of Knobel's commentary, feature the linguistic and textual. Dillmann took over from Knobel two-fifths of the whole, especially the archaeological, geographical, and "comparative religious" material (Dillmann 1897, vi). He tried more than Knobel to represent the views of others, and makes one aware there is more than one possible interpretation of evidence. He is just aware of A. Klostermann's "discovery" (followed by Abraham Kuenen) of "H" (Lev 17–25) as distinct material (see Houtman 1994).

ANDREW BONAR (1810–92)

Andrew Bonar pastored at Finnieston Free Church (Glasgow). An interest in mission—specifically that to the Jews—helps explain a vivid account of the land of Leviticus, around the same time as Holman Hunt's trip which inspired *The*

Scapegoat (1847). *A Commentary on the Book of Leviticus* (New York: Carter, 1851) soon followed. A letter of 1860 reports his joy at "a soul saved through reading my *Commentary on Leviticus*—the captain of a steamer in the Thames." Works such as his *Palestine for the Young* (London: The Religious Tract Society, 1866) show a near-obsessive attention to biblical geography of Palestine, by one who had never been there. It is significant that he used a model of the Tabernacle to help in his gospel preaching.

ALEXANDER MCLAREN (1826-1911)

McLaren was born in 1826 in Glasgow, trained at the Baptist College at Stepney before becoming minister at Union Chapel, Manchester ("the Nonconformist Cathedral of Lancashire") from 1858 to 1908. "Betraying Quaker tendencies, he also downplayed the sacraments of baptism and communion" (R. Chadwick 2004). He seemed, as twice president of the Baptist Union, able to unite liberals and conservatives. His work on Leviticus comes from the mature thirty-two-volume work, *Expositions of Holy Scripture* (London: Hodder & Stoughton, 1904–10). He developed a knowledge of Hebrew at Regent's Park College. Higher criticism, he believed, got in the way of the eternal message of inerrant Scripture.

PRESENT DAY

By the time we get to the commentary of Baentsch (*Handkommentar zum Alten Testament* [Göttingen: Vandenhoeck & Ruprecht, 1903]), even the question of the content of the ideology of the book as "theocratic" has given way to considerations of a documentary sort, an insistence on understanding the book through understanding the process of its composition as a reflection of stages in the development of Israelite religion (e.g., the burnt offering overshadows the *minchah* after the centralization of the cult, to the loss of its function as establishing communion). The twentieth century then witnessed a near determination to avoid anything other than grammatical, literary (source-critical), and historical work and a fortitude to avoid saying anything that could provoke a verdict that exegesis had wandered into interpretation. The commentaries of Noth and Elliger (1966) and, in English, that of Budd (1996), show a tendency to minimalism. This situation changed somewhat with the impact of the work of Mary Douglas (1966), which interested itself in the worldview accompanying the texts yet with a sense that it had something of universal philosophical depth to say to the present. This was followed by the works of Jewish commentators, principally those by Baruch Levine (1989), Jacob Milgrom (1998–2003), Baruch Schwartz (2003), and the "ecumenical" (Christian-Jewish) work of R. Rendtorff (2004), whose scholarly engagement with the ancient text was matched only by their faith commitment and an understanding of the text as seed for the spiritual flourishing of a faith community. If the voice of *classical* Jewish writers is less prominent in this commentary, it is to be clearly heard in nearly all scholarship on Leviticus of the last three decades.

Leviticus 1

Matters Hermeneutical

RUNNING THROUGH SO MUCH of Origen's exegesis is what we might call hermeneutical justification for his spiritual interpretation through what is itself a spiritual interpretation of a text! So, the priest who takes off the skin of the burnt offering in dismembering the animal (1:13) is he who takes the veil off the letter of the word of God and lays bare internal organs of spiritual understanding. Leviticus, Johannes Brenz writes 1300 years later, may seem useless since all Mosaic law, especially that of sacrifices, has been abrogated. He does not expect his message from Leviticus to be very popular in the church. In fact, even the OT prophets in their own time rejected sacrifices. Hebrews is like a commentary on this book of Leviticus. That means that the NT writers did pay Leviticus much attention, the better to understand the sacrifice of Christ. Authors of old have wrongly despised Leviticus as unworthy of God: Lucian, that ancient sceptic, ridiculed sacrifices; but the Holy Spirit laughs back. Leviticus is no more or less a scandal than the shameful cross itself, as signified by the removal of the skin (1:13). Whether one comes to the text through the Spirit (Origen) or one sees it as a fascinating enigma (Brenz), there is a recognition that there is more to Leviticus than meets the eye.

And yet it must be acknowledged that for all those who urged blessing from the external—whether the letter of the text or the *realia* of the sacrifices—there were others who wished attention to be quickly diverted to the Christian doctrines and figures which these things symbolized. The spiritualizing interpretation was viewed as a gospel interpretation according to those following in the tradition of Augustine's *On the Spirit and Letter*.

Peter Cantor therefore writes: "When the Lord through Ezekiel (20:25) witnesses that he had given not good precepts to them, who does not see that in these there is not the goodness of his justice but only an image and figure of his justice."

There is in some strands of Christian commentary a premise that the laws themselves were harmful since, from the golden calf incident onwards, the OT Jews failed to obey even though these laws remained just. That Christian hermeneutic felt itself to have the OT prophets on its side, not least Ezekiel. That did not mean that Leviticus was not worth reading, but that it should not be gazed at. "And it is no wonder if we say that Moses gave signs to the people instead of words since that was always the way of the wise in those times. But Leviticus out of the other books of Moses as ceremonial is more full of mysteries, so that it needs almost everywhere more spiritual intelligence and mystical exposition than others. Its matter is twofold, for it is written 'inward and outward'; history and the killing letter are its outward matter, the spiritual understanding the interior" (P. Cantor, *Verbum Abbreviatum*).

The Puritan Andrew Willet maintains a view that affirms the law as eternal (if read in the light of the NT—here agreeing for once with his adversary, Lorinus)—while holding the practices (i.e., the OT Jewish use of the law) to have passed. "This also may bee observed, that whereas the Morall Law was delivered out of mount Horeb, shewing the firmenesse and continuance thereof, durable as the mountains: the ceremoniall Law of sacrifices, was given out of the Tabernacles, which was but as a tent to bee removed, shewing the immutabilitie of those Ceremonies." It seems that as part of the written law they last for ever even though in physical terms they are no more. Whereas the moral law bound them before it was given, the ceremonial did so only once it came into being.

Calling (v. 1)

The Hebrew title for the Pentateuchal books is taken from the opening word. For the third book this is *wayyiqrāʾ* ("And he called"). While Rashi makes much of this (call "implies" affection and the communication of privileged utterance), Nahmanides explains that the Lord called from the tent so that Moses would enter it to converse with him. For Pseudo-Bede (and the text seems to presuppose some early Jewish discussion, possibly *Sifra*) the "calling" of verse 1 does not come "out of the blue." "Now there was a calling that happened before this, that is he gave the knowledge of himself in the laws of nature. This natural law does not get left behind but grows in the laws and from the letter into the new and universal . . . The Lord Called from the tabernacle, can also be understood as God the Father calling Christ from heaven to the incarnation." According to the *Glossa Ordinaria*, Hesychius, as relayed by Rabanus, tells us that this "he called" in verse 1 links back to Exodus just as the start of Numbers does to Leviticus. The verb is used concerning Bezalel in Exodus 35:30 and maybe this hints at looking back to previous instruction, as well as looking ahead to the higher things (*usque ad*). Thus Moses stands at a halfway mark on the way to salvation. The whole spiritual intention is to call us back from sin and that is the sense of the Latin "*revocavit*" as the LXX has it (Denys). Yet it has to be admitted that the Christian tradition pays much less attention to verse 1 than the Jewish tradition does.

The Point of Offering (v. 2)

Theodoret made his mark on the tradition of interpretation by suggesting that the sacrificial cult served to realign their basic instincts. Since in Egypt the people were taught to sacrifice to demons God allowed sacrifices in the desert. "This has been made clear through Ezekiel the prophet (16:6) *I saw you in your blood and I said in your blood life and increase*. Seeing you rejoicing in the blood of sacrifices, he permitted you to follow these desires. For these and other reasons he prepared a safeguard from evil by means of a strong remedy (*pharmakon*). For he ordered them to sacrifice the things which were worshipped in Egypt . . . He specified unclean things so that they would not make them gods but only worship the one to whom they were sacrificing." This interpretation became perhaps the widely accepted rationale for the OT cult from then on, although it might be fair to say it needed to be reintroduced in the early modern period through reading Maimonides (Stroumsa 2001).

Theodoret emphasizes that God commanded according to the capability of the people and they brought forward their gifts as offerings of salvation not from legal necessity but from their own pious will. Abraham took care not to separate the heads from the bodies of the birds he offered. There is here a sympathetic view of OT religion as "grace-full" in which law is not the condition of election but the foundation of life in the covenant. Theodoret also thinks that deliberate sins are included (see also his comment on 7:20). The priestly offerings were made for sins and mistakes and ignorance. Sin is a willing transgression of the law, but a wrong is a transgression arising out of a circumstance.

Lyra on Leviticus 1:2 offers three reasons why these offerings were commanded: he gets the first reason from Moses Maimonides (avoidance of idolatry) and the second from Thomas Aquinas (encouraging worship) and the third is that of "pre-figuring Christ." This "interfaith" approach is reinforced: Hebrews 9:22 after all has exact parallel in *Yoma* 5a and *Zebahim* 6a (Hailperin 1963, 212). Rashi was very explicit about Moses officiating as a priest during the days on which Aaron was consecrated a priest (on Exod 40:29). This, Hailperin (1963, 207) muses, was possibly an idea Lyra shared with his Parisian contemporary Marsilius of Padua, who downplayed the role of the priest in forgiveness. The agent is the believer more than the priest, so for Gersonides (d. 1344), as well as his Christian contemporary, this included any penitent Gentile. Mirroring the three reasons are three goals: first, *confession of false worship* (idolatry): it is important that even the priest "top up" his holiness by first offering himself and the priest's own confession at start of the Mass is mentioned. (This provides the rationale for Psalm 42[43]:4—"I will go up to the altar [so, LXX, Vg; Heb. 'hill'] of God"—as that which becomes the start of the Western Mass, down through the Council of Trent and beyond the opening lines of Joyce's *Ulysses*, where Buck Mulligan equates morning Mass with his shaving ritual. There is an almost univocal equation of the OT altar with the church altar.) The second aim is *to become aware of God's goodness* (David in 1 Chronicles 29 confesses: "of your own do we give you"). The third is *to teach virtue*: the bull signifies Christ's courage, the sheep his innocence, the goat his "likeness of human flesh." The very presence of the Hebrew term ʾ*ādām* ("man") in the text seems to inspire a democratizing treatment in Jewish and Christian interpreters, with the Christian mention of Christ as "everyman" reinforcing this emphasis.

From an early modern providentialist outlook, such as Cajetan's, truth was retained even in the unrighteous use of these laws, when Hebrew idolaters turned towards cruel *human* sacrifice in their misuse of such commands; for even then there was a (ironic) foreshadowing of Christ's coming to human sacrifice. The Reformers felt the need to insist that *only Christ's death justified*, and therefore there was a dissimilarity between what the priest in the Eucharist should intend "today" and what his counterpart did in Israelite times. Hence Conrad Pellican comments that the placing on of hands signifies devotion and faith with acknowledgement of God's benefits and recognition of our need for justification from outside ourselves, although we must supply faith and devotion. Chytraeus delights in the variety of sacrifices, which indicates the variety of benefits Christ gives. He cautions that in the offering of 1:6 the significance is not its being daily repeated, but that it is of a *lamb*. It is also clear that there is only one place for worship, in *Stiftskirchen* (mainline churches) worship is to be regular as ruled by the Word as God, who tells his people how to worship, and that is never in private! Paul spoke in 1 Corinthians 11 of a *receiving* not of an oblation of Christ's body and blood. The priestly function is to pass on to others the good news of Christ's death, not to placate God's anger.

The Burnt Offering Specifically (vv. 3–9)

Rashi held this offering to be *in lieu* of a punishment for sins of violating a prohibition and failing to perform a commandment, and Nahmanides unpacks this by explaining that it includes sinful thoughts which require a burnt offering, as in Job 1:5. Unwilling sins will be dealt with in Leviticus 5–7. This perhaps skewers the assumption prevalent in more modern commentary, that the offerings in the first chapters are symbolically offering up one's life through identification with the beast which does so literally (Janowski 1982, 220) or even have little originally to do with atonement (Rendtorff 2004, 43). "Basic sinfulness" is seen to be in view, whatever the other purposes of the burnt-offerng. The LXX term *holocaustos* and Vulgate *holocaustum* can be Anglicized as "holocaust" (as in the Jerusalem Bible of 1966), but this is "no longer a good translation" (Hartley 1992, 17), and K. S. Davidowicz (2006) represents this objection when he writes that "holocaust" as an offering brought before God is an unsuitable term for what happened to the Jews. (Many Jews refer to the holocaust as the *Shoah* [catastrophe].) The English word might have lost view of its etymological origins, but in using it to equate the amount of Jewish destruction to that of Hiroshima, there developed the connotation that the literal cremations had a symbolic resonance.

The word "holocaust" was actually used before World War II, denoting huge fires with casualties, disasters, or liquidations. As an article in *Ha'aretz* (Thursday, March 13, 2008, Adar27, 5768) shows: "The casualties of World War I were referred to, in the press, as 'holocaust,' and that was also the term *The Times* used when reporting on the book burning in Berlin in 1933. Winston Churchill writes in his book *The Aftermath* (1929): 'As for the Turkish atrocities . . . helpless Armenians, men, women, and children together, whole districts blotted out in one administrative holocaust—these were beyond human redress.' The article then argues that the word is too biblically (and Christianly) loaded to be serviceable and concludes by quoting: "To turn the Jewish genocide into a sacrifice makes it a 'biblical' event rather than an event of our time—a myth rather than a reality . . . The Holocaust should not be isolated, labeled as *sui generis*, the cataclysmic event, the discontinuity in history—all those things that necessarily follow when the Holocaust is seen as 'The Holocaust'" (Garber and Zuckermann 1989, 207). They also note that the OED and Webster continue to give the "sacrifice" definition first. If God *were* punishing Israel in any sense then he was doing it in the way of the Akedah, i.e., in the framework of love. The authors of the Ha'aretz article reject this parallel, but they affirm that some Jews have thought this way, on the grounds that putting the hideous fate of the covenant people of God outside of the providence of the covenant God is a concession to the secularizing and nihilist-"shoahistic" forces of destruction whose deeds necessitated the search after a *mot juste*. "Holocaust" might not be such a bad word. It is worth remembering that *shoah* as annihilation is equally biblical in resonance (Isa 10:3) and captures the radical bleak nihilism of the events. Yet Leviticus 6:9 (It is the burnt offering, because of the burning upon the altar all night unto the morning), however harrowingly, recalls the cremation that lasted day and night in the death camps.

It can be argued that the clue to the spiritualizing of sacrifice lies in the text itself, in that the burnt offering, where what is solid turns into vapor, is the very first thing a reader encounters.

In Homily 1, Origen makes clear that here it is humanity (*anthropos*) that, according to the (LXX) text, is making this offering. So Origen thinks in spiritual-cosmic terms, but not without an anchoring in the particulars of Christian salvation history. He also notes that Jesus was offered up by Annas and Caiaphas, the sons of Aaron. There are heavenly as well as earthly sacrifices (cf. Heb 12:23; Col 1:20), such that Origen can speak of a double offering (*duplex hostia*) of Jesus wherein he offered his vital power as a spiritual sacrifice (Origen 1981, I, 78). The divine "fire" which then comes down to accept the sacrifice symbolizes a third dimension to Christ, a fire which draws or assimilates all the Savior did in the body to his divine nature, an idea not unconnected with Origen's insistence on the spirit of Christ as a mediator between divinity and humanity (cf. *On the Principles* II, 6–8). There is also a moral sense for the end of the sermon: one can offer one's own flesh up as sacrifice in order to have access to the entrance of the tent, where the pure soul can then gain a hearing of the divine books. Virtue gains access to wisdom.

Of course, "spiritualization" of sacrifice had been going of for a while and not just in Christianity. Spiritualizing in the sense of matter disappearing into air is there from Leviticus 1:2 itself. The Dead Sea Scrolls manifest belief in a temple that is invisible now yet "quasi-physical to come" (4Q *Florilegium*). For a while the Jerusalem church could play the role of the Levites over against the rest of the Gentile church (Himmelfarb 2006), but in Gentile circles the priesthood had not been hereditary and later NT such as Hebrews and Revelation set it to one side because cultic sacrifice had had its day. Klawans (2005, 220) suggests the importance of sacrifice remained in the metaphorical employment of its categories. Hence one could speak of a "sacralization of behavior and prayer" as much as a spritualization of sacrifice. It might be better to see some sort of meeting in the middle through some mutual metaphorizing effect, such that there was little awareness that Leviticus 1–16 and Leviticus 17–25 were about different things. In Romans 15:16 Paul portrays himself in sacerdotal terms as a priest who "offers Gentiles." The church's being a royal priesthood might mean less "democratization" of priesthood than a "sacerdotalization" of ecclesiology.

What Christianity *introduced* was not internalizing or spiritualizing—there was plenty of that in Porphyry's vegetarian *On Abstinence*, while Iamblichus's two-tier vision is also individualistic and has a remarkable similarity to the Eucharist in the city and watchful sacrifice of prayer in the desert (cf. Chrysostom, *Hom on Hebrews* 17, 3; Aphrahat, Dem 4; cited in Stroumsa 2009, 74)—but monotheism's associated idea of "insurmountable distance to God," such that *metanoia* had to be achieved morally not intellectually. True, *Verus Israel* had to *see* behind the text, but it then had obediently to *do*, and thus it was a public religion (Stroumsa 2009, 24f). Christianity changed ascesis from discovering to reforming the self. Still, unlike post-70 AD Judaism, "Christianity defined itself precisely as a religion centered on sacrifice, even if it was a reinterpreted sacrifice. The Christian *anamnesis* was the reactivation of the sacrifice of the Son of God, performed by the priests" (Stroumsa 2009, 72).

Yet with the ripening of allegorical interpretation the idea of whole/burnt offering was an obvious candidate for the metaphor of self-sacrifice. So, Isidore of Seville, reported in the *Glossa Ordinaria* on 1:3, claims "from the flock" means "from the stock of the patriarchs," who "by the plough of his cross subdued the land of our flesh and very much made the seed of the virtues of the Holy spirit to flourish." The reference to Christ's sacrifice is almost lost in the rush to get to a spiritual-moral interpretation, which, while dependent on a christological reading, almost obscures it: "We now morally offer a bull when we conquer the arrogance of the flesh, the lamb when we correct irrational emotions, goat when we overcome lasciviousness, dove when we are simple, turtle-dove when we are chaste or keep chastity; the unleavened bread when we dine not in the leaven of evil but in the unleaven of sincerity and truth."

Of course, this spirituality is meant to be Christ-focused. The *Glossa* continues: "The sense of offering 'all things' (as in verse 13) means that we offer our whole person to be conformed to the spiritual scriptures which are written about the intelligible altar of the Lord's body..."

Or, to take a twelfth-century example, the place where the ashes from the sacrifice were poured signifies the righteous humility of the person who does not boast of the tasks he has taken on nor the greatness of revelations, but remembers that he will return to dust (Rupert of Deutz). The high point of medieval spiritual-moralizing interpretation, where the referent of the text is the soul and its parts, comes with Ralph of Flaix's highly popular commentary on verse 6: "We remove the skin of the sacrifice when we, not content with the superficial in life, see past the things which are only good to look at and see the hidden vices. The wood is the virtuous thinking which encourages the Holy Spirit to blaze so that doing good becomes a pleasure ... some people abandon carnal lusts but don't rise to spiritual desires."

Engaging Leviticus

The point is that Leviticus mirrors the soul's anatomy. Denys the Carthusian wants also to spiritualize: "The work as it works (*opus operans*) pleases him, i.e., the interior intent and devotion and the exterior too in those who possess love, who prefigure the sacrifice of Christ which truly pleased God. As Aquinas puts it (*ST* I–II, q101), the human person is ordered into God, not only through interior acts of faith, hope, and love but by external effort—to show we are God's servants."

So with Denys, these sacrifices were intended not just to divert people from idolatry but to enable them to give honor to God by using his chosen methods, and to show them to be sinners. This sounds little different from what Lyra has already established, until we look closer at Denys's argument: "The altar in the soul is faith in which all deeds need to operate, or else they are sin. As an ox ploughs the land, so the Lord and Savior throws up the heavenly word and supernatural grace, and spiritually ploughs the church on earth, then soothes it, opens it and fertilizes. The Father in offering up the Son was not angry with him but that the Son for his honor placated the father 'accidentally.' Priests once wrongly offered up Christ, but since his resurrection they can do this in a good and saving way."

This tradition of interpretation endured and was given a new lease of life in early modern Puritanism as with Andrew Willet who, concerning the dividing of the parts of the burnt offering (v. 6), wrote, "Whereby is signified, that hee which cometh unto God must, *singula examinare,* examine all his parts, yea his inward thoughts, and consecrate them unto God." Willet sees sacrifices to be classified as serving mystical, spiritual, moral, civil, and one or two other ends. The word "ceremony" does not come from *ceres* or *cereis* (wax) candles but *cherem* ("set apart")! Nothing was to be brought into worship without God's direction. As Hebrews suggests, these sacrifices had no power to justify or purge consciences in the time of the law. And since Christ's resurrection they have lost their power to do any good or harm.

A more positive, less intense form of this surfaces in the "enlightened" comments of Jean Leclerc: the fire of the burnt offering is the flame of charity from the Holy Spirit, and the wood symbolizes holy thoughts. Some people abandon carnal lusts but don't rise to spiritual desires. Is it the case that goats, which signify lusts, are being offered to God!? But the goat is a dead one. *Extermination* of sin is what is acceptable to God. And yet there is a cosmic dimension to this that is not to be overlooked. The whole context is the temple of God, his presence along with the saints in heaven. There is also the importance of study and meditation as the means of bridging the cosmic and the moral. It is the world of the mind that matters and anyone who inhabits it to desire the bridegroom will have his mind enriched. There can be no prayer without desire. Don't bother praying if your heart does not want eternal life!

Reaction against Spiritualizing

In the Christian tradition such literal concern as with Rashi for the aesthetics of the offering (e.g., avoiding faeces and feathers) or Abarnabel's concern that ashes (v. 16) be disposed of is absent, but instead there is a warning that care ought to be taken with the Christian cultic *realia*, i.e., the offerings of bread and wine. With the formation of a *Corpus Christianorum*, any spiritualizing idea of *un*bloody sacrifice in the Eucharist was slowly lost; already by 804 AD Pope Leo III believed that the actual blood of Christ had been found in Mantua. In some medieval Eucharistic theologies there was a concomitant literalism—that the heart was written on by the transforming power of Christ's "blood infusion" (Angenendt 2000, 377). Amalarius of Metz was on the losing side at the Synod of Quierzy in 838 when he challenged the fully realist view of Eucharistic offering and was seen to loosen the identity between the Eucharist and the historical body of Christ. As the Middle Ages advanced, the notion that one *encountered* salvation history (and hence the offering up of true body and blood), rather than having one's mind directed to it where it resided (in the past or in heaven), came to dominate and a realist-objectivist view of the sacrament became more prevalent and therefore *as* strong as any moral internalizing tendency (Angenendt 2001, 141).

The Christian cult needed to be controlled by the priests (nothing gets offered except through them, and there are "those who offer" and those for whom these are offered—Andrew of St. Victor). Leviticus offered some principles. It started with an offering that was about rendering thanks, and that too is what drives the Mass. There can be very basic accounts of this: for instance, where Stephen Langton hails the outward forms of liturgical worship as helping us to be holy since singing and reading restrain wickedness (not only in his commentary but also in Langton, *De mysterio missae* [PL171, 1177]).

The medieval majority seemed to favor keeping a place for lessons from Leviticus for church worship. Bruno of Segni agrees that Jesus' sacrifice is the great and special sacrifice, which is brought to mind daily by priests and also in the suffering of martyrs, and yet the very beating of the animal flesh signifies also the heartfelt contrition of the believer. Bruno covers all angles when he adds that to touch the sacrifice is really to believe that Christ is God. Even when the infant Jesus is portrayed one never says—"wait until he looks like a forty-year old then we will worship him!"

Hugh of St. Victor, on the other hand, shows some sign of wanting the definitions right, not only for the sake of historical accuracy, but so that NT events can be given the correct interpretations in light of a correct interpretation. "Although Scripture tends to call sacrifice 'offering' and offering 'sacrifice' it is more proper we think to keep sacrifice for animals, offering (oblation) for dry goods, and libation for liquids" (*On the sacraments of the Christian faith* II.2.3, 255). This seems at least to hint at a three-part hierarchy of (a) Christ's sacrifice, (b) Eucharistic oblation, and (c) moral self-offering as per Paul in 2 Timothy 4:6.

Lorinus had stated the Tridentine account of sacrifice and Leviticus as part of his discussion of that topic. That it is the nature of men that they cannot be lifted up to divine things without the help of exterior things. In the OT, as now, there were these ritual symbols and actions.

When Johannes Brenz reacted to this, it was not to spiritualize to the extent that ritual actions did not matter, but simply that the historical cross of Christ mattered more. If Christ had thought the Mass was that which forgave sins then he would not have bothered to endure the cross. The text in Malachi (1:11) that oblation is to be made in his name in every place does not refer to the Popish Mass but to the spreading of the gospel—that Christ was sacrificed for our sins on the cross—among all peoples. The variety signifies the variety not of sacrifices—since there is only one Christ and one true sacrifice—but of the benefits. For David Chytraeus, in a polemic that claims Irenaeus (*Adv Haer* IV.32) for his side, the Fathers never thought of applying benefits to others through the Mass.

Particular Details and Universality of Sacrifice

In worship, Brenz insists, we should not be seeking another Christ or trying to please God without reference to that specific Christ, as the Turks try. We learn from this that it is not enough to bring the offering to the door (that is, to believe that this Christ was indeed Christ); we must go further and transfer our sins to him through faith and believe that he is the sole expiator. The other religions and hypocrites put hands on their own works, not on Christ (vv. 3–4).

Such ceremonies could not offer salvation but they had the civil use of keeping people in a place or a disposition where they *could* hear the Word of God. The energy Brenz expends shows how he thinks the matter of direction in worship is important. Brenz adds: Why facing north (v. 11)? Is not facing east more worthy? Well, explains Brenz, many of the pagans worshipped the sun, facing east then west. Facing north avoids this by turning away from the sun in the meridian and looking to Christ for his light of celestial splendor (v. 15). Killing the animal "on the northern side of the altar" (v. 11) reminds Pellican that Christ was crucified outside Jerusalem, on the Way (*caminus*) of the Lord. Willet observes that the *Gloss* took the worshippers to be eating on the east side "as did Adam and Eve." The *Gloss* here is wrong, he claims (it should be "north" not "east") and errs in its interpretation (i.e., it has nothing to do with sinful Adam and Eve). Instead "it should be signified, the feare of the saints, who are uncertaine of their works." Christians are *not yet* in Paradise and they have to pay close attention to God's revealed will to receive assurance.

The view that pagans copied Moses became standard in Early Modern times, in part due to a rediscovery of Maimonides who had mentioned that the Greeks also excoriated their bulls (Stroumsa 2007, 79)—and they also probably got the idea from Noah, who was common ancestor to them and to the Israelites whose practice is recorded here. Borrhaus shows his training as an alchemist when he concludes: "Just as in the realm of nature it is not the size but the power of things like herbs and blood of goats which can soften diamond, the sap taken from the hellebore plant whose smallest drop counters bile, that divine dust known to the wise, whose smallest part turns impure metals to perfection!"

There was something about the ordering, classifying, and detail that appealed to the early modern mind. However, where the interest in details appears (e.g., Calmet's frustration at not knowing quite which body parts were to be burned in v. 14) it is a symptom of at least a partial shift from the exegete as theologian to the exegete as historian.

In a presaging of recent interpretations by which Leviticus 1's "canonical ordering" suggests that sacrificial offerings are not first and foremost about sin, Grotius first says that this is a *voluntary* offering, not a commanded one (cf. Deut 23:22). He is very quick to point out that the Hebrew of vv. 3–4 is about gaining access to God—not "for the propitiating of God"—and that *kpr* does not mean "expiate" but to "commend" someone to God. On the matter of "burnt offering" (v. 9) he adduces numerous writers including Vergil and Seneca. But the whole point of all Hebrew sacrifices was to be the vehicles of praise, prayers, and blessings (1644, 88).

The "Catholic Enlightenment" view represented by A. Calmet hitched together the universal need and desire to worship with a defense of outward ceremony as essential. It is only the offerings of the righteous that are acceptable to God because they are done in righteousness and a heart of love for the Creator. However, the prophets were attacking only the *abuse*: the instinct to sacrifice is a good one, as enshrined in natural and written law. They would have the minds of the participants remember the figurative nature of these, and the fuller reality that was to come. Calmet explains the need for a priest to give a stamp of approval that an offering is whole, as has been the practice of other lawmakers, from Solon to Mohammed (2–3). It is also important that, as the LXX emphasized with its repetition in 1:4, hands be placed on the head of the beast.

Perhaps a fitting justification of Leviticus being allowed to inform Christian worship is given by Pope Benedict XIV in his *Ex quo* ("On the Euchologion") (1756, 67): "Then to our purpose he [Leo Allatius, d.1669] concludes that it cannot be absolutely asserted that that man judaizes who does something in the Church which corresponds to the ceremonies of the old Law. 'If a man should perform acts for a different end and purpose . . . which resembles the ceremonies of the old Law, he must not always be said to judaize.'"

Keil concluded that "the relation which the sprinkling of the blood (v. 11) and the burning of the flesh of the sacrifice upon the altar (v. 13) bore to one another was that of justification and sanctification," meaning the work of Christ and the Holy Spirit respectively. The comments of Rashi, Ibn Ezra (atonement "to serve as a ransom for life"), and Nahmanides (atonement to allow "closeness" with God) in speaking of sacrifice in place of capital punishment imply that sacrifice does deal with deliberate sins and that their purpose was not merely symbolic or educative. So too for some recent Jewish interpreters, the sacrifice is more like a passport or protection as one comes into the sphere of divine holiness (Levine 1989, 7) or it is decidedly moral and yet also increasingly about joy of restored innocence as expiation became the focus of the newer sacrifices described in Leviticus 4 and 5.

Leviticus 2

The Soul Who Makes the Offering

THE USE OF THE Hebrew word *nefesh* ("soul," "person") at the start of chapter 2 is then echoed in the LXX's *psyche* and the Latin Bible's *anima*. Origen viewed the whole human race as included in Leviticus 1:2's choice of "*anthropos*" (Heb. *ʾādām*), however the subject at the start of Leviticus 2:1 is a more tricky notion with moral connotations. It denotes the one who is merely *psyche* or *anima* (Heb. *nefesh*), which Paul calls *animalem hominem* (1 Cor 2:14–15) who, even if not bound by sin, still does not have anything spiritual which could be figuratively called "the flesh of the Word of God." In other words, it is the *ordinary* believer, the "psychic" one, the one who has the choice whether to sow to the flesh or to the Spirit. (Of course, if he chooses right, the Spirit will guide.) Such a one is not able to offer the big sacrifices as he is unable to test it all, but can only offer things of ordinary life and he certainly needs to have the oil of divine mercy added to his sacrifice if he wants to escape this present life's pull. Lay people too are called to play their part. Ephraim Syrus (d.373) took advantage of the ambiguity of Semitic grammar to see the soul (*nefesh* or *animal*) as object here: "*And if a* nefesh *you bring as a sacrifice* (Lev 2:1), surely, then when one offers a life (*nefesh*) it is as if one is offering up one's *own* life" (Ephrem 2001, 71). On verse 6, he writes that the priest's taking the rest of what is offered need not mean all the offerer has—though "the man from Apamea" (probably Numenius, fl. 150 AD) would receive merit for such total surrender. Again the Leviticus text challenges Christians to high levels of self-giving. Theodoret finds it noteworthy that the one who offers the animal in chapter 1 is called "man" but here in 2:1 is "soul," i.e., the logical (the man) offers the illogical (the beast), and the soul offers the soulless (grain).

In the Middle Ages Ibn Ezra did connect *nefesh* with the sense of "willing spirit" from Psalm 51:14, but the intense, anthropological interest is Christian. Rupert writes that while "the soul" is simply a part representing for whole man, yet the fact that the soul is emphasized reminds us of the importance of the intention of the offerer. During 1125–28 Rupert was criticized for ascribing to the perfect soul or Mary what could be said of the whole church (Van Engen 1983, 291). Mary was the hinge of salvation history he argued. Here on Leviticus the wisdom is more ecclesiological, but he expects much from individuals. For Stephen Langton, the "poor soul" who here offers only vegetable produce denotes the soul or the body that does not concentrate on the salvation of the soul alone. For what are they doing with the "psychic" (non-spiritual) teaching of the Platonists? They are to be examined and prayed for. He rages against those who would put philosophical words and not the true word of God on the altar.

According to Denys, the church itself is like this grain offering. Isidore and admittedly others like Irenaeus (*Haer.* V.2.3) had said this, but Denys expands on the idea: the church, like the grain, is gathered from many faithful, washed and united in baptism, anointed by the oil of chrism and made firm by the fire of the Holy Spirit, offered up to God through humility and devotion to God. The soul offers this to God through keeping church unity, through trusting the merits of the church, and through commending the church to God in prayer. This is hardly an ecclesiological reading since the individual soul is viewed as the motor in all this, co-operating with divine grace. Additionally one can see figured here purity of conscience or contemplation of divine things, which draws things from the active life and is led to the grace of contemplation from good deeds.

Qorban-Eucharist

Theodoret seems sensitive to the requirement of priestly mediation at all stages of the offering ritual. The fact that it is a "bread" offering suggests (to a Christian readership) the Eucharist. Hesychius shows that his understanding of the Eucharist is as a memorial and as a means of receiving Christ's passion. The sacrificial meal denotes the dispensation of the passion of the "only begotten," judging that the cross can be likened to flour. Just as it is only firmed up once put on to fire, and is not consumed nor sustains any corruption or loss, and once firm is soon ready for use, likewise the cross of Christ is strong only as it subjects every creature to crucifixion, his flesh, which for eating was unsuitable before his passion (for who was capable of eating the flesh of God?) but was made ready for food after the passion. For if he had not been crucified, we would not eat the sacrifice of his body; but we eat, taking as food the memory of his passion. A page earlier he has spoken of how offering the meal in the OT is equated with believing in the incarnation.

Rupert thinks that the inner mind is like corn and wheat. And what is Scripture if not the bread of God? And the ear of the corn is the spiritual sense. It is not enough just to be aware in making offerings; one must also add to them love and the aroma (2:3) of goodness. It is not enough just to be aware in making offerings; one must also add to them love. To cook the likeness of God's word in a pan is to treat Scripture in the Spirit and making bread should be done without any heretical or puffed up yeast but with the oil of love since persecution is close, especially from false brethren. One should challenge them to add the oil of charity not the zeal of bitterness. The ill will of those outside presses on the vessel (2:5–6) and this means those inside it (the church) need to hold together while dealing with false brothers whose aim it is to cause division. Interestingly this is not about the Eucharist, as we might expect, but about the Christian life. The idea that liturgy is where God stamps humans with a remembrance of their part in his unfinished history of salvation was all-important for Rupert of Deutz (Kahles 1960, 47) but that is something that happens in the mind through symbols rather than by means of created sacramental grace. Rupert elsewhere observes (*De Divinis Officiis* II, 22) that the church has incense which it offers on a daily basis "for the aroma of sweetness" (Lev 2:3), and has bells instead of trumpets, although what is important is the moral significance participants draw from these *accoutrements*.

Something very similarly "intellectualist" is observed by Stephen Langton—with a little variation. By "pan" (v. 7) he designates the cross of Christ: just like a frying pan it is a means like a crucible of holding the impassible divinity within the passible humanity, and as in the pan the soft things harden and vice versa, so in the passion of the cross hard hearts are softened and soft and wavering hearts are firmed up. This resonates with what Ralph says about the need to be "in Christ" with contemplation of the cross as the means to moderating moral extremes into a virtuous mean.

The *anonymous medieval commentator* is summarized by Smalley (1981). After a number of useful examples, she concludes that like Peter Chanter there was a sympathetic view of the *legalia* as having an ongoing moral purpose: they confer virtue to those who read them spiritually. His comments on Leviticus 2:10 ("*sancta sanctorum*") show he believed that these sacrifices *had remitted actual sin*, as circumcision had with original sin (a commonly held view by the mid-twelfth century: Landgraf 1954, 67). This conflicts with Hugh's opinion, faithful to Augustine, in *Contra Faustum* XIX that the sacraments of the Old Law *signified but did not confer* sanctity. The Anonymous Commentator thought they had done so, *if* used worthily by the Israelites (thus not *opus operatum*—as the Christian sacraments—but *opus operans*). Thus some remission of sins was possible under the Old Law.

In these interpretations, intended for the "advanced" Christian reader, the Eucharist is not as prominent as one might expect. Ralph asks: What else is the bread tin which receives enormous heat, other than the pressure and trial of this world—cf. the psalmist of Psalm 117 who was a type of the martyrs, and the pre-Pentecost apostles were like this in that they were persecuted as in a fire. The adding of oil symbolizes the preparation of the mind with virtue prior to the burning of tribulation so that it is cooked, not burnt up. Strengthened continuously by virtue and after coming through "the baking tin" of trial they are translated into heaven just as the martyr Ignatius (Ign. *Rom.* 4) said that he was the grain of God so as to become bread for the world. The grain being baked means the determined fixing of minds. Those saints in the time of war on the church showed the way; now during the church's time that same zeal should be shown in combating vices. Benedict "our legislator" (Saint Benedict of Nursia, founder of Western monasticism) has said that the softness of mercy should not be only in the heart but in speech to others, for the one who is corrupted will more freely accept the wounds of love when he is made aware of their utility to him. Paul, writing to the Galatians, mixed hard and soft words in his rhetoric of moral teaching, as did Cicero.

The Jewish medieval commentators (e.g., Nahmanides) remark that the priest is somehow a buffer and that the word for the portion offered (vv. 2f) is related to the idea of remembrance (Heb. *zkr*) "before God," i.e., for God to remember the offerer, as Ibn Ezra explains, for incense, of course, plays on the olfactory sense, which has a close connection to the memory, even apparently, in God. One should not be persuaded from the large amount of monastic writing that the connection between the Levitical meal offering and the Christian Eucharist was totally forgotten. It was used during the preparation of the gifts from Carolingian times (Kunzler 2001, 140). As Durandus puts it (*Rationale Divinorum Officiorum* II, 30, 34), "The rite of the synagogue was carried over into the religion of the church and the sacrifices of the carnal people were changed in the observance of the spiritual people." Hugh of St. Cher, aware of Rashi here, thinks that the "memorial" (v. 3) being put on the altar has nothing to do with *our* anamnesis: No, it is *God's* remembering. The offering needs to be done with pure intention. Yet little connection is made between incense then and incense in the Church's liturgy.

This emphasis on the objective propitiation achieved continues in the exegesis of the early modern period where objective satisfaction elided with penal substitutionary metaphors. Thus Borrhaus writes that those who lack such a memorial remain in the divine wrath and can never buy off their punishment. We need to keep Christ in scope or else we will be like those accused by the prophet (Isa 66:3): he who offers a *minhah* (an offering) is like one offering (Christ's) blood. The priest eating the rest of the offering (2:3) speaks mystically of the mystical communion of Christ and the church, for the NT tells us *we* are the priests now. All that at first sight was hard in Christ is made soft and may be spiritually consumed by us.

Yet in Brenz's hands this is made to serve Eucharistic theology. For the Hebrew word usually translated "baking tin" (v. 5) means "a flat instrument for frying," like the iron instrument, shaped like pincers, with which we lift the white discs that are used in the Lord's Supper. The memorial works on both God and humans. So Brenz is happy to draw correspondences with the Lutheran Eucharist in a way that the less sacramentalist, former Anabaptist Borrhaus would not. The memorial is not only to remind spectators but even the Lord, who is some way adds a record of memory. God, because of sin, comes almost to forget human salvation and only remembers everlasting damnation. But if he looks on Christ his Son then he is not able to contain himself but to forget all wrath. So one raises Christ in the Eucharist as a memorial so that God forgers his severity. Piscator comments that that which gets eaten shows that Christ is spiritual food for all the faithful. The text holds this food to be a very holy thing, and this means that Christ is not given as heavenly food to the impure, which is also Eucharistic and reflects a more "Reformed" view that unbelievers simply cannot receive anything other than bread and wine.

This accent is shared by contemporary Catholic commentators: "*his* memorial" conveys the sense of each Christian's mind being jogged to remember God (and Cajetan observed that "his" refers to the offerer). And that fits with what the Eucharist is about (so, Lorinus). It is thus in the early seventeenth century that a Eucharistic interpretation of Leviticus 2 really comes into its own. Lapide contends that if the *animal* sacrifices signified the sacrifice of Christ killed on a cross, then the *grain* offering signifies the sacrifice of Christ in the Eucharist under the species of bread and wine: this can be called a true sacrifice and not just "offering," since there is destruction and consumption. Just because the grain offering was not one of the three major types of sacrifice, that does not mean it was not a sacrifice (*pace* Abulensia). A little later Calmet contends that "remembrance" is not the best translation of Hebrew "*sacharah*" (he means *azkarah*: vv. 2, 9, 16) but the more neutral and sacramentalist "worship and celebration of the divine name" is more suitable. Of course, humans need signs by which we are reminded that God is always looking over his church and guarding it.

Rich and Poor

Ephraim Syrus reports (2001, 40): "once a woman brought a handful of fine flour, and the priest despised her, saying: 'See what she offers! What is there in this to eat? What is there in this to offer up?' It was shown to him in a dream: 'Do not despise her! It is as if she had sacrificed her own life.'" Procopius asserts that true piety is not manifested by size of offering; more important is having an attitude which comes from divine hope: no murmuring. Our own cleverness is not to be offered, even though we are called to be cunning as serpents.

In other words, poverty is a subset of humility. Now for Lyra, the main point of chapter 2—which he has learned from Rashi (cf. also Talmud *b. Menaḥ* 104b)—is that this grain offering is for the poor people's offerings: since the offering of a poor person is seen by God as if he had offered his own life (cf. Matt 12 on the poor widow). Rashi has informed us that "honey" can mean any sweet fruit, which is quite a cheap offering. As if almost to counter this, Denys writes: the rich are those who neglect the things of the soul, while by "poor" one could understand the "not yet perfect," lacking in godly things and called "soul" (i.e., neither spiritual nor fleshly). They can only offer up mediocrity of virtues and they realize the need for divine grace. There is much less emphasis on the spiritual advantage of being literally poor in Denys' scheme. Since our works are of mixed quality we need to plea with the Lord to accept them, as he himself will "judge righteousnesses" (Ps 74).

Lorinus is happy to approve Abulensia's interpretation that God really ordered this sacrifice so that the priests would have bread as well as meat for their sustenance. Lapide's view is more the Lyra-Rashi one, when he comments that the cereal offering was made the standard by God so that the poor could also take part, as well as to provide this staple for the priests.

Leaven and Honey, Salt and Oil (vv. 11–13)

The insistence in Leviticus is on *unleavened* bread made with *fine flour*; in other words, that which is not simply in "common use." This has metaphorical value, although the Christian tradition is somewhat ambivalent as to whether something being unleavened is meant positively (Mark 8:14–22) or negatively (Matt 13:33, but also 1 Cor 5:7f). Philo could see leaven here as symbol of self-aggrandizement (because to be consumed is the opposite of self-aggrandizement). In the story of the sacrifice of Isaac, in Genesis 22, Isaac was not consumed, just as here, in Leviticus 2, leaven and honey are not consumed. But, according to Clement of Alexandria, Christ, unlike the offering in Leviticus 2, was consumed (*Paed.* I, 23). For Clement the story of Genesis 22 is not about Isaac being wholly offered (ibid., 90). Rather, he focuses on the *contrast* between Isaac and Christ—whereas Isaac was, in fact, not appropriate for sacrifice, *Christ was appropriate*. Theodoret thinks that leavened bread was here prohibited for the reason that no one should have the Egyptian habits. And honey is prohibited since the bee sits in unclean places. Human labor is called for, since by honey self-indulgence is condemned.

Jerome observes that Solomon, as one who knew about luxury, at least knew to keep it out of the temple (Letter 128; NPNF2 6:2582; CSEL LIV, II, 83). He cross-references Proverbs 5:3—"the lips of a strange woman drop as honey"—and concludes: "this is the reason that neither honey nor leaven was offered in the sacrifice of the temple and that oil, the product of the bitter olive, is burned in his temple." Also in his Homily 75 he notes that honey is a sign of pleasure and sweetness, which brings death (FC 57, 127).

The West Syrian liturgy in the following centuries would delineate a three-fold sacrifice in the Eucharist: that of "Melchisedek" in the bread and wine at the start of the service, that of "Aaron" at the point of incense being offered, and thirdly, that of Christ's sacrifice (Jungmann 1962, 92). In some sense the Syrian church saw a progression of worship through history, and it even dramatized this in its liturgy.

For the early medieval period Bede (in the Gloss) interprets the salt as sign of the covenant is that which restrains lust, while oil denotes willing spontaneity. There is to be no honey, as Eucherius of Lyon (d. 449) has it, for those who seek the sweet life are not able to recognise the Lord's mercy. Instead we should cultivate the salt of reason and discretion.

The Canterbury School of Theodore on v. 11 observes that yeast signifies pride, whereas Hesychius (PG 93, 810) has it as "foreign doctrine" and Ps-Melito's *Clavis scripturae* (Pitra, *Analecta Sacra*, 35) has it as "corruption of the mind."

Yet there was also a literal interpretation to serve spiritual ends, allowing a direct correspondence between the OT *minha*-offering and the Christian Eucharist. Augustine wrote of the unleavened bread of the OT as a figure of Christ not abrogated, since the "leaven" of "later" Judaism had been removed by Christ (*Contra Faustum* 19.10; CSEL 25, 508). The *practice* of using unleavened bread was introduced from 700 onwards. It was regarded as continuous with the *minha* offering which was also unleavened. It would seem wrong for the divine body into which the visible elements pass (Isidore Sev 1, 18, 30–35l; CCL 113, 20) to be fermented since that denotes deceit (and honey, insincerity). Rabanus Maurus (*De inst. cleric.* I, 31; Fchr, 2006, 222) teaches on the basis of verse 11 that the Eucharistic bread should be unfermented. This is standard in the West (cf. Rupert, *De divinis officiis*

II.23), while offensive to the Byzantine church, as represented by Patriarch Michael Caerularius around 1053–54 (PG 120), who called the Western churches themselves "fermented" for imitating the ancient Jewish practice of unfermented bread.

Ralph reminds his readers that Romans 12 tells us that one does it right if the intention is right. The Lord has anointed us with the oil of gladness and we should do our duty lightly (2 Cor 9) and, when we work, to call insistently on divine help. The founder, St. Benedict, tells us not to murmur in our heart and he also tells us about the incense (Latin: *thus*) when in the preface of his work he tells us to pray. Putting incense on the altar (v. 15) means to offer prayer. Love for God is needed if there is to be the desire that gives birth to praying people who ask in their hearts. With Lyra one finds a less sacramental interpretation which prefers to speak of incense as mental devotion, oil as the anointing of godliness, and salt discretion. But as Paul (1 Cor 5) warns us, yeast represents the corruption of the Mosaic tradition.

Brenz asks, "Why is honey not allowed when it gets good press elsewhere in the Bible?" Well, honey is sweet to begin with, but leaves a bitter aftertaste. Christ is quite the opposite; and his sweetness has a utility making us faithful. Our offerings need the salt of faith in Christ or else all that we are will perish. For Piscator, "no ferment" simply means there was no sin in Christ. There is to be no honey since that at length goes off, whereas Christ is always sweet to those who eat him.

Calvin mixes the metaphors, or the recipe perhaps: Jesus speaks of a *seasoning with salt* (Mark 9:49). In these words he (Christ) signifies that, when we are searched and tried by fire, we shall be acceptable sacrifices to God, and that this is the seasoning of salt when our flesh with its affections shall have been well macerated. Meanwhile, let us firmly hold to this, that our service of God is not what it should be without the savor that is sought in the word; since in all the brains of men not one particle of salt is to be found. In good Protestant Word-Eucharist balance, Chytraeus interprets salt as the essential condiment that the offering must have, i.e., the Word of God that accommodates to every situation. For salt "bites" and cleanses all sorts of pastoral problems. Piscator adds that salt reminds us that we be savory and not rot in our sins, achieving this partly through Christ's satisfaction, partly through our sanctification.

In Calmet's observations, which often tend towards the "dietary," there was no honey or leaven, since these things were incompatible with salt and oil and wine. However, later he says that the Greeks mixed oil and wine to make a health drink. Interestingly he then reports Plutarch's slight that the Hebrews forbade honey because it ruined the wine. The two sides of Calmet (pietist and pedant) are shown in (with Theodoret) his refuting any idea that the "no honey" rule was simply to stop flies being attracted. Honey could include that made from dates, and this is in fact more likely, given the Arabic.

Matthew Henry's peroration takes the reference to "oil and frankincense" to mean that "wisdom and humility must soften and sweeten the spirits and services of young people, and then their green ears of corn shall be acceptable. God takes a particular delight in the first ripe fruits of the Spirit and the expressions of early piety and devotion."

The nineteenth-century critics strike a wholly different chord. Salt is the sign of a theocratic covenant which "Jehovah" and Israel contracted (Knobel). Rendtorff (2004) observes that sacrifice is not just about blood. Abel was as good as Cain and the offering is more about the placating odor than about the value of the offering: as it were, the material is immaterial! Milgrom (2004, 26) delights in observing that Abarbanel and Robertson Smith (1894, 222) concur in showing that the accent is on fellowship, with basic bread as the basis of hospitality (akin to the widow's mite of Mark 12:41–44). In their view a symbolic amount serves to encourage reconciliation.

Leviticus 3

Peace Offering? (v. 1)

THIS CHAPTER AND ITS content, the sacrifice of peace or "salvation," seems to have had relatively little attention paid to it in the early church period. Likewise *Leviticus Rabbah* skips it, and Rashi views it as having more of a "horizontal" intent (i.e., to unite humans in fellowship), while Nahmanides explains the "whole" as meaning "the whole of the species" (i.e., not just male animals) and thus "both male and female animals may be offered." Origen points out that if sacrifices are to be called "saving," as in Leviticus 3:1 (LXX translated *shelāmim*, peace offering, as *thusia sōtēriou*, salvation sacrifice), there can be no substitution by a little sacrifice, as in the previous two chapters, but it always has to be one that is full and perfect. Allegorically Origen and Bede speak of the fatty protective part as the soul of Christ that covered his divinity; this was the seat of his desire and devotion. Theodoret thinks that what matters more is that God and the priest in this offering shared peace. And this offering pacified each in rendering to each what was his. It is called "saving" for it was given for salvation already obtained, or to be obtained or maintained.

Hesychius thinks that the "salvation sacrifice" or "peace offering" is for those who are not spiritual enough to offer a burnt offering, which he defines as a life of chastity. The two basic types of sacrifice (whole and peace) were delineated in Exodus 20:24. The relative strengths of virtue are shown in the fact that here a female animal may be offered whereas in Leviticus 1 only a male could be. For Peter Comestor, whereas Gentiles used to derive the term "victim" from enemies about to be conquered or already conquered, the Hebrews derived the term from the word "to tie." How this works in the Hebrew we are not told, but he adds that no one should think that God delighted in the literal aroma of flesh but rather in the thing signified and in the devotion of those offering.

Leviticus 3

Hugh of St. Cher holds that in this offering God is the one who offers and is the priest of his own offering and he feeds and satisfies individuals, being given to gain or maintain their salvation. Similarly, for Brenz, Christ was the fattiest inward part offered up so as to show that the whole church receives the fruit of Christ's sacrifice by faith, by which it is sanctified. Here is the interesting idea that sanctification, like justification, is by faith rather than by grace as such. Thus by faith alone we receive Christ and so too our heart is purified by faith. What do we now offer? First, ministry, like the Levitical priests, and, second, our lives and words of praise.

Brenz notes that the Vulgate translates the Greek "offering of salvation" as "offering of peacemakers" (3:1). Brenz sets up the question, and Calvin seems to give an answer by offering another possible translation. Calvin thinks *shelāmim* should not be translated "sacrifice of peace-offerings" or perfections. Rather its plural number might aptly be translated "prosperities," on which account, David calls the libation which used to be made in this sacrificial context "the cup of salvations" (Ps 116:13). By this outward sign he intended to denote thanksgiving. Calvin comments: "I admit that this sacrifice was not offered in acknowledgment of gratitude, but also when they sought of God peace and success; yet still the epithet will always admirably suit it, because they confess by it that God was the author of all good things." A certain amount of scrupulosity inculcates a sense of mystery and earnestness, and so too should our "thanksgivings" be performed. For Calvin there is in this sacrifice a sense of thanksgiving for *all* of God's providence, not just for salvation through Christ.

Piscator makes the point that in verses 1 and 6 where the Latin Bible translation of S. Pagnini (1528) has *sacrificum Eucharisticum* the Hebrew is more like *sacrificum retributionum*. Yet for his commentary he sticks with the non-Hebrew "Eucharistic" translation, as if the New Testament turns an ominous-sounding sacrifice into a gladder one. Today these thanksgiving (Eucharistic) sacrifices mean the spiritual sacrifices of Christians, which we offer gratefully to God (cf. living sacrifice in Rom 12 or 2 Tim 4:6). This also happens when, from our riches, we give generously to sustaining the ministers of the church. Willet's commentary on Leviticus 3 amounts to little more than: "not works but thanks are to be offered in a healthy religion." Calov is aware that chapter 7 will say more on these, but overall the idea of the sacrifice is "peace," or a family meal as sign of peace and friendship with God. The mystical sense is to get rid of passions—in honor of God.

Leclerc's concern at verse 2 was that this was different from the Egyptian practice, which made it an offence to sacrifice bull calves, and at verse 11 any pagan idea of eating a banquet with the gods is thankfully missing. His overall interpretation is that this is both for giving thanks and turning away divine wrath, as William Outram

(*De sacrificiis* I, x) has shown. Yet we do not have here any system of laws in Leviticus such that we can be quite clear what this offering was. Knobel points out that in this "peace-offering" the priestly share is not so holy that others too could not eat it. He takes it to be a recompense offering of thanks (cf. Josephus, *Ant.* 3.9.2). Some such as Philo, Calvin, Leclerc, and Outram prefer "offering of salvation." The LXX uses *sōtēriou* in the Pentateuch but *eirēnikē* in other parts of the OT. But both translations of the Hebrew are too general and hence wrong!

Dillmann disputes Knobel's claim that this offering is all about giving grateful thanks but not also about asking for something. For it was also offered in hard times (Judg 20; 1 Sam 13:9) and here God could be paid for something yet to come as well as for service already rendered. There is nothing wrong with thinking of this as currying favor. And it was not the opposite of the sin offering (*khatta't*) or to be defined over against it since it is much older than the latter. Knobel's explanation is echoed by Milgrom—joy is the theme that unites this with the freewill offering and the vow, and it is about rare occasions where meat was eaten (Milgrom 2004, 28)— while Levine takes it to be a "tribute (*shalōm*) greeting." The suspicion with which Rendtorff holds this (following Janowski 1980), preferring to see the emphasis (with Sifra) as a public one, of the individual "bringing and sharing," and having nothing to do with anxiety over uncleanness. It is proof that ritual can be closely connected to everyday life, even if eating meat is not "everyday"—agreeing here with Milgrom that for once there is relaxation from anxiety.

Choice Parts of the Animal

Hesychius adds that the fact that one offers up the entrails and the surrounding fat demonstrates the need to offer to God our thinking and desiring. For the heart is the stomach of the soul in which we first conceive our actions and then try to fulfill them. This seemingly "biblical" anthropology is complemented by what the medics say—that the lower part of the stomach, or the kidneys, is where the habit of the passions that arise is stored. In any case we are to offer what is irascible to God for its destruction, not that anger *per se* is bad—God has his own anger after all—but *anger towards a bad end* is bad, as is inordinate lust. Offering a goat symbolizes someone converted out of a life of sin, while the sheep are the law-abiding; both belong to the flock.

Theodoret seems to emphasize the idea of the parts and distribution of sacrifice: our offering the tail (3:9)—that which comes last—means that we offer our prayers through those whose virtue is imperfect, giving credit to the church hierarchy. Yet

Isho'dad of Merv writes that "all the innards" mean the intelligence; not least the liver because it converts food into blood and eases the pain of the lower part of the soul.

Theodoret's ecclesiological interpretation is to some extent lost in the West. Hugh of St. Cher draws on Andrew of St. Victor to point out what is implicit in the text—that the innards of animals other than these (i.e., other than "consecrated" animals "from the herd") were allowed to be eaten. The intellect as the life of the soul (and the soul in turn the life of the body) is to be offered to the Lord. Again there are details that stimulate the Eucharistic theology of the Middle Ages. With Rupert of Deutz, the innards are burned here as a way of giving thanks that with God's help they have burned all their vices with the fire of the Holy Spirit; this is the experience of those who, according to the apostle, delight in the law of God according to the inner man (Rom 7:22). The meaning of giving up all is illustrated by Paul's claim to beat the body and reduce it to servitude (1 Cor 9:27), but this cannot happen unless the inner root of concupiscence is burned out by that fire. The "whole tail," as being the end of the body, represents those who persevere to the end and will be saved (Matt 10:22). In other words, this sacrifice of virtue comes after "cross and Eucharist."

Ralph warns that "delight" can be an open door for death. The liver and surrounding area signify the appetite for harm, and the liver, he adds, with a passable medical wisdom, is the source of the blood, which in turn signifies cruelty. Yet two things can be represented by one word in Scripture. And since many examples teach this, faith is one for all the elect. The innards represent holy affect and godly devotion, by which God is served. And the end or consummation of holy devotion is signified by the mention of the tail, which reminds us to persevere to the end.

Cocceius discusses the meaning of the word *yoteret* ("appendage"), in the Vulgate translated *reticulum* (v. 10). It is something near the kidneys above the liver, and comes to settle on the liver when the animal bends down, but is actually part of the liver. The reference to kidneys or "inward parts" (v. 4) reminds him of "the sinful ones," who chastised the psalmist (Ps 16:17, Vg: *et noctibus erudierunt me renes mei*). Yet in Christ they signify the humblest and holy hidden thoughts, leading to wisdom. There is a general principle in verse 9: one must not eat what is meant to honor God (cf. Gen 9:5).

Commenting on verse 9, Patrick tells of sheep tails so thick that locals of the Syrian Desert melt the fat and keep it to butter their rice; whereas the suet is something other than the fat, that can be separated from it. He follows Maimonides in claiming that suet is too rich for the human diet and so is more suited to being offered up to God. Calmet, commenting on verse 3, says that the Egyptians and Greeks take special care to separate the fat from the rest of the offering, whereas Strabo tells us that the Persians offer up only a part of its stomach fat on the grounds that the gods want only the soul. Some think that verse 16 means a literal prohibition on eating such suet at *any* time, whereas blood is *never* to be eaten. However, 7:23 makes clear that suet is prohibited only in the case of sacrifices.

Offering and Distribution

Denys then brings in Thomas's figurative reading (*ST* IaIIae q102) concerning the three-fold divide of the offerings—to God, to priests, and to the people—to show that human salvation and peace come *from* God *through* the ministers of the church *to* those who cooperate and are hence saved. The eating of these parts means avoiding lasciviousness and it shows reverence to God to give "life" back to him from whom it comes. However Denys wants to add his own spiritual interpretation. The fact that both male and female animals may be offered represents the Lord's rational soul (male) and his innocent body (female), and his spiritual sufferings on our behalf. "Laying on of hands" stands for rigorous discipline; the fat to be offered means we are to be abstinent in fasting, and the overall point is that we try to impress the superior intellect on to our senses.

Piscator reminds us that the cattle that are to be offered in this sacrifice are to be whole or free from flaws, by which we are warned that we should not declare thanks to God if we then give cheaply to him. The laying on of a hand represents putting our sins on Christ by faith. And sprinkling the blood shows that our good works please God only on account of Christ's blood. The sweet smell is a metaphor for those works, which come from faith and are of gratitude, which please God. Piscator does not spell this out as his (in)famous doctrine of Christ's active righteousness being ours, but it sounds like part of the groundwork for this view (Mühling 2009, 115–34).

Lapide has little to say except to repeat the mediaevals (Hesychius and Ralph) and to regard this chapter in a tropological way as about the lower levels of piety. The chaste are those victims who have been made peaceful to themselves and to God. The middle-grade Christians and the married (who are signified by the peace offering) dedicate a sincere intention to serve God: works like crafting, plowing, and so on become holy and meritorious when combined with acts of religion and charity.

Cocceius, on finding in verse 1 no distinction between male and female, is quick to reference Galatians 3:28 ("there is no male nor female, for you are all one in Christ Jesus"). Christ would not only be strong in obedience but was also weaker in suffering—not that he was defeated but that he underwent shame and pain and would have appeared worsted. This leads to a "democratic," inclusive approach to the question of the universality of the blessings of Christ's sacrifice: the lamb is Christ in whom *all* have communion and access to God (cf. 1 Pet 1:19). Yet the parting shot is to view present Israel as ruled out of that arrangement for the present age. "*Saeculum*," as he translates ʿ*olām* ("forever," v. 17), here means the time when Israel is detached from the nations until the time of the blessing of the nations. Of the two testaments, the first is for the commemoration of sin! This shows Cocceius at his supersessionist best (or worst!).

In two more modern commentators the emphasis is on the reception of the blessings of the sacrifice, although that is only implicit in the text. Matthew Henry on 3:5 comments that penitent confessions must always go along with our thankful acknowledgments; and, whatever mercy we pray for, in order to get it we must pray for the removal of guilt, as that which keeps good things from us (Hos 14:2). Bonar views the offering as symbolic of the conveyance of Christ's blessing to the offerer: "the pieces presented should be those seated deep within. We approach a reconciled God, to hold fellowship with him as Adam did in Eden in the cool of the day." We should be yielding hearts to God in communion just as Christ did to the Father, even when "the just wrath of God seemed to spurn and thrust down each heartfelt emotion." Christ could be represented by a goat, "to prevent the error of those who would place the value of Christ's undertaking in his character alone."

Leviticus 4

The Individual Who Sins Unintentionally

Hesychius is shocked that some people accuse the body of causing sin, but that is not how it is, for if our soul is healthy no luxury of the flesh can harm it. And the person who sins in ignorance is not driven by the body, but by ignorance of the good due to negligence and through bad example, confusing bad and good. Hesychius is aware of some slight differences in the LXX, which renders "unwilling" rather than "ignorant" in verse 27: presumably one can know one is sinning and yet not fully will it. Procopius notes that Scripture calls some acts "sin" even when they are not deliberate; for one may sin even when one thinks one has not sinned, e.g., Saul when he ordered a fast (1 Sam 14:24).

Some scholars trace a regression from the NT "ethic of intentionality" to what one finds in the Middle Ages where the deed is what matters and the intention is irrelevant. An important place in Augustine's Christology was taken by the idea of "*Christus medicus*," which would be especially important for penance (Angenendt 2000, 131). Angenendt (2000, 635) contrasts Augustine's playing down sins of weakness and ignorance in order to focus on the serious ones of ill will (*De diversis quaestiones 83* CCSL 44a, 32) with Gregory the Great's stricter concern about all sorts of sin as needing penance (*Dial.* IV, 43), resulting in a simple religion expressed in the Penitential Books. Eventually with the help of Abelard and others (Lutterbach 2003, 243) a process of the internalization of a grid of sins and a slow refining of consciences took place, opening new space for the NT ethic of intention and the renewed establishment of the inner man. Lutterbach also traced a move from a corrective-medicinal to a retributive form of justice that took place in penance.

One does have to question whether NT ethics were so much about intention (Lutterbach 2003, 239, sees Acts 15:19–20 as an exception), and whether Augustine's medicinal approach or the *Christus Medicus* idea in general (Knipp 1998) really elevated either intention or the deed above the underlying sinful condition. Kottje (2005) argues that certainly, by the time of the early Middle Ages, there was an emphasis on the deed (*Tathaftung*) as in the earliest Irish penitentials. Yet even Lutterbach admits that, in cases of murder and indiscipline, intention always *did* matter: in the Penitential of Finnian intention and knowledge were taken into account so that sinning with heart or only with body made a difference to the punishment. Kottje adds examples from the Ambrosian, Bedan, Columban, Cummean, and Bigotian Penitentials. Even anger or duress could be used in mitigation. Both act *and intention* became significant in fixing the penance.

Yet what Kottje then concludes seems questionable, that these Penitential Books always meant to contribute to the improvement of people. It would also seem that Abelard's intervention made no great difference in practice: cf. Caesarius von Heisterbach, *Dialogus miraculorum* of 1223 (Nosges 2006). Reconciliation could be achieved without feelings of regret (also Ohst 1995, 130f). Grace from sacramental penance seemed to have more to do with correcting particular distorted relationships than correcting attitude and intention.

As for the canon law of Gratian, Joseph Goering comments: "it is asked whether sins are dismissed through contrition of the heart alone. And one may answer yes, by the intervention of God's grace; but it is nevertheless necessary that confession of the mouth and satisfaction of good works follow, if possible, otherwise the penitent who does not do this will sin gravely through contempt [of the church]" (Goering 2008, 224). External order mattered for spiritual freedom. This was reinforced in practice by Pope Innocent II—who stipulated oral confession and works of satisfaction in addition to contrition—yet we should add that it can be plausibly argued that people wanted this guidance. However, when one turns to the commentaries from the High Middle Ages onwards, one can also see a fairly gracious view of human weakness.

For Ralph of Flaix the use again of the word "soul" (*nefesh*) means "man," though is not used to signify substance (*the* soul) but to highlight the idea of man as alive yet infirm. It denotes human beings as active life forms in the lowest parts which do not know God's will *or cannot obey it*, which is what the LXX alternative (see Hesychius) allows. Whereas when it came to deliberate sins an offender was to be thrown out "with the lepers."

Lyra contends that "soul" is simply "anyone" since soul is the principal part of the human. And if anyone through ignorance omitted what was commanded to be done, since in Scripture a command in transgression through commission is held to be the same as an omission and vice versa, then the sacrifice was just as much instituted for that sin of omission. In Denys's view this theme of imposing order has a curious correlation to the apostle "wrestling wild beasts" (1 Cor 15:32) in that the major part of a human follows the movement of carnal affections and passions, and the soul—as something unfixed—shuttles between good and evil depending on what is contained in it. Hesychius was right, thinks Denys, that it is the *soul* and not the body that sins. The ignorance here (v. 2) is that of *fact* which caution should have been able to avoid, or an ignorance of the law which one is not obliged to know and so does not sin directly as a result of that ignorance, although occasionally someone could sin from such ignorance. Denys thinks this includes both positive and negative commands.

Calvin plays lawyer, psychologist, and linguist simultaneously. For *shegāgāh* (4:2) means "error," not "ignorance": what is in view is not occasions when we mistakenly think we are right but when we just do not think. "For many do not search themselves, and therefore slumber in their sins; whereas if they honestly examined their doings, their conscience would straightaway smite them." Likewise, the best translation in verse 22 is not "shall have offended," but "shall have known/felt that he has offended." "The word *hodaʿ* which they render tentatively 'to make known' may fitly bear my translation, unless this preferred, 'if he shall have known.'"

Lapide notes the Hebrew *shegāgāh* which more recent translators render "through error," as if it was some sort of disease. But really the words means "ignorance," and it is translated that way by the Targum, Philo, and Jerome. All the commands of the Lord means that natural, ceremonial, and judicial are all included, and these are positive just as much as negative commands (so, Cajetan). Abulensia wrongly thought that this passage was only about actively obeying *ceremonial* commands. The point of the command is to expiate cases of non-intentional disobedience of a command to do something, whereas in the case of intentional transgressing of a commandment not to do something the individual gets punished. For the judge does not admit ignorance as an excuse, since when the legal matter is a crime the accused is presumed to have known the law and the form of his deed, unless he establishes the contrary. So it is not just about ignorance of how to sacrifice correctly but of all laws.

Lorinus contends that it is one thing to sin *through* ignorance and another to sin *because of* ignorance. Ignorance is either ignorance that could not have been overcome, and is thus excusable (this is sinning *through* ignorance), or that could have been overcome, and is thus inexcusable (this is sinning *because of* ignorance). And therefore all sin is ignorant, as the Philosopher (Aristotle) says, so that all can sin *through* ignorance without sinning *because* of ignorance. Non-ignorant sin (i.e., sin not *caused* by ignorance) becomes malicious when the intellect forms the idea of sinning and it is not just passion that is the cause.

Matthew Henry seems unaware of the discussion on the subjective state of mind, and following Simon Patrick limits the sins to committed *acts*: "(1.) They are supposed to be overt acts; for, had they been required to bring a sacrifice for every sinful thought or word, the task had been endless . . . (2.) They are supposed to be sins of commission, things which ought not to be done. Omissions are sins, and must come into judgment; but what had been omitted at one time might be done at another . . . (3.) They are supposed to be sins committed through ignorance. If they were done presumptuously, and with an avowed contempt of the law and the Lawmaker, the offender was to be cut off, and there remained *no sacrifice for the sin*, Heb. 10:26, 27; Num. 15:30."

Calmet admits "the rabbis," followed by Grotius and Vatable, think that this chapter concerns offences against negative commands ("commissions"). But the majority of interpreters think that sins of ignorance can include those "committed" against positive commands too, since there is no real difference. For positively and negatively are two ways of saying same thing.

After two centuries of indifference to this question, the last thirty years have seen a renewal of interest. Such concern is reinforced not only by sensitivity to the form, i.e., that this is a new section marked by "and the Lord spoke to Moses" at verse 1, but also by a (post)modern interest in the depths of subjectivity. Rendtorff argues that Milgrom is wrong to argue that this law is about a situation in which someone knows what he is doing but not its consequences. However, he agrees with Milgrom that the force of *shegāgāh* is that the person who acted consciously first becomes conscious of the act as sin at the point of the offering. Through this offering it comes to consciousness that (s)he is guilty, as holiness provokes awareness of fault, however unintentional. (This seems quite different from the traditional view of Ibn Ezra and Nahmanides that it is realizing sin that occasions the bringing of the offering.) The link of subjectivity and altar is so tight that the altar, not merely the conscience, needs to purified. A "sin committed anywhere" threatens to cause the divine presence to withdraw from the sanctuary, such that the altar needs purified. Its impurity acts like some early warning system of moral dis-ease for the whole community (Milgrom 2004, 31f). Rendtorff is also unsure that the text casts the offerer as *homo peccator* (a sinning man) who somehow manages to cast off sin onto the sacrifice. There is, says Rendtorff, no close connection with Leviticus 16 (*pace* Milgrom). Certainly the expression of penitence seems to turn a heavy sin into a lighter, pardonable one. "In light of the conceptual framework above, it appears that, in priestly legislation, there is a fuzzy line between physical ritual impurity and moral sin" (Boda 2007, 52; Gane 2005, 200; *contra* Klawans 2000, 22–31).

The Sacrifice for Sin

Origen has confidence to assert this the young bull was offered for service in heaven, but for sin on earth. "Outside the camp" means "outside heaven" and that means "on earth" where he suffered (Heb 13:12 and Gen 32:1f). The bathos of discoursing about entrails (v. 11) demonstrates Christ's true human nature. What follows is highly christocentric: the "innards" (*adipes*) can be thought of as his holy soul, which veiled the secrets of his divinity, while the "kidneys" stand for the bodily material. His "soul" was to be given over for heavenly service, and "the kidneys" were given over to fire, which casts doubt on any notion that there was any motion (i.e., sexual arousal) of Christ's genital parts. (In ancient medicine the kidneys and the genitals are seen as closely connected.)

Cyril of Jerusalem (on whose penchant for the particular and the concrete in religion, see Walker 1990) had no doubt about the christological value of Aaron as presented in Leviticus 4:5: "Moses gave these titles to two men eminent above all, changing the name of his own successor as leader Auses to "Jesus" (Num 13:16), and giving his own brother, Aaron, the surname "Christ." This was so that through these two chosen men Moses might represent at once the high priesthood and the kingship of the one Jesus Christ who was to come."

Ralph sees here (v. 4) the young bull (as in Ps 21[22]:12), which on account of the crosses of its horns has triumphed over the devil and refreshed the whole world like the voice of the Lord breaking the cedars and making them dance like young calves (Ps 28[29]:5). Christ is like the Lebanese calf whose human origins were in a pure ancestry like the snow-capped peaks of Lebanon. The cedars are like the powers of this world cut down by the weapon that is the word of the Lord, cast down from a height. It is the Lord who is being offered here. As for the devotion and prayer of the priest and the one offering, which were in the faith of Christ to come, they will not be left without power of his, Christ's sacrifice, for as the apostle says it is impossible for the blood of bulls and goats to take away sin (Heb 10). This is offered for a single person from the people.

Christ, thinks Langton, had power in own hands to lay down his life, but that the ritual took place "before the Lord" ("*coram domino*": v. 7) means more than just *in the Lord's presence*, but *for his pleasure*. Christ did not triumph by power but by wisdom, and endured his passion by both the power of his divinity and the patience of his humanity. The flesh of Christ was the means. Do even we rightly deserve this? His flesh was tougher than horn.

This seems very good news for the people of the former covenant, although whereas Rashi had confidence in the people to make this system work, Lyra comments that they often erred through ignorance of their elders. Indeed, on verse 26 Calvin insists that these sacrifices are to be considered as sacraments with real spiritual effect and are not merely political in purpose, as Lutherans like Brenz might have emphasized: "And assuredly those who do not acknowledge that the legal rites were sacraments, are not acquainted with the very rudiments of the faith . . . a pardon was truly promised to the fathers, who reconciled themselves to God by the offering of sacrifices, not because the slaying of beasts expiated sins, but because it was a certain and infallible symbol, in which pious minds might acquiesce, so as to dare to come before God with tranquil confidence." As Zachman puts it, "for Calvin, Moses goes one better than the patriarchs" (Zachmann 2007, 195).

As one moves into the modern period, the interest shifts towards parallels with ancient societies, which makes the OT practice, as reflecting "the ancient mind," seem to have a rationale of its own. Patrick comments that sprinkling blood is unique to the sin-sacrifice for the whole congregation (v. 17) and indicates that it was serious. The "whole congregation" means all the people, not the Sanhedrin for whom atonement is made, as Selden has argued against "the Talmudists." He compares Apuleius, *Metamorphoses*, Book 6, which describes a pagan equivalent; although this Pythagorean practice was in fact borrowed from Moses. He follows Maimonides in suggesting that the pouring out of blood (v. 30) was done in order that it not be kept in a vessel for gods to eat. And blood was used by some gardeners to fertilize ground, as Constantine L'Empereur (Professor of Semitics at Leyden, 1627–48) observes, so perhaps that is another reason why Leviticus commands it.

Knobel draws a parallel in Euripides *Iphigenia in Aulis* (1591ff) for vicarious satisfaction, which was also known to Cato, and many moderns have followed the rabbis in seeing this, although they misunderstand the ancient mind when they think that it is not just the punishment but also the sin and guilt that gets transferred to the beast. That would be to make the animal unclean, which it nowhere says it is; it is vicarious *execution* that counts, not vicarious *sin bearing*.

The Sinning High Priest and the Ruler

Philo had commented that if the high priest sinned it would not be "of himself" but rather in the sense of being caught up in a sin shared by the nation (*Spec* I, 230). Origen is also aware of this question: for the high priest (4:3ff) we should note that it is not specified whether the fault was deliberate or not. He represents the pious soul, ignoring any association with "Christ" (even though the Greek of v. 3 contains the term *christos*). As for "the Ruler" (*ho archon*) (vv. 22ff), this means the power of reason (*vis rationis*). Rather shockingly he comments on verse 4 that Jesus in his incarnation drew the Jews to sin in allowing them to deliver him up to death. Hebrews 7:28 tells us that such OT mediators are weak, for to be men they have to be able to sin. In fact, we admire such a man for recognizing his sin and understanding it.

However, Hesychius's interpretation makes *Jesus* to be the referent of "high priest" here. So, if Christ is the intelligible anointed priest, how can he here be said to sin? Well, in the sense of carrying the sins of his people he did, as he willingly offered up his flesh, in the presence of God, as the Father looked on. Furthermore, because Christ's priesthood is eternal, he is, as the LXX has it, "consummating (*teteleiómenos*) his hands from the blood" (v. 5) in the mystical supper at the moment of the breaking of bread. Somehow, mystically, the priestly agency of Christ is transmitted through the consecrated elements. Of course, Hebrews 10:20 tells us that Jesus is the veil (*katapetasma*), mentioned here in verse 6, but Hesychius manages to make this reference in Hebrews apply—by association or synecdoche—to the incense altar, so Jesus is *that* too. However, the holy of holies itself is heaven, so the christomonism in Hesychius' interpretation is not quite total. Procopius briefly notes that the implication is that priests are of a higher office than rulers, although in earlier times kings liked to honor themselves with priestly titles.

Ralph thinks that although a priest might sin, the high priest would not sin, although, (following the Augustinian theory of "head and members") Christ has conformed himself to sinners. The guilt of others as his members, however, is imputed to him and that is what is going on here. To Denys it seems quite possible that priests could indeed sin from ignorance. Thomas Aquinas offers him a helpful answer in *ST* I–II 76: nescience is simply a lack of knowledge, but ignorance is a lack of knowledge in cases when the person *should* know, and that *is* sin. Given this status, it is a terrible thing to lead people astray, and one deals with this by offering to God lust, filth, and the unruly flesh by subjugating it with fasts and disciplines, mortifying it until purified and in every way subject to reason. Yet since we are not able to satisfy or be reconciled to God in our own powers we offer up the grace and merit of Christ and hence Christ's very most pure body.

Brenz is much more interested in the prince's than the priest's sinning: The high priest here was no angel but a man liable to sin and who made an offering for his own sins. Just as there was a difference between sacrifices for the high priest and for the whole people, so too between that for the prince and that for the individual. For if a prince sins, he offends many. That which in private is called drunkenness gets called "magnificence" among the powerful, and what in ordinary people is called adultery is called "being human," but it is by no means the case that they have the prerogative to sin against God; in fact their sin is all the greater for their status. Accordingly, David's punishment for adultery was not dealt with just once but continuously.

In God's sight, states Chytraeus, sin is one and the same and needs the expiation by Christ's death, yet there are degrees of sin in this life, which can be discerned in efficient causes, objects, and other circumstances. Here there are rites for different people but in Christ there is neither Jew nor Greek, etc. Lorinus believes one can translate the types of offering into types of penance or punishment depending on the seriousness of offence, which in turn depends on the perpetrator's status in the community. Serranus takes all this to be about post-baptismal penance. Lapide mentions that the prince is to offer a goat (*hircum*), that is a strong and harsh penance.

Knobel sees this chapter as dealing in offences to God that can be reckoned as "theocratic sins." In a theocracy it is of more moment when the leaders fail, and the amount of sin determines the price of restitution.

The Sinning Community, Penance, and "Outside the Camp"

Origen sees mortal sins as vincible through serious penance; mortal sin is, by definition, to be left outside the camp (cf. Rahner 2005, 411). Procopius takes the unintentional sin of the congregation (v. 13) to refer to the Jews shouting "crucify him" (or just, he admits, more generally to the crowd's instinct to act ignorantly). The Jews did not discern the Word made flesh; they sacrificed the true paschal lamb, which should not have been done, and, like Abel's blood, Christ's blood cried out to God. To follow Christ "outside the camp" will mean sending a repudiation of a life in this world stained by sin. It is at the very root of the monastic journey into deserted areas.

Yet new communities in new places need to be hallowed. The need to purify the community was particularly poignant in an age when Christianity was taking public space away from pagans and establishing its own sacred places. In Carolingian thinking the vision of the purifying ritual, even that of verse 18, was an inspiration to faith and monastic settlement, as in this story of Otto, bishop of Regensburg, persuading those after Charlemagne what made his city a sacred site (Tischler 2005,133):

> And the king and bishops came to the high altar and saw the signs of canonical consecration on the substance of the altar and the Greek and Hebrew letters written on the four horns, unknown to the Latins, as today can be seen by all who look. And in the way they looked round the whole church and they found it consecrated in the right and canonical way . . .

> And blessed Marianus replied: "And I saw with the eyes of my body a heavenly light illuminating the darkness of the church and I saw Saint Peter in the style and clothing of a bishop and the twelve apostles with him and a countless host of angels consecrating the altar in the manner of ecclesiastical consecration, as there appeared on the horns of the altar the writings of unknown words and the sprinkling of the walls with blood (Lev 4:18). All this happened that you might more readily believe . . ."

In this we see the foundations for the practical theology of the medieval church as enacting a liturgical-Eucharistic theology in which the death of Christ is offered up as part of a cosmic drama. But in accordance with this, those who become impure as a congregation need some way of taking this impurity "outside." One goes out of the camp for a short time in order to qualify to re-enter it without the sin (v. 12).

The *Glossa Ordinaria* adds, simplifying matters: If one can return a free odor of good works, giving back to God what pleases him, how much more the saints (presumably those in heaven) remain in the purity of nature (i.e., in pre-lapsarian innocence). This hierarchical idea is continued in the *Glossa*'s comment that the basin (vv. 25, 30) represents human beings or the church militant at the bottom of the celestial hierarchy. Christ has managed to direct our desires (inward parts), which he leads towards God, although, of course, some desires were not found in him, such as gluttony and sexual desire.

Ralph solemnly reminds his readers that the blood of Christ does not atone for all, nor does faith alone suffice to be numbered among those for whom he atones. We need to have penitence congruent with his for that. In a moment of pastoral sensibility, Ralph adds:

> It is not enough to know one has been shamed when sin is made known: but one must blush over it, and hate it. Putting a hand on it fits the requirement that penance must be freely undertaken, not forced, except by divine love and care for one's own salvation. All who are born in relationship with God and continue in innocence have a gate to the east [after Ezek 40:6] since for them the entrance of the heavenly kingdom is unveiled by the light they receive . . . The friends of Job were only reconciled through the one they sinned against and Cornelius and Saul in Acts needed mediation. Yet human grace is not enough. Grace is to be begged for with the whole heart for without it there can be no hope of salvation. As the entrails are burned, so are we to burn our passions so we do not sin again.

Denys appeals to his community that sometimes to purify the place, people need to come out from it. To go outside the camp as Christ did (Heb 13) means to leave behind lusts, since we are upheld in the face of adversity and mockery by the watchful care and love of Christ. The Son of God died for you and still you sin?—this is the question Denys leaves his reader with.

Lapide responds to this. Question: why is the burning outside the camp? (v. 21). Answer: to strike fear into the people, that their sins also deserved to be burned in hell. We also see how important the high priest was in his adding the prayer, that God would abolish the very traces of sins, just like these sacrifices. (Lapide sees the high priest's turning the sacrifice to smoke as referring to prayer—cf. Rev 8:3.) Of course, Hebrews 13:12 tells us that these ceremonies signified Christ outside the camp in order to start the church among the Gentiles, for the cross of Christ was not on the altar of the temple but of the world (cf. Pope Leo's *Sermon 9. On the Passion*). The moral sense is given through Hebrews 13:13, that this ceremony signified that all who wish to accede to Christ and the Eucharistic altar must go outside the camp of luxury, this fallen and unfixed world, to carry Christ's cross by embracing poverty, abstinence, humility, and contempt, in order to reach the city above (Heb 13:14), with the priest praying for them God would be propitious (v. 20) and would not punish his people in this life (which he would have otherwise done). However, as for the blame and punishment of the *other* life, this was removed, not by the sacrifice or prayer of the priest, but by the contrition of those who had sinned, and through their contrition this sacrifice was a sign and declaration that they offered for sin. Taken mystically, the sacrifice for sin is penance and contrition. It is not enough to change one's ways but one needs to make satisfaction for the wrong done. Let those like Luther, who do not recognize penance except as stepping into a new life, realize this. Augustine in *De penitentia* is against them, as is Gregory (*Moralia* 21) and Bernard (*Sermon on the Song of Songs* 10). Compunction should come first from fear of hell and only then from love of God and kingdom. Baptism is a fount of tears according to Paphnutius and Palladius (*Lausiac History* 46) and John of Damascus in *The Life of Barlaam (and Joshaphat)*.

In early modern moral theology, as reflected in commentary on the passage about the community's unknowing sin, we find a curious sense of the liminality of the church, oscillating between a state of salvation and damnation. Ainsworth notes: "All the congregation" (v. 13): "This showeth that the Church may err—both in its people and its judges."

Calmet comments: theologians remark that external sacrifices remit only the exterior punishment. It is only faith, love, hope, and contrition—when joined to the sacrifices—which can remit sin itself. There is something quite similar in Bonar: "It would be with many tears and strong crying from the depths of his soul that he touched the altar's horns—a type of Jesus in the garden, when he fell on his face and offered up supplication." Also verse 12 reminds Bonar: "We are not to forget sin, because it has been atoned for; . . . God wishes his people to retain a deep and lively sense of their guilt, even when forgiven." Four miles outside the camp is a type of hell—where Christ's suffering could be seen from the city.

Rendtorff's view is that the *ḥattāʾt* ("sin offering") sacrifice in Leviticus 4 is more about participation with the divine through a blood offering of symbolic value, rather than any "washing" (Levine, *contra* Milgrom). However, Milgrom (with Abarnabel) thinks the interchangeability of individual, common, priestly, and princely "fault" concurs with a view of impurity as collective and contagious, even where not in its root a "moral" or willed fault (see Gane 2005, 69.)

Leviticus 5

Cases Requiring Sin-Offering (vv. 1–13)

For Hesychius the sins in 5:1–13 certainly flow into each other. To touch an unclean beast (v. 2) is to come into contact with the devil "in the voice of swearing" (*phônên horkismou*) with those who live in his idolatrous way, when we connive at what they do (v. 1). Thus Hesychius can link verse 1 with verse 2. Becoming aware of a negligent sin is like Herod's situation after promising the head of John the Baptist. This is the kind of thing that this "wrong" (*ʾāshēm*) means. "Touching unclean things" (v. 2), as one example of this, reminds Grima of Paul's injunction in 1 Corinthians 7 against those who sin against their own bodies by fornicating. Yet there might be also a mystical or higher meaning, that the soul might be touched by the suggestion of the devil.

Lyra is happier to allow that in these verses we find just a miscellany of wrongs with no obvious connection. However, Denys will strain to see the connection: for anyone who gazes lustfully on a woman "touches the unclean." And the animal killed by beasts is one whom the devil led into mortal sin, and then one is, through association with him, corrupted by the bestial motion of the flesh, even without consensual contact. However it becomes *deadly* sin when—whether from immaturity, lust, weakness, or similar fault—one is overcome by an external force, whether man or devil.

Brenz thinks that to demand the death penalty for one who makes such a mistake, say, in eating holy things seems harsh. However the law does teach us what real sins are. The scope of the law is not merely to establish among people a civil, external honesty and cleanliness, but has another aim and a greater use by far, as Paul often mentioned: the acknowledgment of sin. And not only the moral law but also the ceremonial does this, to show that by nature (on account of original sin) we are so affected that nothing stays unaffected by our unclean touch. When the law declares those unclean who touch an unclean thing, we should note that a corpse is not *in itself* unclean in God's sight, but the person touching it is unclean, and *he contaminates the corpse*, rather than vice versa (although we should say that the thing brings out the uncleanness from within us).

For Calov the *ḥaṭṭāʾt* (sin) is a fault in *omission* and the *ʾāshām* (*delictum*) is a wrong by *commission*, although he admits there might be some confusion. The Hebrews say that the *ʾāshām* is any sin against affirmative precepts. Yet the point is that the one who doubts whether he has sinned is already caught by this law: so, when in doubt we should assume we have sinned. In verses 1–14, it is about a *sin* and not an uncleanness unknowingly received (as in verse 17), which is a different kind of offense. In the supplement on verse 5 he follows the Hebraist Fagius (d. 1549) and "the Hebrews," that Numbers 5:6–7 confirms that sacrifice can only benefit where there is penance and confession. Calov does some work of clearing up the confusion: Fagius and others hold that *peccati* are sins of omission and the *delicti* are sins of commission, which Augustine in his Question 20 and Gregory the Great inverted when he wrote: "a *peccatum* in deed is a *delictum* in thought." Lapide along with Jerome and Procopius had *peccatum* as "knowing" and *delictum* as "unknowing" which Vatable (French Hebraist, d. 1547) called "lesser sins." But it is better to see it the other way round, argues Calov: chapter 4 is about sins committed through error and chapter 5 introduces what are *more* severe sins.

Patrick affirms a real difference between *ḥaṭṭāʾt* and *ʾāshām*, but finds it hard to say what this consists in, for Maimonides thinks *ʾāshām* to be the lesser offense, but Bochartus thinks the opposite, following the sense of the LXX *plemmeleia*. And perhaps Ibn Ezra sees the difference as that between ignorance and forgetting, but has no evidence for this. Patrick comments: "From whence a very learned Person of our own (now with God) concludes, That an Offence was peculiarly called *Ascham* . . . about which a man was dubious . . . or did a manifest damage to other men"; whereas *ḥaṭṭāʾt* results when the offense was known.

Hearing False Witnessing (v. 1)

The essence of the offence is perhaps best shown by the examples of unintentional—as opposed to a deceitful and active (a contrast stressed by Ibn Ezra and Rashi)—omission: omitting to speak up, or to purify oneself (as Nahmanides helpfully clarifies). Origen in *Homily* 3, (1981, I, 126) values the historical sense (against conniving at false testimony) as morally edifying, since it instructs that to keep quiet is to accept someone else's sin (cf. Matt 18:15–16). The spiritual sense is that it indicates the offence of not giving vocal witness to Christ's advent.

At the very beginning of his treatment of Leviticus in his *Quaestiones in Heptateuchum*, Augustine gives a fine pastoral interpretation of Leviticus 5:1 (*if a soul has sinned and he hears the oath spoken and was himself witness . . .*). It seems to say that we sin if in our hearing someone else swears falsehood and we know him to have sworn falsely yet say nothing. But between the fear of sinning in this way and the fear of a betrayal of men there is quite a large force of temptation. We can be ready by warning or prohibition of perjury to recoil from such a grave sin. But if no one else heard what was said concerning the matter—if only we know that the person has sworn falsely—it is a most difficult question to know whether to betray him, especially if he might face the death penalty. But since it does not specify here to whom it must be told—whether to the one who received the oath, or to the priest, or to anyone who not only cannot prosecute him by applying torture but can even pray for him—then it seems to Augustine that one can release himself from the chain of sin if action brings forward the medicine of confession.

Here Augustine imagines it was a case of a conflicted conscience eventually offering up the truth after being "economical" with it. By early modern times there is no such easy way out, and Augustine's darker view reaches a stern conclusion. According to Calmet, the apodosis of the conditional sentence in Leviticus 5:1 is: "he will bear the punishment for his sin"; that's to say: the judge will punish it or God himself will exact vengeance from it. But, Calmet objects, "he will bear his sin" (v. 1) means he is not covered by the sacrifice and will surely remain guilty until the Last Judgment and be cast out from his people, for it is not a sin of ignorance or weakness at all but is a crime punishable by the ultimate Judge when the guilty will be convicted. This, of course, is bad news for those guilty of such an offense and indicates perhaps that this in some way is as serious as those crimes whose punishments are mentioned in Leviticus 20. Kant (1949, 346–50) would be almost equally hard on those equivocating about truth-telling.

Touching Unclean Things (vv. 2–3)

To Origen it seems crazy to think that that touching a prophet's corpse would be bad, since Origen's view was that the relics of holy people were beneficial. For Ralph, only sin is unclean to God. So "touching something unclean" cannot mean to touch a dead body physically. For it is "*anima*" not "*homo*" here! A soul touches the unclean when it gives consent to another's sin and corrupted this way tunes the will towards blame; an "animal killed by beasts" is when, by the suggestive seduction of the enemy, one slips in sin, when one by his own deliberation subjects oneself to sin. For Willet, touching unclean things means keeping too much pseudo-Christian company "who did adioyne himself with those, which were dead in sinne."

Swearing to Do Harm (v. 4)

Origen had more of a problem with the person who promises something that might be bad (or good) (v. 4) and then does not do it. Why should it be wrong not to follow through on a threat, for example? Unless we see "*malefacere*" to mean "opposing someone," or something clearly wrong, say when we set out to fight the flesh with an oath of chastity, and then fail to do that. However, the literal sense of the rule seem a bit foolish, so there must be a higher meaning to the statement. Augustine tries harder to hold to the letter of the text. If we compare him with Origen on this, Augustine is much more committed to the text as it stands and therefore to particular words. On verse 4, the verse which gave Origen particular problems, Augustine points to similar examples in Psalm 65:13f, Ezekiel 3:18, and Numbers 30:4. This distinguishing (*distinctio*) seems to be a way of speaking that separates something from the rest, which are not included in such a term. Augustine understands this to text to refer a case where someone did not know whether that which he was swearing to do was a right or wrong or he swore before he knew or that he did know just what he swore but then recognized that it was not to be done or sworn, and he confessed. And when it adds "*adversus ipsum*" [against it] that means against *the sin* he will confess, i.e., he will in a sense "accuse sin" by his confessing.

It is again some question—not a trifling one for Augustine—what it is that Moses means immediately following: "after he knows this, he offends." This suggests that there is only sin *once there is knowledge*. Moses does not say, "after he knew this and repented" but "after knowledge he sinned." That is, if someone is doing what he knows should not be done (i.e., doing it "after knowledge") then a purification for the wrong is owed. But that is not what was being said before, where it seemed to be about sins committed by the ignorant and the unwilling. Augustine sees the conundrum. So better to say that the words are in reverse order to the meaning. Perhaps—since Scripture has such types of speech—what was said in other places in straight order may sometimes be said in reverse order. For since it is written often elsewhere, "and he commits wrong and [then] becomes aware of it," here we have the reverse: "he knew and [then] he committed wrong." No less than the *Mishnah*, knowing seems to add intention to an initially unintentional sin.

Ralph is unsure: some say that this is to be understood to be about the evil of punishment to be inflicted on him, whenever he swore that he would afflict himself with a fast or some other mode of mortifying the flesh. Others say that this can be understood about the evil of guilt—that of swearing to condemn a neighbor unjustly or anything of this manner. Not that such an oath should be fulfilled but simply that one sins by swearing it in the first place.

Willet name-checks Tostatus (Abulensia), following Hesychius, in proposing that a man who swore to do evil must still repent of breaking his oath when he fails to do evil. But what the Law here is opposing is not the lightness with which people make their oaths, but their not taking care to keep them, and *that* is what the sacrifice is for. But in the case of an unlawful oath, no satisfaction will be achieved. This chapter deals with sins of ignorance that come from negligence or weakness, but not sins directly against God, committed out of malice.

Matthew Henry on this passage discusses rash swearing: "Such wretched dilemmas as these do some men bring themselves into by their own rashness and folly; go which way they will their consciences are wounded, sin stares them in the face, so sadly are they *snared in the words of their mouth* . . . Wisdom and watchfulness beforehand would prevent these straits."

Graduated Offering and Penance (vv. 6–13)

The Rabbinic commentary places a good deal of weight on the idea of *korban 'ole veyored* (graduated offerings, according to one's economic capabilities) and Rashi, Ibn Ezra, and Nahmanides are also keen to make sure that no one should delay from offering on account of financial means. In an analogous way the Christian writers are sensitive to the "wherewithal" of the offenders. Hesychius observes that the lawgiver wished to keep many doors open by suggesting a variety of ways of penance according to type of sin and sinner: sackcloth, fasting, tears, continual prayer, vigils, and the like. The old and the weak have another non-penitential way of gaining forgiveness and that is by offering oneself to the contemplation of God and the scrutiny of his law, dedicating the mind to heavenly intercourse. Normally, however, penance should be exercised so as not to cut the sinner off, but to submit them to the mind of Christ, observes Hesychius. One needs to spend time away from those who do evil for he will be too anxious to avoid offending them, and he must not give them cause to relax and commit further sins.

What we get here from Hesychius is almost a list of "tips" on penance. Christ loves to save the one who comes to him. It is a question of laying oneself on the altar, even the one who it seems impossible that he be saved. It pertains to Christ alone to take on sins. Those who have lost hope through prevarication should know that Christ even prays and takes on penance. But penance can be repeated in Hesychius' view (Jüssen 1934, 77), although he is aware in his comments on 5:11 that penance can be abused (cf. Heb 6:7f). It would seem, however, that *public* penance cannot be repeated for some *serious* sins. But even a person who commits such sins should not despair but as a backslidden sinner should turn to Christ, who is also outside the church.

Procopius comments on vv. 7–13 that the Father was pacified by the death of the Son from which he received sweet fragrance. The life that we then enjoy is Christ's. Virtues that are "in Christ" pour out the sweetest smell, like the mind influencing the lower parts or enhancing their odor. That is what he interprets from the injunction *not* to add oil or incense (v. 11). Amalarius (*Liber Officialis* III, c.44) in his "On the Mass for the Dead" writes that death is the punishment for the first sin and so is celebrated without "Gloria and alleluia," without oil and incense just as in the guilt-offering (v. 11). For the same reason we do not give a kiss of peace when celebrating the death of the Lord.

The *Glossa Ordinaria* prefers to shift attention to the details, phrase by phrase, rather than attempting to grasp the meaning of the passage as a whole. Thus it excerpts Gregory's *Homily on Ezekiel* on v. 8: *Retorquebit*: This means to "twist back" our senses towards virtues. By the head we understand the mind, which directs our actions. To remove it part way from the body means to distance it from the delights of the flesh but not from its needs (Rom 13), etc. We are not to serve the body but nor are we to hate it nor consider it to be made by the devil as the heretics do, but rather as joined, subordinate to the head. Nothing other than the imitation of Christ and the obedience to the preaching of the gospel can snatch one out of sin. It could be also that this is the very center of the chapter for the *Glossa*, since even when the subject of the action changes back from the priest to "the soul" bringing the offering (v. 11), the focus remains with the priest. One commits the hope of salvation to the divine godliness, i.e., the priest. There is a high regard for priests here, as those who imitate Christ. Especially given the fact that the one who is in the habit of prevarication does not know whether his prayer is of a sweet odor or not. A priest can reassure.

For Langton, the dove (v. 7) symbolizes the groans and tears of penance. There are two types of sin, the doing of evil and the despising of good. Two types of offering are required so that we might do good. For occasions where we have neglected good we must offer ourselves, burning with the fire of sorrow as well as making restitution. There are thus two types of tears depending on the level of foulness. That the head of the dove is not separated indicates that the penitent remains joined to Christ. As deposit the soul has to be given back to God and if we corrupt it by sin we are breaking the deal. Paul, in 2 Timothy 1:14, reminds us not to neglect that deposit.

It is not that *all* senses are condemned, only the contrivance (*ingenium*) which aims clearly at wicked practices.

For Denys there is direct application of the plain moral sense. With Jerome, the person who swears to do something bad and does not do it, sins, in that he has broken an oath. There are three companions of any oath or vow; namely, truth, judgment, and justice. Now if someone swears to do something spiritual which relates to their worship of God and the salvation of souls, but then cannot fulfill this, then the law touches not just the fraudulent person but anyone who takes money from church offerings and delays in paying it back. For even according to the letter the Law ought to edify its hearers. For its observance is useful and necessary to those who have power with ecclesiastical dispensation. They ought to be careful with this power. As well as culpability for ignorance of the Law, those who are ignorant of fact (as in Leviticus 4) will have some fault if they are seen to have been less than circumspect. How much more, if the OT people were guilty, are those today who go nonchalantly into church and the mysteries. If one cannot perform the heavy exercises of penance then one should offer doves, i.e., groaning with all one's heart, or at least the external behavior should be sincere and exemplary. This chapter teaches us the danger there is in ignorance of things that each, according to the demands of his calling, is expected to be aware of. For 1 Corinthians 14:38 has: "he who ignores, he will be ignored," and, Ambrose reminds us, that ignorance is a great sin.

Willet dislikes Lyra's "Romanist" interpretation that the lack of oil in the sacrifice means no sure mercy, such that the sinner should always fear that he is not forgiven (cf. Trent Sess 6, 9). But David's confidence in divine mercy in 2 Samuel 12:13 shows us differently. Further, "The Doway glossemen [Douai Bible, 1609], doe give this marginall note upon the vers 16. *Beside restitution, satisfaction also is necessary for the offence to God.*" No, cries Willet: "I read of Peter's tears not his satisfaction!"

Keil thinks that the command of vv. 11–13—that it be offered without oil and incense—was to ensure it did not to have character of a *minḥāh*. "But the reason why it was not to have its character was, that only those who were in a state of grace could offer a *minḥāh*, and not a man who had fallen from grace through sin . . . he was not allowed to add oil and incense as symbols of the Spirit and praise of God."

The Guilt Offering (5:14–26: English Bibles—6:1–6)

Origen emphasizes immediate confession and penance for this more deliberate, hence serious, offense, reacting before the devil can accuse us, for if we wait for his accusation we might end up with his confederates in Gehenna. Origen elsewhere makes this distinction: it is one thing to be merely "polluted," another thing to have to be abject or "thrown away." Doing extra private penance is what "destruction of the flesh" means for a Christian (cf. his Homily in Ps 37:2). Yet, on the other hand, what "we" have to give is our faith as the smallest of admission charges—and Jesus can tell whether our coin of faith (v. 15) is counterfeit or real, heretical or catholic (1 Cor 11:19).

Ralph follows this Christ-centered line of approach at much more length: The person who dares to question church teachings should correct himself through the teaching of Christ, that by now having him as his teacher in the faith, through him might deserve to be reconciled: the silver coin (v. 15) hints at the confession of faith and the one who confesses that Jesus in the Son of God, will be indwelt by God (1 John 4). Christ's sacrifice is gained by the price of confessing the faith (Rom 10:9). It is two-fold in that there has to be true belief and spoken confession, as is the measure of the church in its tradition—only there will one be able to exchange faith for the ram. The Septuagint (LXX) has inflated the two to fifty coins. Now fifty coins is the worth of a horse or any big animal. (On verse 15 he is very exact that a shekel coin—and the Hebrew dual makes clear there were two of them—was worth four Spanish reals or one Brabantine florin.) Yet spiritually the LXX means here the fiftieth day on which the Pentecostal Holy Spirit was sent. That confession of faith by which Christ is acquired is given to people through the Holy Spirit. One cannot ask for the forgiveness through the sacrifice unless, having been corrected, he is now following the teaching of Christ. We should note that the ancient Jews put the heretics [Protestants] to shame by their readiness to be specific in their confession of sins. Mystically he approves Ralph's use of the LXX *fifty* shekels, which signifies that the confession in the Holy Spirit is the way to acquire Christ as the sacrificial ram for ourselves.

Grima comments that the very sacrifice of the lamb reveals the sinfulness that comes from the lust that belongs to the flesh (Jas 1:14–15). Langton is more interesting when, on verse 6, he writes that to offer a lamb is to offer to the Lord that which is innocent as to work; to offer a goat is to surrender share of one's action; it is well said that "a lamb from the flock" is preferable since many are the active and few the contemplative. Yet it would seem that these are of equal value.

Brenz contends that external signs in worship help back up the word of forgiveness. They are signs that we should impress on our minds, and they let us express thankfulness for spiritual benefits and keep the public ministry. The provision of a pauper's offering indicates not only that God is merciful, but also that it is faith in the offering that matters. Some (Catholics) teach that one should doubt the divine mercy towards us. Some impious people are happier in this world than are godly folk. We cannot judge God's favor from external events—that's the true meaning of Ecclesiastes—but we can be sure from the Word of God which comes forth from the promises of God (in Scripture), on account not of our perfection but that of Christ.

Sinning in the Holy Things (vv. 15–19)

Theodoret, on verse 17, comments that it happens sometimes that by inattention someone sins in not bringing at the right time to God consecrated things such as firstborn, firstfruits, or things promised. He points out that verses 15–16 make it seem that a greater penalty will be given to the one who sins through carelessness (*plemmeleias*). First, he is ordered to pay what he owes and to add a fifth of the value; and then to offer a ram worth fifty coins and thus obtain the remission of sin. This was fulfilled by Zacchaeus. Brenz thinks that from Leviticus 4:1 to 5:13 the focus has been on *peccatum* (sin, error), but from 5:14 it moves to *delictum* (fault, wrong): in which case an extra offering of money is required, and always a ram. For it is an offence against the sanctuary, in cases when one doubts whether he has done wrong or not. The Hebrews call it a "wrong (*delictum*) of doubt." But other "wrongs" are intentional, such as sacrileges, theft, and rapine—*delictum* is not one of these. However Brenz does not consider the sin in verse 17 to be a sin directly against the sanctuary for he goes on to talk about restitution to one's offended neighbor (which is absent from the text), with a great concern to make ceremonial law work for public morality. Christ thus demands penitence, whose works are many, including reconciliation and restitution of things to a neighbor. He concludes that sin will not reign unless "you do not want to be reconciled with your neighbor and restore to them what you owe—even if there is no public court case, you should still do it quietly as Augustine said (Ep 54 *Ad Macedonium*)."

Where 5:19 speaks of guilt "against the Lord," Patrick tells us that Targum Jonathan paraphrases "against the *Name of the Word of* the Lord." He, Patrick would not over-elaborate and did not trust this Word theology. "Were not the impious pamphlets that have lately been spread abroad, against the Doctrine of the ever-blessed Trinity?" More positively, it was already known in that in Genesis 28:21 the word of the Lord is so plainly made the object of his Jacob's adoration, and the Targum on Genesis 3:22 has "The Word of the Lord said."

Milgrom (1991) has drawn out the logic of this sacrifice as not simply an offering for impurity, but for *guilt*. Here confession translates *deliberate* sin into *inadvertent* sin so it can be dealt with. The phrase in v. 5 often translated as "when he realizes his guilt," Milgrom translated as "when he feels guilty." "Bearing the sin" means *feeling bad* and it motivates confession allowing the guilt to be dealt with. He applies this: finally, to delay apologizing for the hurt inflicted on others may lead inevitably to serious reprisals. Every additional moment that someone feels hurt by us allows that hurt to fester and grow (2004, 49). The serious sin (unintentional sacrilege or intentional fraud) can be given an amnesty on the condition of such a reparatory offering. "[The Priestly author] postulates a new category of jurisprudence: repentance as a factor in the mitigation of divine retribution" (2004, 60). As with Alcoholics Anonymous, so with the "prophetic" view that repentance before the Lord of the universe is the *sine qua non* of divine- and self-forgiveness. This might sound controversial enough (and the medieval Jewish commentators are much more interested in the objective sum of reparation to the victim), but there is something even more awkward in Gerstenberger's claim (1993, 73): "a cross in Bergen-Belsen and a memorial Mass in Auschwitz can have reconciling character" where there is a receptive attitude to symbolic acts opposing the powers of destruction. But the principle that jurisprudence includes the religious (already sounded by Rabbi Akiva) offers a challenge to modern, secular distinctions.

Leviticus 6

ALTHOUGH THE HEBREW TEXT and the "moderns," as Calmet puts it, are aware that 6:1–7 belongs with chapter 5, most of the history of interpretation sees commentators failing to read them as one unit. Most commentators, however, have managed to link the "trespass" or "wrong" of these first verses with the *ḥaṭṭāʾt* (sin-offering) and *ʾashām* (guilt offering) of the end of the chapter (vv. 24ff) and the beginning of chapter 7. Thus, while as so often the interest is less in the logic of the whole chapter and more in the meaning and significance of phrases, nonetheless commentators do mostly make the right connections, or at least not obviously false ones.

Spiritual Fraud

Origen announces that John 6:63 tells us that the words of the Lord are spirit and life; and we should believe the same of the words he spoke to Moses. In other words, the letter of Leviticus 6:1–6 is for those stuck in carnality who defraud each other, and one would hope none of that faithful have such morals. So there needs to be a spiritual sense of this to be applied to believers. What could this be? Picking up on *depositum* (v. 4) as that which is entrusted (*parathēkēn*), for Origen this means the body and soul (as image and likeness), and one carries a large responsibility to return it to God in the condition one received it. One keeps the image's deposit (cf. 2 Tim 1:4) by being merciful (Luke 6:36) which is to be perfect (Matt 5:48). Here Origen glosses Matthew with Luke. Imitating God keeps the deposit of the divine image kept safe. But if you behave badly you receive the devil's image (1 Tim 6:20). There is some literal sense to be salvaged in Origen's eyes. He notes that there is no mention of the amount of money to be added, unlike at Leviticus 5:15. He considers the difference between sinning against holy things and outside them. 1 Samuel 2:25 makes the distinction of sinning against God (holy things) and against men ("outside them") (1 John 5:15).

Procopius, commenting on verse 2, states that Christ takes away the sins by which we are injurious to our brothers, and the one who has faith can escape the charge. Yet we are still to make it up to our brothers, as Zacchaeus did by his fourfold restitution.

Hugh of St. Cher operates as if the instructions were written directly for the church (cf. Dahan 2002). The historical sense for the Jews is of some interest, but the straight moral sense is what he is occupied with. Hugh relies on Josephus to instruct that while in such cases money was to be returned with twofold increase, animals were to be returned *four*fold and cattle in *five*fold, to correspond to the loss of usefulness sustained. And this principle can be applied today: in cases where the stealing was owing to hungry stomachs, he will have to pay sevenfold, the number of perfection. If one lets such people off lightly we will soon have others saying they *needed* to commit adultery because their hearts were empty. Of course, the "part for the Lord" given to the priest (6:6 in English Bibles) refers to that which is due to bishop or archdeacon today.

Calvin believed that God commanded precision in order to get obedience in small things. Shuttling between verses 2 and 25 he concludes that Moses begins to distinguish between *ḥattā'ṭ* (sin) and *'ashām* (guilt)—which the Latins call *peccatum* and *delictum*—though he had before used the terms indifferently to express the same thing. "What the difference was, I know not; I see the guesses of others, but nothing certain." The rites seem very similar for dealing with both.

Lapide tells us that Calvin wants to extend this to other intentional sins, but really such sacrifices are only for injuries to the neighbor. For willful idolatry, divination, schism, and the killing of parents there are no such sacrifices, and for internal sins there are no sacrifices either, only for external. It is certain that all these can be expiated by an act of contrition to which all the prophets refer sinners, promising them forgiveness. Moreover they do nothing towards satisfaction of sins since they work only for the redeeming of temporal punishments. For the Catholic doctors (notably Bellarmine and Suarez) call "satisfaction" the redeeming of temporal pains. There follows a patristic florilegium (a chain of patristic statements) about the importance of confession. On verses 4–5, fraud is intentional so it requires a ram rather than just a goat. Yet Moses does not mention here priests or princes or people as a whole, which presupposes they will not sin deliberately.

Willet, with his semi-Presbyterian ecclesiology, sees some kind of precedent for church courts having a place, where confession and a sacrifice with a smaller penalty (restitution plus one fifth) can serve as an alternative to the full force of the secular (civil) law (fourfold restitution). Willet rubs up against the Catholic use of the language of "soul" (*nefesh*) in verse 2 in order to speak of traducianist view of original sin whereby the soul was conveyed with the seed through sexual intercourse. No! In Scripture "the soul" means "the person," as in Genesis 46:26 ("all the soules that went out of Jacob's loynes").

Calov is concerned to tell us that the extra "fifth part" (v. 5) is not what expiates but is added simply to acknowledge the insult to God. Calmet notes that it may seem strange that serious sins like these here in 6:1–5 can be dealt with by sacrifice. Yet one might say that Moses acts here like a wise legislator. For these are hidden sins that are hard to prove in law and have to do with a religious mistrust of God—thus a softer, non-juridical sentence is provided. In the case of verses 4–5, when you knows who the true owner is yet keeps the thing until your conscience afflicts you, it is really more a case of self-regulating morality, seeking an amnesty by volunteering a confession and bringing recompense and sacrifice at one's own initiative.

The Appropriate Sacrifice by the Priests (vv. 8–13)

The Jewish commentators, sensitive to the new section (*tzav*) from the formula: "And the Lord spoke to Moses," tend to see the focus on action *by the priests*, whether selecting the right clothing or attending to the fire.

Origen wants to discuss sin (so spends more than half of the sermon on 6:1–6), then Christ, and then "behavior" and "Scripture," avoiding the details of the sacrifices. Augustine was also to the point: Why is the victim offered as a holocaust (v. 8)? Well, this is to show that the holy things are not to be given in *part* but rather one is to give oneself *whole* to the God of the whole. It is remarkable that after such a strong resistance by Origen to the idea that this chapter had anything to do with the priesthood, that those who so often follow him should reverse this. An exception is the monk Rupert of Deutz for whom the linen tunic of the priest signifies the life of the new person (in contrast to the covering of skins put on by Adam after the Fall). The soft linen stands for the chastity of those so surrounded in their hearts with divine love that marital love has no appeal.

The view that these verses are indeed about the Christian priesthood goes back at least to Hesychius, who writes that not everyone requires the most perfect wisdom, yet the priest should be perfectly wise. He orders the offering of perpetual sacrifice—that is, a continual burnt offering every day and evening—that by beginning from perfect wisdom he will end with the same and will have composed his whole life for perfection. Thus a higher holiness is demanded of priests. This meaning is allegorized from the sense of holocausts and their continual burning—not letting the fire of the Holy Spirit go out, as Paul said in 1 Thessalonians 5:19, and in the night there is a need for burning as the day approaches (Rom 13:12). Christian priests are made a burnt-offering so as to be spiritual while all others remain earthbound. Hesychius does not dwell on the garments of the priest but on the essence of "priesthood" in righteousness and chastity, and on the priest's connection to Christ. It is not just a matter of literally keeping sober day and night but also of spiritually keeping sober during that spiritual night (John 4:24). For the body of Christ is the intelligible altar, and one must put on that the inextinguishable fire of the ministering Spirit. Those men supreme in wisdom are not to offer up *their own* ideas but rather what Christ has revealed. By "the altar" (v. 14) it means the humanity of the Only Begotten. The incarnate Lord passed on to us that we should think of the Father-in-him and him-in-the-Father and know of the Holy Spirit that he is of the Son himself and proceeds from the Father. This is enough theology for salvation and anyone wanting to delve deeper commits a sin!

Cyril reports on the ritual prescribed in verses 14–18: The burnt offerings show the perfection of those once most hallowed things. Now the sacrifice shows the life subject to God, whose apt figure is the finest wheat presented with oil and incense by the priest's hand. For a life dedicated to God, even if in part, must be extremely fragrant and flourishing with all sorts of shining hope. Or do you not say that our every good work is most fragrant? Cyril then continues in this dialogue to work out what these priestly things mean: that which is not wholly burned (vv. 20–23), he warns, is not appropriate for the Christian priest, who must be *totally dedicated* (every sacrifice of the priest will be a holocaust) and not divided between God and world, but crucified with Christ so that Christ lives in him (Gal 2:20). A softness of heart will result from the process of trial. But Cyril is then quick to advise his charge Palladius that this can only take place through Christ, in who resides all purification, who endured his saving slaughter for us. The offering for sin is none other than that by Emmanuel, who as pure lamb was wholly offered. And since, as God of God, he was the Holy of Holies itself, the Son sanctified creation in his own spirit.

The Carolingian period also saw emphasis on the power of the divine Crucified One being channeled through the Eucharist, which was the one worthy means of grace and visual aid (cf. Alcuin, *Carmen* 109.11 or *Commentary on John* 3.15; Chazelle 2001, 24, 33). What emerged was an interesting elision of the figure of priest and sacrifice, to the point that they became almost indistinguishable, through both being referred to the action and passion of Christ on the cross. The influence of Hesychius in the *Glossa* should not be overlooked, especially the addition: "this is a perpetual law for the Lord" (v. 22), which is interpreted as to do with Christ's eternal priesthood. It is the flesh here that was burned up, whereas he who descended from heaven in the incarnation was not burned up (Heb 9:14) Christ's sacrifice was indivisible or "whole," as Aquila translated, and cannot as such be divided to be eaten.

The qualities of a priest and Eucharist are what interest Langton. Aaron, as the "mountain of courage," helps people to be faithful and the day of anointing truly means the day of incarnation. Aaron, that is Christ, laid down his flesh as an offering and his sons offer him daily while they make a memorial of Christ's passion.

Hugh also reminds us that in Exodus morning and evening sacrifice is described, to signify Christ who was to be sacrificed at the evening of the world, who was fuller and more effective than others, and who yet was also slain from the foundation of the world (Rev 13:8). He is prefigured by Abel. Therefore, the church offers twice daily, making a general confession first in the morning, and in the evening prayers as supplement. Fuel is fed for the nourishing of the flame of love in us when we remember what Christ endured morning and evening in his passion. There is to be no day's business of other offerings until that lamb in the morning is first sacrificed. "They shall eat it in the place of the tent of the sanctuary" means around the tabernacle, not *in* it. For nothing is to be done in the oratory except prayer, as Augustine says in his *Rule*.

Langton in the same way in his commentary here teaches that Scripture gives in these daily burnt-offerings a model for the church to follow in its daily office. For the general confession is designated by the morning sacrifice, whereas the confession of the more spiritually advanced is represented by the evening sacrifice.

The Catholic Reformation drew comfort from a daily sacrifice that only the priests could make. Lapide reports that Jerome and Bernard on the Song of Songs thought that "eat the sins of the people" happens when clergy become corrupt: but this is not what Scripture means. It is better (with Cyril, Theophylact, and Theodoret) to see Hosea 4 and this passage as meaning "they *deal with* the people's sins," so as to remove them.

Willet is as "secular" in inclination as Origen was: just as the priest renewed the altar fire each morning, so we are to first of all think of God and put all earthly things out of mind. For the Pietist Henry, religious leaders now (as then) are required to model high standards which lay people are expected to attain to "in their slipstream" as it were. Yet: "We are all undone, both ministers and people, if we must bear our own iniquity; nor could we have had any comfort or hope if God had not laid on his dear Son the iniquity of us all, and he is both the priest and the altar."

The Flame

Augustine asks if the flame on the altar (vv 12f.) burned all the time? Perhaps verse 22 explains: "everlasting" (*sempiternum*) means that every high priest would re-light it on the day when he succeeded the one who had died. This is an important point: that it is not the flame itself which is to be understood as "eternal" (i.e., without interruption), but rather *the law* of keeping the flame going on such repeated occasions. Thus, even when the things, the *realia*, of the cult have passed, as shadows must, the law concerning them remains. Grima thinks that the altar burning with perpetual flame is the heart afire with love, just as fire in its own way does not impede a vision of the stars. Thus love as situated in God finds its own matter and so love then comes to be immortal. Love does not distract but shows up what is disordered. Of course, love in this present life needs the fires of Hades (*inferno*) to make the heart good in what it lacks. But the damned remain forever in their inordinate love and wicked lust, just as the rich man was forbidden to cool his tongue (Luke 16). Deuteronomy 32 tells us that a fire is lit in God's anger and endures to the last, impeding the vision of God. Just as in Psalm 57:6 (LXX)—"fire fell on them and they did not see the sun"—it is right to burn oneself in good works out of love of God. It should be noted that the threefold state of love is to be devoured by this fire. For Christ the high priest breathes down from heaven saying: "Receive the Holy Spirit" so that their hearts were burning. Fire is found mystically in the church below and on the road into Jerusalem, that is the church above.

Denys adds the spiritual elucidation: it will burn all night until morning. As Christ was an offering who exposed himself to burning, the flame should burn in our hearts too as we remember what he endured. And we should do this the whole night, i.e., throughout the time of this present life, which is like night in comparison to the life to come.

It is not surprising, thinks Brenz, that pagans like the Chaldeans worshipped fire, since it can burn up all other gods. Nevertheless Canopus of Egypt outwitted them with water. Some say that holy blessed water can extinguish the fire of purgatory. The fire was not, even for the Israelites, any sort of reality, but rather a symbol of Christ's death for us, i.e., the fire of his affliction. The everlasting killing of Christ is foreshadowed by the everlasting fire of whole offering. It reminds us not to make a show of lights, as the hypocrites do, but that the preaching of the gospel on the afflictions, passion, and death of Christ might always gleam in the church and remain. Christ makes all those believing in him to be priests.

Chytraeus adds that fire was from the beginning of the world a sign of the presence and grace of God, but since the Gentiles did not know these things they started mistaking the sign for God in their worship. Xenophon and Plutarch tell us of Persian spectacles. But even Romans committed sacred fire to vestal virgins, in imitation of Leviticus 6. For the Greek word *hesia* and Latin *vesta* come from the Hebrew *ish yah* ("fire of the LORD"). More importantly, the perpetual nature of the fire mirrors the doctrine of Christ, died and risen, to be *always* held forth. One may compare Jeremiah 23:29: "are my words not like fire?" Such fire disperses the darkness of doubt.

Spangenberg uses the mention of flame to speak of believers doing the work that is preaching the gospel (rather than preparing themselves for saving grace). The tending of the flame, however, shows how "we" are, by the burning passion of Christ, to test and return to God believers tested and found righteous before him. Lapide sees the perpetual nature of the fire as suiting God's majesty, which is constantly to be adored and honored. It is not about worshipping the fire as some pagans, Persians and Romans, do.

A skeptical note is sounded by Calmet. Theophrastus tells us that guarding the flame is one of the most ancient acts of religions (see Eusebius, *Preparation* 1.9), while "the Rabbis" believe it was miraculously kept and anything added was not of necessity but to hide the miracle. Calmet is not so sure, nor does he know whether the flame was kept during desert marches—probably not, although Numbers is none too clear. As for Maimonides's claim that the temple, once built, had *three* fires on the "Holocaust Altar" . . . well, he our sole witness, so we cannot be certain.

Abarbanel had equated the flame with the compelling love of God, with reference to Song of Songs 8:6. The image of fire as purifying and offering up the living soul is also found in Charles Wesley's great hymn, "O Thou Who Camest from Above"—written in 1762 and based on Leviticus 6:13—with lines such as "Kindle a flame of sacred love, Upon the mean altar of my heart . . . There let it for Thy glory burn, With inextinguishable blaze," in which Wesley mixes the Levitical metaphor with that of Pentecost (Lloyd 2007, 215). We might contrast this with Bonar's interpretation of the same verse, almost a century later: He writes, "There is no 'putting out' of the fire. 'The fire is not quenched,' is Christ's own expression"; perhaps in reference to this type (Mark 9:44). "There will be no putting out of these flames in eternity—no waters to quench them—no interference of God's mercy to end them."

Sanctification through Contact

Origen muses that it seems counter-intuitive that even an evildoer could be sanctified (v. 27) by contact with something sacred. Well, the gospel tells us that this *can* happen as, for instance, when the woman in Mark 6:25 touched Christ, whose flesh was the Holy of Holies. Of course, she did not touch that but only as far as the hem of the cloak, in her faith. But once someone is a Christian one can come closer and touch the flesh of the Word of God whenever able to discuss and explain his hidden mysteries. If we can teach with clarity and authority then coming close is what we have done. Procopius sees the ritual of the offering as an illustration of penance. He makes the connection with Mark 6:25 and advocates the right attitude as the woman who was bold to touch Jesus in her self-dedication. Incense stands for hope and oil stands for a life with a seriousness of morals, as one free from all yeast of evil.

Augustine expands upon the sense of "Whoever touches its flesh will be cleansed (sanctified)." The people as such are not to touch but to stand far off. The one who dares to approach and receives bloodstains is ordered to serve in the temple, as no longer lord of himself. So the point is that there is a calling to holy service, which is not for everyone. "All who touch will be made holy" (v. 18); this verse shows that in discussion about God it is enough for theologians to *touch*, just as the one who wants to be warmed touches fire, but if he goes too close he will be burned. In other words, one should not delve too deep in doctrine. The basic stuff is enough. Hesychius's doctrine is focused on the Incarnate One, rather than on speculation. The "one-tenth of an *ephah*" is like the humanity of the Only Begotten who is capable of receiving three measures, that is the Trinity. The reference to morning and evening indicates Christ's passion, since that, in fact, started in the morning at Caiaphas's house. The cross of the Lord, just like a stout frying pan, was not harmed by the heat of human sin. With the lordly flesh placed on it, it returned that flesh, now edible for human beings. Without this we would never have seen the body of Christ mystically. Lapide is more practical and negative: as for "everyone who touches," that means they ought to be sanctified and made clean lest they go on to touch sacred things and contaminate. So the future tense here is to be read as imperative, not indicative.

Calmet comments on verse 18 that one needed to be pure in the sight of the law as a Levite to partake of the food and that those who do not become sanctified in a *negative* way. "Sanctifying" can often have the sense of making *im*pure. Verse 27 concerns not whoever but *what*ever comes into contact; not only (as we have seen) all people who touch need prepared holiness, but also things that come into contact with sacrifices can no longer have an ordinary use. Knobel is able to explain simply be saying that a thing cannot be holy and unclean *at the same time*. Touching them does not make the clean things impure, and it is certainly not to be thought of as taking the load of moral sin off the person who touches them. In this Knobel confesses himself proud to stand in the tradition of Grotius, Spencer, Outram, and Michaelis.

Gerstenberger describes the priestly garments as "radiation protection suits" (1993, 85). It reinforces the idea that that there are two worlds: cultic and everyday. Even if lay-folk are clean they must not touch. This places a lot of responsibility on to the cultic leaders who are under Moses. Hopi Indian sacred dance can be nullified by sexual impurity, but the standards here are stricter. The prophetic criticism against the Israelite cult (e.g., in Malachi) was not anti-cultic *per se* but rather an objection against its *abuse*. In Ezekiel 44:19 the priests who go out take their clothes off so as not to sanctify the people, which presupposes that holiness was regarded as much more contagious than in the Pentateuch, for which the area of priestly operation is an exclusion zone (Milgrom 2004, 63f) so that people could not benefit from holiness as things could (vv. 8, 27) and claim "sanctuary," as had happened with Adonijah, according to 1 Kings 1:51. In keeping with this the medieval Christian right of sanctuary was restricted to cases of accidental murder. In medieval England sanctuary or asylum would be followed by voluntary exile, or, in the case of Tudor England, to a sort of house arrest (Field 1991, 225).

Putting the Ashes Outside the Camp

The ash which remains until the next morning (v. 11) represents, in Rupert's view, unclean thoughts, and to remove those ashes is to bring them to Christ, who cares for our whole salvation. And this is done through repeated confession of heart and mouth. The burnt-offering (v. 12) is the secret sacrifice of true love in which the faithful soul longs for the sight of God. Grima comments that to put ashes by the altar is to think on how the sinner's way will be burned up, and will be thrown out of the camp as being of no profit (cf. Luke 19:11–25: the Parable of the Talents). Denys observes that although the *Gloss* takes "ashes" to mean the completion of good works, they could also be seen as "meaning the lowly consideration of our mortality and weakness." For Brenz, ashes being taken outside the camp signifies the burial of Christ, i.e., of one who was not going to putrify in body but was to be made holy by resurrection: "you will not abandon my soul to hell" (Ps 16:10/Acts 2:27). Lapide is much more literalistic and wants to draw a conclusion for contemporary liturgy: verse 11 instructs that the remains were to be burned again outside, and the implication has to do with care about not leaving the sacrament "surplus." The law demands even the smallest details from holy men, so as to show that nothing which is to involve the sacred cult it to be taken lightly, as Cyril says in *de Adoratione* 12.

Leviticus 7

Another Attempt to Define "Wrong"

IN GIVING THE REMEDY for the offence, the tradition needs to specify just what needs dealt with. Roman civil law traditions described "*delict*" as arising where negligence leads to harm in a situation where a duty of care can be held to exist. Augustine, commenting on 7:7, does not think there is much difference between *peccatum* and *delictum*. But perhaps *peccatum* is the perpetration of evil, while *delictum* is a lack of good, so that, just as in a praiseworthy life it is one thing to desist from evil and another thing to do good, just as Psalm 36:27 warns: "turn away from evil and do good." After all, *delictum* sounds like *derelictum*, which is a sort of negligent omission. The Greeks have two names for this one thing: *paraptōma* and *plēmmeleia* (which it is in this verse in LXX), yet in Galatians 6:1 Paul prefers the former. And that word (*paraptōma*) carries the sense of falling. The one who does evil in sinning has first fallen away from good. *Plēmmeleia* has more the sense of not caring, or of not deliberately choosing what one does.

Hesychius has a completely different understanding of "wrong." The kidneys (7:4–5) mean "wrong desire" which needs to be offered up to God. This is more than just sin against neighbor, but is a sin against God. The sinner needs to receive a share of Christ's sacrifice in one person. Only that which is offered is efficacious, and really not only that but the sacrifice of the Only Begotten, which excels them in value and allows the sinner to share in the resurrection of the dead, the judgment of the devil, the liberation of the curse, and the restitution of paradise, each of which would be too much for the virtue of the penitent, who needs to add in his share of the Lord's sacrifice. For a "wrong" deserves something extra.

Commenting on verse 20, Theodoret asks why is there a need to sacrifice for "mere" touching. He answers: through these small things God heals large passions, for if the physical things contaminate according to the Law, how much more do the things of the will which are properly called transgressions? Here we see that negligence, especially if it offends against the worship of God, is a serious matter.

Nicholas of Lyra follows Augustine by explaining *delictum* as *derelictum*. Lapide admits that it is very difficult to know how to distinguish sacrifice for sin (*peccatum*) and sacrifice for wrong (*delictum*). Ribera (in *De Templo* 6) replies differently from Augustine's omission/commission classification: it is sin if priest and people who, ignorant of fact, take what is not theirs or eat what is sacred, or touch what is unclean, and it is "wrong" when there is ignorance of law or rather a *delict* of an announced law and forgetting of the law, as when people do what is outlawed. This is a subtle and plausible response, but no more than that.

Willtt has much to say. He contends that Pellican and Vatable do not really get it right that the only difference between *ḥaṭṭāʾt* (sin-offering) and *ʾāshām* (guilt-offering) is one of degree. For the latter is an offering for *delictum* or "trespasse." Both Osiander and Cajetan are however wrong to deem that to be greater than sin. For *ʾāshām* is the term used for sins made from infirmity, as in Galatians 6:1: "if anyone be overtaken in *paraptōma*." As Lorinus rightly notes, *plēmmeleia* is not used in the NT. Furthermore, in Ephesians 2:1, 5, the Apostle distinguishes *sin* from *trespasses*, "but because the difference is not great, neither is there any great diversitie in the ceremonies and rites of the sacrifices for both." This seems to take away what he had given when disagreeing with Pellican and Vatable. In any case, with Junius he thinks the point is: "for so our sacrifice of thanksgiving must be offered with a prepared and devout mind."

Oven, Pan, Griddle (7:9)

Origen, as he often does, turns the cultic *accoutrements* into aspects of Scripture. We cannot believe that God is propitiated through cakes in an oven (v. 9). So, he asks, what is going on here? Well, our hearts are either to be cooked by God or burned by the flames of the devil, just as things that cannot be taken raw need to be cooked to serve to people (just as in Ezekiel's vision). The oven (*clibanus*) evokes the most profound things in Scripture, the pan (*sartago*) those things which if examined become clear, and the griddle (*craticula*) denotes those things that are patent.

Hesychius with his christocentric perspective views that which is from the oven as signifying the birth from the Virgin; and that which is from the frying pan the passion of the cross; that which is from the griddle, the resurrection from death, restoring reason to all and adding the proof that is required. Langton's approach is similar, but he wants to include an application. Christ was conceived in the womb of the Virgin like bread cooked in an oven. The bread in the pan is Christ suffering on the cross. The bread on the griddle is Christ rising or ascending since the fire in the griddle ascended, and so too Christ ascended from death to life. One needs a devoted mind to be allowed to eat it. The three types of bread represent history (in the frying pan), allegory (in the oven), and morality (in the griddle). The bread with oil on it signifies that in the gospel grace tastes much better than in the Law.

Priestly Mediation

For the *Bigotian Penitential* 31–32 (Bieler 1963, 202–3), there are the seven types of remission of sins. The seventh type occurs when anyone turns a sinner from the error of his ways. This is modeled by the priests offering for someone else and then being paid back by those they serve. Rupert has a much less sacerdotal emphasis with the priest as almost incidental. "To hand over to the priest" (v. 7c, Vulgate): first one needs the intentions to be brought to the judgment in God's presence, so that conscience might accuse, and fear bind, and reason adjudicate, and when it accepts this response, then it proposes a change of ways, and then finally he might offer a pure confession to the priest. For who thus draws close to confession but he does not yet wish to leave his sins behind does not then consecrate the innards and breastbone of the peace-offerings, and thereby he hands over what he has brought to the priest in vain. Where the confession is not followed by contrition and correction it may rather be said that it is shameless proclamation rather than confession of sin!

Lyra breaks down the priest's ritual into six movements. However Rabbi Paul thinks there are only four, so as to make a sort of four-way sign of the cross, but this number can be reduced to two, Denys thinks: one, that it was offered to him who was to be crucified for the redemption of the world; two, that the sacrifice prefigured that saving sacrifice, offered on the cross for the world's redemption. The point is, as Thomas (*ST* II–II, q102) confirms, no appearance of magic is to be given. The priestly right hand symbolizes the fortitude of the mind needed to sustain the defects of the lower parts. (He directs us to Alexander of Hales, *On the Third Part of the Sentences*.)

According to Chytraeus, the dividing of victim by the priests connects with that saying from 2 Timothy 2:15: "rightly dividing the word of truth"—a metaphor also beloved of Melanchthon.

Penance, which is preparatory for receiving the Eucharistic sacrifice, is to be seen as something heroic, Lapide thinks. In fact the mention of "every male" in verse 6 makes one think of the heroic penitents before the Law in John Climacus' (d. 649) *Ladder*, chapter 5. Tropologically "skin" (v. 8) symbolizes patience, as our father Job showed (Job 2:4; 19:10), as related by Gregory the Great in *Moralia* 5. Whatever in this life seems bitter, think of it as sweet and count all affliction as rest. Like Rupert,

Lapide's emphasis is on the state of those receiving from the sacrifice, rather than on the priestly performance.

Leclerc claims that on verse 18 the rabbis stray far from Moses, in that they, like the Latin Scholastics, say that the effect of the sacraments depends on the intention of the priest. This doctrine was made up to inculcate reverence for the priests among the people, but is the opposite of the text's intention. Patrick observes that the priests got to keep the skins *only* (v. 8), perhaps in recognition that Adam was given them for garments after his first sacrifice. This interpretation puts the priesthood in its place. The ritual, adds Patrick, is unlike the games played with beasts' skins by the Romans in the Eleusinian mysteries.

Fresh Worship

Origen takes the flesh of the sacrifices (v. 15) to be the word of God which is taught in the churches; they do not proclaim that which is yesterday's—as the flesh in the literal historical sense had to be consumed on the day of the sacrifice—but by the grace of God they find and bring forth fresh spiritual things (an allusion to one of Origen's favorite verses, Matt 13:52). The sacrifice of praise (Ps 49:23) must be fresh: otherwise when we open mouths the mind will be blocked by yesterday's meat. Thus the Lord Jesus told them to take and eat right away (Matt 26:26).

According to Cyril of Alexandria, worship does not always mean that we have to be gathered together, for what matters is being joined into one body and soul by the one faith, and we can worship at home at any time of day or night. Nevertheless there is place for common assembly (*parastasis*) of the baptized along with catechumens to sing hymns. In this non-Eucharistic service, this sacrifice of praise is what the *fermented* bread offerings symbolize. A song of praise should be poured out like oil, with each person, beginner or advanced, making a contribution to the whole. That all should be eaten before the third day (v. 15) means we should approach praise as something which does not belong to the passing of time.

For Hesychius, the eating of the sacrifice is to be immediate because it concerns the present age, not the one to come. Mary chose the better part: the simple life, swift and ready to cross over. So *crastinum* means the third day of resurrection. As James 4:14f reminds us, the second day is today. Anyone who thinks that after the "third day" resurrection there will be any *literal* eating, such a person will not be accepted. The "flesh" that touches the unclean (7:19) speaks of virtues from which a saving sacrifice is composed: e.g., chastity, mercy. It can also mean when our thoughts come into close contact with evil notions (cf. Matt 15:17ff). Theodoret has a moral interpretation of the command in verse 17 to burn any meat still uneaten on the third day: the rationale is that God did not want them to dine alone but to share the meat, and the prohibition on keeping it made them generous.

Rupert thinks the three days (vv. 15–17) are the three stages of human life. The third day (v. 17) is one of burning and disposal, that is the last stage of the life of sinners. It is unclean and flesh touches this when an offering is brought forward by an impenitent sinner to a worshipping priest. Pollution happens today when priests demand what belongs to them and their stomachs, not what, after the model of Jesus, could be done for an offering for sinners that might be given to the Lord. For when the priestly dignity submits to rich sinners and indulges them by not telling them their sin, such a priest will be lost from his people (ideally defrocked).

The second day of eating the sacrifice (vv. 15–16) is interpreted by Bruno of Segni as the gospel—in which Christ is much more clearly sacrificed and believed—eaten and drunk. Let us come now to the third day, but not to eat together on it so as not to believe him that it is dark; for it is without sun and light, wholly blind and errant. So we understand the corrupt doctrine of the heretics who utter many blasphemies about Christ. If anyone will follow their teaching as he will sacrifice, believe, and eat, it will do him no good, but rather his soul will be harmed by such a feast. By believing them he will go astray and be guilty of dereliction of duty. Such was Berengar (of Tours, d. 1088), who invites us to think impossible things concerning the Eucharistic body and blood. Yet we do not grasp by reason but ingest by the fire of the spirit and love and put our trust not in arguments but in the faith and authority of the saints; for we cannot resist heretical arguments by reason.

Langton interprets the first day (of eating) as this present life. And that is acceptable to the Lord, and even on the second day (i.e., as death approaches), but if after death it is not acceptable since here is the place of deserving and the future is only for the enjoying. Or by the first day the teaching of the Law can be meant; by the second the teaching of the gospel. By the third the teaching of heresy—by those who think that they can change after death and do works and thus "eat the flesh" on the third day. Hence they will be consumed in fiery *gehenna*. It is to be noted that a lack of continence comes in three forms and its replication was three-fold. And the first kind of incontinence is when evil thoughts come to someone who then ought to drive them away, the second who enjoys such thinking and gives them space and resource to operate freely. The third is in the deed itself. The point is that lust could be restrained by a belt so as to combat the first, or by having one's back turned to it, or by reflecting on the heart in which the action of evil can be restrained and by thinking about the Last Judgment. The basis of baptism is penance and the baptism in the oil of anointing is to know the hope of grace since grace is given there and sins are remitted, a basis which is the penance of baptism because the death of Christ is spelled out in its actions.

Denys reports that Origen said that the reason for not leaving it to eat next day was—for the Jews—simply because God said so. (It was important to Nahmanides, against Rashi, that for the votive or freewill offerings, the permission to eat on the second day was not an encouragement to delay eating.) But such a response is inadequate to meet the arguments of unbelievers. And it is fine to look for causes, since blessed are those who examine his testimony (Ps 118). Actually the point is simply that God wants them to receive the benefit right away, for their good. Rabbi Paul opposed Lyra, saying it was too harsh to think death was the penalty for late eating, and that such a person was rather to be left to the judgment of God and not killed then. But Denys thinks that eternal death is the right punishment for mortal sin, and whoever deserves eternal death, deserves also to be removed from this life according to the firmness of justice, as Thomas puts it in the *Summa Contra Gentiles*. As to whether this sentence was in fact carried out in OT times, the Jews know best. Hebrews 10 seems to suggest that those who disobeyed the Law of Moses before three witnesses were killed. Such a person is not a sheep but a wolf and so needs to be destroyed. Willet takes "cut off from his people" (v. 20) to mean a sentence of death, which seems harsh (cf. Exod 12:9; Num 15:38) until one realizes it is a moral commandment which came from God after Moses had consulted him. Therefore the phrase "to be cut off from God's people" is better understood of the judgment of *God* than that of man. Such a person would be left to divine judgment (otherwise it would say "die"); so the phrase does not always have a sense of physical death, but of God's judgment in the future. Denys spots the difference between a thanksgiving offering (*zebaḥ*) and freewill or votive offerings, and is more interested in the spirituality of the first. The person who gives thanks to God ought to renew himself spiritually right away and not prefer activity, however virtuous. He is to delight in the Lord, giving thanks to him every day as if anew. We have to give thanks to the Lord without delay, since we are not able to save up benefits, unless the Lord grants the grace of staying and progressing to the end.

Spangenberg comments that "eat before the third day" is a warning that Christ's benefits will not be of use after death. Lapide observes that it would be unseemly for sacred food to rot and this is simply what verse 16 is about, so that this cult did not get a bad name. And also that it is not to be held over but given out to all the needy and poor, as Philo and Theodoret affirm. The thanksgiving offering is seen as more worthy because there is no compulsion but is the act of a free godly mind, which spills into praise of God. One loses grace if it eaten on the third day. Spiritually speaking, none of the work is to be left to the day of resurrection, and the present life is the second day. So, do what needs to be done in time!

Willet targets the practice of reserving the sacrament, so votives offerings (v. 16) could be eaten the next day but not the Eucharist, since one should be even more reverent towards God in the latter case and eat it as it is consecrated. He dislikes the impertinent applications made by the *Glossa*, "that a man must not leave his works imperfect here," or "touching the incarnation, nothing should remain undiscussed"—an interpretation which goes back to Origen. No, it is better applied to our making speed in keeping God's commandments, and to our laying hold of Christ by faith. As meat offerings are not kept, "so neither is the Sacrament to bee reserved, as is practised in Popery, in Pixes." And this means that vows must be performed in this present life, as the *Glossa* says, and not in purgatory. He who does not receive remission of sins here will not be there (Ambrose, *De bonis operibus* c2).

Bishop Patrick has a more down-to-earth, perhaps "Enlightened" explanation of verses 15–18. Claiming the unlikely support of Philo's moral interpretation, he contends that the command to eat all on the first day is to encourage hospitality to be extended to many friends. One is allowed to leave some for the second day in cases where the offering is for mercies not yet received, and one might want to take more time. Bonar comments on verse 15: "The Lord . . . commanded it to be immediately eaten, thus speedily assuring the worshipper of peace and acceptance. The love of our God is too full to be retained one moment longer than is needful for his holiness." So after confession forgiveness comes immediately, without penance and process.

Most Christian discussion of eating fat, blood, and its consequences (vv. 23–27) is held over until the interpreter reaches chapter 17. Yet these verses were important for the Jewish commentators. Nahmanides thought that Rashi and Ibn Ezra's claim that it concerned only fat from *offered* animals offered misses the parallelism with abstention from blood: Moses means that consumption of fat from *any* animal. However, being "cut off [*kāret*] from people" for eating the fat or blood of an offering (v. 27) means being cut off from being gathered to one's fathers in the afterlife as well as not having any physical descendants (so, Milgrom 2004, 66). The ancient Near East did have a belief in the afterlife but it was suppressed by the biblical authors. Nevertheless, verses such as this (v. 27) affirm its existence. This raises all sorts of interesting points for a biblical theology of "death," but highlights how much the pre-1600 Christian tradition, when discussing the church's judgment of penance, had in mind post-mortem divine judgment as a backstop in cases when wrongdoers seemed to escape sanction.

Elevation of the Breastbone (vv. 28–36)

On verse 34 Jerome (*Epist.* LXIV, 1) comments that the breastplate is also called or "excellent and outstanding." As in Malachi 2:6: the lips of the priest keep knowledge and the law is required from his mouth, and hence we learn that knowledge of teaching and law ought to be present among priests, and such power of spiritual grace as well. This is someone who is able to resist those standing against them in argument, and who has nothing of those hell-bent wicked works in him, but who has a "separate" right arm (vv. 32–33) of works of a special holiness.

Hesychius takes the breastbone to stand for faith and confidence. For Christ offers up the souls and the desires of the saved, who is from the sons of Aaron, not on account of family line, but on account of due dignity excelling all others and for his right arm, i.e., every good action that applies or makes the work effective. Here we see the interplay between Eucharist and the contribution made by the lifestyle of the people. The mention of a perpetual law shows that time and place does not matter as much as faith does. It is an everlasting law that comes from Israel.

Hugh of St. Cher comments: the heart is first to be cleansed from sin *then* filled with grace. Therefore the remission of sins happens first as Master Gerard (presumably Gérard d'Abbeville [d. 1272] who defended the rights of the secular clergy against the religious orders) admits. The elevation of the breastbone in God's presence (v. 34) happens from necessity not from religion, as Jerome explains.

Chytraeus holds the burning (v. 30) as concerning the bringing to mind in worship of Christ's passion as well as penitence, true faith, and invocation at the time of the Eucharist. He argues that those allowed to participate at communion must be clean, i.e., "doing penance and believing their sins to be remitted through Christ," and having a good determination not to sin more; and not to "throw pearls before swine." Further, he thinks that the dedication of the breastbone (v. 31) to the priests is a sign that reason is useful in giving them controlled behavior in a way that the lower faculties (represented by entrails) are not. In fact the burning of the tail and entrails symbolizes recognition of God's judgment on our mortal nature. We teachers are to instruct our hearts with true doctrine that we can teach control of life to others.

Brenz thinks that the offering being elevated on high signified Christ's being raised, since he was sacrificed firstly in the cross (Spangenberg and Calov also emphasizes this), then *through* the cross in his supreme majesty of the kingdom of heaven: "and this should give us cheer that through the cross we have exaltation." The moving of the offering up, down, and from back to forward signified the spreading of the gospel from the sacrifice and exaltation of Christ into the whole world.

> The hypocrites directly copy this rite in their mass, but they should know that these rites were abrogated by the revelation of the gospel of Christ, since shadows must give way to truth. Why if they want to imitate don't they shake about a breastbone and an arm rather than wafer? For the Lord's supper is not a sacrifice and Christ is not first offered in the Lord's supper but rather his body and blood were offered once on the cross and are distributed by the sacrament of the supper. Distributed, not offered! He said "do this in memory of, not in sacrifice of me"!

Calov adds that while Grotius follows "the Jews" in giving natural and medical-dietary reasons for why these sacrifices are offered, really they are symbols of what we offer up, body and soul, as acknowledgement of God as author of life (in OT terms). Still one can learn for Jerome (*Epist. 128 ad Fabiolam*) that in offering the breastbone pure thoughts, knowledge of the law and the true doctrine are proffered, while in the arm [or thigh—v. 34] it is good works and striving against the devil. That which one thinks one will later show forth by example. On the matter of forbidding the fat to be eaten (vv. 24–25) Calov is clear that Christians are not bound by Acts 15:29 any more than Leviticus when it comes to what they eat, and he suspects Willet of Judaizing tendencies.

Keil is happy to sum up the sacrificial rituals with a positive note: "The forgiveness of sin which the atoning sacrifice procured, was only a *paresis* [an overlooking] of past sins through the forbearance of God (Rom 3:25, 26), in anticipation of the true sacrifice of Christ . . . a sanctification of the fellowship already established by the covenant."

Leviticus 8

THE IDEA THAT LEVITES were to be equated with church deacons and Israelite High Priests with Christian priests (one per altar) was expressed by Jerome in Epistle 146.2 and taken up in the *Sacramentarium Veronense*, prior to the time of Gregory the Great. Chydenius (1965, 34–36) has given a very useful summary of the church's thinking during this period (the second half of the first Christian millennium):

> According to the typological outlook, not only the mystery of Christ taken by itself but also the sacramental order of the Church by which it was extended to the faithful could be regarded as the antitype of the prefigurative order of the Old Covenant. The Christian institutions could, then, be looked upon in two different ways. On the one hand, as part of the fulfillment in Christ, they were the *antitypes* of the OT institutions. On the other hand, as belonging to a sacramental order distinct from Christ, they were symbols of him. As such they were analogous to the OT institutions . . . [A]s soon as this analogy became a commonly accepted fact, the christological basis was partly forgotten. It was simply assumed that every Christian institution had its counterpart in the OT, and that this was true irrespective of whether it was a symbol of Christ or not. The analogy between Israel and the Christian society thus emancipated itself from typology and sacramental symbolism alike, and became a principle of interpretation in its own right.

There can be distinguished a "triptych" approach where the OT priesthood is mediated to the Christian priesthood only through Christ, and a "diptych" approach, where the relationship between the two is immediate, even if the latter is seen as a more spiritual institution than the former. Spiritual does not mean "pale" but "more real." What has come with Christ is more of a reality than what was in the Old Covenant (Chydenius 1965, 50). Pseudo-Alcuin (*De divinis officiis* c. 950) mentions six degrees of Levites, which meant six degrees of status existed below the priesthood. Rupert of Deutz moved towards almost an identification of OT institutions and church institutions and Alexander of Hales (d. 1245) took priesthood as institution to be common to both covenants.

Moses, Aaron's Consecration, Christ, and Authority

The early verses of this chapter become the occasion of reflections on the function and status of that which is conferred through ordination and consecration. Despite the recognition of the canonicity of the Epistle to the Hebrews, the high priesthood of Christ (Heb 7:12ff) was not a theme mentioned in the early church, apart from Hippolytus. It seemed too Arian a theme and then later too Nestorian to speak of Christ that way (Hossfeld-Schöllgen 1994, 26). Now Christian *prophets* were called "high priests" in *Didache* 13:3, and the term was used for Christian bishops in Tertullian, *Bapt.* 17:1, but, as Grässer emphasizes, the church was not thereby inferring their status from their representing Christ. As Dassmann (1984) has shown, already in Clement of Rome there is a direct appeal to the OT hierarchy in order to call the young church to order, and "High Priest" was occasionally used for bishops to set forth his difference over against other clergy. The point is that, to begin with, this usage reflected a view of Christian leadership as *corresponding to that in Leviticus*, rather than to Christ (Grässer 1993, 238). Clearly by the fourth century one can speak of some amount of "sacerdotalization" of the Christian ministry.

Yet Origen in the third century was a representative of an early church practice whereby "anointing" was primarily part of making *Christians*, not of making ministers. Basing his understanding on 2 Corinthians 3:14–16, he said that prayerful Christian interpretation of priestly dressing is not to follow it literally, but is to keep its distance from that of carnal Israel. Origen sees that in verses 1–9 the order is "washing then dressing," and the same order of applies to Christians spiritually. But, curiously, he adds that Christians are purified by law first before baptism: "you who wish to receive holy baptism and qualify for (*promereri*) the grace of the Spirit, you must first be purged by the law, you must first by hearing the word of God distance yourself from pagan sins . . . so that by taking on meekness and humility you will be able to grasp the grace of the Holy Spirit." In other words, Moses is the one who prepares the Christian for baptism (cf. Junod 1994, 52). Thus the catechumenate is a time of showing character in response to the word/law so as to qualify for the Spirit's grace in baptism, and Isaiah 66:1–2 is used to reinforce this pattern for renewal, as also was the observation that Moses (the law) and Elijah (the prophets) were with Jesus when he was transfigured. The tent for the law, the prophets, and the gospel is one tent, i.e., the church of God. So Moses first washes the priest of the Lord (i.e., each Christian) and then dresses him. Anyone can perform ministry, but to be a real priest one must have equal stature in knowledge, action, and teaching. The job of the priest is to stay near the tent (church), learn from God (by reading Scripture and prayerful meditation), and to teach people. This is to give Christian priests a quasi-rabbinic role.

A change came with Cyprian: it was not the priest's empowerment through ordination that bestowed forgiveness—that lay within the sacrament itself. However, the bishop became, in his view, the lord of penance and right liturgical order (Campenhausen 1963, 313). If Christ is High Priest then the bishops can be equated with the priests and deacons with Levites. The bishop is never called "High Priest," though in Cyprian's Epistle 67:4 deacons like Levites serve the altar, but presbyters share in Christ's priesthood in such a way as to be subordinate to him. As Donovan (1970, 575) puts it: "A striking aspect of the whole development is the centrality of the role that the Levitical typology played in it. The NT proclaims not so much the end of the religious traditions of Israel, as their transformation . . . Striking is the very early application of Malachi 1:10f to the Eucharistic assembly." Yet this christological development of "priesthood" builds on the correlation of OT and Christian priesthood.

The variant of this view that the carnal or physical aspect of the OT priesthood continues in the church is evidenced in Athanasius, *Sermon to the Newly Baptized*: "You shall see the Levites [i.e., deacons] bringing loaves and a cup of wine, and placing them on the table. So long as the prayers of supplication and entreaties have not been made, there is only bread and wine. But after the great and wonderful prayers have been completed, then the bread is become the Body, and the wine the Blood, of our Lord Jesus Christ" (PG 26, 1325). Even more explicit is Moses Bar Kepha, in his *Explanation of the Mysteries of the Oblation*, for whom, "The deacons [also] fill the place of the former levites" (folio 151b) and that "the stoles [*orarium*] which are upon their left shoulders declare their subjection, like subordinates who are in subjection; for he who is in authority wears the stole upon his head or upon both of his shoulders." It seems to have been the *Constitutions of the Holy Apostles* (2.4.25), which is unreserved about the equation of Christian priests and bishops with priests and High Priests of old, that the "holy bishops . . . are your high priests, as the presbyters are your priests, and your present deacons instead of your Levites . . . but He who is above all these [i.e., Christ] is the High Priest." Then, at chapter 8 of the *Constitutions*: "Thus you also today, O bishops, are priests to your people, and the Levites who minister to the tent of God, the holy catholic church, who stand continually before the Lord God. You now are to your people priests and prophets and chiefs and leaders and kings, and mediators between God and His faithful, and receivers of the Word and preachers of it, and proclaimers of it and knowers of the Scriptures and of the utterances of God, and witnesses of his will, those who bear the sins of everyone, and are to give an answer for everyone ... And as he has taken our sins, so you also take the sins of the people."

It would be wrong on the strength of another passage in the *Constitutions* (2.7.57) to suggest that the term "High Priest" could also mean any high officer within the church, when it seems to have been identified with Christ alone. Jerome's Epistle 146 has: "Bishops, presbyters, and deacons occupy in the church the same positions as those which were occupied by Aaron, his sons, and the Levites in the temple." On verses 7f Jerome, in his *Ep. ad Fabiolam* (*Epist.* 64:20), while complaining that he cannot find a copy of Tertullian's *Liber de Aaron vestibus* in his library, goes on to say that the cleansing of Aaron and sons by Moses represents the purging of the world and the sanctity of all things, the sacrament of baptism. (This gets repeated in Amalarius, *Liber Officialis* II; 235.) Jerome explains that although in Exodus 28:9 the priest put on eight pieces of clothing, here in Leviticus there are only seven, since it wants to avoid any laying on of hands on the genital area. Gregory the Great's view of Levitical "teamwork" meant that a bishop's ordination being performed by a lone bishop was to be avoided, as in his letter (*Epist.* 64) to Augustine of Canterbury (PL77, 1191). Elsewhere Gregory insisted, with reference to Leviticus 8:30, that the *pallium* (an ecclesiastical vestment) sent by the pope to each new bishop is such that he not to wear it outside of the context of the Mass (*Epist.* 3; Martyn 2004, 54).

Certainly in his *Etymologies* (VII, 12:21–22), Isidore (c. 620) allows for a strong continuity of the Christian priesthood and diaconate with the OT. The former can be called "*sacerdotes*" because they give what is sacred (although only those priests who are bishops can confer the Holy Spirit), while the order of deacons takes its beginning from the tribe of Levi, and implies that Christian deacons can trace their inheritance back to the patriarch Levi. A few decades later, the third Council of Braga (675), canon 5, describes the use of reliquary altars in processions in terms of the ark of the covenant being carried by the Levites (PL 84, 589–90): "bishops, when carrying the relics of martyrs in procession, must walk to the church, and not be carried in a chair, or litter, by deacons clothed in white." The spirit of continuity can be found still later (c. 1150) in Peter Lombard's *Sentences* (IV d24, 9): the order of the priesthood takes its beginning from the sons of Aaron.

Amalarius of Metz in his liturgical manual *Liber Officialis* (II, 13: *On the priesthood* [c. 825]), writes that according to Leviticus 8:12 the bishop's consecration "for sacrificing" is made in his ordination as priest, and this was the view of Paul, Ambrose, and Jerome, although Leviticus 21:10 ("the High Priest among his brothers") reminds us that his ordination to bishop is best done *collegially*. Further, he reports (II.11) that the *Statuta ecclesia antiqua*'s canon 92 (C 5, possibly by Gennadius of Marseilles and hugely influential) was contrary to the spirit of both OT and NT in reserving the laying on of hands for deacons to the bishop and excluding priests—out of a stated fear that for them to touch would confer priesthood on the deacons. The bishop, however, has and confers something that is functional—to do with being elevated to bishop—rather than ontological (as in the case of his priesthood: see Gibaut 1989, 240). What seems to have been allowed as a compromise (according to the old Gelasian Sacramentary and at least one other; see *Liber Sacramentorum Gellonensis* [CCSL 159; 1981], 386; also *Liber Sacramentorum Augustodunensis* [CCSL 159b; 1984, 184]) was for the priests to put their hands *beside* or *on top of* the bishop's, yet without touching the head of the deacon. As Riché and Lobrichon (1984, 616) comment, it was because he was able to have a spiritualized view of both the Aaronic and the Christian hierarchy that the connection between them appears most strongly in Amalarius. And for the consecration of churches the sacramentaries borrowed their ritual from both Exodus 29:12–18 and Leviticus 8:11.

By the high medieval period (Schöllgen-Hoßfeld 1994, 44) sacerdotal terminology can be applied indiscriminately to bishops and to priests, yet the term "High Priest" seems still to be reserved for Christ, or at least hardly used, even for Metropolitan bishops. Hugh of St. Victor comments that the sacrifices are to be offered by no one in particular, lest the necessity of sacrificing daily would mean he would be prohibited from carnal intercourse, following that command that a man from whom semen issues is prohibited from entering holy places and is held to be unclean until the evening. Hence the daily sacrifices can be offered by all priests, except that one sacrifice which once a year the High Priest is ordered to enter through blood into the Holy of Holies. Whatever sacrifice he offers, the portion to all the priests is equal and is divided the same for all.

So Hugh does not take the opportunity to argue for priestly celibacy from this and assumes that OT priests were married. What does seem to matter (*On the sacraments* 2, 2, 3) is that the clergy are seen as forming one side of the body of Christ and that the Levites "supported by tithes and oblations and victims of sacrifices" are a good precedent for this (Hugh, *On the sacraments*, II, 2–3; 256). Literal garments seem especially important, "by means of what appears externally it may be shown of what nature they should be within. The ceremony was . . . taken partly from the Old Testament, partly expanded by the late Fathers. We read [Lev 8] that Moses placed his brother Aaron with his sons at the door of the Tabernacle as a testimony to be sanctified . . . the sacerdotal garments amounted to eight."

Hugh of St. Cher claims that Aaron, not Moses, was appointed as High Priest to mediate between God and people, because the will of the people did not want Moses, since they thought he would boss them too much. The theme of a chain of mediation runs through Hugh's considerations. Yet how could Moses do the consecrating if he was not consecrated? Well, Moses consecrated Aaron in place of the Lord, and he exercised the office of a priest without being one. This is just like when the cardinal's deacon is sent by the pope, or when a bishop is present he can give the blessing from the pope since he has his authority. Who anointed the high priest after the deaths of Moses and Aaron if no one else was high Ppriest? Augustine had argued that all that needed to be done was for the one elected to put on the high priestly garments as these all had already been anointed, but to Hugh this seems hardly an answer.

For Denys, Moses has pontifical and sacerdotal dignity, albeit in another form from that of Aaron. It is the type of a fullness of power which Moses could hand on to Joshua and which the pope, as *Pontifex Maximus*, has in respect of the church militant (so Thomas). Elections have to be open; there should be no aspiration to the office and it would be a mortal sin if a candidate were in a state of even minimal sin. Josephus, Denys tells us, thought Moses was told to present himself as a priest due to all the work he did for the people and that he was a friend of God. But God chose and called Aaron as priest, not Moses, and this shows the mercy of God.

Hebrews 7:12–18, where Christ is compared to Melchizedek, was a passage that played a big role at the Council of Trent in regarding the church priesthood as sacerdotal. Luther had said that Christ far excelled Melchizedek as well as Aaron (Hagen 1974, 108) so Catholics might as well use the Aaronic imagery for Christ's and their priesthood. *Pontifex* was used in the *Vetus Latina* and Vulgate, both for the Jewish High Priest in John's Gospel and for Christ in Hebrews. For the Jesuit Lapide that is precisely the import: "in his Church through his ministers, to be sure through priests appointed by him, Christ continually offers even to the end of the world the sacrifice of the Mass: that is what it means for him to remain priest forever according to his two natures" (Lapide, *Comm in Heb 7*, in Demarest 1976, 37). "Aaron and his Sons" (v. 2) becomes a saying of some importance, since it signifies "Christ and his priests." If Christ is greater than Aaron, then he subsumes Aaron's functions on earth.

Calov comments that Moses anointed Aaron since he was prophet of the Lord; just as elsewhere kings were anointed by prophets (1 Sam 10:1; 16:13; 1 Kgs 19:15; 2 Kgs 8:18; 9:1–6) until the line is set up and the priests take over the consecration. Bellarmine used this passage to claim that pastors are appointed by the High Priest (Pontiff), not by a prince. However, it is wrong to apply this to the present situation, objects Calov, to make it seem that Moses was a priest in whom spiritual and temporal powers were blurred. Moses was a political prince, not a pope. In any case, even Aaron, the anointed of the Lord, has to put on the equivalent of Christ to cover his own uncleanness.

The Function of Aaron Understood through His Clothing (vv. 6–9)

Under the influence of Philo (*On the Life of Moses* 24), who discussed at far greater length the symbolism of the priestly garments (8:6–9), although much of the detail about the jewels in the breastplate comes from Exodus 28, Clement of Alexandria (*Strom.* 6; ANF translation) writes with reference to Leviticus 8 to explain the priestly function of this consecrated humanity:

> Moreover, there was the breastplate, comprising the ephod, which is the symbol of work, and the oracle [*logeion*, used in v. 8 of LXX for "headpiece"]; and this indicated the Word by which it was framed and is the symbol of heaven, made by the Word, and subjected to Christ, the Head of all things, inasmuch as it moves in the same way, and in a like manner . . . And they say that the robe prophesied the ministry in the flesh, by which He was seen in closer relation to the world. So the high priest, putting off his consecrated robe (the universe, and the creation in the universe, were consecrated by Him assenting that, what was made, was good), washes himself and puts on the other tunic—a holy-of-holies one, so to speak—which is to accompany him into the adytum; exhibiting, as seems to me, the Levite and Gnostic, as the chief of other priests (those bathed in water, and clothed in faith alone, and expecting their own individual abode), himself distinguishing the objects of the intellect from the things of sense, rising above other priests, hasting to the entrance to the world of ideas, to wash himself from the things here below, not in water, as formerly one was cleansed on being enrolled in the tribe of Levi.

For Origen tunics of animal skin symbolize mortality coming from the fragility of sin's corruption, as per Genesis 3:21. But for those who can presuppose the Law and its purification the dress will be one of incorruption. The epaulettes are to be put on before the turban (*logium*) since one is to do works and then seek wisdom as a second step. But the showing-forth of wisdom in Christian teaching comes after the turban of wisdom has been acquired. On verse 7, the "two tunics" signify the carnal ministry and spiritual intelligence; although, of course, the apostles have only the one, since Jesus told them not to have two tunics. This implies that the OT priesthood contained a mix of carnal and spiritual, and that post-apostolic Christian priesthood is analogous, yet in the sense that a priest's chastity must be so in body and in mind, including works and wisdom, status and the fullness of knowing God, for that is what Christian priesthood means. There is a nice contrast preserved in the *Glossa Ordinaria*: the curious and bathetic comment by Jerome which would be lost in the thick of his Epistle 84, that just like Roman soldiers the priests had linen undergarments for the purpose of quick movement!

It was important to Rabanus Maurus to show how monks were a "different kind of priesthood" and this meant a clericalizing of them. Tonsure is dealt with right at the beginning before any treatment of hierarchies. There is a much more literal approach to vestments than Amalarius's allegorizing. So in *De institutione clericorum* (I, 2, 292f) Rabanus writes: it is as priests that anyone can be like Levites, and this following Isidore of Seville (*Etym.* 7:12–15). Then he comments: this order is lawfully proposed in the church, since the priests serve as did the Levites: the Levites were chosen to serve through various offices in the temple, therefore as priests in a special way they were chosen to serve God day and night in a special way. Christian priests operate in the church in the same way that the Levites operated in Israel—they work in the present-day church, the true temple of God, in the things that concern God, with the roles of atoning for ignorance and discerning between clean and unclean. Increasingly more monks became priests as the Eucharist became more and more precious. Brothers could receive the Eucharist in both kinds. Any unused host was to be stored like a relic, although the Eastern custom of consecrating bread and having it last for a week was sneered at by Cardinal Humbert in the mid-eleventh century (Browe 2007, 389).

For Hesychius, the dress of the priest (vv. 6–9) spells out the incarnation of the Only Begotten who assumed the two parts of humanity—the earthly ("tunic") and the heavenly ("robe"), and it was the old man which was crucified and the perfect soul made to triumph. Following the same line of thought, the *Glossa* on verse 10 comments that Christ was anointed according to his divinity (in tandem with the Father and the Spirit) and was anointed according to his humanity. So there is a trinitarian correspondence to what went on between the two lead characters in this chapter. Moses anointed and yet he also offered (an anointing to Aaron), since he bore the figure of Christ.

One can see how much priestly language can be appropriated for the monastic order in Ralph's treatment of verses 6–10: The priests are the stones of the sanctuary who should always be in the hidden place of God and not in the world of action and events. Yet these stones are distributed around the "head" of every cloister. The point is that virtue is not ornamentation, but is to be located on the heart. Right reason constrains all thoughts and is an example for others: such a person "brings new and old out of treasure" (Matt 13:52). There needs to be patience, not just toleration. "For, as Gregory says: the hiding of anger is not the same as gentleness."

Ralph is very happy to translate "anointing" into moral-spiritual categories. The seven pieces to put on are the seven gifts of the Spirit: two are supreme—wisdom and understanding; the lowest is fear. Yet that must be fear born from faith and mixed with hope, and that is what is the beginning of wisdom. Cornelius of Acts 10 works as an example of godly fear. A pastor ought to be not only close through compassion to individuals, but also suspended in contemplation on behalf of others and those able to hear what is said far away. That priest of the Law, whose forehead was decorated in gold and who wore bells at the bottom of his robe supplies us with a noble image of the teacher who by the height of contemplation communicates to the people by preaching. There is an important link between contemplation and preaching. To sprinkle seven times is to purify our faith from all error with the work of the sevenfold Spirit. We should interpret the altar of burnt offering as the church above, and its "horns" those who are there in fuller sanctity and elevated in wisdom. Moses principally touches the horns with the blood of a young calf, since Scripture imprints the memory of Christ's passion more deeply on those who abound in knowledge and love. Moses touching the ear of Aaron is like Paul passing the faith on to Timothy in 1 Timothy 6.

Denys reports that Josephus had said the priests had ten pieces of clothing, but here it seems that the High Priest had eight and the other priests have four (Exod 28), as Thomas had observed (*ST* 1.II, q102). Cajetan relates Jerome's comment (*Epist.* 64) that clothing sets people apart by status in both biblical religion and among pagans (e.g., Roman "grades of senators"). Well, Cajetan adds, in the same way the Lord orders that his priest dress in an impressive way so that his dignity be commended to the Israelites.

Lapide writes that Aaron was at home in the tabernacle. The breastpiece represents the ark, which contained the tables of the Law and the wisdom of doctrine and truth (Urim and Thummim). In fact in the clothing the whole world is represented. The High Priest differed from the other priests with five prerogatives: being oldest in age, unique at any given time, allowed once a year into the Holy of Holies, with more pieces of clothing, and on his death fugitive manslayers could return to own places. The effusion of grace is "pontifical" and God wants to teach here the importance of order and submission in the church. For Piscator, the splendid clothing of Aaron prefigures Christ's authority, which holiness of life gave to him along with divine eloquence and boldness.

Willet sneers that "papists" give priests six garments and nine more to a bishop, corresponding to degrees of virtue according to Bellarmine (*On the Mass* c14): "The priesthood is changed, so also the law of the priesthood . . . faith [is] more precious than gold." Yet, objects Willet, Peter had no silver and gold, so they (Roman Catholics) have to resort to Aaron's crown as precedent for the pope's triple crown, which actually makes him more like Cerberus, "for so he arrogateth unto himself power to keepe out and in his hellish purgatory whome he will." Willet thinks that the wearing of Urim and Thummim (v. 8) signifies that the priest should, by word and example, edify the church. Vatable thinks the divine name was inscribed there, but there is no proof in the text. We can apply the spiritual sense to Christ, but it is too curious to apply it to a minister! Maybe we just say they should be clothed in gifts of grace. Willet makes it all sound as perhaps it is—mysterious.

Without their dress, thinks Calmet, with a slight whiff of enlightened yet possibly also "monastic" anti-clericalism, "off-duty" priests were regarded as lay people, i.e., their priesthood was functional, and the rabbis tell us a priest approaching without the right clothing would be killed.

Anointing and Its Effects (vv. 10–13, 22–24, 30–31)

The earliest Christian commentators on Leviticus 8 concentrate on the moral symbolism of anointing: Theodoret, on verse 23, asks why the right ear and hand get touched with blood and oil. He answers: "this is a type of our benefits; the blood is the blood of salvation, the oil of the most holy chrism. The right ear is the symbol of praiseworthy obedience. The right hand and the foot are those of good deeds . . . For there are left-handed deeds of obedience which are doom-laden." The monastic non-liturgical spirit is also reflected in his contemporary, Cyril, who comments on verse 31 that those who eat yet who may not approach the altar are those weaker believers who can receive Christ's blessing and whose task is to cease from sins so as to be able to receive Christ's new creation in the manner of medicine, rather than those "militant" holy ones who make progress in virtue. Thus appears a distinction between passive and active levels of holiness, and negative and positive conceptions of it.

Hesychius' liturgical theology sees the anointing of Aaron as predictive of the apostles at Pentecost. By the "canister of consummation" (here reading with the LXX's *thusiastérion*, a thurible in which incense is burned, rather than the Hebrew's simple "offering") we should understand by this the tongue "in the Lord" which alone brought to us the excellent and perfect doctrine. If you ask why Aaron commanded his sons not to go out of the tent of testimony door, we may answer that this means that the apostles were not to start the evangelical preaching without the Lord and wander into error. For that reason Aaron was consecrated and perfected like the apostles who waited for the Spirit. When they preached it was only through the gate that is Christ (John 10:9).

As for the Christian practice of anointing, it seems that it happened to rulers in their coronation ceremonies at least two centuries before Christian priests were anointed (at some stage in the tenth century AD) (Köttje 1970, 103). Gildas (d. 570) writes of the anointing of a British king, with reference to 1 Samuel 10:1, and Julian of Toledo (*Qu. in Leviticus XIII* 3.4; PL 83, 330) around 700. So verse 12 along with 1 Samuel 16:13 was applied to royal coronations, despite Isidore's silence on the issue. Köttje thinks Isodore wished to reserve these biblical references to anointing for Christ. But Köttje perhaps here reads too much into the silence of Isidore, which is as ambiguous as the silence of the Eighth Council of Toledo (653) about such things. By the late Merovingian period the practice of royal anointing seems to have been well established, and would remain until forbidden sacramental status by Innocent III.

From a position where the bishop was called "*sacerdos*" on account of his eminence, as Gibaut (1989, 238) puts it, "later, *sacerdos* and *presbyter* would become interchangeable. The emphasis on the sacerdotal definition of the episcopate and presbyterate affected the diaconate and the minor orders as well. As the presbyter became more associated with the Levitical 'priest' of the Old Testament, so the deacon became associated with the 'Levite,' his liturgical assistant and subordinate."

It might be asked why the sprinkling of oil occurs now, if Aaron was already anointed. This gives Ralph the occasion to apply this verse to the Christian life, quite apart from the sacraments, with a very non-sacramental view. According to Ralph, every man though baptized, so long as he lived among the temptations of this world, cannot be without sin. Christ repeatedly purges us from all sins (1 John 3), not only those in the past but also in the present life. For in the church is the grace of the Holy Spirit which is faith in the passion of Christ by which one receives pardon for one's sin. It signifies the purification of a daily penance and the washing of the feet after baptism (John 13:10). Grima turns to his reader and prays: the anointing which you have received, may it remain in you, on the altar of your body and in all vessels, that is in all your members for the making of satisfaction—which is what God receives on the altar. Anointing can give strength and also has a softening power. And contrition renders the hard heart soft. There is no fruitful confession without contrition—here speaking to a very important medieval debate.

The Jewish medieval interpreters notice a little (Ibn Ezra) or some (Nahmanides) discrepancy between what God ordered (Exod 29:5–9 to which Rashi refers the reader) and what Moses did here in the preparation of Aaron. Rashi is very explicit about Moses officiating as a priest during the days on which Aaron was consecrated a priest: this Lyra asserts, possibly in dialogue with his Parisian contemporary Marsilius of Padua, who de-emphasized the role of priest in forgiveness (Hailperin 1963, 204). Lyra says Moses did this by the Lord's command through whom comes all consecration. Both Lyra and the midrash contend that God's Word is what does the consecrating so that Aaron can be consecrated though Moses.

It is important to Lyra to avoid too much "anointing" with something that resembled intervention from on high. Hence he argues that the Hebrew does not have "and he consecrated Aaron's sons" (v. 13), but only that he clothed them. How were High Priests consecrated?: simply by clothing being put on, as we see with Eleazar in Numbers 10. Some say they are consecrated by the inferior priests, just as pope is. The unguent here is called "oil of unction" in Exodus. Denys repeats Ralph's explanation for Moses being allowed to consecrate Aaron, but, adds Bonaventura (IV Sentences, d22), that according to the Apostle in Hebrews 7:7, the minor is always blessed by the major. To which Bonaventura responded: true, thus a bishop who consecrates an archbishop or pope can only give him an episcopal consecration. But can Moses even be rightly called "priest"? Yes on the authority of Psalm 99:6, even though, as Augustine admits, he had none of the priestly clothing.

For Brenz, like the oil on Aaron's beard, the divinity overflows Christ for our benefit (Lev 8:12 in Brenz, *Romans*, 132). In his later Leviticus commentary Brenz adds that all Christians are granted life in the love of God himself, yet they experience tribulation (*Anfechtungen*), so that this is not a theology of glory (see Brandy 1991). Anointing foreshadows Jesus' majesty, authority, and the nature of his office. But in Christianity there is no such genus as those priests who "do Mass" (*missatores*) with those sacrifices, for since Christ there is no place for anyone to sacrifice for sin. It is in the gospel that there is remission of sins today. The papists make it seem that it is not Christ in heaven's interceding that matters, and that the once for all sacrifice is not sufficient.

The Aaronic priesthood was not set up to foreshadow church's priesthood but *only Christ's priesthood*, while the NT equivalent of the *sons* of Aaron are *all* believers who feast on the aftereffect of Christ's offering. The ministers of the church can be said to sprinkle Christ's blood when they preach the gospel about remission of sins. The papists are trying to rely on their own merit by adding to Christ, and then they go even further than the Levitical way by employing pagan fire worship (presumably in their use of candles). The Levitical sacrifices were imperfect: therefore they were repeated, just like the Papist ones. The sons of Aaron are the whole church of Christ who is fed through faith by Christ's sacrifice, i.e., become partakers of his merit.

Spangenberg comments that we need our lifetimes to be consecrated in holiness, so that we might become heavenly priests. These sons of Aaron look a bit like suffragan bishops, but it is clear that the sacrifices stopped with Christ and what the Papists have are concocted and remote from God's Word. Calmet, commenting on verse 15, sees the marking with blood as the high-point of signing the whole person to the service of God, as one step beyond anointing. This ritual was quite unlike that of the Romans in which blood was made to cover all his body and clothes before, while wearing a golden crown, he was taken underground with bull blood dripping. Piscator comments that the oil on his head signifies Christ's optimal preaching: the oil and blood together remind us that remission of sins and gift of the Spirit are all-important. Moses anointed the tent, i.e., the place where God dwelled, to consecrate or destine it for the worship of God. There is to be no sense that what happened was anything magical. The sprinkling in the first verse is to pronounce an invisible state of affairs, and in the second to make the place fit for worship rather than to invest things with any ontological change. More important for Piscator is the blood that *expiates* the altar (v. 15), or "takes away sin" (*entsündigen*). The right ear lobe, the right little fingers and toes of Aaron and his sons are dipped in the blood and this is to symbolize that the good deeds of the faithful are no more than hearing the word of God sincerely and trying to live it out, except for the imperfection which clings to them yet is removed by the blood of Christ.

The establishment of a holy space or place instructs that only in the church can the consolation of Christ's death touch people. Willet is especially unhappy with the idea of anointing of non-human objects. One must not see anointing here as encouraging the consecrating of churches, as Lorinus does; such are superstitions and they help to reinforce the superstition of the Mass.

It was observed by Keil that Aaron was anointed with oil full on his head, whereas other priests (his sons) were just smeared. Knobel will observe how "sons of Aaron" is the mark of a Priestly (or an Elohist) writer, and is never found in Deuteronomy. These sons too were considered priests in this "theocratic society." Dillmann adds that there would be plenty of rural places with their own Levites who would be seen as priests just as much as the temple priests; but through Hizkiah and Josiah their position would have become untenable. Thus there is a distinction in the late composition of the book that seems to downgrade the Levites.

Keil insists that what it meant for the sanctuary to be holy was the filling of it with the power of the Spirit "which proceeds from God and fills the natural being of the creature with the powers of the divine life." The Romantic Pietist here insists that even inanimate things can receive divine power (against modern views that "leave a hopeless abyss between spirit and matter"). He attacks "Talmudists" who think that the "once-for-all" anointing of Aaron sufficed for all future generations of priest.

What is noticeable is that, Reformed theologians apart, there is little attention paid to the role of blood. The Reformed, through the agency of the Jewish convert Tremellius (d. 1580), became aware of the importance in Jewish commentary of the sanctuary being cleansed in order to serve the function of expiation (Rashi and Ibn Ezra on v. 15). The Hebrew of verse 22 *millu'im* ([ful]filling) encourages the idea of this ram-offering as specially connected to the making holy of the priests.

Waiting Seven Days (vv. 33–36)

For Augustine verse 35 raises concerns regarding the historical plausibility of a requirement to sit for seven days and nights at the temple entrance. What, without moving? Hardly! Rather, it just means that they dwelled somewhere around there, and it does not mean they had to stay in the one spot all the time (just as in 1 Kings 3:38, which tells us that Shimei sat in Jerusalem for three years). Augustine argued that it was not that they could not go out but that they were to be based there for seven days. Some in the East seem to have observed the letter of this law as binding on monks just after their consecration, as per the Canterbury School's Commentary (Bischoff and Lapide 1994, 480): "The *multi* who observe the custom that a monk is not to leave the church until the seventh day are evidently eastern monks, for the practice is attested in both Palestine and Syria" (cf. *Canones Theodori-Iudicia* II.iii.3).

Lyra adds that during that week they received moral instruction: for seven days and on the eighth day they obtain where seven things are understood as what they ought to abstain who are newly consecrated as priests: the overlong sleep, the indulgence in eating, the uselessness of action, the multiplicity of distraction, the emptiness of lies, the variety of fiction, the use of affection for which they ought to offer the rigor of penance (signified by the bull calf) for sin. Piscator finds the consecrating of the sons of Aaron to mean the vocation of the apostles as they waited. The washing of Aaron signifies the fact that Christ was pure; the washing of sons of Aaron that pastors of the church should announce Christ blamelessly (Phil 1:16) and be an example to the flock (1 Pet 5:3).

Patrick is aware "about the necessary Easements of Nature, for which they had no convenience. It is more likely they were not so confined, as not to be allowed this liberty." Calmet concurs with this common-sense view, but likes the symbolism he finds in Cyril (*De Adoratione* 2) that the seven days mark the whole life of a priest. Matthew Henry gives a fuller account of the typology: "And those that are thus solemnly dedicated to God ought not to depart from his service, but faithfully to abide in it all their days." On a more "anthropological" account, this rite of passage required a weeklong exposure to holy service for the priests' own benefit (Milgrom 2004, 87).

Leviticus 9

THE MENTION OF "THE eighth day"—so significant for Jewish interpreters (especially Rashi) with its use of the word *ḥānak* ("to dedicate," whence Hanukkah), as the inauguration of the public cult and the subsequent focus on the altar (cf. Milgrom 2004, 88)—is all but missing from the Christian discussion.

Preparation for the Revelation of Glory

The continuation of the installation of Aaron and his sons requires sin offerings for themselves and for the people. The purpose is that God's glory will appear to the people. The rare (for Leviticus) mention of "glory" in verse 6 in its Greek translation (*doxa*) can also mean "that which is given to learn" (as in its Platonic usage, as in Exodus 16:7 where it is something "educational"). There is a curious interplay between grace and moral effort that Hesychius explores: penance prepares the heart for the offering that is Christ, who is gift as well as example. For the altar of the burnt offering is the church, which is sanctified by it. The morning offering was when Christ appeared to the world, while the church is sanctified by him until "the evening" of the world, as it believes in his righteousness and in his sacrifice which, as often as he is offered for "us," gets bestowed on us. The Redeemer, when he came, transcended the Law's precepts; for he removed not only the lust of the flesh but also that of the heart. The one who gave the law now gives us his blessing as he helps us to keep what he commanded.

Hesychius comments further: The Lord then commands: "Do what I say and you will see my glory." Therefore on Sunday, the Lord's Day, we stop, and when we celebrate the Eucharist the Holy Spirit comes. This is just as it happened when after resurrection Jesus ate with disciples—especially in John's account. We are his "house" on whose behalf Aaron is told to offer for (v. 7 LXX—not in the Hebrew or Vulgate), if we maintain the faithfulness and glory of hope till the end; so those who progress and are more perfect are rightly called "his house." And if the Lord preached one doctrine it was penance and perfect behavior, which introduces them to an understanding of God. As people who are corrected just as much as anointed we too can be saved, even if our behavior is not heavenly. The church must gather good patterns of living and take on the manifestation of God's glory. With verse 24 there is a renewed interest for Hesychius in the coming of the Spirit at Pentecost. This is paralleled with the different visions, such as those of Ezekiel, who saw cherubim, Micah, who saw a host of seraphs, or Isaiah, who saw one seraph. The point of Pentecost is not that it made people understand, but that it caused them to wonder and not really understand. Cyril too holds the manifestation of the glory of the Lord on the eighth day to be the main point of Leviticus 9. Likewise Hugh of St. Cher maintains that it is a case of "*do* this and his glory will appear" (v. 6), which means that it has nothing to do with saying the right words, but requires holiness of life.

After attempting to argue that there are also only really three main offerings for individuals, Augustine notices that this chapter deals with the sin of the people with one mind and will. And, as for the sacrifice of salvation, the calf and ram are offered for all the people. It is hard to say why the choice is restricted to these two animals, unless one is for the salvation of individuals and one for that of the people, as with the sin-offering above. Augustine wants to propose the idea that the sacrifice of salvation is properly for individuals, not for a large amount of people (*publicum universorum*). It is of universal benefit, true, yet while singular things can exist without the universal, universals are made up of singular ones. This reflects Augustine's desire that the baptized move on to *personal* faith and perseverance.

Chytraeus notes how verses 1–6 speak of the sinfulness of human priests but also of preparation for the manifestation and presence of the Son of God during the age of the church. In the style of a Renaissance theologian he adds: since it is the glory of God, when we glimpse it we are changed into that image. Calmet elaborates the "preparation for presence" theme (vv. 4f): making these sacrifices expiates faults and increases merit. To state that the Lord will appear means, specifically, that the cloud will halt above the tabernacle, or fire will issue with miraculous signs of his presence. Calmet, with a historian's eye, yet as one who wants to make OT religion appear plausible, investigates what might have been expected to happen. With Knobel's interpretation the priests are achieving something that the people are to applaud. This "theocratic" performance was a way of claiming authority for the priesthood. Any sense of the text's application "for now" has fallen away.

Hierarchies of Blessing

It is clearly to be noted, thinks Augustine, that "consummation" or "perfection offerings" (Greek: *krion teleiósis*; Latin: *oblatum consummationis* of v. 22) are ordered so that the priesthood can function, whereas the people have these offered for their salvation. Augustine asks: is it a sacrifice that is *salutaris* (v. 18) in the sense of *salus* merely as "of health" or as "of salvation"? Well, it could be understood as the latter: for there was salvation under the former covenant in the OT; as Psalm 115:13 has it: "I will accept the cup of salvation." Then also Simeon in Luke 2:30 whose eyes saw "your salvation" was known to Christian faith. But the idea that prevails in Augustine's thought is that the priests have this blessing for the sake of their function, not that some kind of Christian perfection is bestowed. However Hesychius approaches this chapter with the rubric that Pentecost signifies perfection. Christ was the intelligible Aaron, whose sons are ministers of the order of presbyters. Hesychius is not afraid to make room for the non-priestly figure, such as *Moses* who beats the image of Christ so that *every righteous person* on having Christ in him can give out a blessing. The Aaronic priests bless on account of Christ and are allowed to give the *fullness* of blessing. In any case, while the priests have the consummation as Aaron, the non-ordained can still have the image, as Moses.

Yet for Cyril of Alexandria priests are very much set above the people in the distribution of blessing. The Christian High Priest is the bishop, who is "a type and sits in the place" of Christ, while the priests (presbyters) are his collaborators just as the holy disciples were Christ's (cf. Dragas 2003, 6). Thus, what was said about Christ's and his disciples' calling is also applicable to the bishop's and his priests' calling. For Cyril there was and is a twofold sacrifice, one to redeem and the other for living communion with God; or Christ and the life in Christ (cf. Dragas 2003, 18). One requires Christian redemption to have revelation of glory, but one needs to have priestly virtues in order to give, though not to receive, communion.

Ralph indicates that there is a tripartite classification of Christian society (*Corpus Christianorum*). The purity of the perfect is one thing, as they offer themselves to God as a burnt-offering, and bind themselves to the religious life out of contempt for this world because of joy. It is quite another thing to be "peacemakers," i.e., those who, although they try to please God, are still taken up with worldly activities; and it is yet another thing to be one of the penitents, or those who have recently turned to godliness and have just renounced lusts and so are embattled with inner desires. The perfect are those who empty their minds and are fixed on meditation or prayer, and even avoid the distraction of thinking.

Grima mentions that "the eighth day" (v. 1) denotes that, due to his enfleshed state, eight days after Christ was born he was ordained to be circumcised and given the name of Jesus. And for that reason in all different places when they are ordained priests celebrate along with Christ. Yet the Lord says, "whoever today is not with me, his mouth will be empty and will not be counted worthy." The challenge is to priests to keep their pristine Christ-likeness. Denys also has an interpretation that focuses on priestly living as enabled and inspired by Christ.

The Sin-Offerings (vv. 7–21)

Augustine gets worried about the order in which the various sacrifices are made. Why here (v. 7) does it say *first* that offering should be made for sin *then* the burnt-offering, when earlier he ordered the sacrifice of sin to come second, by going on top of the former? Yet nor is it how he spoke about offering the birds in Leviticus 4 and 5: *first* do this and *then* that, for here it is simply "do this and then that." The instruction given earlier tells us what is to be done first, where he says to put the sacrifice for sins on top of the holocaust. Although it may vary much, what Scripture relates is that Aaron did as he heard rather than as he was told, in that he first offered for sin then gave the burnt-offering. Perhaps he in fact did this first and then Scripture *narrated* that it was done afterwards, as it tends to do in many places. Augustine's solution is that whether salvific or for sin, it is not necessary that the offerings be put on top of the burnt-offering.

Incense was put on the horns of the altar, according to the *Ritual of Soissons* (c. 1180) (Martène 1, 4, xxii in Jungmann 1952, 94), modeled on verse 9. According to Ralph, the sons of Aaron offered the blood of the victim just as the church pastor rebukes the blameful things the people have done, yet also alertly catching what is vicious within himself. The priests' offering means "correcting, admonishing." Hugh of St. Cher writes that although five different offerings get mentioned, only three are really described: the ram for the people's sin and the bull and the lamb for the peace-offerings. Perhaps the omission is for reason of brevity (and Hugh will later affirm this, even though he admits Augustine does say that this is problematic, since five are indeed mentioned). Something can be made of the offering of the lamb, namely that God by such a sign assures us of his grace. The various animals and other offerings stand for various things that the church as bride offers to God in his various children: the goat is penance, the bull is good works, the lamb is innocence, etc. The peace-offering means that which saves. "Do this and his glory will appear." Again, this has nothing to do with saying the right words. Peter Chanter has asked why the innards are placed on top of the breasts offered (v. 20). Perhaps only a symbolic reason for this can be given: that the innards belong to the Lord and have higher dignity than the breasts, which belong to the priests. Exodus 20 disallows the use of ladders so Augustine is right to comment that "Aaron descended" means there was a sort of ramp they used to go up and down.

There is little Christian attempt to offer a rationale for the series of offerings, such as atoning for the golden calf incident or any sins of Aaron (as Ibn Ezra thought). The peace offering means that which saves. In other words all the essentials are covered. The animals point backwards as well as forward in salvation history: e.g., the mention of "ram" is in memory of the one in Genesis 22. The lamb is in memory of the paschal lamb when the firstborn of Egypt were visited by the angel. The goat is an animal chosen to show the seriousness of sin.

According to Denys, as Aaron offered *first* for himself *then* for people, charity begins with one's own self. Anyone wanting to be heard by God on behalf of others let him make a personal effort to be reconciled to God and to please him. Aaron went into the tent of testimony to pray to God so that he would show by some action that the sacrifices were accepted. Although Moses knew God already by revelation and had spoken, still he prayed that what was preordained by God would be completed by the prayers of the saints, just as Christ prayed for his elect and for the glorifying of his body even though he knew that was preordained to happen. This self-sacrifice Jesus made in his own power to God the Father, or rather to the whole most-blessed Trinity, was completely free: and the celebration of a good priest does not as such work more than that of a bad one, yet as to the things joined to this sacrifice such as prayers, praises, and some ministrations, the Mass of a virtuous presbyter does avail more than that of an unrighteous one. The prayer of a bad priest, which he issued in the person of the church, as if acting on its behalf, can achieve some amount of effect. So a priest should be chastising his own body before Mass, and offer himself totally to it in a burned offering. He does not stop offering praise and thanks for benefits granted and does not stop praying to receive greater things.

Brenz is an example of widening the non-clerical interpretation of Aaron which would result a century later in the pietist notion of "the priesthood of all believers," on the basis of Luther's "das eynige gemeyne priesterthum" (WA 8: 254, 7; see Wengert 2005). Although Aaron offers for his own sin, Brenz insists that Aaron is not the person on whose account and with whose sacrifice God is truly pleased. The Papist sacrifices are even lesser than the Aaronic ones, because at least the latter were instituted by God, not men. Where the text says that Aaron lit the altar, it should be understood that Aaron did not light it with fire he made himself, but that he placed the things on the altar for *the Lord* to light. In doing Aaron was showing faith in divine promise. Christ has made us all priests of his blood who can share a blessing with each other in the name of Christ, and God wished that to be confirmed if it can be seen by faith. The popish blessing, with crosses and hidden murmurings, is a mere human replacement for this.

As for blessing, Lapide sees verse 22 as denoting a double blessing from Aaron on the people: first when he offers and second when he leaves the tabernacle. Of course, the form of words for benediction is given in Numbers 6:24–26, but also in 2 Chronicles 20. These are figures of the truth in the blessing by Christ, and not only at the point of his ascension. Calmet on the same verse tells us that holding out hands was usual in ceremonies. It marks the authority and superiority of the one who blesses all the assembly (cf. Num 6:23). Matthew Henry asks: "How can we expect to be accepted in our prayers for others, if we ourselves be not reconciled to God? This charity must begin at home, though it must not end there." What is interesting is the failure by the tradition to relate the entering the tent after the offering to Christ's own resurrection and ascension.

Fire from the Lord

The fire is the form God takes here just as it had been encased in cloud at Sinai (Exod 24:17), although this is not much emphasized in the Jewish tradition until later (e.g., R. Sforno, early fifteenth century). According to Isho'dad of Merv, the "stupid disciples of Zoroaster" have stuck to their doctrine and think that fire is the child of Hormizd. But they do not understand that there are not two natures of fire in the world, i.e., fire does not have a hidden metaphysical nature: it is just fire! Likewise when verse 24 reports that fire leaped out, this did not happen by the nature of the fire, but by dint of its being a gift of God.

Rupert, in a "history of salvation" manner, comments that on the eighth day of consecration a fire comes from the Lord, for he is a fire, who now on the first resurrection of souls consumes their sins and then later in the second resurrection devours also the mortality or corruption of bodies. This fire ought never to be lacking on the altar, which is the faith by which Christ dwells in our hearts. Ralph's interpretation has more to do with the Christian life, taking the fire that came out from the Lord to be the Holy Spirit who proceeds from the Father and the Son. This fire sent into the world devours the burnt-offering, i.e., the hearts of the perfect caught up into his love and separating from worldly effects, enlisting all their power and effort for divine service. "For today the Lord will appear" (v. 4) is added as if to say that it is right that such sacrifices happened today, since the Lord will appear not in himself but "in effect" by giving fire from heaven onto the holocaust altar. By the time of Nehemiah the fire was restored after being hidden in a deep and dry well in Babylon by the priests of the time, and restored at the time of Nehemiah, as 2 Maccabees 1 tells us.

Luther, commenting on verse 24, observes that God does not ask the priests to prepare any fire. He then radicalizes this: Fire comes from heaven when we account ourselves nothing, dead before God. The fire is the Holy Spirit, which brings a new mind. To serve God we do not need to be monks but to believe in Christ. Brenz is agnostic about the Maccabean story of the flame being preserved through exile (2 Macc 1:19ff.) Possibly such a miracle happened, but if God allowed the temple to be destroyed by the Babylonians it seems likely that the fire of the altar was also completely extinguished. Lapide writes that mystically speaking fire is a symbol of chastity and divine purity, which men, and above all priests, ought to copy: compare the accounts of the pagan vestal virgins in Ovid's *Fasti* and Vergil's *Aeneid* IV. Christians, while they would keep and kindle this flame, do not fear it ever going out (with a strange interpretation of Deut 32:22). For the Holy Spirit, having descended at Pentecost, stays. He can melt iron. Such is God and his love, which like fire can be foe or friend. It can show the way and it also makes hard. So with God one must be respectful, for the Spirit is active not restful. He gets into cracks with his sevenfold subtlety. As fire is to light and heat, so is the Father to the Son and Spirit (John Damascene, *On the Orthodox Faith* 1.9). The fire consecrated and sanctified, so to speak, the offerings as much as those offering them. Heraclitus was right to say that God is an intelligible fire. Lapide continues: in 503 AD St. Abba Euthymius often saw angels ministering to God alongside him as he sacrificed and he would elsewhere see fire and a huge light coming down from above which engulfed him with his action until the sacrifice was over. The "fire coming from heaven" (v. 23) reminds Lapide of 1 Kings 18:24, 28 and also the approving of Solomon's offering in the temple (2 Chr 7:1). Now the pagans claim the same, as with Servius in his commentary on *Aeneid* 12. However these things are either fables or they were brought about by the art and skill of a demon. The Jews report the tradition that in this fire a lion's face can be seen, or that the Messiah can be represented, being the lion from the tribe of Judah, and that this fire cannot be extinguished by water, even if rivers washed over it (Song 8:5). God willed that the priests added fuel though it did not need it. It is a "Jewish fable," Lapide thinks, to suppose God willed priests to add fuel: why would they have to tend it if so many waters could not extinguish it? And the Jews are wrong to say the second temple lacked this flame (see 2 Macc 1:19). Abulensia is mad to think the fire went out after this eighth day and stayed out for thirty-eight years until they got to Canaan. Ribera (*De templo* c17) is right to argue that it was a perpetual flame after all.

Calov prickles at any mention of pagan parallels to this ceremony as related by Grotius. He follows Junius in taking the fire "from the faces of the Lord" in verse 24 to mean "from the propitiatory" where God commanded the visible proof of his presence. Calmet, showing an interest for detail without emphasizing Moses' intercessory role to "enable" Aaron in the way Rashi and others did, observes that Moses does not tell us how this fire issued, but it does seem connected to the joint blessing. The fire comes out and joins with the already present altar fire and makes it burn up totally the offering there. It is like an ether which turns into fire (cf. Philo, *Mos.* I, 12, 65) and perhaps this was a special action for Aaron's first sacrifice. (Cf. 2 Macc 2:10—fire came from heaven on to the holocaust.) Josephus thought it to be like lightning, and this lasted until temple of Solomon, when God then sent a new fire for that occasion (2 Chr 7:1, as Abarnabel had spotted); and during the exile that fire was kept in a cave. Whereas the Rabbis tell us it went away at the time of Manasseh, Maccabees tells us it was back during the second temple. Those who do not accept this are those (i.e., Jews and Huguenots) who do not view Maccabees as canonical. Calmet wants to maintain a post-exilic continuity to the story of salvation. Keil however argues that there is nothing to back up idea that the fire was sustained even only until the time of Solomon's temple either by miracle (so the "rabbins") or natural means (so Christian interpreters). Levine (1989, 58), in the tradition of *Sifra*, notes the double-edged nature of a fire from heaven via the tabernacle: it can mean either blessing or destruction.

Leviticus 10

Unholy Fire (vv. 1–7)

Leviticus Rabbah 12:1 has: "R. Ishmael explained: Aaron's sons died because they entered [the tabernacle] drunk with wine." But the *Rabbah* seems to prefer a divine tenderness in this episode, and verses like "those who are close to me/those who draw near to me" seem to give a gloss to the story (see Kugel 1998, 745) of a more positive sort, one which might mean they had ascended to heaven.

Theodoret soberly reports on verse 1 that the Lord God instructed that the fire be kept alight and wood to be added to the fire day and night, but no human-made fire was to be brought in to be mixed with the divine. Since Nadab and Abihu, the sons of Aaron, transgressed this law and brought in manufactured fire, divine fire consumed them. We learn from these things not to quench the Spirit but to enflame the grace we have received. We also learn not to add anything to the Holy Scripture but to be content with the Spirit's teaching and to hate heresies, which add myths to the divine words and prefer unseemly ideas to the thoughts of the Scriptures.

Hesychius finds a note of consolation: but if we have put on Christ in baptism we work as priests and will not die, nor bring wrath in the congregation. This chapter serves as a reminder to Procopius not to mix human and divine agency in the work of salvation. With grace appearing the letter of the law is useless. For the divine fire shows its power here, lest anyone imagine that the divine fire is imaginary, for God is a consuming fire (Heb 12:29). Yet part of this work was to reconcile Israel "according to the flesh" with what it had heard from Moses. Procopius is not saying that the law is not to be obeyed in every detail, but that only Christ's power could make it work. Isho'dad reports Yohanan of Bet Rabban, who had led the School of Nisibis in the mid-sixth century, relating the Jewish interpretation that thinks their bodies were not burned, just that their souls taken out of their bodies, since (v. 5) "they carried them by their tunics," and here too Isho'dad has no strong preference for an explanation.

Lyra, party to Jewish traditions of interpretation, argues that the two were not consumed in body since not even their linen clothes were. From this comes the argument that Nadab and Abihu were saved, just as in 2 Kings 13f, when the "man of God" led astray by the false prophet returned to Bethel only to be killed by a lion, the lion did not touch his corpse out of respect. For God in this life punishes holy men even for a light fault by his just judgment; even for a hidden fault. Still he is clear that they did offend against instruction. The flame devoured, that is killed, their souls since their bodies were not consumed nor even their clothes. From the fact that Nadab and Abihu were buried with their priestly clothing, the custom grew that the priests of the New Law (i.e., *Christian* priests) also be buried with priestly clothes.

Denys laments how imprudently those blessed by God forget him. So God took this drastic action, this to instill fear in all the priests who would follow, so that they would carry out their office reverently and fearfully. The miracle is that the bodies were not totally burned up by such a great fire, but remained intact, just as when the body of the prophet and his donkey were untouched though killed by that lion in 1 Kings 13. So it is to be believed that the two priests escaped damnation after receiving this temporal punishment, for the Lord will not double a punishment. True, they seem to have sinned mortally in what they did against the instruction of God, but in being so killed they were mercifully spared through this ritual of penance by Aaron. Being buried in full robes perhaps indicates they were already forgiven. Maybe Moses absolved them from guilt, or from at least part of it. Denys notes that Lyra followed Rashi's opinion that Aaron not only deserved to die but also to lose all his posterity (as in Deuteronomy 9 where the Lord was fiercely angry with Aaron). But Rabbi Paul disagreed, arguing that Aaron's sin was not so large as to deserve to be blotted out along with his progeny. God alone knows how serious our vices are, and what were the causes and mitigating or penalizing circumstances. We know only what is revealed to us in Scripture or elsewhere.

From Leviticus 10 Luther draws the lesson that the proud may not teach, however respectable their background. Such a shocking story should shake the complacent. For those who show no respect, the fire is the Spirit who will put up with much but not heresy. Luther lapses into the vernacular: "*Da ist kein Schertz.*" It's no joke, especially as their responsibilities were light compared with those of the ministers of the gospel (*Predigten über das dritte und vierte Buch Mose* 1527/28; WA 25:414).

Calmet judges that the fire on the holy altar was not good enough for Aaron's two oldest sons. Or perhaps they were punished because they had not washed, or were wearing only tunics (see Lyra, and Estius the Jesuit Pauline commentator, d. 1613), or because they were drunk. This is unlikely as the Israelites would not have had any wine in desert (Deut 29:6), and in Numbers 3:4 and 26:61 God accuses them only of offering "wrong fire," nothing else. Calmet's enlightened conscience seems troubled. Now Scripture had not forbidden such a thing, though some think God had forbidden it implicitly in 6:12, by not commanding it. Yet did the punishment not rather exceed the crime? It is easier if we follow Lyra and others who think God had forbidden it expressly, which made their offence mortal and for which they would suffer in life to come. If not, then the severity can be explained by God's needing to set an example. And so the pair probably found God merciful to them in afterlife, and, as Philo observed, they were given an honorable funeral.

Drunkenness and Abstinence (vv. 8–11)

Origen feels his charge in a homily is not so much to explain the Scriptures as to build up the church. Sobriety is the mother of all virtues and church leaders are to practice this, as 1 Timothy 5:23 specifies. Jesus also warns against hearts heavy with "drunkenness" (Luke 21:34) for it makes body and soul feeble. Of course, passions in general can do this to the soul.

As for a mystical interpretation of passage, Origen muses: We need to examine how the Savior—the true Priest—and his disciples drank wine before approaching the altar but when they began to approach it abstained (Matt 26:29). Our Savior mourns our sins even now and cannot rejoice so long as one remain in iniquity. As he was being made sad for my sins he could not drink the wine of gladness (*vinum laetitiae*; cf. Matt 23:27). Just as it is not just Aaron who must not drink, but his sons too, so likewise the apostles are waiting for us too to follow their example (Heb 11:39–40).

Ephraim interprets the drunkenness as what led to the fire going out, which necessitated the offering of foreign fire. Cyprian in his *Unity of the Catholic Church* 18–19 comments on the sons of Aaron in his context of dealing with schismatic and heretical baptism. These examples are being followed wherever the tradition that comes from God is despised by lovers of strange doctrine and replaced by teaching of "merely human authority" (i.e., in Cyrpian's context, heretics trying to rebaptize). Theodoret thinks wine was not forbidden at all times, but only at the specific time of ministry. For the Apostle Paul commands a priest (*hierea*) to be sober and only a little wine is to be taken on account of wearisome weaknesses, as per 1 Timothy 5:23. For it is necessary that a priest be perfect since entrusted with the advocacy-prayer of the people. So let us learn once more from this (v. 17) as those who eat from what the people bring, that if we do not live by the Rule and do not offer up prayers for them, we will receive judgment from God. As the Lord mysteriously spoke through Hosea: "they have eaten the sin of my people" (Hos 4:8).

Augustine finds it unclear whether "the eternal law" (v. 9c) is the ban on drinking altogether or on that which interferes with their priestly duty. They are to be sober and able to instruct about holy things (i.e., how the lay people should approach the sanctuary) and to be able to tell holy and unholy people apart. As for the High Priest, it surely just means he was not allowed to drink wine when he was about to go into the tabernacle or before the altar, which he has to do daily for the sake of the incense-offering. Perhaps God foreknew that at a future point there would be a number of High Priests at the same time, some of whom could drink, while others would be on duty.

For Procopius the prohibition of drunkenness (v. 8) symbolizes a wider range of sins. A priest should not lose his reason and be taken over by earthly things. The Nazirites offer an example to priests to be sober for all their life long, so they can rightly sprinkle the seeds of doctrine, or they should at least be mindful of sobriety so that their life of sins can be lamented and confessed when they turn to do sacred works. Likewise Bede (*On the Tabernacle* 3.2) observes that some in our time "are consumed by the fire of heavenly vengeance because they prefer the fire of cupidity to the fire of heavenly love."

Grima takes Augustine's opinion on verse 9 to be that they should never drink wine. But if we ask why our students are allowed wine today then it has to be said that it is because there would be very few of them if they were not able to drink that which intoxicates! (For Thomas Aquinas's view that restraint applies more to the old who need to be able to think and teach see *ST* IIaIIae q149, a3–4; cf. Dahan 1999, 286.)

Lyra concludes that since people are prone to drink beyond measure, this therefore is simply a prohibition, though not for always but only for the time of ministry. Lapide comments that the Hebrews thought the two sons slipped up through drink and diminished responsibility, and yet if they had been completely drunk they would not have been able to get the fire going. It is most likely they were very excited and disturbed by seeing the fire fall, such that they wanted to thank God, but fear stopped their approach and so they turned to something they could control. So it is a fiction of "the Rabbis" that Nadab and Abihu were consumed because they did not wash their hands and feet or had only tunics on, or because they did not want wives, or that they opposed Moses. Their crime was worse if we appreciate the full symbolism of it as to do with heresy, although Abulensia is probably right to say they suffered death in this life so as to escape eternal death and therefore sinned venially; or if it were mortal then they had time to remove it by contrition. A sign of this (that their sins were only venial) is that their bodies were unwounded, for Moses is said to bury them in holy clothing and the people to mourn for them. God is rightly able to judge venial sins by killing people, although human judges should not. God will show himself holy in his priests by punishing the sacrilegious.

Leclerc has it that the context of an alcohol ban in Israel should be realized, namely that the Egyptians were big drinkers with their libations to Osiris. What Nadab and Abihu did *is* commanded on the Day of Atonement, so the timing rather than the deed itself was wrong. They were punished for temerity, not drunkenness. Leclerc thinks chapter 10's point is that small changes to the divine command lead to big changes and set a bad example.

Aaron's Grief

Ephraim provides a masterly study in the psychology of bereavement. On verse 19 ("And such things have come my way"), he asks: "What sort of things? Aaron said: 'My sons, who burned with anger; my mind, which was enflamed and fired with love for them, and for which there was no comfort or relief from the boundary you had set, not to rub my head, not to rend my garments, not to raise my voice, not to go out of my tent, nor to embrace my sons and bury them . . . But you Lord are honored with goodness and justice . . . perhaps the Lord is not pleased.'" When Moses heard this, "he was pleased."

Jerome in *Epistle* 105 paraphrases verse 6 as follows: One is not to mourn, lest the soul is missing from the sacrifices of God and while he should be busy in his mysteries gets distracted by emotion. Echoing Luke 9:61–62, one is to "let the dead bury their own dead." Jerome comments that although an innocent, quiet behavior can be of profit, keeping silent can also harm, since the madness of wolves can be kept at bay by the barking of dogs and by the stick of the shepherd. Augustine is not sure whether it was a general ban on their mourning: it was more likely just for their seven days of service, and then they could mourn, as soon as they were off-duty. Hesychius sees symbolized in Aaron's silence the suffering ("pierced to the heart": v. 3 LXX) of Christ, "the intelligible Aaron."

Hugh of St. Cher observes: Job was the same as Aaron, in that he kept silent. The priests were prohibited to mourn on the grounds of their being so newly consecrated, so it is not a general ban on grieving, except for the High Priest. So many people have cried, including even the Lord over Jerusalem and Lazarus. The priests are prohibited to cry over their dead, since they ought to conform their will totally to the divine will. Sometimes crying is permitted so they can express the emotion of compassion. But one is not to cry as those who have no hope (1 Thess 4). They are not to go in to the temple, that is, not go in for the purpose of grieving.

Lyra's main point is also that one should never overdo it with signs of mourning, and links this with idolatry. For priests who use idols in their rites, such as bones and flesh of the dead, are not to be thought of as the priests of God and the Lord comments that the minor priests should not grieve the dead, very close relatives excepted. Especially in the early days of their service they should distance themselves more from these things. Here the guilt of omission is highlighted, since Aaron and his sons, upset by the death of Nadab and Abihu, forgot the goat for sin in the fire. Denys opines that, as for the mystical sense, Aaron asked how he could please God with a mournful heart. This shows that disproportionate and worldly sorrow leads people into a place in God's discipline where one cannot be deserving of salvation. Rather we should rejoice in the Lord always, under all conditions.

In the modern era, Keil notes that Moses does not reprove Aaron (*pace* Knobel) but just explains the divine judgment to him. "Don't cut your hair at all" (v. 6) does not mean to avoid the "pagan" shaving of the head here, rather he is just told to stop basic care, as a sign of moderate grieving!

Unforgivable Sin

There is no explanation in verses 16–18, according to Hesychius, as to why they were beyond mercy. Perhaps, although every sin is wiped away through penance, those who preach strange doctrine and commit blasphemy are not saved. In the similar case of Ananias and Sapphira (Acts 5:1–11) they were unable to be penitent, in fact it was just not possible since they were self-condemning. "Thus if you hear his voice today, do not harden your heart" (Ps 104:8). Aaron here is the person of the church, which cannot offer penance for those who attack the priesthood. Jesus wants to find his church holding to his doctrine.

Gratian in the *Decretum*, c.35, has: "Namely since the sons of Aaron did not eat that which was in the holy place for sin, that is they did not perform within the church the penitence for committed sin . . . Since they sinned against the Holy Spirit; by the intelligible force of the Holy Spirit the chance of any sacrifice in place of penitence is forfeited. There is no offering for sin left for those who sin willfully. For just as true penitence deserves pardon, thus false penitence annoys God."

Their rashness was seen as a sin against the Holy Spirit because he was the fire, the one who, as Rupert of Deutz puts it, lights up our darkening mortality as Christ lifts all believers up into an eternal burnt offering to God (Kahles 1960, 86). This action tried to usurp his place and role.

Hugh repeats what he finds in Gratian and emphasizes the psychology of the impenitent as "hopeless." Aquinas (*ST* IIaIIae, q13, obj4) reports: "Further, Bernard says (*De Dispens. et Praecept.* xi) that 'to refuse to obey is to resist the Holy Ghost.'" Moreover the *Glossa* on Leviticus 10:16, says: "a feigned repentance is a blasphemy against the Holy Ghost." Denys adds: The bishop, the judge, in fact any Christian, on hearing a reasonable explanation, ought to be ready to forgive the penitent and not to be austere and judgmental. Yet nor should he just believe the excuses, but should investigate with great diligence the cause when he does not know it.

Lapide explains that the Targum has "do not cover the hair of your head," but the Hebrew has the opposite: do not *bare* it. "Lest perhaps you die": "perhaps" here is not a note of doubt for it was certain they would die if they do what is forbidden here, i.e., mourn their brothers. But Scripture uses in sure things this phrase of doubt to show that humans have free will and that the outcome is free and not set, although this conditional proposition would be certain. Ambrose in a letter to Simplician explains this saying that people are prone to excuses because nature hates to be penitent. Calov complains that Willet, on verse 19, seems rather to justify a mitigation of the offence when he mentions Moses tolerating Aaron's weakness. The others such as Calvin said it was the priestly duty to eat the offering on the same day. Leclerc adds that Josephus praised Aaron's silence for constancy; it compares with other stoical figures like Marcus Horatius Pulvillus in Livy, *History* II, 8.

For Keil, Moses reproved Eleazar and Ithamar for burning the sin-offering instead of eating it. They are meant to "bear the iniquity," which means, as it does in Exodus 28:38, *to expiate sin* for someone else. The priests do this by eating and that act does not just declare sin removed but actually symbolically removes it. This was "an incorporation of the victim laden with sin, whereby the priests actually took away the sin by virtue of the holiness and sanctifying power belonging to their office." Aaron is sober at the end, not because he is grieving (Knobel) but because he is penitent and feels disqualified to eat.

Gerstenberger (1993, 115) shakes his head at that anthropological constant—the demand for standards to demarcate holiness with which to exclude others: *that* is what motivated the Priestly writer's desire for order. Milgrom's approach is more sympathetic and "personalist." Aaron had failed to consume the *ḥattaʿt* as *Sifra* observed, but he was teaching Moses a lesson, that the recently defiled sanctuary required purification (Milgrom 2004, 97–99, spots the tragic irony here). The eating of the offering has remarkable symbolic poignancy. Milgrom mentions the custom as late as 1900 of the "sin-eater" at English funerals who consumed bread and beer over the corpse. "Just as those who are closest to the battlefront are more likely to die so those closest in the service of the sanctuary are more prone to err" (Abarnabel; Milgrom 2004, 94).

Leviticus 11

Holistic and Gospel Hermeneutic

AT THE HEAD OF Christian interpretation and some Jewish interpretation stands Philo, for whom there were strong medical reasons for the Jews to avoid unclean animals since these are fat and fleshy, producing indigestion, which is the cause of all illness. These rules find a middle way between abstinence and luxury (*On the Special Laws* IV, XVII). There is a principle of becoming what one eats: one should eat herbivores if one would be gentle in one's lifestyle. Philo helpfully lists the ten animals that are clean to eat. These are, of course, also symbols of instruction: e.g., the rumination signifies the bringing back of what we have learned and making it our own, thus cementing ideas together), and then he impresses the image of it all firmly on his soul (XVIII). Here we see a gradual progression from a literal/medical to a figurative reading.

Origen's interpretation is a moral one specifically in terms of response to the call of the gospel. He defensively insists that it is not just Leviticus that uses animals to speak of humans. Indeed, Paul does it when he remarks that all these things spoken of in the Jewish Scriptures are a shadow of future things (Heb 8:5; 10:1). This chapter's instructions are not to be taken literally by the NT-informed Christian, who, like Peter at Joppa in Acts 10:9, has ascended in mind and spirit. But we should only eat with such who give us a certain "flavor." Theodoret observes that Acts 10:11–15 and its aftermath revealed the faith of Cornelius who was a Gentile yet desired salvation: the Gentiles are the "food" with which God commanded contact. The early medieval Irish *Pauca Problesmata*, citing Eucherius of Lyons (*Formulae spiritalis intelligentiae* 1.37), looks back to creation and resolves the question as to why clean and unclean animals must have been distinguished before the flood, and yet were put together in the ark. This was because the law had not yet made this distinction, and this all under the guidance of Moses by the Spirit.

Reasons for Avoidance

The straightforward moral allegorical interpretation, that animals stand for bad moral attitudes and behavior, came to triumph in Christian interpretation. Novatian (c. 240; 1972, 89) had already insisted on a symbolic interpretation in the tradition of Philo but also on the grounds that if the NT made all things clean literally then the unclean in Leviticus could only be *symbolic* of spiritual impurity. Isidore repeated this (PL 83, 330): there is nothing wrong with created nature as such. So for these foods or animals to be unclean, they must stand for actions and wills. The law provides a mirror by presenting animals in which images of axioms can be seen. Take the camel, for instance: it exemplifies an unformed life twisted by crimes.

Eusebius of Emesa (1953–57) is clear that all those things that were worshipped in Egypt God now commands to be eaten so that they thus despise them; and what they gluttonously used to devour, such as the pigs, he forbids. There is another reason. The common nature that often presumes it can do what it likes, sometimes out of haughtiness, sometimes out weakness, here receives condemnation. Habit of nature and convenience in all things needs to be challenged. Aphrahat follows Eusebius on the first reason (to avoid superstition as they had in Egypt, especially a temptation when things got even harder for them in the desert), but his second is quite different and reflects the "gospel" hermeneutic mentioned just above. After they made the golden calf, God gave them commandments which were not good (Ezek 20:25), which were hard and too numerous to keep, such as in this chapter. But Christ (Matt 11:28–30) has lifted the yoke. Hesychius explains that not all animals are clean and this is not because of nature, but because of our excess and that we have spoiled nature through evildoing. The unclean animals are vicious in the sense of being opposed to the four cardinal virtues. Not to touch means not to imitate those whose virtue is only a sham.

Langton thinks that to eat unclean animals can mean to eat the sins of others in the sense of delighting in imitating them in their vices. Hildegard of Bingen's *Physica: 7 De animalibus* furnishes a moral reason that is also medicinal. The animals that are not to be eaten instruct us in the way of virtue and "possibilities" or things to be avoided, but the edible ones are eaten by way of concession for the sake of promoting health (here she is presuming a vegetarian diet for monks, etc.), and even the pig may be allowed for those who lack warmth/vitality. Albert the Great, whose botanical knowledge and skills were put to good use in his bishop's garden in Regensburg, comments on Luke 8:32 that the pig is dirty by nature, for it even looks monstrous, and with the elephant is exceptionally monstrous! For it has a stronger lower jaw which it moves, not least to defend itself, and it loves to sit in mud and with hardened skin armed for battle to eat filthy things. This is all according to long-held customary knowledge, the custom driving the law of Leviticus 11:7. Nahmanides cites medical evidence for drinking pigs' milk as a cause of leprosy.

Hugh of St. Victor (so, Smalley 1969, 41) "also taught that *legalia* had had a moral function. They inculcated obedience, kindled devotion, and signified that uncleanness was to be avoided, by forbidding pork, for example." The northern French anonymous commentator of the twelfth century (for details see Smalley 1969, 34) from that same period consulted local Jews, to discover that the command in verse 34 on eating meat which had been in contact with unclean things had been relaxed. Yet with Peter Chanter there was a sympathetic view of these *legalia* as having an ongoing morally edifying purpose for Christians as for Jews: they confer virtue, and even just in reading them there is a blessing, not a curse.

Conversely, Hugh of St. Cher was clear that at a literal level this chapter has nothing to say to Christians since the NT's declaration of all foods to be clean. So it is what these *signify* that counts and this means the Christian life of penitential virtues. So in animals we can see human morals painted. But what about the serpent who was *created* evil—as Gregory the Great and John Damascene hold? Well, Hugh agrees that only prelapsarian *humanity* was pure. It is false to say that those who do good are good; no, those who do evil are evil, but those who are good do good, as Aristotle and the fathers agree. Purity is double: one is being clean from guilt and the other is to be clean through grace, which precedes action. Shockingly, Dominique Grima writes that the hare is like the soul lulled by the devil into playing games until tired out and the devil kills with his sharp teeth of sin. Yet too often with the *Glossa Ordinaria* and Ralph of Flaix even where the readings are original, they are still predictable: for Ralph the camel, porcupine, and hare (11:4–6) are people too busy with worldly cares and fears, and, if we think of porcupines, does not Jesus mention the spiky thorns of anxiety (Matt 13:7)? The lesson of purity is not so much about avoiding these sins in oneself as avoiding those who have developed these habitually, so as to lead one astray.

As for Jewish interpretation, Maimonides states a principle of a close soul-body connection (*Guide* 3.27): "The general object of the Law is twofold: the well-being of the soul and the well-being of the body." Or, at *Guide* 3.48: "I maintain that the food which is forbidden by the Law is unwholesome." For Rashbam: "These foods heat up the body and harm it on other ways." The priests were to look out for the people, as Nahmanides observes, so the purity laws are given to Moses and Aaron who would make sure that nobody would try to claim that, for example, non-cleft-hoofed, non-ruminant animals not specifically mentioned were in fact permitted. Abarbanel sees it as instructing priests to maintain right good and just, and "pour holiness into the people," and the mention of abomination means, he adds in a voluntaristic manner: "do not enquire after the reasons for these commands."

After reviewing the individual cases, Lyra—who follows Rashi in claiming that the food laws are about eating, not sacrificing—leaves a literal interpretation for today open by concluding rather generally that spiritual purity is achieved by the obeying of the command not to touch. Thus one is to be holy in soul and body. What marks his interpretation out, apart from some "originality" in mixing Jewish and pagan lore—the pelican (v. 18) is unclean because it eats serpents; these come to the nest to poison it, and the father has to come back and clean with own blood!—is his "voluntarist" insistence that even when it is hard to say why something is unclean, uncleanness is transmitted in part from the willful inward disobedience to the taboo.

However, any movement to find wisdom from the literal sense suffered a setback when Luther complains that the pope wants to set fasts during which only certain things can be eaten, and that means that prices go up and he starts to act with secular power. No, the spiritual meaning is that one eats food spiritually when one believes and preaches Christ—that he has done all for us. In our bodies we are to obey parents, to mortify passions, and not commit adultery. But in our souls we are free. If one's father says "don't believe such and such" then he is not to be obeyed. To eat is to believe and enjoy the word in the soul or to receive sound, nourishing doctrine. The law kills the old Adam, so that the gospel be led over the conscience and the conscience be strengthened.

For Brenz, God appeals to humans that just as much as they shrink from disgusting foodstuffs that would do them physical harm, so too they should shun impiety. He takes care of our souls even more than our bodies. We must reject some things to have more space for his blessings. The Law as pedagogue talks in symbolic language. Of course, since the NT letters (Rom 14; Col 2) and the story of Peter at Joppa (Acts 10) we know that no food is unclean to us if we are clean. But at that time since Christ was not yet revealed God wanted this people to remain in servitude and God somehow was pleased by this limited obedience. Dead things foreshadow dead works, which are sins.

Calvin repeats the wisdom that the NT passages prove what was the case pre-Fall: that of course no animal was ever unclean *in itself*, only as to its *use*. The same goes for the tree of knowledge of good and evil; it is the prohibition that matters. God was strict with them lest they fall into other perversions; these commands to the Israelites were "acts of discipline whereby he might accustom them to study purity, which is so generally neglected and omitted among men." However, the Jews went astray when they made too much anxious labor out of washings, even when "unconscious of any such pollution." Calvin's point is that the law of purity is pure as law and in its content and so should be precious to the saints. Chytraeus concludes on a more negative note, that to the unclean (i.e., those not purified by Christ's death) all is unclean in mind and conscience (as the corollary of Titus 1:15). Nature strives for its own conservation, and so it abhors the decay and impurity that pervades it. Although Mosaic laws are abrogated, still the nature of men and of other things stays the same, and so principles like forbidding incest, avoiding leprosy and unhealthy food, still obtain. There are, he adds, unhelpful papal imitations of these fastidious laws, although he does not specify or describe these.

Lorinus comments that no food that enters the mouth pollutes a person in respect of the soul. But God and the magistrates, especially the ecclesiastical one, are able to forbid certain things so that the soul is not spoiled by sin of disobedience. One of Jovinian's errors, repeated by the Protestants following the tradition of the poor of Lyon (the Waldensians), was that the church cannot rule on such things. It seemed to others that this was a distinction concerning sacrifices from tradition, given to Seth or Enoch, and not that which was permitted to Noah and his progeny after the flood. Here there is some resolution given on each, in that whatever may not be eaten cannot be sacrificed. Those foods that cannot be eaten as well as not sacrificed are mentioned on grounds that they produce sickness and stop people concentrating on worshipping and serving God. Anyway, the NT is more about inner purity, the OT about outer and political purity. Some foods were disallowed for symbolic reasons for Jews; for Christians however, food is good for human society, as Pope Nicolas I wrote in his letter to the Bulgarians (chapter 43) in 866. The sense is that the church can also rule on which external props to inner holiness are to be allowed or prohibited.

Willet wants his reader to be sure that although Leviticus 11 tells us of sin and how to avoid it, both it and the natural world cannot instruct in righteousness. So the chief reason for the chapter is figurative, to show the separation of God's people. The meaning cannot be a moral meaning either, since many of the beasts are unknown to us, so how could we copy them?

The uselessness of these laws even to teach morals becomes a "quaintness" in the treatment by Grotius, who relates that the classical sources tell us that the Hebrews must have adapted many of these food laws from the Egyptians who forbade eating any four-legged with horns, which were sexually overactive (Pliny, Book 10). Both were variations on a universal and natural principles. Herodotus tells us that the Egyptians abstained from pigs not because, as Tacitus had it, pigs were prone to scabies, but because their flesh is so sweet that over-indulgence causes such a disease in humans.

Calov, like Willet, sees Moses and Aaron's teamwork as representing the dual task of civil and priestly legislation about foods. There is some link of unsplit hooves with sexual proclivity, as Pliny reported. Yet we should have no faith in Maimonides and other "blind" Jewish doctors, and we should not try to find a reason in the natural causes of the good and bad "foodstuffs," for laws are simply based in the free choices of the Creator. He was looking for obedience as much as for temperance. Grotius, reports Calov, has followed Novatian in thinking it has to do with the fact that luxury is inimical to sanctity. But we should not mix up human and divine reasons. So that means we see them as unclean symbolically, that is by divine *will*, not by nature (*contra* Grotius who viewed them as natural principles in the minds of the ancients). One can and should learn that whatever God wills that might seem odd in the judgment of posterity, one should nevertheless obey it!

Leclerc is sure that the chapter is about animals that are judged unsuitable for eating, not simply for sacrifice. Moses took a religion from the Egyptians and cleaned out the superstition from it. One such borrowing lies in the fact, as Josephus showed us, that the Egyptians also abstained from pigs; and Arabs and Phoenicians too, according to Bochartus (d. 1667). These laws were not intended to be useful to the Israelites, since the very reality of the experience contradicts this, for they ended up no better-tempered than the nations who did not have food laws: so it cannot be that it was meant to sanctify them. The things are not *in themselves* abhorrent, but become so *through the command*, which was given for the purpose of restraining greed. It is a matter of abstinent reverence in eating, not of reflecting holiness as an attribute of God through being "different."

Bonar wistfully remarks: "they [the Israelites] could never gaze on these merely with the feelings of one admiring a creating God; they were led to think of them as connecting with a holy God, who discerned between the clean and the unclean, and sought the redemption of fallen creatures." Nature is not to be admired sentimentally: "I remember while in Palestine in 1839 the vast number of insects . . . near Magdala . . . These creatures on the wing were like messengers sent to admonish the saints of God that the sweetest spots of earth were polluted." The distinction reminds him of God's holiness and human sinfulness. "It is not till next morning that his complete deliverance is apparent to all. It is at the resurrection morning . . . that all effects of yesterday's defilement are gone."

This moral pessimism resounds also in Keil's commentary: Universal human horror is the same thing as a common awareness of original sin. "It is in this penetration of sin into the material creation that we may find the explanation . . . leading to a *horror naturalis*, an inexplicable disgust. It is as if humans as they began to fall into sin yet still somewhat innocent looked on horrified as the natural world reflected back at them their true state, whose childlike mind, acute perception and deep intuitive insight into nature generally, discerned more truly and essentially the real nature of the animal creation than we shall ever be able to do."

This idea that nature reflected the moral ambivalence of humans after the Fall was opposed by Knobel, although "the theocratic author," he believes, would have believed in some primal state of order to which he hoped all would return. The idea that death results from sin is a Pauline "invention" and is not found in the OT. In Knobel's view, the left-wing Hegelian Bruno Bauer (d. 1882) was just as bad as the orthodox theologian H. A. Hävernick, when he wrote that nature makes humans self-seeking and draws our souls into sin. The OT recognizes the weakness of nature and human nature, but that is not the same thing as malice.

Rumination and the Cloven Hoof

The ruminant are understood by *Barnabas* 10:1–12 as those people who meditate, and the cloven-footed as those who are "divided"—who are in the world yet moving towards a holy state. In the *Letter of Aristeas* 161, rumination is glossed as "remembering God's benefits." Both of these are devotional in their emphasis, but Irenaeus (*Haer.* V.8.3) has a more obviously confessional interpretation, taking verses 3ff. as pointing to those who have faith in Father and Son (the cloven hoof somehow suggests a binitarianism) and who meditate with this in mind. If Barnabas brought the behavioral avoidance aspects of the Philonic interpretation to the fore, Clement of Alexandria emphasizes the instructional. So, although Clement warns against licentious "pigs," which Egyptians loved to sacrifice (*Strom.* 7.3), and those who plunder others ("birds of prey": vv. 13–18) (*Protrept* 3.11.75), he is more interested in "the split hoof," which "obviously is the sign of evenly balanced justice, of them which chew the cud of the true food of justice, the word, which enters from outside through instruction. And once within it is recalled as if from the stomach of the mind for the musings of reason" (*Protrept* 3.11.76). Barnabas demands that one should not associate with those who are characterized by the following: ingratitude (swine), being parasitical (birds of prey), loving filth (sea creatures), promiscuity (hares). David understood the spiritual force of what the three types of animals stand for when in Psalm 1:1's three strophes he names three types of evil people to avoid, denoted here by the three categories of fish, swine, and birds.

Discernment is what Origen calls for, yet his own comments are not without inconsistency: the camel illustrates one who meditates and discerns in his mind, but who in actions cannot tell the things of this world from those of the world to come, and such a person is still unclean. Also unclean are those whose lives are virtuous but look down with pride on the humble form of the truth and then depart from it.

Theodoret advises that the divided hoof signifies the discernment of good and contrary actions, so as to live not only for this life but also in the one to come, devoting all one's powers to that end. To be ruminant means to meditate on divine oracles and not just to mouth them. Jerome made use of the distinction in Homily 23 (CCL 78:152) by saying that while the Jew is single-hoofed, the Christian is cloven-hoofed because the latter takes the two testaments to ruminate on. Hesychius notes that camels are referred to in Isaiah 21:6 and so too here as there signify Jewish conversion. Such a beast is also a figure of the letter of the law whose heavy yoke the Jews carried. The camel is half clean, hence on the way to conversion: accordingly the scribes and Pharisees ruminated but they did not "divide" since they could not discern the spirit of the text. While Origen thought of "ruminate" as the ability to discern in one's mind, Hesychius has the cloven hoof as standing for discernment in mind and action, something "the Pharisees" lacked (Tampellini 2003, 813). In the Coptic world, in Rufus of Shotep's Homilies (c. 600), the camel actually stands for the OT law, which, while spiritual (Rom 7:14), "does not split the hoof so that those who adhere to it may adhere to it without discernment." OT law requires a NT spirit to make distinctions and explain its true meaning (Lienhard 2003, 1026).

In the 1188 pilgrimage book of St. Fiacre, the saint is seen as one who ruminated on Scripture in the way of a clean animal and used his discretion to break down the material (Dubois 1995, 292.) A generation before this, Ralph was especially interested in those who are signified by animals who chew the cud but do not have a cloven hoof. These are those who have the heavenly teaching in their minds but do nothing with it, as with those in the Parable of the Sower in Matthew 13. There seems a concern with Waldensian-style "paupers" who simulate a form of unvirtuous poverty and who do not ask God for eternal delights. Such people are like weasels (*mustelae*) (v. 29) or chameleons (i.e., those who flatter all sides when they lack power, like Absalom). Similarly, Rupert of Deutz writes that the story of Peter in Acts 10 tells Christians to be spiritual in their interpretation and so "to have a cloven hoof and to ruminate is to have the understanding of the Holy Trinity and diligently to draw on the memory of the Trinity with word and deed, and to guard especially against dividing the Trinity." Rupert reminds us that we know that all evil comes from within and moves outwards (Matt 15:16–20). Yet there is a place for movement in the opposite direction—outward-inwardly working discipline according to a sense of holiness as discipline: the oven is the youth who naturally burns like one and the only remedy is smashing, that is being afflicted with beatings or considerable fasting that they might improve.

Langton points to Zechariah (Matt 1:6) as one who meditated on the law in ruminative fashion. There has been a welcome shift in the meaning of "meditation" from the sense of the Hebrew "to mumble, repeat," to the sense of "digesting the content of what is being said," partly under the influence of the metaphor of rumination on the concept of meditation. The content of one's contemplation is what matters, not that one is a contemplative. It is alarming when some see the divine gift in the lucrative offerings or who become preachers that turn the grace of the good news into money. The camel pretends to be gentle, and even if it sweats on the heat it will pretend friendship. The chewing metaphor expands, in Langton's treatment, beyond the early verses. Hence those insects with long back legs (v. 21) are those who praise temporal things more than eternal, but to eat these is meant in a good sense; that is, foods of this sort are works that are difficult to "chew." Presumably (not certainly) Langton means that part of "digesting the word" is to deal with difficult people in the pastorate.

Lyra seems happy to work with Aristotelian-scholastic virtue ethics. The cloven hoof is a sign of a temperate disposition, for the cleft shows that their flesh is not too humid, and that they are not too earthly and not too dry; for an uncloven hoof is a sign of excessive earthy dryness. Ruminating fiercely is actually a sign of a temperate disposition. Calvin, with a flash of humor, says it is fitting that in this very difficult-to-interpret chapter "dividing the word rightly" is what is signified by a cloven hoof. Of course, there was a literal sense for the Jews in the former times: perhaps the uncloven hooves are wild and the animals non-ruminating feed for the most part on filth and excrement. This seems to go back on his insistence that God meant something more mysterious than health advice. Spangenberg makes sure that to have a divided hoof is to be able to distinguish between Moses and Christ, between the law and the gospel, nature and grace, the letter and the spirit, the fleshly and the spiritual, the earthly and heavenly man. Lapide shares Lyra's point about over-dry meat being unsuitable for human consumption, and that those that ruminate have better flesh. Lapide does not want to spiritualize at first, but then adds that "morally speaking," these are the holy men who have hidden God's word in their hearts. Willet perhaps self-consciously sees in the case of a camel some beast with "encyclopedic" knowledge (not unlike himself!). "The bottom of his foot is fleshy as in Beares, for that in long journeys, *they doe shoe them with soles*, because of the tenderness of his foote . . . Aristotle writeth of a camel, that having covered his damme, that was his by his keeper, having a cloth cast over; which afterward the camel perceiving, did runne upon his keeper, and bit him that he dyed." Further, according to Willet: "Hare is dainty meat and Emperor Alexander Severus ate it every day. It runs faster uphill owing to longer back legs. Hereby may be signified, that a good man, whereas most men in the world goe down the way that leadeth to destruction, he cheerfully climbeth up the way to Heaven . . . Hare hathe a great heart for size of body and [the] Philosopher says the heart is not proportionate and so they fear."

Sea Creatures

Origen admits that this passage does not mention any beasts of the sea which are *clean* but for this we have the parable of Jesus in Matthew 13:47–48, where good and bad fish are sorted out. What is more important is the quality of immaterial nourishment we can give to neighbors in need. In the waters, those who do not have fins are like those who are pressed down by the waters of life to be on the bottom; whereas those with fins can rise up and can be caught for the kingdom. Theodoret thinks that as scales are to the fishes so is the panoply of virtues to humans. And just as fins are to them, so is faith to humans. So says Paul, speaking of the scales of grace and the armor of the spirit (Eph 6:16).

Hesychius comments that the fish that can be eaten are those from the nations who have come through regeneration in the water of baptism. But fish that have scales for skin are they who are stuck in their ignorance of the Word of God and who resist the dagger of the Spirit. They do not have fins and corrupt the waters of baptism and penance. One should keep away from these people (1 Cor 5:11.) The *Glossa Ordinaria* echoes this and adds to it Isidore's comment that hirsute, serious men are here approved: those without are unclean since they have effeminate and oversmooth mores. Only if ignorance is soluble to them they can have sublime cognition and heavenly life. In the *Glossa*, Gregory the Great's moral lesson is repeated: in the fish with fins and scales who leap through the sea are figured the elect souls who alone go into the body of the heavenly church; they do things well on the outside but are still seeking stillness on inside (cf. *Homily* 31; CS 13:255).

According to Ralph of Flaix, fish stand for those unclean thoughts deep in human minds.

Thomas Aquinas (*ST* 1–II, q102, art6, ad1) has something quite different: fins signify the heavenly or contemplative life; while scales signify a life of trials, each of which is required for spiritual cleanness. To have fins is to reckon oneself to be a sinner, which is a good thing and to be admired, as Gregory the Great would say

Engaging Leviticus

(drawing on Origen's association with the Parable of the Net), so that we too might be fish in the Lord's net.

Lyra—going his own way with a more literal sense and appreciation of Jewish perception of the world—comments that Gentiles, when they find such animals in waters and other liquids, repute them as magical, offer them to the gods, and use these concoctions to gain special nocturnal powers. One can tell that when he writes about the reptile being unclean he is not very convinced! Lapide, however, claims that reptiles are so unclean that even to *touch* them is forbidden. Calvin notes that there is less account of fish in detail because the Jews were not all that informed on maritime species. Spangenberg equates things that are in water without fins with those who are baptized but do not have the knowledge of divine things and so corrupt the vocation (ministry), and who are to be avoided. Calov tells us that Luther, commenting on Deuteronomy 14, understood by "fins" the doctrine of the faith which rules and works hearts in this world, and by "scales" the fruit of that faith.

Then Leclerc, on verse 26, reassures us that purity laws do not apply to those who throw back unclean fish caught in net. For Bonar, a test of faith would arise when fishermen were tempted to keep the sea creatures without fins and scales caught in their nets. It was the same principle as that of the forbidden fruit in Genesis 3. This common-sense view continues on verses 32ff: a spring could not be polluted but a cistern of still water could! On verse 34 (*delapsus ex iis humor*) "water" could mean humor or urine; so it is talking about some body fluid coming from a corpse, not just the presence of water. The rabbis, when they stretch "water" to mean "rain," are as bad on the OT as the scholastics are on the NT! He finds it "typical" that superstitious Jews got worried more about washing water than drinking water supplies. It is what comes out of a person that pollutes (Matt 15:11).

Corpses and Carrion

What is apparent is that the Christian exegetes remain true to the negativity of the Mosaic legislator and, at first, even to his intended referent. Adomnan's Penitentials teach that if a human or animal corpse is found in a well it must be emptied and the earth that had been sullied dug out before it is clean (Adomnan 1958, 177). The same goes for an animal found on the shore (Canon 9). Extending the principle that the Lord forbade flesh to be eaten with its blood, Canon 14 asserts that things that have drowned are not to be eaten, for the blood will have coagulated, as is also the case with a stag found dead in a trap. As many commentators have observed, there seems a belief in a mixture of medical and supernatural reasons for direct application. There is a general horror of carrion through their literal association with corpses, and this follows through into what seems like a pre-modern horror of wild birds as tokens of death, imminent or recent. This horror reinforces the rhetorical power of the metaphorical spiritual sense.

Hesychius assimilates rapacious birds to those in 1 Timothy 6:3–4 who lead widows into sin, whereas crows simply are those who have no feelings: Noah's crow went astray, and so did Christ's Judas. The cormorant (*larus*) of verse 17 can live in water and earth, which is a bit like those who want to keep both practices of circumcision and baptism, despite Galatians 5:2. This sharp rejoinder gets repeated in the *Glossa Ordinaria*. Finally Hesychius answers an objection: But one might say, are not some of these birds good? Does not David compare himself to the pelican and night owl, and Moses call God an eagle? Well, prophets call Christ a lion while Peter calls the devil a lion: so, on account of high flight, the eagle is good; but in that he is rapacious, he is not to be associated with. And in any case, talking of David as a night owl is talking about man in state of sin and living at night an as pelican living alone deprived of likeminded folk: this is not something David rejoiced in being!

In the case of the eagle (v. 13), this is the contemplative who from a height looks down on corpses, that is, he is tempted down to temporal things. Ezekiel 17 provides a warning! In similar "penitential" manner Bruno of Segni says, what are owls who have wings but can hardly fly other than religious hypocrites. And to touch a dead thing does not literally mean that but means to knowingly and willingly sin and to fall over it means to do it unknowingly. "Until evening" means until the end and consummation of sin, which is the end of the duration of penance, but also a state of maturity in which sin has at last died down. Peter Comestor provides an ascetic reason (PL 198, 1201): Jews abstain from eating carrion but they will use their suet for fuel. But the food laws were generally just given for reasons of encouraging abstinence.

When one bears in mind that medieval illustrated Bibles were be read by (higher) lay-people, the *Bibles moralisées* "contain an inordinate number of texts concerned with money lending; in the vast majority of these cases, textual references to usurers are accompanied by depictions of Jews" (Lipton 1999, 32). Thus the raven in verses 15–19 or toad in verses 20–31 represents such people. Yet, as Lipton admits, it is significant that also a worldly bishop is depicted alongside the Jew. So Christians are portrayed as doing all these things and with even greater frequency than Jews. Money lending is to be seen as an unchristian activity. There is little of this in the medieval Jewish commentators, who can be seen as not so much subverting the text as reinforcing a framework of a doctrine of good creation: the ornithological fascination of Ibn Ezra displays this. (Nahmanides redresses the balance by reminding his reader these birds are cruel by nature.)

And this concern did seem to rub off on Christians. Aquinas (*ST* I–II, q102, art6, ad1) takes two examples from the world of birds: "The vulture, which follows an army, expecting to feed on the carcasses of the slain, signifies those who like others to die or to fight among themselves that they may gain thereby ... The coot ["*porphyrion*"] ... drinks only when it bites, since it dips all its food in water: it is a figure of a man who will not take advice, and does nothing but what is soaked in the water of his own will." Likewise, Denys the Carthusian is very interested in the medical healing qualities of birds, which indicates he viewed them as having powers for good or ill. The "*charadrion*" is an all-white colored bird, the lower part of whose leg can clear up occluded vision. There is a ritual: if the person is to be healed the bird will look at him as if supporting the cure; but it now becomes unclean as a result. This seems an odd diversion, as if unclean things contain in them antidotes to more serious poisons.

Lapide is keen to get the literal sense right, but in doing so his eye is for the monstrous and the nature of moral uncleanness such represents. He continues: Some, such as Abulensia think griffins existed; other (Pliny and Origen) rightly think not: Moses probably meant to refer to a bird of great strength and rapacity, which contributed to the germination of these tall tales. A huge eagle was found, according to Fabricius, in 1550 in an area between Misniam and Dresden whose nest took up three oak trees; one chick had a wing seven fathoms long with nails the size of a man's finger. The eagle is a symbol of a demon (cf. Augustine on Ps 123:7), while the pelican or Hebrew *qāʾāt* (v. 18) vomits up the meat of the seashells once digested, so that Jews and Christians do well not to eat that bird. Nobody really knows what the *herōdion* (LXX v. 19) is. Augustine (and Lyra following him) thought it was a falcon (in Ps 103:18). To Albert the Great it was the noblest of eagles, deriving the etymology from *heros*, "hero." Actually, retorts Lapide, these birds signify power, arrogance, and the cruelty of carrion. He can think of twenty negative associations, but all of them signify saints mired by worldly motives.

Small Animals, Contagion, and Cleansing

The Theodorian Penitentials specify that if the mouse (v. 29) that had fallen into the soup was dead, then the soup could not be eaten, but if it was alive then, on the sprinkling of holy water, it may be eaten. The point is that in the case of a dead mouse the pollution is double as we have an animal that is *both* unclean *and* dead. It would seem, according to verse 32 and the Penitential, that their pollution tends to spread mostly by contact with their corpses (Firey 2009, 69).

"Hrabanus Maurus used his commentary on Leviticus to turn the pollution taboos against Jews and to proffer prescriptions for purification and correction [with] penitential formulations for correction of spiritual failings. The animals prohibited in the dietary codes become emblems for human vices, many of which Hrabanus ascribed explicitly to Jews. Conversely, clean flesh, for Hrabanus, is the salvific Word that was made flesh in Christ" (Firey 2009, 95). While there is something of this in Rabanus and his main source Hesychius, the Jews are hardly prominent in this rhetoric, except as examples. Those being admonished are over-casual Christians, especially those meant to be following a rule. To speak of Christ's flesh as pure would be a truism and so such christological discourse is hardly central to Rabanus's aims.

A good case of this can be seen in Langton's preaching: while some study "like on all fours" to sin, David with Bathsheba was like someone on whom a corpse fell and was negligent about it. For evil intention can spring upon a good intention and pollute it. The vessel of unclean water stands for the lust for vainglory. The baptized as signified by the water of cleansing (11:40) have less excuse than David or those ignorant. There are three ways of sinning: by suggestion, by delight, and by consent. We teachers should be careful (with allusion to Jas 3:1).

Lapide informs the reader that the Hebrew word *saphan* (as his fellow-Jesuit F. de Ribera has shown) can mean "hidden" and can be applied to several animals, not just a hare. The mouse is forbidden to be eaten, not on the grounds of its greedy manner of eating which ignores God (as is reported in Polycarp's *Letter to the Philippians*), for its grunting is quite natural, but for the symbolism that it has nothing but its food and does not think of higher things (so, Cicero, *De Natura Deorum*, 2). It could also be that the hare symbolizes usury, or is effeminate (cf. Cyril of Alexandria, *Against Julian*, 9).

For Willet, unclean small animals are reprehensible in all sorts of ways. The coney leads him to a historical matter of fairly recent significance. As *shaphan* ("hider") it seeks shelter; and so is prudent and yet also fruitfully reproduces. According to Pliny (*Nat.* 8.39), Majorca was once overthrown by digging of conies. "By them are signified underminers of common-wealths . . . Such were our later underminers of the Parliament house." (Here is a reference to the Gunpowder Plot of 1605.)

Lapide concludes his treatment of the chapter and its theme by insisting that a moral reading of the natural world (note, rather than Leviticus 11, in keeping with Lapide's baroque preference for *realia* over text) leads then to an account of human holiness that means clinging to the sacraments. The reference to washing at sundown alludes to Christ's death, the eve of the age, by which all uncleanness was removed for the new age. When verse 44 tells them to be holy, that means *clean*, as in Deuteronomy 23:14. The people are to represent God's own spiritual holiness in bodily form. Holiness means to abstain from polluted and execrable things (as Bernard, Sermon 22 on the Song of Songs puts it). The Protestant heretics should note that sanctity does mean some amount of abstinence and fasting. That which makes the people of God special is their rites in which they are given over to the worship of the true God. This is the first and greatest foundation of Christian communities.

Jewish scholars were concerned more for movement of corpses (Rashbam quoting *M. Zavim* 5:3); questions of decomposition; practical questions of primary and secondary uncleanness (Rashi on vv. 34–36); the teaching of the Sages on touching unclean things just before going on pilgrimage; an awareness that in everyday life people rarely touched fish or birds or even insects, such that verses 24–28 concerns only unclean mammals (Nahmanides) and water-immersed food being unfit to be offered; and that touching an unclean animal is only a problem when it is dead (Ibn Ezra, against "crazy Karaite people"). Becoming unclean is not a misdeed as such (Schwartz 2003, 229). Such separation was a constant reminder of Israelite-Jewish status: these laws were "vehicles to the higher ethical life" by means of imitation of God (Milgrom 2004, 108), including not over-fishing (ibid., 111). For creation to be good presupposes moral choosing: in that sense Genesis is subject to Torah. Mary Douglas was right to spot symbolism, in that the animal classification (sacrificial animals, clean animals, unclean animals) corresponds to humanity (priests, Israelites, the nations) but she (and Countryman 1988 following her) made a "serious error" to think the opposite of holy was "common." It is impurity that is the opposite of holy. Moreover "pollution" is only a matter when humans ingest rather than it being about some obsession with cultic tidiness, and pigs reflect the underworld not intermarriage (Milgrom 1991, 721ff).

More recently Mary Douglas opined that Leviticus really means that animals are holy and *that* is why so many, especially vulnerable ones, are deemed unclean (i.e., to be left alone). This might encourage one to eat as few as possible, following a humanitarian yet anti-anthropocentric lesson. "Unclean is not a term of psychological horror and disgust" (Douglas 2001, 151), but rather of *protection*. But swarming (with reference to Genesis 1:25) is a positive thing, in conveying the sense of being fertile: *sheqets* means simply "shun!" in the sense of "leave alone!" It is *harming* these creatures, not the creatures themselves, that is unholy. As an account of the Priestly author's intention, Douglas' more recent interpretation can be accused of being too "sentimental" for ancient tastes, if not for modern ones. It packs an ethical message, but the subjective dimension of holiness seems undeveloped.

Leviticus 12

THE UNIQUENESS OF ISRAELITE circumcision was in its timing: at the beginning of life as a rite of covenantal initiation, and not at puberty (as in many cultures) or for the ordination of priests (as in Egypt) (Milgrom 2004, 124). Maimonides (*Guide* III, 49) says that circumcision was performed on the eighth day because if it was done later tougher foreskin flesh and increasing parental affection would cause more pain to the child, and if it was done earlier the baby would be too weak. It all reflects a deep commitment to life and a symbolic need to eliminate waste as representative of death. Few Christians would object to what Milgrom affirms in the following comment: "The forces pitted against each other in the cosmic struggle are . . . the forces of life and death set loose by people themselves through their obedience or defiance of God's commandments." In the medieval Jewish commentators (Ibn Ezra and Nahmanides) there is sensitivity to the ill-feeling that comes with menstruation. "Even her glance breeds danger and seven days must pass after childbirth or menstruation before marital duties are thinkable. Her body will take a longer period to settle or the impure blood be flushed out by the menstrual cycle and the sin offering is 'to atone for anything improper she said.'" Abarbanel, on the other hand, emphasizes the burnt offering as simply an expression of *thanks* for safe childbirth.

The Problem

According to (Ps-) Hippolytus Canon 18, even midwives are to be refused communion until purified, but instead they should stand with the catechumens, for twenty days in the case of delivering a male child, forty if a female (Bradshaw 1987, 20). This means there would have been a need for many midwives and it denotes a negative view of childbirth! Although this interpretation originated in ascetic, encratite circles, as reported by Clement of Alexandria (*Strom.* III.46.5), it finds resonance in Origen's treatment. "Origen does not interpret the woman as an image of Israel, the church, or the soul, as one could expect. She simply is the mother of a newborn child" (Klingbeil 2007, 98). Origen considers the womb to be an unclean place. Jeremiah needed God to purify him (Jer 1:5: "before you came out of the womb I sanctified you"), and even he cursed the day of his birth, as did Job, David, and Jonah. Iniquity, although mysterious in its causes, is real enough and so baptism is needed to remit the sins of infants. Thus every soul has received a human body that was contaminated (as in Origen's Homily in Luke 14:3, where he has resource to his favorite verse, Job 14:4: "Who can bring a clean thing out of an unclean thing?"). It could be that Ambrose transmitted a version of this to Augustine (Beatrice 1978, 215). It is even touched on by Athanasius, who says that the infant has done nothing yet receives filth from the body (233; *Fragmenta in Matt*; PG 27, 1368), while Dionysius of Alexandria in the mid-third century paints a picture of the "impure women" listening to the Psalms from outside the church door (PL 10:1281–84 in Roll 2003, 121).

Leviticus 12 then, was patent of being read in what one might call a "psychical traducianist" interpretation, according to which the sinful soul is contained in the seed. Augustine makes much of this idea, although, as we shall see, not in his interpretation of this text. Augustine is clear that every child is born in original sin (Rom 5:16–12; Ps 50:7). So why is the mother unclean rather than the one who is born? For surely it is the latter who needs to be cleansed from original sin. Typically, Augustine advises that have to be careful how we read: the sacrifice is not offered for her child (*pro filio/filia*) but for *herself* (*pro ea*). She then sits another thirty-three or sixty-six days with her blood purified. So all this is for *her own* purification. Now there is the problem that in the Gospel (Luke 2:27) it is explicitly a purification rite for *him* ("*pro eo*") as part of Christ's undergoing our penance for sin, though he had no sin himself. So it might be right, or at least a happy mistake of "our translators" to have here in Leviticus 12 *pro filio aut pro filia*; for the Greek *eph' can* mean "on someone else's behalf."

In the account by Diodore of Tarsus (Deconinck 1912, 149) the reason for her rest has much more to do with physical weakness and not moral or spiritual reasons. "For marriage is meant for reproduction . . . So that she does not suffer from her pains thus she stays in a state of uncleanness and has her rest." Theodoret likewise resisted the overly allegorizing tendencies of Origen (for whom the eight days symbolized moral self-purification), and held that the stipulation of a period of purification after childbirth had nothing to do with original sin, but with the rest that a new mother required, with twice as long rest (eighty days) needed for the harder work of bearing a girl (Rouwhorst 2000, 186).

Gregory the Great deals with *inter alia* this question: May a menstruating woman (or husband having had sex with her during that period) come to church and take communion? Certainly she should not have sex during this time, since the Bible takes this very seriously ("the holy law would condemn to death"), but she (and presumably the husband as mentioned) should be allowed to come to church—as in the case of the menstruating woman in Gospel—to seek a remedy for illness, just as the food we eat even though being hungry comes from Adam's sin. "For menstruation is not a sin at all for women, because of course it happens naturally. Yet because our nature itself is so corrupted that it appears to have been polluted even without the consent of our will, the corruption comes from sin, and in this way, human nature itself recognizes what it has become because for the judgment on it." So, let the women decide whether they should express their love for the mystery or keep a respectful distance from the sacrament. "If therefore (Matt 15:11, 19; Titus 1:15), no food is impure for him whose mind is pure, why should what a woman with a pure mind suffering from natural causes be brought against her as impurity?" (Gregory 2004, III: 540).

However, Gregory reveals in the following question that he was by no means a liberal in these matters. A man should not enter church after sex if his mind is still on it: he should wash and pause (Lev 15:16 gives the answer here); even the pagan Romans did that. For "the desire in sex is a sin," even though married intercourse might be legal and legitimate. "Yet in doing them we are somewhat defiled." Paul's saying that he allowed it as an indulgence in 1 Corinthians 7:9 implies that it is offensive. It would seem that there is corruption in childbirth but that due penance is done through her labor pains. In other words, while Gregory does not insist that women who have given birth or who are menstruating should be kept away, the sense is not that there is *nothing* wrong with her state in these cases. Also, as Helmholz (2004, 10) notes, the ban on sex in the time after birth concerns any woman spending time suckling her own children, that she should not use this convenient time so that as to seek sexual intercourse without the chance of procreation. In the eighth decade of the twelfth century the lawyer Gratian backed Gregory on the matter of menstruating women: "The excess of nature cannot be counted as a sin, and it is not just to prevent a woman from entering the church because of what she endures against her will" (Gratian, canon 4, dist. 5).

Hesychius, as transmitted in the *Glossa Ordinaria*, comes straight to the point: As for the mother's uncleanness, this is due to the man, as inheritor of Adam, having infected her; for it was *after* he left paradise that he (sexually) knew her and thus propagated the human race. Peter Comestor in his historical approach treats them literally (PL 198, 1205): one sacrifice is to be offered for the mother's own sin, or for the origin of the child in the case of a girl (which circumcision would take care of in the case of a boy; though Augustine says that a offering was made for a boy "just to make sure"). The Jews do not think that infants carry sin, but that is an error, thinks Peter. Yet another, harder line from Augustine could be quite easily found in the widely read *City of God* VI.9. This was preferred by the Synods of Rouen (1074) and Köln (1279), who went so far as to forbid women who had died in childbirth to be buried in the churchyard (Staubli, 1996, 111).

Rupert of Deutz is clear that the chapter teaches the radical nature of original sin. No one is to boast about how clean they are: if we as Gentiles used to be reptiles and unclean serpents, then we give thanks for the change. Job 14 reminds him (as it had Origen) of that seed which the devil corrupted in the garden with his poison. All have sinned and need God's transforming grace. Rupert is able to make the connection of menstruating (even though it would suit Leviticus 15 more) to the passage in Isaiah 64:6 ("our righteousness like menstrual rags"). Those who do not believe have no intention of cleaning themselves up, yet mercifully the remedy is close to hand. This is "moralized" as love for God and on the other hand "compassion to redeem one's neighbor."

Bruno of Segni is aware that some teachers of the church do not think it sinful if the mother goes to church to say thanks to God for the safe childbirth. So the sense has to be an allegorical one: the seven days is the length of time from Moses to Christ, and the synagogue was unclean for that time, even though she did good work symbolized by the son she bore. She only became clean at the end of the seventh day when Christ's blood was poured (foreshadowed by the circumcision) and then the synagogue had to wait for the thirty-third year without whose blood she could not be cleansed. Spiritually speaking she must not so much offer up a lamb as adore the Lamb.

Lyra backs up Augustine's understanding on two counts: to be "in her pure blood" means that she had been partly purified, yet needs thirty-three more days. Indeed during that time she is prohibited from sex for those days but also from holy things. So there were six days of major uncleanness and thirty-three of minor. The sin was in the act of conception, which frequently is disordered. She is offering for the remission of *her own* sin: the Hebrew has "for her." Denys contends that Lyra was wrong to argue that the offering was for *original sin,* since it was clearly for the mother's, not the son's purification. However, her purification was not from sin but a more "physical" one, from some irregularity. The text leaves it open as to which sin the priest is praying for.

Cajetan makes clear that the "seed" in its effect, not in its receipt, is what is meant here and so it refers to the *child*, not to the father's sperm. Both mother *and* child are unclean in sin, a thing that can be removed only from "the elect" through the sacraments: baptism for the child, penance for the mother. Where it says "and she will be clean or cleansed," this is to be understood in a historical-legal sense; we are not given many details about the ceremony, only that the passing of the required period of time was necessary. Cajetan wants to suggest that the mother is offering for her sins, and *not* for some original sin, since only the NT can deal with that. The passage has nothing to do with Mary. In his gloss he is keen to relate the longer penance simply to the fact that, as some say, a girl weakens the mother more, even though the traditional explanation is that sin came first through the feminine. Here there is a hint of humanitarian concern.

Borrhaus is far more specific and graphic: "the old man" (sinful nature) is not impure *per se* (since God made him in his own image, who made all things and approved it, pronouncing them to be good) so neither conception nor birth nor the propagation of the human race (which are divine works) are as such judged to be impure. Yet, as sin corrupted our first parents, so also conception and birth are depraved. So a double impurity can be counted in this propagation, one of bodies, another of minds (*animorum*): that of the bodies through impure blood, that of the minds through foul lust, among which the sacred letters understand all wicked emotions and desires. The problem here is with the impure blood of the mother's body, in which there is all sorts of boiling, fetid blood, just as the prophet knew, who cried: *In peccatis concepit me mater mea* ("my mother conceived me among sins"). A twofold remedy for body and soul is needed and this physical outward purifying here described. A very brief biology lesson is then given. It takes six months for the human to be perfected in the womb and this compares to the six days of the creation. The Hebrew word *tsarat* indicates that the woman takes the place of the earth, that is, she supplies the material, which the virile power of the man forms and shapes into the members of the human body, while the seed of the menstrual flow by way of coagulation at that very time of ensoulment, and embodiment gathers in a ball into itself. Borrhaus then jumps to a theological conclusion: As the impure spring of blood in her who is menstruating, so a vein and pure spring of blood is in him (*eo*) of whom Zechariah spoke above 13:1: *In that day she (illa) will be an open spring for the house of Jacob and for the dwellers of Jerusalem*. This blood of Christ is given a contrasting type in the sinner, (*viz.*, Eve) who is the menstruating one and the one to be saved. Lastly, the passage tells us that both the offering and the prayer of the priest matter, just as Christ's atonement has to be complemented by living faith, which is both "Marian" and "Pauline" in its formation.

Brenz is bold enough to take enough exegetical liberty with Hebrews 13:4 as to turn an imperative into an indicative, and state that the marriage bed *per se* is unpolluted [*impollutus*]. Indeed conception and birth are not sins but are the creation and ordination of God who blessed them to increase and multiply. And even if a baby is conceived in sin, in as much as it is created by God it is a good and holy creature of God. Childbirth can be considered unclean, not spiritually in the sight of God, but civilly because of infirmity in the sight of men. So there is no necessity for observing this rite of childbirth, nor the forty- or eighty-day period, but what is demanded is natural honesty that each person possess his vessel with holiness and honor. For since the Virgin Mary observed the days of childbirth, she did not do this because she had to do it, nor because she wished to present an example to Christians of keeping this instruction, but because Christ wished to be born under the law so that he might redeem those who were under the law.

Pellican is more sober, but not less hopeful. He thinks that verse 1 shows that God cares for not only the soul but the body too. The "uncleanness" of women after birth arises out of the nature of things in the sense that they need to rest, lest their health be endangered or subsequent conception be made more difficult. Sensing those who would despise such a law, Pellican claims that it has much usefulness and should not be condemned, for women are weaker and need to be looked after more than men. This divine law is much neglected, for it offends human civilization but it depends exceedingly on the necessity of nature. So the law is as much about her weakness as any requirement to keep her away from others for their good. Likewise on verse 3 a boy is to be circumcised on the eighth day and not before, for until he is over a week old he would be too young and weak to take such a wound. The prohibition against coming to the holy place (or having sexual relations) is not because of her blameworthiness but because of the holiness of the holy-making things (*sanctificatorum*), lest by nature she pollute externally what the divine election had consecrated in spirit. The realm of grace is not only distinct from that of sin, but also that of nature, containing a (theology of) gift. Indeed, on verse 6, he observes that the gift of seed and posterity is not so much a gift of nature as of divine mercy: a one-year-old lamb for is to be sacrificed for the redemption of child. This means that Christ's death and the virtues of the lamb by imitation and meditation purify the whole of one's life, not because to have given birth is to sin, but because what is born is believed to be harmed with original sin and so all involved need expiation in line with the will of God. It is not that sin has been given birth to, but that what is born is tainted by original sin and needs redemption.

Calvin saw the impurity as simply residing in original sin: the practice and law were reminders of this (*Inst.* II vii 14, 16–17). The impurity lay not in the intercourse but in the generation, which is much more shameful than intercourse; it is the human condition as such which is so disgusting that it infects our mothers. It is only by God's "indulgence" or grace that the marriage bed is free from stain (*pace* Brenz), and the state of children will only be supernaturally removed from that natural stain if there is marriage between believers, because the sanctity of marriage covers what otherwise might be imputed to blame, and purifies the very defilements of our guilty nature. It is interesting that it is not baptism which is mentioned here, but rather marriage which sanctifies children, as if it were almost a sacrament for Calvin, with the New Testament coming to the rescue of the natural order (*Inst.* IV, xix, 35–37, where he is clear it is not a sacrament, notwithstanding!). The sacrifice after birth and the added circumcision are for the sake of the child—for although Moses seems only to speak of the mother, St. Luke, his faithful interpreter (Luke 2:21–24), includes also the infant, which is symbolic of how great and wide-spread corruption is. The woman's time out is ordained so that she and her husband should learn to detest original sin. Male children need less time because a circumcision ceremony deals with some of that corruption.

In later medieval Judaism the literal sense of Leviticus was preserved at least in the purity rules as affecting menstruating women, with only Rashi seeming to question why this is so. There seems to have been some understanding that the medieval synagogue be understood as an *ersatz* temple. A tradition starting with Bachya ben Asher (c. 1300) holds that while there is no primordial sin through the male line, it does come through the female, and daughters are born when, according to Ezra of Gerona, the father climaxes before the mother during intercourse. This is given fuller expression in Ephraim of Luntshits' *Keli yaqar* Torah commentary of 1602 (Cooper 2004, 458) where it is a question of a "wholesale appropriation of Christian anthropology." Women are the more deceived (as suggested by 1 Timothy 2:14).

Mary and Symbolic Meaning (vv. 2–3)

Any such "human interest" is missing in the history of Christian interpretation. Leviticus 12:2 helped Christian interpreters to understand that Mary was not unclean, since she had not conceived from a human seed. However the Mariological content is not disconnected from the virtues the commentators want to see inculcated in believers, or the honor motherhood receives, not least at Candlemas. In that sense, it is hardly significant enough among the commentators to be seen a theme in itself. It is something mentioned in passing. For instance, Rabanus Maurus (*De Inst. Cler.* II.33) writes that the reason for this statute (Lev 12:2) is the festivity that celebrates that the mother of the Lord was purified in his day, not because she needed it, but to show that Jesus had come to fulfill not dissolve the law. She humbly obeyed this law. The feast takes place at the start of February with a theme borrowed from paganism of "light out of the underworld" fitted to Mary's story (cf. Bede *De temporum ratione*, c12; CCL 123B). She obeyed Sirach 3:18 ("As much as you are great, humble yourself"). Rupert of Deutz, whose Song of Songs commentary might lead us to expect lines of Mariological interpretation, merely states that Mary was the sole "exception," before returning to the "rule" that sin came into world by woman, to whom the devil is closer than to man, so that she needs double purification. Even Denys the Carthusian, in speaking of the Virgin Mary, mentions that she offered a dove, proving she was poor, though her parents were rich enough! Moreover, she did not hold on to the gifts the Magi gave her. Lorinus teaches that it is not wrong to think that the mother of Christ was subject to the natural uncleanness that affects even virgins. And if we are to argue that "having received seed" was added in order to exempt her, how much would this have mattered if no one at the time thought she was a virgin? Christ, as Canisius and Alphonsus (Abulensia) remind us, was born in a place fit for shepherds, which was hardly a place of purity. So the phrase should not be referred to his human birth, which, despite the "pseudoevangel" of James was quite ordinary, but to the divine wonder of the mystery of the incarnation, as Bernard and Suarez (d. 1617) suggest. The bathos of the scene in chapter 12 is wholly appropriate to our Lord and his mother in respect of their common humanity.

Purification Ritual and the Practice of Churching (vv. 4–10)

Augustine, on verse 4, is happy to affirm that purified women are allowed to the *sanctuarium*, yet that can only mean the outer court or atrium (as in 6:26). Women were allowed to bring their gifts only that far. That would seem to be, although it is left unclear, an invitation to women in the Christian church to attend services.

It was Gregory the Great, in his letter to Augustine of England, who introduced an apparently liberalizing interpretation of the teaching of the OT here. The thirty-three or sixty-six days of the new mother's quarantine as prescribed in Leviticus "must be understood figuratively. For if she enters a church to offer thanks during the same hour as she gives birth, she is burdened by no weight of sin." He adds that she is punished enough by the pain of childbirth. Although Gregory ruled there was no need for postpartum or menstruating women to be excluded from church,

Theodore of Canterbury (*Penitentials* 17 and 18) did exclude them, following an Antiochene literal reading of the text (Bischoff and Lapidge 1994). So in Irish and Anglo-Saxon Christianity the practice of "churching" arose, by which a woman is excluded from church for a month and then re-admitted on fulfilling a brief purification ceremony. After birth she was to abstain for thirty-three or sixty-six days from church attendance (*Paen. Cummeani* II.31; Bieler 1963, 116). This, after all, was good enough for Mary, the mother of Jesus. She did this to fulfill all righteousness, although she was not sinful herself.

So Gregory's position was not always followed, as the widespread practice of "churching" throughout the medieval church and beyond indicates. Already Bede's position was unclear: if there is penitential action demanded, then it is because of the original sin of disobedience which is "given expression" in the unclean blood, as Bede has it (a view widely published in the *Glossa Ordinaria* on verse 7). It might, he says, be asked where will she be cleaned who has legitimately conceived? Well, "from the flow of her blood"—that is, in her disobedience from where uncleanness and punishment flow, through the meditation and contemplation of the law, the negligence of which brings uncleanness into humanity. There is an "Augustinian" sense that nature provides its own remedies for sin, but the church should observe that by giving her space and time. The Merseburg Penitential of 850 compromises by ruling that she is allowed to visit church to observe (*percipere*) but if she absents herself, she is more to be praised (Browe 2007, 445).

In his *De Institutione Clericorum* II.33 (mentioned already above), Rabanus Maurus—in describing the practice of celebrating Mary's superogatory fulfilling of this law at Candlemas—seems to suggest that the church has mutated the Roman practice of a festival of purification in which candles were carried and congregations from throughout the city came together. Only now this happens in perpetual memory of the kingdom of heaven, like the virgins of the parable, taking care that the light of their virtues would guide them to the heavenly groom. Bruno wanted this passage not to indicate a short period of penance but a life-long practice. The law was not abrogated by Christ, so it has not passed away. But how should the church fulfill this spiritually? This "birth" is when the old mind receives the seed of the Word, resulting in a good will that comes forth in a process of deliberation and action. So the child represents the new man of interior renewal out of the old. The uncleanness does not start with this process but one recognizes how sinful one is since that only happens when righteousness comes close. Penance is to be a life-long task of long "pilgrimage" to the Lord. We stay in the blood of our uncleanness when we do penance. Those who are still stuck in worldly affairs will have to do a double

Engaging Leviticus

time of penance (purgatory). One has to take action now in this life to purge or one will be purged in the hereafter. We must confess on our deathbed; we cannot trust our conscience altogether for remembering our sins: the Lord will judge.

In the Byzantine Christian world too women were kept at the church door where the purification might take place, just as in the West (Franz 1909, 219). The Greek ritual took seriously the need to purify sin and shame yet with added penance only if the child has been stillborn. But in the central European version, the NT "filtering" of this meant the woman was celebrated, as Mary was in Luke 2:22–39. She was put on a throne in the church, wrapped in a white alb and violet stole, and blessed with water while holding a candle. The two currents of distaste and respect ebbed and flowed: the Synod of Rouen (650) viewed the forty days abstinence as her "human" right, as if for her own protection, yet church practice continued to resist burial in church land of a woman who had died in childbirth.

The "churching" ceremony, which allowed a woman back into the church, was modeled in imitation of Mary at Candlemas and was never seen as too Jewish or pessimistic but as a joyous ritual family time and blessing of the vulnerable woman. However, in this the practice there remained traces of the apotropaiac, despite the attempts of early modern religion such as that of English Tudor Protestantism, expressed in the *Book of Common Prayer* (1552), which wanted to call it "the thanksgiving."

Brenz states that although Christians are free from the Mosaic law, they are not free from the natural law. Therefore it will not be useless to consider this chapter on childbearing in the Mosaic polity. Some interpreters explain the difference of forty/eighty days on physical grounds, because it takes a female twice as long to form in womb. Others think Moses is considering the weakness of the childbearers. Brenz does not really know. So although there may be physical reasons for these injunctions we should respect the divine authority even if we do not understand the reasons for the laws: for it is clear that God spoke them to Moses. As for the remedy, why do we need a remedy, given that through Christ no believer is unclean, there is no sin, and the child is not unclean but is part of the good creation? Women are cursed with the pain of childbirth: but this curse was turned round by Christ; and these remedial expiations foreshadow his: one of curse turned into blessings. Women these days, maintains Brenz, no longer need this to confirm their faith but rather they keep the gospel in mind through the two sacraments of Christ. Paul teaches that the task of women is to be saved through childbirth if they remain in love and sanctification and modesty (1 Tim 2:15). It is not to be thought that the generating of children is by itself a cause of salvation, but that it is the ordaining and calling of God in which women can and ought to exercise true piety and divine worship and pursue true salvation, which includes their marriage and household duties!

Pellican offers an account which is humanist in more ways that one: the offering mentioned in verse 7 is made by the priest not for sin, but for the recovering of bodily and psychological health on behalf of the children begotten, for the gift of prudence for the education and protection of the offspring since it is increasingly dangerous for little ones, so that without the special grace of God and the safekeeping of angels they would not manage to make it to an age they would be able to look out for themselves. Hence not only the private prayers of parents and nurses are needed, but even public and solemn ones. Also, if the fetus is commended before birth then we will not have to worry about danger in birth and the impossibility of baptism (i.e., if still-born), since God cannot deny the prayers of the faithful offered for the glory of God and the salvation of souls. Here there is a humanist "whole of life" interpretation.

The Council of Trent's similarly "positive" emphasis was ignored in the taboo-ridden piety of much early modern spirituality. Pope Martin V (d. 1431) had already condemned the Augustinian Nicolas Serrarius of Tournai when he opined: "women have no need of this blessing, because it is a Jewish custom." Likewise Counter-Reformation Catholics upheld the practice against the "Judaizing" taunts of Reformation. It was in imitation of Mary. It was also a joyous ritual family time and blessing of the vulnerable woman; candles refer to Eucharistic piety. A more "enlightened" view was expressed in Lorinus, who explains that, having dealt with external uncleanness in Leviticus 11, the law now turns to internal. This is why chapter 12 is much more readily applicable to Christians and to Jews who live since the loss of the temple and its rites. The upshot is that internal purification is something to celebrate in a public manner. Yet for all this emphasis on joy, the more negative interpretation did not give up easily.

There is, in fact, a mixed account in the Roman ritual from 1614. It presents the mother as clothed in white with freedom to ask for blessing, although she must kneel and Psalm 24:3-5 ("who may ascend the hill of the Lord?") is spoken. That Catholic Roman rite of 1614 tried to shift the balance a little away from purification and on to thanksgiving in the process of "churching," yet in many places, in fact in most of Catholic Europe (Roll 2003b, 130-35), the action was often experienced as and intended to be demeaning.

Lapide comments on the rite that is found in the Roman ritual published by order of Pope Paul V (1606). After childbirth a woman goes to the church and is met at the door by a priest. He prays over her and sprinkles her with holy water.

Then holding the hem of the priest's stole, she goes up to the altar, genuflects before it, and offers thanks to God for the benefits she has received. In the Latin church, however, this blessing of the woman after childbirth is not obligatory and there is no sin involved if it is omitted, although to omit it out of contempt would be a sin, as P. M. Quartus warns in his work *de Benedictionibus* (1659, tit. 3, sect. 12, diff. 1). But others remarked wisely that some, surely, of the ceremonial rites of the old law of Moses could be observed under the new law so long as they were not done as obligations of the old law, which was abrogated, but merely as customs, or lawful traditions, or as a new precept issued by one enjoying the recognized and competent authority to make laws and to enforce them (as Vasquez observes; vol. 3, in the 3rd part of the *Summa*, disp. 210, quest. 80, art. 7). It was decided that there was no real ground for surprise that the observance of a period after childbirth should be simply a *counsel* for Latin women, but *obligatory law* for the Greeks.

Calmet tells us the state of play in French churches of the eighteenth century: a new mother must serve one week of impurity, then a second week of purity before being received back to communion. She is offering for the shame that accompanies the concupiscence that goes with conception. But how would women in Palestine be ready to travel to the temple so as to make that offering on the fortieth day? Maybe the rule was only observed by those near the temple. But common sense is reflected in 1 Samuel 1 where it was the *husband*, Elkanah, who made the offering.

An official statement came in Benedict XIV's *Ex quo* (On the *Euchologion*) of 1756:

> Then to our purpose he [Leo Allatius, d. 1669] concludes that it cannot be absolutely asserted that that man judaizes who does something in the Church which corresponds to the ceremonies of the old Law. "If a man should perform acts for a different end and purpose (even with the intention of worship and as religious ceremonies), not in the spirit of that Law nor on the basis of it, but either from personal decision, from human custom, or on the instruction of the Church, he would not sin, nor could he be said to judaize. So when a man does something in the Church which resembles the ceremonies of the old Law, he must not always be said to judaize." Hence: Still if they want to stay away for some time out of a feeling of reverence, We do not believe that their devotion should be condemned.

All of the post-Reformation Protestant commentators were agreed that these rites should *not* be literally observed in the church. Grotius saw the reasons to be sanitary, for a desert culture very different from his. Grotius observed that the seclusion of the postpartum woman is known in other cultures from the Greeks, as in Chrysippus and Euripides' *Iphigenia in Tauris*. Leclerc develops this with an anthropological interpretation, again inculcating reverence this way for the sanctuary. Rules of external purity cannot only be for health reasons for God does not care about bodies, only the vices of the mind. Mental purity is what profits humanity and pleases God. However the illiterate can learn from these actions.

Bonar, representing an Augustinian Reformed position, considers the woman to be made unclean by the birth of a child. Why is this? "Because the child is born a sinner, an heir of hell." His near-contemporary Bertholet admits that this passage shows that the Israelite view of nature was hardly exclusively optimistic, but then so are cultures from the Greeks to the Cree similar in periods of enforced separation. Here we see an anthropological interest in the interpretation. And it was not just the Cree. In the twentieth century, the folksy light festival in Germany would be joined to a Nazi motherhood cult, resulting in almost an ordination ("Priesterweihe der Mütter"), which, Staubli (1996, 90) assures us, was actually experienced as demeaning (cf. Ruether, 1985).

Leviticus 13

Literal or Physical Leprosy

WHILE MEDIEVAL *LEPRA* SEEMS to have been a form of elephantiasis, it is hard to be sure what *biblical* leprosy was. From Leviticus 13–14 it seems a strange condition that affected clothes and houses too. It is a condition of half-death (Num 12:12) where one mourns for oneself by ripping clothes, etc. From Miriam's example the rabbis concluded it was the sin of defamation (*b. Bar.* 16b), or some moral poisoning that grace has brought to the surface (Maimonides, *Guide* III, 47; see Krochmalnik 2003, 31). Already in antiquity the idea that Jews sprang from a leper colony (on one interpretation of Exod 9:9) was prevalent (Josephus, *Contra Apionem* I, 262; cf. Hartwich 1997).

The association of the Hebrew *keret* through an Arabic cognate with "stricken, prostrated" is to be rejected. Rather it denotes the epidermical symptoms of some disease (Sawyer 1976, who mentions the World Health Organization's having just banned the term for being too pejorative to be medically useful). Whatever these chapters concern then, it is not modern, Western, Hansen's disease (*elephantiasis graecorum*), which is not particularly contagious. Yet what connects the two is a revolting physical appearance, which might have been deemed sufficient grounds for shunning in ancient and more recent times.

When one considers the treatment of lepers in Christian circles, one of first leper houses was founded by Abbot Lanfranc at Harbledown in 1080s (Cowdrey 2003, 109), but already in Ireland before the middle of the tenth century there were leper houses. Henry II, trying to atone for his murder of Thomas Becket, offered relief to lepers, and the shrine to Becket at Canterbury would offer cures. There is a mixture of reverence and disgust throughout the High Middle Ages. "But whereas theologians invariably regarded plague as a collective retribution, *lepra* almost always ranked as an individual punishment, incurred, like madness, because personal misdeeds." Such a one was King Robert the Bruce in the Chronicle of Lanercost, completed in 1346 (Rawcliffe 2006, 53, 64). Baldwin IV of Jerusalem (d. 1185) was much admired by Saladin for holding on to power despite repeated bouts of this infirmity. Cresseid, the eponymous heroine of Robert Henryson's Scots work *The Testament of Cresseid* (c. 1490), does indeed illustrate the connection that many made between sexual promiscuity and leprosy, but the emphasis lies on her noble embracing of her penance. In England the writ of *De leproso amovendo* demanded, from 1100 onwards, separation along Levitical lines, when disfigurement made the disease clear. Despite medieval medical authors identifying leprosy with Greek *elephantiasis* and giving it the same title in Latin, "their insight was not shared by the Church" (Richardson 1977, 10). It continued to be seen as a biblical plague and highly infectious.

However, in the preaching to lepers by Jacques de Vitry (c. 1230), Gilbert of Tournai (c. 1260), and Humbert of Romains (c. 1270) there is hardly a mention of Leviticus. This is perhaps to be welcomed: less time was spent on categorization and more time was spent on offering consolation through, for instance, the mention of the saintly leper Lazarus in paradise (Luke 16:25) and Christ as the one accounted a leper (Isa 53:4). The fusion of the two Lazaruses in the Gospels—the poor man from the parable in Luke 16 and the friend of Jesus that Jesus raised from the dead (John 11)—produced a "composite Lazarus, who became one of the most widely venerated saints" (Demaitre 2007, 80f). Presented positively, becoming a leper could be even seen as a vocation, discipline, and occasion for conversion; lepers were even considered blessed to be with the disease (Bériou-Touati 1991, 13). The approach of Francis of Assisi in embracing a leper at Gubbio at the moment of his conversion (*Life of Francis*, 4) inspired the early Franciscans to encourage an "order of lepers." All these things were positive. This constructive view was given official sanction by the papal instruction of Innocent II in 1131 that those sick with leprosy should live together and sustain hope of the eternal prize by a community that could help them endure opprobrium and loss of familial love.

Ivan Illich (1987) gives a powerful account of this: "The hospitalization of compassion also gave a new personal status to those marked by deformity... Most came to the hospital to die. By rule, the beds of the sick were oriented towards the altar in the center of each ward. This altar was surmounted by a cross. By mid-century, the naked body of Christ was nailed to it. And for these centuries, Christ's body is the central icon of the body in pain."

By end of the fifteenth century, fear of infection became the dominant reason for separation (Rawcliffe 2006, 36, 58) and by then lepers had lost their former appeal as holy innocents. Ironically, it would seem that medicalization progressively removed the air of sanctity. "The first medical representation at a judgment for leprosy appears to have been recorded at Siena in 1250" (Rawcliffe 2006, 37). Marsilius of Padua in *Defensor Pacis* cited Jerome, that the priests have the right and duty to discern the sickness, but Marsilius questions this as "ultra vires," arguing that the priest may *enforce* the judgment, but the judgment should be made by one trained in medicine. Yet the lines between the physical leper and the spiritual leper grew quite fuzzy. Krochmalnik (2003, 27, relying on Bériac 1988, 88) claims that Masses for the dead were said for living lepers. Much more in France than in England was the leper associated with the heretic—wandering and uncontrolled. There was a massacre of them in 1321 in southern France.

A Levitical connection is made when the cause of being born leprous is declared as coitus during menstruation, as in Robert of Flamborough, *Liber poenientialis* (c. 1210), or at least a child's predisposition to leprosy through menstrual coitus. Gluttony and fornication are also mentioned as possible causes (Rawcliffe 2006, 182). Demaitre (2007, 97) draws attention to the three grades of leprosy in the late Middle Ages: touched, infected, contaminated. The Parisian master Jean de Bierville in 1411 found three physicians who pronounced him safe after being accused of the disease before ecclesiastical authorities. Just as important was the priest's being able to "cleanse" (Lev 13:15), which, for legal purposes, in Köln and Ieper as late as the 1570s could make the difference between practicing a trade (if clean) or, if "touched" (*tactus*), being allowed only to beg in public places.

The *Decretals* of Gregory IX (xv) had allowed for leprosy of a partner as grounds for dissolution of a marriage. In the 1540s Bucer likewise allows for divorce in cases where one partner is leprous beyond hope, since that is a case where God by not healing them has shown his will that they separate (Bucer 2004, 360-64). In this he is aware that he is out of step with the Catholic position. Those who want such people to still be legally married are "Pharisees" who do not understand that the Lord on occasion bent the rules (1 Sam 21:7 and Matt 12:1-8).

Borrhaus explains in his commentary that leprosy comes from vitiated blood, and the appearance of whiteness (v. 4) is explained as coming from a cold humor or bile. Such leprosy does seem curable and does not have those marks of incurable leprosy: for there is no mention of hoarseness, baldness, varicose veins, sweat, blood thickening, or sleep problems. And this diagnosis is backed up by verse 6's "only an eruption" (*quia scabies est*), i.e., it is not leprosy! Pellican was rather skeptical about getting medical knowledge out of Leviticus. On medical things we are better going to Pliny the Elder's "De psorosis" in his natural history, he thinks: God made him and his science! He wonders why the priests did not take blood, or sample urine as our medics would do. Although that method was not especially reliable either, he muses, and can vary with the person, size, diet, time of sampling. So maybe the divine law was quite right to avoid and just stick with colors of skin. He observes that in verse 13 the name "leprosy" gets used for more than leprosy (e.g., for scabs of all sorts), although such a person, however, would not be actually adjudged and called a "leper" on inspection. Sticking with the literal sense, he advocates stoicism in the face of disease. For the literal sense of verse 45 teaches the manners to have and also charity when it orders that the excluded leper is not to despair and think he is abominated, yet to hold himself back from mixing with his citizens lest he infect them fatally. He is to realize that this is the Lord's will, not merely human impatience; the Lord ordains the good in the good and all things to his glory and one should accept one's lot!

Willet is less liberal. "When there breaketh out a sore but in some parts . . . it is an evil sign, because thereby is signified the weakness of the expelling facultie: but when the humours are expelled over all the body, it argueth the strength of nature, as Valesius well observeth." Having established that the sores were watery rather than bloody and hence not what Job had, he contends, tempering Bucer's liberalism, that there could be a repudiation of conjugal rights (*quoad thorum*) in the case of contagious diseases, and perhaps separate rooms, but no rejection concerning practical support (*quoad subsidium*) in a marriage, and hence no divorce. Christian law is to insist on marital duty towards a leprous wife, although an intermission while contagious is permissible on moral grounds: "2: These contagious diseases are for the most part caused by lascivious and wanton living . . . wherein there is a breach of wedlock . . . and to force this [conjugal] duty offends against charity." So Willett does allow an argument of separation on the grounds that cases of "leprosy" might be considered as sexually transmitted. Jesus' host Simon the leper had been a leper, and he had been long enough excluded so that he was given that epithet, but "obviously" was one no longer when Jesus met him in his private house (Matt 26:6).

Peter Comestor had mentioned that Josephus is right to laugh at those who said a leprous Moses came to Canaan with a bunch of leprous rejects looking for mercy. Willet, also following Josephus' *Contra Apionem*, observes that it is unlikely that if Moses had been unclean he would have made a law about his own shame. Lapide was convinced that leprosy was no common disease but rather was sent by God like a plague upon the Jews for their various graver sins—i.e., simony, blasphemy, murder, and rebellion. It was a different disease from our elephantiasis. Abulensia thinks our form of leprosy is just a more corrosive form of the biblical one, but no, the "Jewish" [i.e., biblical] leprosy touched skin only, while our leprosy affects flesh and bone; and the Jewish one affected clothes and walls and houses. While ours is incurable, theirs was curable. And as Augustine (*Questiones in Evangelium* q.40) noted, it was more a vice of discoloration than ill-health, and that is why the lepers were declared "clean" by Christ rather than "healed." With reference to the famous contemporary medic Franciscus Valesius, Lapide concludes that leprosy was not one sickness, and it was extended by the Jews analogically to vices of clothes and houses; and that happens because the disease is in the air, as verse 45 about covering mouths suggests, and it can affect inanimate things just as much. He recounts the story of the holy leper Abbas in the desert when they brought him money after sixty years and he refused it, saying that God had looked after him well enough thitherto. This idea was taken on by mendicants who received bread that made them feel better in health, as those who gave were inspired by God and angels to give, as St. Francis reported.

Lapide's understanding of it as a plague, a thing common to certain communities, is paralleled by an example in early modern times: Gustavus II of Sweden's 1610 patent for Sjählö leper hospital, Finland, was granted "because we have formed the impression that the infectious plague and disease of leprosy, which is a divine punishment for sin, is spreading and becoming common in Finland" (Richard 1977, 149). A decade later Grotius in his *Adnotationes* on Leviticus 13 would distinguish flowing superficial leprosy as better than quiescent chronic kind: "still waters run deep." This notion goes back to "rabbinical" sources and can also be found in commentators such as Willet and Calmet who, in his *Dissertation on Leprosy* (1720, 587), reports that early moderns like Beza thought it a "mere" deformity like elephantiasis (as in Matthew 8) and not a disease. The Hebrew word is a lot wider than "*lepra*" of the Greek physicians. Willet had noted that the key was the "erupt" connoted by the word *tsara'at*. It was spread to Europe by returning crusaders.

As late as Bishop Patrick in the early 1700s there were some who were sure it was a providentially sent plague. Even the pagan Pliny (*Nat.* 26.1) mentioned several new diseases, such as scurvy, affecting the Netherlands, which he saw as sent by God's displeasure. True, he admits, (echoing Andrew of St. Victor; Smalley 1968, 80, n.152), we do not see leprosy infecting clothing these days.

Already Calmet can report that microscopes have shown that little round discs like tiny white worms are to blame, along with the insects that spread it. In any case, it has nothing to do with melancholy or thick blood. But it was just what Job had! (Willett had thought otherwise.) This was all the more reason to quarantine the outbreak even if it ended up not being a case of leprosy, as Calmet adds in his commentary (on verse 10). The skin turning white is not a sign of healing but of full leprosy, a conclusion which Exodus 4:6 reinforces. On verse 35, the grieving leper is like Mephibosheth in mourning (2 Sam 19:24), with the upper lip covered, for only the exterior signs warn people off from the threat. With moldy Turkish carpets "today" sometimes all that can be done is to burn the whole thing!

Voltaire ridiculed Calmet's science. Leprosy's prevalence in biblical times was due to the nitrous bitumen pits in the desert. Calmet's theory that it was tiny worms burrowing subcutaneously was false. Astruc has shown that this type of leprosy is not from "*la verole*," which is peculiar to South America and was not what Job suffered from, as Calmet thought. And the example from Juvenal that Calmet appeals to concerns some bruises gained from sodomy, so Calmet should be careful with his comparisons.

The leprosy bacillus was discovered by G. A. Hansen in 1873. In a matter of fact way Knobel reports two types among Arabs—Bohak and Barras (dark and white types). In Basra and Damascus "today," he observes, one can see quarters for lepers; most Eastern civilizations fear them.

Spiritual Leprosy

Jewish commentary from Sifra to Nahmanides spend much time discussing symptoms (e.g., on verse 29, the "affection" (*ng*') requires hair to have fallen out, or the difference between superficial and subcutaneous affection). It is part of taking the Torah at its word in making sense of it. Christian commentary is very quick to attend to what such manifestations *represent*, and to speak of leprosy *also* metaphorically, possibly in the light of the plain metaphorical sense ("Away! Unclean!": Lam 4:15), given its role in penitential rites. The difficulty of specifying just what is going on in any detail means that most commentators, when applying the text's regulations of the disease to spiritual pathology, use selected details which fit their interpretation, rather than trying to give an account of discrete sections of the chapter. Even if the Christian view does not specify the particular sin of which leprosy is the result, unlike the Jewish discussion of Miriam and defamation (cf. Maimonides, *Guide* III, 47), there was agreement that the disease was an expression of sin—rare in the Jewish interpreters.

Philo (*Quod Deus sit immutabilis* 122–30) had already explained the person who had fully recovered from leprosy (vv. 12–13) as one who had committed *involuntary* sins, whereas the one whose leprous impurity remained was one who had *intentionally* sinned in his conscience. The moral conscience acts to witness to sins (Philo on verse 34). Clement of Alexandria picked this up, while supplementing it with the remedy as provided by Christ's cross, the *xulon kedrinon* of Leviticus 14:4.

Justin Martyr (*Dial.* 41.1 FC 6:209) had already stated that the sacrifice of flour for leper's purification (14:10) is the type of the bread offered in memory of Christ's suffering in order to cleanse all souls.

Origen is less interested in the relationship between sin and sickness than in giving a clue, through symbolism, to an anatomy of spiritual disease. According to Origen there are six types of spiritual plague, which can be taken as three pairs of types—each pair composed of disease that is curable (in this life) and incurable (in this life, though curable in the age to come). Isaiah 1:6 reminds us that superficial ointment treatment will not work and Jeremiah in a number of places teaches that painful scarring can be healthy, in God's way of cleansing, even when one is left weak and humbled. Bright coloring symbolizes those whose sense is oppressed and who therefore act against reason. The third type is where there is an ulcer from which a white scar and redness results: this shows impurity in the soul with the bubbling up of impure desires and unclean thoughts. Even if cured through the grace of faith and remission of sins, there remains a scar as some evidence of this. There is a fourth type, a burning, which comes from a lust for human glory and arises when someone goes back to their old ways immediately after being healed. The fifth affects the head and occurs when someone does not have Christ as head, such as Epicurus who was ruled by pleasure, or it affects the beard, showing a spiritual sickness even in the supposedly mature. Sixthly there is a baldness that is not unclean, as such, rejecting things that are by nature dead but prone to having new growth and uncleanness.

Theodoret thinks that the law dealing with leprosy reveals the sickness of the soul through the bodily sufferings, and through the involuntary sin the deliberate is condemned. If it seems that physical things can be impure, how much more the intentional things? A variety of types of leprosy is recounted, corresponding to a diversity of sins. The origin of the leprosy is of interest, since there is a start of sin. Just as the priest judges leprosy, so there is a requirement for a judge for the soul's sins. Leprosy has a variety of shades. But it is the evil indwelling the soul that makes it leprous. The law was a shadow, training the Jews through material things. Theodoret notes that through another prophet (Mal 2:15) God made it clear that nothing is unclean in itself except for a bad conscience. For it is necessary to look to see whether the things are unclean by nature, then how to fight them by nature. Leprosy is the fruit of uncleanness, but Moses encourages the hearer to rule over inordinate desire.

The ulcer which formed then healed is sin cured by penance, just as the scar manifests passion, writes Hesychius on Leviticus 13:18. Just how strict penance should be depends on the sin, so there are a number of ways of penance just as there were different offerings in Leviticus. The idea was to humble the flesh and release the spirit from the earthly and sinful. Jüssen (1931, 49) remarks that Hesychius was thinking of a monastic context for strict ascetic discipline in which one's whole life was a whole offering. Becoming a monk was one way of doing penance (Poschmann 1928). However, in Hesychius it is more a case of the lay people imitating the monks who lead; for the former it is much better to have a short period of penance. Moses and Aaron are both mentioned in chapter 13, because Moses had the spiritual sense, which we need to find by contemplation, while Aaron accommodated it to the carnal mind of the people. Full-time monks and lay people are in this together.

It might seem that since leprosy is involuntary the person has already received punishment and he who ought to deserve mercy from the law is further punished by this tough discipline; when he deserved help for his weakness he did not receive this and was subjected to trouble. Weakness would never have overcome him if he has been able to resist it. But that is the point: what could such have done not to fall sick? One can sense a pastoral compassion in the logic. Was Job able to avoid it? True, even he had sin deep down, for all humans have descended into sin. When the color turns white (v. 17), this positive event is viewed as the Gentiles coming to find the Scriptures lucid. Hesychius imagines Pilate as one whom Christ—the High Priest—sees to bear the scar of past sin, yet who will not persevere in healing, whereas Paul, who came from the Jews, had his scar of former sin subside. There is not a thoroughgoing attack on Jews here, even if an occasional dig at their continued literalist reading habits.

"Corporeality was a surprising thing in the hands of Carolingian exegetes, largely because of their ability to merge or elide the spiritual and the carnal" (Firey 2009, 91). What this means is that the Jews' unbelief was regarded as somehow contagious, like leprosy. The *Gloss* abbreviates Hesychius on the point: the Jewish people, as transgressors of the Law, could be counted guilty of spiritual leprosy in a way that the Gentiles, who also transgressed it, were not counted. Why? Because the Gentiles were not subject to the Law. Hesychius takes leprosy to signify transgression of the Law. The true leper is anyone who sins on the second warning, after an interval has elapsed, in other words, once the Law has been laid down. One can see the rhythm of Leviticus 13 here: inspection–interval–inspection.

Rupert, writing in a monastic context, is clear that leprosy is an image that denotes heresy. The priest's job today will be cheerfully to catechize the person in all the Scriptures of the catholic truth and to present him now well confirmed to the mother church, saying it was not "leprosy," only "scabies" (v. 6)—that is, not intentional sin but ignorance—and he will receive this spirit of reconciliation. To wash away leprosy means a brother is to be named and shamed as a fornicator. The means for curing the physical disease in the OT are harsher than in the case of the treatment of adulterers in Rupert's time, he comments. He implies that many a brother is getting off quite lightly.

For Grosseteste the Levitical theology is used to help interpret the Vulgate of Isaiah 53:4 (*Et nos putavimus eum quasi leprosum*)—"that is by unclean sin," as another translation (Symmachus?) has it: for leprosy is reckoned to be uncleanness in the Law. Christ was considered like a leper, since leprosy is an infectious uncleanness and he was thought to be infecting others (II. vi. 6; p. 97). Denys argues that it is wrong for any commentator whether Jewish or Christian to say this law was harsh and man-made for not having compassion on sick people. No, there were good reasons for these commands. Lyra had a tendency to dwell on it as a disease of clothing and not the whole person, and even wanted to emend the text as an addition where it says (13:55) "and it shall be burned in fire whether on the surface of clothing *or throughout (vel per totum)*." Denys accuses Lyra of ignoring Jerome's advice to translators and being too caught up in individual words, such as when he wants to translate "windows" (v. 41f) as belonging to houses, whereas Rabbi Paul carefully shows it is an anatomical term.

In the Reformation times it was observed that priests could not "effect" any healing or make unclean but only pronounce what was the case *already*. Using the Geneva Bible, the Reformer John Knox writes against those who think priests have the power to heal. "The adversarie: The like phrase of speache have we in Leviticus 13:13—'If the Priest see that the scab is growne abrode in the skinne, the Priest shall make him uncleane.'" (Knox's opponent might have been following a translation under the influence of the LXX; cf. the Wyclif Bible: "herfor the preest schal defoule hym.") Knox replies: "How shal the Priest make him uncleane who is alredye uncleane, and whose flesh he durst not touche but by declaring him to be uncleane? The Priests are commanded to pronounce according to the signes which thy see" (John Knox, *Works V: On Predestination*, 381).

For Willet, "Caietanes opinion cannot stand: that the discerning of the leprosie belonged to the priest as he took charge and care of the people." Tostatus [Abulensia] is also wrong to limit it to the High Priest only. In fact, the priests are not doctors but were functioning merely in the context of admission to the sanctuary. As Oleaster (d. 1563) says, there is no need for priest to be a physician, since the symptoms are all observable to the eye. The question is: has it deepened and spread? Today, the ministry is called not to confession and absolution, but to a "spiritual discerning of the inward diseases of the soule, and a separating of the precious from the vile, as the Founder separateth the pure metal from the drosse." 1 Corinthians 5 encourages a balance between advocating radical treatment yet without precipitous judgment. Yet the law can only declare sin, not heal it, which belongs to the gospel.

Willet further opposes the "fancy" of Lorinus in distinguishing mortal and venial sins. Nor has he any time for extreme unction. "Where learned they to build the sacraments of the new Testament upon the ceremonies of the old? And if they will borrow from thence their anointing with oyle, why not with blood also, for the leper was anointed with both." It is prayer, not some oil ritual, that works. And the ceremony reminds us to give thanks to God for our health. Lapide was not so sure, for verse 2 instructs that the leper be shown to the discerning priest who was a type of the priests of the new Law, to whom Christ passed on the power of binding and loosing sinners.

Cocceius calls leprosy an infectious, serpent-like disease. God teaches here that a variable person in whom good words are mixed with bad and whose life is unstable does not have a place in the house of God and congregation of saints. Isaiah 53:8 backs this up, for they were right to exclude even the Messiah if they thought him leprous, for they did not have the word of God dwelling in them. Whereas the Gentiles—who did not have the profession of the true God and thus were leprous—nevertheless were judged by God to be pure as though not having sin and were taken to kingdom of heaven. Those who go around wandering with torn clothes, shouting "unclean" (v. 45) clearly signify the Jews excluded from salvation.

The Curable and Incurable

Augustine gives a lot of attention to Leviticus 13 without anywhere saying why. Where, at verse 3 (also vv. 7–8), it says the priest "defiling" him, this really means *pronouncing* "defiled." A sign of leprosy does not necessarily indicate leprosy. The priest will pronounce the person free from the suspicion of leprosy. The washing is for the reason of something being wrong even if proven not to be leprosy. The idea is that, if discovered, leprosy was very serious and meant life outside the camp, so that suspicions—marks or blemishes—must be taken seriously, and the washing of the clothes of the one who is cleared of suspicion shows there was something unsound even in that sign. It would seem that the analogy is with the average sinner who can have his sin forgiven and be welcomed back in.

On verse 13, Theodoret observes that this law is full of humanity. Just as a vessel that has touched a corpse is unclean but if it has touched a spring or lake is not, so too the many-colored one be kept from the others, as having hope of purification. When he becomes all-white he is allowed to mix with the others so that he is not cut off from other people for the whole of his life. This is a type for spiritual matters.

Engaging Leviticus

The Law orders that there is to be no eating with sinning believers. But it does not forbid dining with unbelievers (cf. 1 Cor 10:27; 5:9–11). This is like what the leper is to an extent, since the one who is an unbeliever has lost all natural color. With such a one we are to converse and spend time with: but not the others. He has called pure that which has become white completely as unsound in body, but no longer legally contaminating those who approach.

Ralph comments that the priest goes out of the camp to find and inspect those who are being cured from leprosy—those to be marked as people who rejoice in the company of the good—and this happens when one is feed from desires and overcomes the world. This cannot be done in their own strength but in believing that Jesus is the Son of God (1 John 5). The field of the mind is to be purged of wicked emotions so that with a serene and peaceful conscience we can find sweet rest in our inward parts. This is a state of rest, *apatheia*, where no one can anger or distress you. In this tabernacle of conscience there is tranquility of the spirit and rest from works and external cares. There are six days for activity, but the seventh is for contemplation. In line with the two-step cleansing of the curable leper, the first makes a person holy, but the second makes him perfect.

Rupert sees the penitent Christian like the one who is being cured in Leviticus 13: he will shave his body of all superstitions but also be washed: that is, informed by sacred doctrine. He needs to remain outside the tabernacle for seven days in case he would mingle again with other heretics, and he will be watched to see if he is mature. And for the heretic it is not enough to confess the Trinity unless there is also love for God and neighbor flowing through him (Matt 25). There is an emphasis on taking teaching from the two testaments as the way to be purified.

Rupert's vision is a lot more negative and does not expect much healing and reconciliation of heretics. The leper rips his clothing like the heretic does the clothing of Christ, which even the Roman soldiers did not wish to do. He is to go around saying that he is contaminated. Thus making bestial noises the heretic deafens the hearing of others even when he thinks he whispers. And in his cell, when he slanders God his king, a bird of heaven hears him and announces it (Eccl 10: 20) and there is fear in the house of God. He who while he lives is not amended by the spirit of reconciliation will spend eternity alone outside the camp, alone even while among a host of the lost. Linen means the subtle eloquence of Plato or other philosophers who were dead to God. Their clothes are to be burned, that is, the writings of those who are unrepentant heretics. Burning the garment (v. 52) is to destroy it, not in any sense to offer it up to God. There is an interesting observation about one who continued to be controversial in this period, namely Origen. If the place of the leprosy was quite obscure (v. 34), say restricted to one chapter, and there are many useful things in the whole volume, that bit can be removed and the rest kept, as some have tried with Origen's works. But if other parts appear now appear leprous, then it is better to burn to protect the simple at expense of robbing the wiser.

Hugh of St. Cher uses the text to inform the ritual for excommunication. Who is the equivalent of "Aaron the priest" (v. 2)? Well, the sinner should not be taken to the archdeacon—who cannot bind or loose—but only to the archbishop or priest. The binding and loosing is of two sorts: jurisdictional and ordinary. The archdeacon has power in the first, but not in second sense, and cannot judge alone. So the message is that no one ought to be expelled from the church without due process.

The waiting is for seven days (v. 6), which Rashi took to mean that sex was not allowed until the eighth day on which purification was complete. However, this cleanness did not, as such, qualify them spiritually for the temple area, claims Lyra. Oil means "divine grace or mercy" by which the leper could be miraculously healed. (However, this time he does not mention the force of nature as an alternative to miracle.)

Borrhaus counsels that not all things that look strange are pernicious. And the Apostle [Paul] tells us to bear with each other. There are some vices to be tolerated in the church of the saints, where the body of sin has the custom of rebelling against the spirit, so long as the rebellion is not being consented to, or a vice that goes no further than "skin-deep," even though it persists. Concupiscence, if restrained within the bounds of the restraining Spirit, is not a capital offence but can be dealt with by the judgment of our absolving Aaron (i.e., Christ). Some vices can be borne, others not, and these should be treated more seriously through excommunication. False doctrine is like cancer creeping through the body of the church. Such people need to be disciplined and silenced, and like those with a covering on their mouths (v. 45). But just because something springs up again it can be confessed and the worse sickness is not knowing and confessing how inwardly ill we are, or refusing to seek healing, just as the Egyptians were affected by ulcers for despising the word of God in Exodus. His medical interests get the better of him when he adds: oil of tartar and heat can help to restore hair, the physicians say.

Calvin had written about the abolition of the priesthood and yet what is fascinating is his identification with it, first when dealing with the unlikely place that is Leviticus 13: "surely to this ceremony corresponds excommunication. Yet he commends moderation less someone who is still able to be healthy be condemned before time." The way to deal with such people is to relegate them to "outside the camp." As is known, Calvin preferred that those who could not identify with the evangelical orthodoxy of his reform should leave Geneva. He can only be readmitted who has protested his repentant determination to walk in newness of life. The religious authorities, both then and now, held jurisdiction only as they prefigured Christ and had this God-given ministry. Calvin justifies his disciplinary strictness by indicating how Scripture speaks of the incorrigible: the white scar and skin type (v. 17) comprise a sign of a past sin indicating an old error of the accusing (satanic) conscience that the person knows well. The second type speaks of *unknowing* sin, and those so afflicted deserve to be less harshly punished than those with the white scar and skin type, who are hypocrites.

Lapide states that the idea of exclusion (v. 46) is to make them long to return to God as they have no human company. It was unfortunate that Luther and Calvin were not properly separated from the people and thus managed to infect many. Willet singles out quite another group: given the mention of white hair (v. 30) he rants against "leprous" clothing that "our daughters of London, and other places in England, farre exceed herein the daughters of Sion" and against dyeing of hair, given that blonde hair was a sign of leprosy in Leviticus! Dissimilarly, Lapide sees the tortured Christ in the outcast leper.

Milgrom concludes that at issue here is something more than physical. "We are dealing with ritual, not pathology... Bodily impurity stands for the forces of death" (Milgrom 2004, 128f). This view, that physically manifest sickness is evidence of spiritual malaise, is not far from the connection made in the Gospels (e.g., Mark 1:40–45; Luke 17:11–19; John 11), yet this is not a connection commonly made by post-biblical Christian interpreters. Lazarus is a *healed* leper (Kremer 1995), yet leprosy was known to be incurable, and pilgrimages to Lazarus shrines were for consolation and some alleviation, not cure (Demaitre 2007, 247). Pity was for exceptional, liminal people (such as St. Francis), but exclusion was the norm, analogous to species of public sinfulness requiring expulsion. As leprosy became less prevalent and public offences such as adultery, then blasphemy, were tolerated, this position of "outsider" (in German "leper" is *Aussätzige*) could be taken by others, notably Jews. Despite the likes of the enlightened Schiller (Krochmalnik 2003, 34) the "civilized" copiers of Tacitus (*Historiae* 5:3–5) ended with the policy of the ghetto and camp for Jews.

Leviticus 14

Dealing with Leprosy

WHAT FOLLOWS IN THE first part (vv. 1–32) of chapter 14 is a close-up view of the ritual for one whose disease has not spread and so may be deemed clean. The ritual reinforces this state. This chapter is more hopeful than the previous (for spiritual sins which have been checked before they can become mortal ones).

Origen writes that the affected sinner should keep his mouth shut and stay outside the camp until the ritual performed for his cleansing has taken place, whereafter the priest will go out to him. The red twisted thread figures the sacred blood that was "pressed" out of his side by the lance (John 19:34). The bird and its blood mix with the water to represent the presence of Christ's atoning death as the believer receives the Spirit along with water baptism. Origen spots the pattern of "and he will be clean" (v. 7) followed by "and he will be cleansed" as showing how sanctification is a process of working through what God has pronounced over a new believer. Shaving means the removal of all impure thoughts. Yet fresh, healthy growth of good thoughts are to be encouraged (v. 9) as with the Nazirites: so there is a three-stage order of (a) sacrifice that removes sin, then (b) the fruit of piety in works, then, finally, (c) a more blessed thought-life.

Cyril in his *Glaphyra* is quite upbeat. The lesson to draw from the cleansing of the leper is that sin was reigning in us *until* God showed us mercy and love. Being made to participate in this we shall be received and will be offered as a sweet fragrant offering to God and Father (2 Cor 2:15). We have been enabled to wash away our sins (vv. 1–9). Christ is the Priest meeting *the church* outside the camp, at the gate. The two pure birds offered form a type of Christ, who is from above. For Emmanuel came to us from above as one pure, not knowing sin. So the sense envisages the cedar wood, which does not decay because the two natures running together in Christ went towards one (here previewing the Chalcedonian Definition). Hyssop is a herb

Engaging Leviticus

known for getting rid of unclean colds and phlegm in the inward parts. The twisted, red thread indicates that God the Word was tortured in his flesh and blood! The bird is put over the running water and it touches it with wing but gets out unscathed; so too, Christ sustained the grave: he was in death, but was above it too. Whereas for Origen, the seven times of sprinkling indicated seven demons needing expelled, for Cyril it is the perfect number to get across the idea of Romans 5:20, that grace exceeded sin.

Theodoret gives less space to the remedies of chapter 14, but does address the meaning of the two birds brought for sacrifice (vv. 51ff).

> This concerns a type of the passion of the Savior: for leprous humanity the master Christ was crucified, whose flesh received death while his divinity indwelled the passion of the humanity. And just as the blood of a bird is dipped in water by cedar wood and hyssop and the rolled red thread shall show the leper to be clean, so the one believing in Christ the Savior is purified by the water of most holy baptism, washing away the stains of sin . . . The rolled thread a symbol of the soul and human body; the hyssop of the most holy Spirit's heat and sweet fragrance. So the baptized take off the leprosy of their souls . . . But the one who remains leprous will live outside the camp, as the sinner who is not penitent is put out of the church.

Hair removal from all one's body (v. 8) is significant in this procedure. Cyril, in *Glaphyra*, writes that like the leper cleansed, whose hair is removed, so too we are purified through holy baptism, and our fleshly growths are taken off as Christ works in us through his word that is sharp to cut off sins and free the mind. The leper does not go back first to his own home, and likewise we do not go to heavenly home each of our own yet, but to the camp, a "holding station."

There were, claims Lyra, three camps in the Hebrew encampment, but the leper would be excluded from the furthest one. "Alone" does not mean he did not have company of other lepers. Lyra then says that this is all about the leprosy of clothing. Baldness is a sign of more advanced or chronic leprosy. However, if someone's hair falls out, one should not pronounce leprosy from that evidence alone. If someone objects that a week's exclusion from his tent (v. 9) for one who does not have leprosy is unfair, then Lyra answers that it is best for priest to err on the side of saying it is leprous and excluding him, even if the leprosy is not manifest.

Hesychius, on verses 19–21, thinks that the portrayal of the burnt-offering actually describes the sinner's contribution of penance. The sacrifice of Christ first cleans us from wrongs and sins and then our holocaust is formed. For when we are made spiritual by the intelligible cleansing, we have our body and soul sanctified; thus we are made worthy to go up to the altar; then we receive full cleansing and we do not need more. For there are stages of cleansing: some are brought into camp and others are brought closer to the altar.

Ralph discusses how often a pastor needs to go out into the world, putting aside care for his own flock, to find souls whom he can pronounce clean. This happens when one is freed from desires and overcomes the world. This cannot be done in one's own strength but in believing Jesus is the Son of God (1 John 5). There are some who give the appearance of imitating Christ but do this as a pretense. In offering two birds, one represents doctrine, the second morals. The earthenware vessel is the body of Christ, and the flowing waters are the floods of the Scriptures. Therapy takes time: one is to reach a state of rest, *apatheia*, where no one can anger or distress you. Six days are required for active progress in virtue and the seventh for contemplation: the first makes holy, the second makes perfect. The eighth day is the new life. The Greeks say that oil is called "mercy" and lights the eyes of the merciful and all-powerful God. So we are to keep up good works after penance.

In a fairly standard "medieval" account Luther adds that the pope wrongly thinks he can extinguish leprosy by the sword. When we kill heretics (whose torn clothing means they tear by dissection the covering of Scripture) we do two wrongs: we take away his body and his soul. Instead, the only way to touch a heretic is through word and grace and blood of Christ and the Holy Spirit (oil) (vv. 6–10). If he cannot be converted let him live alone and we should be careful of him.

For Pellican, the birds in questions are not domestic fowl (as in Origen) but wild fowl. There is a parallel here to the two goats in Leviticus 16. And the one is not sacrificed without wood, for it is impossible for the leprosy of sin to be purged without the wood of the cross, by which the Savior triumphs over the principalities and powers, with hyssop for the purifying of conscience. On verses 7–9 water and blood make one think of the Savior's side. For Christ came not to kill the flesh of sin, but to cleanse the conscience, so that that we might walk in new life.

According to Cocceius, in an attack on the soteriological heresies of Piscator and the Socinians, the pouring of blood over water (vv. 6f) signifies not just obedience but death. This is not to say that the passion of Christ alone is ours, and that his obedience to righteousness must be provided by us; or even that the obedience of Christ alone avails for us as type and example, but the blood of Christ and his death is not assigned to us.

Lapide writes that while the priest could only *declare* that one was cured, the power of Christ's priesthood is much greater, since it can actually *cure* spiritual leprosy, and absolve sin in the sacrament of penance. In the ritual (vv. 4ff/49ff), the bird is the one, like Christ's divine nature, who is not easily trapped and so is free from disease, and the wood, like the wood of the cross, is incorruptible; the red betokens spiritual health, while the hyssop is like the grace of the Holy Spirit (although Lapide adds that Saint Antony referred to the demons as like little birds trapped in the net by Christ). Oil is offered to God but it is not sacrifice, it is just held up to him, while the two lambs and the young sheep signify absolution that is done in the name of the perfect Trinity. Cocceius similarly comments about Leviticus 14: the priest who judges is, firstly, Christ and, secondly, those who come to God in Christ and who judge by his word as to whether someone has faith and confession of the truth. The pure winged creatures that are offered suggest the state of Christ who was forced to hide himself and flee the plots of men. Also, Spangenberg had written that once we have faith then as "live birds" we can fly to our heavenly home.

Leclerc is tired by ingenious interpretations by the tradition, though he is not above thinking that redness is better than whiteness because it relates to the restoration of ʾādōm (Hebrew for "red"). He notes that a purifying of a house takes place in *Odyssey* X, 493, where Euryclea followed Ulysses' instructions. Cedar wood (v. 49) is not porous and its oil is useful for lighting rooms. The Israelites followed the Egyptians here for the remedies for disease.

Jewish commentary is keen to connect the text with Miriam (Num 12:14) and Naaman (2 Kgs 5:10), and, following Rashi's definition of "outside his tent" (wife), Gersonides insists on sexual abstinence to make penance complete, with Uzziah (2 Chr 26:19) serving as proof that those without humility are in most danger. (For Sforno, the ʾashām (v. 12) and ḥattāʾt [v. 20] are offered for any muttering against God when under pressure.) It is not medicine but deliberate and costly penance that makes clean (Abarbanel).

Diseased Houses and Garments (vv. 34–57)

Tertullian in *On Purity* 20.11.12 writes on verse 44:

> If after its rehabilitation and transformation, the priest again observes in that same house any of the old pocks or stains, may he pronounce it unclean and order its timbers and stones and its whole structure to be torn down and cast forth into an unclean place. This is a type of the man, body and soul, who is transformed after baptism, that is to say, after the entrance of the priest, and then takes up once more the scabrous contaminations of the flesh. He is cast outside the city into an unclean place. That is to say, he is "given over to Satan for the destruction of the flesh" (1 Cor 5:5).

There are no second chances after baptism for Tertullian, yet the penitential system in the church was not so rigorous. In any case, most early commentators prefer to refer verses 34ff, about houses and their contents, to the Jewish synagogue. Thus Theodoret asks, What is meant by clothes becoming leprous (Lev 13:47)? These things, he declares, show the amazing love (*philanthropia*) of God once again. For he bears the sins of people, who sin in their clothes and houses. Since they had committed sins, the house of Israel was like a leprous house that was removed, like leprous stones, by the Assyrians, then the Babylonians, and then the Macedonians. Since they had a leprous rock, the lawgiver ordered the house to be knocked down. It was unfit for any gathering. It might seem strange to think that the demolition of the House of Israel by foreigners demonstrated God's mercy, but the implication is that God did afterwards restore them from exile, and this might be instructive for disobedient Christians.

Cyril is less positive about willful sinners. On verses 33–53 he writes that in these words the mystery about the Jewish synagogue is revealed clearly along with the things that have happened from beginning to end and will happen through Christ. Their leprosy was incurable by doctors. Indeed, in the laments of the prophets we hear the leprosy of Israel deplored (Jer 14:7–9; Mic 7:1–5). The priest orders the house to be demolished, for the Lord is to be feared in his watching over our negligent deeds, and so he calls on the priest as the one who bears the face of God. Verse 42's discourse about replacing old with new stones points to how the prophets tried to cure Israel, and the inspecting priest is Christ. When he became man there was a real change from the old corruption to the exceedingly fine commonwealth. He took them who were still stuck in their original passions and in a state of permanent sickness, and ordered the rest to be purified, sending them out to an unclean place. For the whole system of the Jews, based on Law, has been dissolved and scattered to an unclean place (Jer 39:42, 46). Jesus was right to say that no stone will be left on another (Matt 24:2). Verse 46 indicates their being left outside with only a future hope of return ("until the evening"), as Romans 11:25 indicated, as fulfilling Micah 4:6. Cyril enjoys the detail: "The last section (14:48–53) clearly relates to the mystery of our Savior and the purifying by the holy baptism; the two birds indicate the heavenly man who at the same time is God by the two natures which he had for different reasons fitting to each . . . The red thread means our confession of the death of the Savior." For in the Song it says, "your lips are like red thread, my sister bride." The lips of the church announce salvation through the blood of Christ and order profession of this faith to be made, thus the lips can be rightly compared to red thread. The cleansing the whole house (vv. 51f), which takes place through the blessing of Christ and confessing in him through baptism, is the only way back for the synagogue. Look how through these words (of Leviticus) Christ is depicted and faith and confession in him is shown. By the "living birds" one should understand, according to Cyril, the ever-living and life-giving Word, and through the sprinkling one should see the precious blood of his suffering "temple." For we say that he suffered in flesh, i.e., only in a body of his own. In the incorrupt wood we receive his incorrupt flesh; by the hyssop, the Spirit (warming in his properties); by the scarlet thread, the confession of the testament in his blood; in the living water, the grace of baptism (cf. Ezek 36:24). The bird is sent out to the field (v. 53) and the priest prays for the house, so that it will be cleansed. The city, as that made up of many buildings, stands for the whole world with the firmament for walls. This, therefore, signifies Christ who was sent out of this world to the heavenly field by ascending to heaven (like a bird). Cyril's interest has moved from the synagogue to Christ as the only solution.

Procopius thinks that verse 34 means the Jewish synagogues—for the Jews did not accept the warnings of God long before the coming of Christ. The visit of the priest signifies the visitation of God that is terrible and fearful. Yet there is, and more explicitly than with Theodoret, an application for Christians. God does it so we might embrace purification from vile thoughts, as we wait for him who looks at things much more deeply. God will try to root out the occasions of weakness and sin. After a warning, if plague is still there, there no hope of salvation. And indeed the Jews were scattered like stones.

Hesychius argues that God today makes his displeasure known to the church and not to the synagogue. The church is blessed with marks of discipline, like leprosy in the walls. The house of the promised land is the Gentile church. But Hesychius's emphasis is on Christ healing every sort of sinner.

In the sixth century the direct meaning is the Christian penitential one. Severus of Antioch, commenting on verses 49–53, observes that the Law purifies also the leprous household, showing the greatness of penitence. If a person has come to such a progress of virtues that he is worthy to be a dwelling place of God, and if after that—through an unguarded life—he runs towards evil, he can still, through penitence, remove the leprosy with the help of the blood of the Lamb of God. Likewise, on Leviticus 13:57, Gregory in Paterius (Lienhard 2001, 181) has: "A roaming and wandering leprosy lays hold of a garment when, by an unreformed fault, guilt takes hold of that soul that seems to be faithful . . . First he took pride in his possessions; then he took pride in his generosity!"

Lyra sees here rules for leprosy in houses to be applied when the promised land is entered. There were two reasons for these: the health and safety of inhabitants, and because the heathen liked to use these houses for idolatry, invoking demons, etc. Denys saw it as meaning the infection of the *whole* congregation by moral, especially heretical, depravity or schismatic or hypocritical tendencies. Where the pastor complains to the bishop, the bishop should step in to support him and denounce such things out of love and zeal, for they break up congregations. The bishop should remove those who will not be corrected by using public penance, even treating the obdurate like Gentiles. There is little sense here of the bishop exercising investigative or inquisitorial functions, but of taking the parish priest's word for it.

For Pellican, on verse 37, houses are to be destroyed for reasons of purifying the surrounding air. From these laws we can learn spiritual things such as the atmospheres of places, and that there should always be a public air of honesty and virtue, and one should avoid mixing with superstitious in their places. Calvin is not very interested in the details of the treatment of leprosy, so he skips to verse 34: this stands for those who take God's gifts (houses) and are too ungrateful to keep them sound. They are to confess, even before the evil has overrun them, even when there is only a suspicion; yet some are treated with mercy and God wants them to take steps to improve.

Willet reports that Lorinus refutes Oleaster who thought that the disease was unique to Jews; yet Lorinus does not see that it is specifically an eastern disease. The disease of the buildings *is* particular to Israel as a symbol of judgment. Tertullian was wrong to interpret verse 45 as precluding penance, when, for Paul (1 Cor 6), penance is restorative.

Calmet, on verse 36, notes that Moses decently wanted to spare the house owner embarrassment so ordered him to leave before priest arrived. This all happened more for the sake of reassuring the people than for effecting anything in the nature of the infected thing. The same worms which infiltrated the human flesh could even make stones crumble eventually (see Lev 13:37). To pray for the house means only praises of God, vows of his infinite purity, or recognition of human sins in general, for a house as such cannot really have impurity in God's sight.

Bishop Patrick reports a dream of Rabbi Levi ("Barcelonita") that the plague was sent so that houses could be pulled down and Amorite treasures be discovered there. In any case it was a divine stroke on the holy land for offences against his Majesty. Abravanel has helped him to see the link to Habakkuk 2:11, i.e., the stone crying out and the timber beam answering, "turn unto the Lord." The repair work involves a long process and if the man ignored the scourging of the walls, then it would affect his stuff, then his skin. Even with Job the discipline did not start with his body. Post-Enlightenment commentators seem to have wearied with the detailed account of ritual and the leprosy of houses, which Keil calls "nothing but mildew."

So the chapter concludes (vv. 34–57) with less cheerful news for houses. On this, Rashi, commenting on verse 43, thinks that the phrase "if the plague come again" implies that houses should be given a second chance with only certain stones being removed and prayer being said, since the disease is a sign of sin (Abarnabel, with reference to Hab 2:11), before being torn down. Nahmanides blames "evil spirits," even though these are ultimately sent by God. On verse 40, Milgrom concludes concerning chapters 13 and 14: "Thus one can deduce that the land is not inherently holy . . . Israel's behavior alone will sanctify the land or defile it" (Milgrom 2004, 139). Perhaps that remains true for any nation.

Leviticus 15

Male Emissions

THIS CHAPTER MOVES TO treat "hidden uncleanness" (Ibn Ezra). In cases of male "abnormal" (gonorrhaeic) emissions, a small sacrifice is needed, along with washing, although Rashbam insists this must be vigorous and localized, including persons or things in physical contact. In the tradition of Philo (*Spec. Laws* I, 119), who related this discharge to nocturnal emissions, Clement of Alexandria (*Strom.* II, 61) insists that the Law here treats those who have sinned unwillingly "whether in killing or accidental discharge." And according to Clement this should still be punished because it arises from the weakness of sexual self-control. The thought of the desert fathers on this matter finds its *locus classicus* in *Conferences* 7.2.1 where Cassian relates the story of Abba Serenus who prayed for and was given the freedom from all bodily unrest, even emissions at night. Thus "for the rare few, there is a state beyond restored nature in which even 'natural' physical processes are stilled" (Stewart 1998, 76). It has to be said that Cassian was usually more interested in "attack as the best way of defense," cultivating active virtues, to help keep monks from waking sexual temptation. The battle is the heart and the intention rather than the body, and there are no ritual ways of coping with any such emissions. Yet what should be driven out are those emissions caused by vivid dreams, so that any emissions should be for physiological causes only because the sleeping heart will be still (*Conf.* 12.8.2) The ideal is for a state in which even at night there is no desire because sexual potency is possessed by God. The ascetic interpretation is still very demanding.

Hesychius is quick to allegorize the details: just as a flow could be natural (during intercourse or menstruation) and unnatural (outside intercourse or menstruation), so too teaching could be "chaste" or "against nature." He thinks the LXX duplication of *andri* (man/husband) in verse 2 means that it is a teacher (no simple but a "double" man!) that is subject to this command. Teaching that is out of place is not life-giving. According to Paul, that from which the body of Christ subsists is the generating Word, but it can be easily misused and in that case no sons of God will be born from that preaching. Paul himself was a seat (v. 4) or vessel (v. 12) for that teaching Word—one who, like a good chair, accommodated his divine teacher. But those who teach falsely infect others who will then need a time of penance (the symbolism of "evening"), while the teachers themselves whose impurity is intentional are beyond penance. The vessel (v. 12) is his preferred metaphor for those who can repent (wooden) and those who cannot (clay), and, being brittle, will have to be broken. Their whole selves, inward and outward actions, will need washing with what Hesychius indicates is immersion in sound teaching, the grace of Christ, and the workings of the Spirit. This will involve coming to the tabernacle—which is where Christ dwells, i.e., among the apostolic language, wisdom, and behavior—to be perfected in the age to come. Verse 16 tells us that the sin of Adam gets passed on through sexual procreation, and only Christ can give the washing. He is allusive but seems to indicate that they will be unclean until the end of the age, although baptism will stop them being lost. The contagion is not deliberate sin.

Another way of dealing with what seems a very rigorous requirement is to suggest that it does not concern *lay* people. Cyril of Alexandria interpreted this chapter as giving principles for *priestly* holiness, not general holiness. In *De Adoratione* (PG 68, 840) he urges that the scope of the "new letter of the law" says that *priests* must be those who suffer from a genital efflux as being pious, lovers of God, so as to be good mentors for those who require training in faith and piety.

However, in the West Gregory the Great treated these verses as providing rules for *all* in the church community by relating emission to that of sexual intercourse rather than the previous monastic "nocturnal emission" interpretation. In his *Responsa* (which would be an influential command through being included in Gratian's *Decretum*, Distinction 6 on the question of whether a lay person can receive or a priest preside at communion), he writes that a man should not enter church after sex if his mind is still on it, but should wash and pause (Lev 15:16). He rules that the desire in sex is a sin, even while the act is legal and legitimate. "In the doing we are somewhat defiled" and so should only come to church if sex was purely for procreation, for Paul allowing sex as an indulgence showed it was some sort of offence (1 Cor 7:9). He does, however, specify that *nocturnal* emissions—if caused by natural superfluity or sickness—are unproblematic for holiness, but where there is consent (i.e., masturbation) they are problematic. In the old law such a man was "polluted before the Lord and, unless he has been washed with water, he is not allowed to enter the assembly until the evening." The application of this today is:

"Spiritual people, however, consider a man who is tempted to impurity through a dream and then defiled in his imagination through actual fantasizing to be polluted. He is to be 'washed with water,' that is, guilty thoughts are to be cleansed away by tears; and, until the fires of temptation have subsided, he should count himself guilty until evening, as it were." Lastly, "if anyone was a captive, he was not fighting at all, but he who was fighting was not a captive" (Reply 9; cf. Godden 2001).

The application to nocturnal and general "pollution" is illustrated by two early medieval documents. The *Penitential of Fleury* (ninth century) commands expiatory prayer to be said after any nocturnal emission, its wording based on the seven penitential Psalms. There is a sense (as early as Ps-Alcuin) that this kind of law views such things as manifestation of the otherwise hidden seven deadly sins, which are the foundation of all other sins. The medieval *Glossa Ordinaria* is gloomily abstract: the trouble required to cleanse even that on which semen has come into contact shows the misery of original sin which has polluted the human race without our even sensing it. It is lust that drives sexual intercourse even at a natural time.

A return to allegorizing inspired by Hesychius (whose commentary continued to be read) was made by Rupert who halfheartedly suggests a spiritual meaning: that an "impure flow" is related to the loquacity of heretics, and their scandal-dissent-making. Ralph does much more and comments in a very abstract way that in the mind the "flow of seed" is the sequence of the hearing of thoughts, and the quality of what is said is affected by how it is heard. Now, if the mind is subjected to too many voices (i.e., troubling thoughts) it can be soiled by them. In the Fall, through wanting to become divine, humankind became human, knowing good and evil. We are reduced to the grace of the Creator: since after the time of our mortality, after the seven days have passed, the blood of Christ cleans our cheeks and the redness of our shame so that we will be received into the society of the angels. The making unclean of the saddle (v. 9) indicates "when people are raised up and made unclean by unrighteous praise." The wooden vessel is the incorruptible soul, which unlike the body is unbreakable by penance, although it benefits from the body's penance. The soul is called by some a "bronze vessel"; yet "wooden" captures the sense of its mobility, for it is not heavy but can be cleansed.

For Lyra, the flow of a man's semen can give a fetid humor, which can affect him. For in such emission there is bodily pollution, which is obvious, but also often a spiritual uncleanness, even in the marriage act, wherein, although it can be exercised without sin, nevertheless inordinate desire is often present.

The Reformer Chytraeus thinks that the efflux symbolizes unchaste living, as condemned by Hebrews 13:4. One should avoid unchastity for ten reasons, the ninth of which is: "Lest we draw down punishment on the whole commonwealth, as when Paris's lust was ruin to the whole of Troy." Brenz establishes that chapter 15 deals with nocturnal emissions which are *not coital*: and in the case of the woman it is not she whom the man came towards, but rather she who touched the polluted man or was near him in the night. The Jews tell us, he continues, that demons and ghosts are generated from such emissions, such as Lilith. But no, that flow is natural and so it is a "civil" not a moral uncleanness, and as such needs civil and ceremonial expiation. (Moreover, the chapter is not about *sexual* infection, for that is treated in chapter 20.) So why these rules? Well, they tell us to please God even in matters of external and political cleanliness. This cure concerned bodily not spiritual health. The temple in those days was external so God willed external cleanness. Secondly, such external instructions serve to remind us about the inner uncleanness of original sin, which is present even in reborn and godly men. Just as with Abel's offering, the good works of the godly please God, yet not on account of their own value or purity but on account of Christ in whom the godly have been reborn and whose works are done in faith. We must not be complacent but always seek the true and perfect righteousness in Christ through faith. Leviticus is part of the Law that leads us to acknowledge sin.

Likewise Calvin (as on chapter 12) wanted to insist that it is not sex as such but the human condition that is shown to be filthy by these commands. And yet it does have to do with lust, shame, and so it *could* relate to the seventh commandment, though not exclusively:

> This appendix, as I have said, can be added to the seventh commandment. The principle ought not to be restricted to modesty alone. Thus God wanted to inculcate horror so that they would be careful to flee filthiness. The principle is that what came out of the person made what it touched unclean not the person out of whom it comes . . . So even the one who was conscious of no blame in the flow of semen ought yet by that sign to confess to the corruption of his natures; and at the same time by an example to others, that each might learn carefully to watch himself since vice possesses the whole human race.

Yet good pastoral practice is added. For any confession of evil, unless joined with the hope of pardon, gives birth to desperation. In the French edition of his Pentateuch commentary Calvin adds that 1 John 5:6 reminds us that Christ appeared on water and blood to cleanse all stain. This law is about efflux that affects many, not just "someone too much given to women." On second thoughts, perhaps since this law signifies *general* moral purity, it is better not to place it as explanatory of the seventh commandment.

Spangenberg thinks that an unclean flow that pollutes health refers to teachers spewing forth false doctrine. Such a person is unclean until evening, i.e., when mindful of his baptism, by faith he receives Christ who came in the last days. Because of disobedience, the human body is made filthy, such that even insensible things can be polluted through contact. Yet, through faith, bodily washing (i.e., external political cleansing) pleases God. It does not bring salvation but has physical rewards such as health, etc., and reminds us that we have unwilling sin. Spagenberg, as is his wont, is far from clear, but he seems to indicate that baptism and Eucharist have the function of keeping people within a religious community that will have some restraining effect on them.

Lapide quotes Abulensia, with no obvious disapproval, that this effluence from the male happens when warm water is drunk before bedtime, for that loosens the digestion, and so it would better to drink nothing or to drink wine! Abba Moses, in *Vita Patrum* 7.1.64, gave the monks reasons for any nocturnal emissions: too much food/drink/sleep/laughter. It can also come from soft clothing, which breeds softness in the body and then the imagination, and all this provokes pollution.

Grotius regards emissions as diseased and notes that in places of Syria gonorrhea was just as contagious and epidemic as leprosy. It is the disease's *spreading* that has to be taken seriously. The Hebrews knew of three types of flux: mucus, saliva, and thickened blood. Calov plagiarizes him on these details but wants also to have the spiritual lesson: Theodoret is right to say that by natural things we are instructed concerning the vices of the mind. So that we acknowledge the filthiness of our lips, we restrain the pride of our heart, and we fear spiritual uncleanness and guard against punishments fixed for the impure (Rom 1:24, 28; 1 Cor 6:10; Gal 5:21); by the seed of the divine word and the precious blood of Christ we are set to be cleansed. Calmet is dismissive of Grotius's argument that this was the type of gonorrhea common in Syria and infectious—there is, he says, no proof of this. This symbolic law helps us to realize to what extent God wants us to maintain the interior and true purity that he demands of his servants or true Israelites.

Matthew Henry spots this as (v. 2) "the running of the reins," a very grievous and loathsome disease, which was usually "the effect and consequent of wantonness and uncleanness," with "the pain and anguish of a rotten carcase and a wounded conscience . . . It was also sometimes inflicted by the righteous hand of God for other sins (2 Sam 3:29) . . . Let us bless God that we are not under the yoke of these carnal ordinances, that, as nothing can destroy us, so nothing can defile us, but sin . . . And the defilement we contract by our sins of daily infirmity we may be cleansed from in secret by the renewed acts of repentance and faith."

Henry is forgiving yet warns of our record at the judgment to come. For Leclerc, a male emission was a serious matter. Since there was something lustful about it (for it did not happen without some arousal), the Law is right to deem it *unclean*. Although the rabbis want to read "hands" (in v. 11) to mean "whole body," they here are distorting the Hebrew language. The change of situation envisaged in verse 16 means that an emission is not the same as when it takes place in intercourse, when full bodily bathing is needed. What follows (see his note on Exod 19:15) is in accordance with Egyptian rules. Perhaps the premise is that intercourse took place daily, as suggested by the "until evening." It would certainly be inconvenient to find water in such dry areas. Of course, it was difficult for the poor without access to water to keep these rules, which is why Ezekiel 20:25 speaks of "statutes which were not good," but were given to discipline the people with Egyptian ideas of cleanness. This was not part of God's grace but most pernicious, since there was no real uncleanness, just anxiety about it harming their well-being which drove them to great lengths. The gospel of Jesus set such poor people free (Matt 9).

Keil held that Knobel was wrong for thinking that conjugal intercourse *in itself* defiled. No, it is not the *concubitus* in verse 18 but the emission of the seed in the coitus that brings about the defilement. He also seems to know what kind of disease it was: it was not one that was sexually transmittable but some infection of the bladder.

Female Menstruation

Clement, in *Paedagogos* II.10, maintains that there is no admission in the Hebrew Law of men to sleep with pregnant wives and those who have given birth; conjugal desire is a lawless and unrighteous thing. Theodoret was one who was troubled by the idea that something as natural as menstrual blood should be unclean (15:19). As the Law affirms, there is nothing truly unclean in nature. But although sex and related areas of human life are not unclean as such, the Law wanted to moderate the amount of it by adding a burden to discourage too much willful delight.

For Hesychius, the excessive flow of blood signified demonic idolatry of pagan mystery religions, especially after the knowledge of the gospel should have put an end to this. The lawgiver wanted men to stay away from women when infertile, for that is to behave in an idolatrous way. The remedy is to wait for the day of Christ while abstaining from such. This is what it means not to approach a woman. But in verses 25–27 there is something amiss in the state of the woman herself, that idolatry has taken over the "temple" of her person. Yet she who touched the garment of the

Lord was healed of her suffering. Those who wish to extend the literal observance of the Law beyond its time are like those who menstruate out of time.

The *Bigotian Penitential* (II.8; Bieler 1963, 222) demanded twenty days of penance if a man has intercourse with a menstruating wife. It appealed to Theodore of Canterbury to forbid entry into church let alone communion at the "time of the month" (*menstruo tempore*). And for men: "Whoever sleeps with a woman at the time of the month shall do penance for twenty days." In the *Glossa Ordinaria* menstruation signifies depraved thoughts, which flow from inside outwards. The only person polluted in such a case is the woman herself, and even when there is no physical expression given to inward thoughts and desires, in God's sight such intentions are punished. So that which is unwilled signifies that which is willed though not acted upon.

Intentions matter in sin. The touching of a woman during menstruation connotes idolatry, which is to be abstained from along with its practitioners. It was this emphasis on purity that promoted a further pollution-avoiding custom—that of the Eucharistic host being put directly on the tongue, and that only once a year. This custom then became established as the norm (Angenendt 2008, 460).

Rupert is clear that there is nothing impure about menstruation as a superfluity of nature. A woman in that state should be encouraged to go to church but not blamed if she holds back. Ralph sees this flow of blood as a case not of the depravity of will but of something which has gone wrong within nature. The soul lives on its affections. By "woman" is meant here the human mind that is made heavy when it receives the seed of the Word. The mind is very much a battleground between desires. Conflict ensues and the outcome is uncertain. It is one thing just to touch a menstruating woman, another to sleep with her, since that means to become one with her and to transfer into oneself by long custom the uncleanness of her mind and depravity of mores. Such a person is not unclean until the evening only, but "it takes seven days." In other words, this symbolizes those whose sins are more ingrained and will take a long time of life to die. If the tabernacle was to be spared from uncleanness how much more that place where the Eucharist is consecrated daily and the death of the Only Begotten is represented under the sacrament?

Despite verse 19, Peter Comestor is reluctant to see this chapter as not about menstruation. In John 8 the Lord told "the haemorrhaging woman" (*sic*!) after she was healed to "go and sin no more," through which it is clear that she was afflicted with sickness *because of sin*. Curiously Peter fails to read either Leviticus or John very carefully! For Lyra, emissions are still worse in the woman's case because she is "colder" and can less easily digest humors.

Denys interprets the issue as one of a lack of cultic cleanliness, or offence in worship. He then observes that this uncleanness was not a fault in itself and does not always imply guilt for it sometimes arises from guilt-free cause. But it was a bodily uncleanness by which that flow is in itself physically foul and there was an irregularity so as to be an impediment to entering the temple. God expects a high level of righteousness. Here Denys thinks that whereas the woman's flow in chapter 12 was from natural causes, here the causes are not natural, and such a passion often implies sin. Thomas Aquinas has written in the *Summa Theologiae* that various sins are signified by external forms of uncleanness, so that the woman's blood signifies pagan idolatry using blood (I.2. q.102). William of Auvergne in his *On faith and works* has written that a menstruating woman was counted unclean according to some of the "Zabaeons" (Arabs). This extreme view prevailed in Egypt and Canaan and it was linked to worship of the moon, when menstrual blood was offered, just as in Jeremiah 7, where placentas were offered to the Queen of Heaven. The corruption and contagion of menstrual blood is of such great foulness that it is like a mirror in which a woman can examine her own face. Thomas informs us that in Isaiah 64:6 sins are compared to menstrual rags and so they should keep clear or else they will conceive handicapped children. The command not to sleep with a menstruating woman was ceremonial inasmuch as it related to uncleanness, but inasmuch as it related to the underlying cause of the command's institution, it was moral.

Now as for Denys's spiritual interpretation of this chapter, it is about coming into contact with heretical opinion. The woman having her menstrual period illustrates the lower reason and the sensory appetite in which the torrent of carnal desires prevails. For it is not continuous but comes at a certain time from heat or natural overflow, or from diabolic or human suggestion. And the continuous form of the flow symbolizes someone overwhelmed by sin and temptation. One needs to guard against this.

Lapide allows the sixth-century John Moschus in the *Spiritual Meadow* to remind us that a woman is foul on the inside. An infant touching her is not unclean, of course, since that is necessity rather than something chosen. Pliny (and Lapide adds other classical authorities) instructs us that menstrual blood (*Nat.* l.7, c15) is horrible and destructive and so a menstruating woman is rightly thought unclean. Tropologically, the sense of the passage, following Hesychius, is to keep away from blood-loving idolatry. The rule is that things unclean in themselves could transmit uncleanness by contact; but that person then touching something would not make them unclean. For, on verse 24, he seems more liberal: that the man is not unclean because of sin, if his intercourse was legally marital, but because of the legal uncleanness which arises from the conjugal act, which is naturally and therefore legally unclean. So any sin there is comes not from touching her, which just makes him irregular, but in not dealing with this by expiation. The Jews still see some things as unclean for which they no longer have the means of expiation, and this leaves them in a state of wrong conscience.

Calmet believes that God wanted all people to be consecrated like priests in a temple. According to verse 17, a man needs purification after sex only if he is going into the temple courtyard. As for the woman in verse 19, it used to be taught that such impurity was contagious but modern medics do not agree. Pliny (as above) was a bit dramatic in asserting that menstrual blood contained poison that renders things infertile. It was all about keeping far from the holy place all those who had legal or real, interior or exterior soiling. Leclerc is similar in finding mixed moral-medical explanations for the laws here. A woman is called "impure" so that a man who is salacious would not approach her. Pliny (ibid.) was outraged at such a thing since menstruation so disgusting.

Knobel similarly adds that no Greek was to enter a temple unwashed after sex (Romans too) and that it would be death for having sex with a menstruating woman and only slightly less an impurity if you lie next to her as she menstruates. It is even worse when one's wife's flow is irregular, since she is impure for all that time (as in Matt 9:20). Dillmann notes the Islamic parallel, as well as those found in many ancient societies, that one must wash if one then wants to pray (Quran 4:46). Around 1900 there is an interesting change in the interpretation of this chapter, from Bertholet (medical reasons for the taboo) to Baentsch (reason of avoiding the demonic), from the nature of the disease to the religious aspect.

In cases of irregular female bleeding—in which case a man might not be blamed for having sex with the woman, a sacrifice is required in addition to washing. Menstruation and male ejaculation during sex are likewise causes of minor uncleanness requiring only washing. Only that which was underneath the menstruant can be affected and in this she is, practically speaking, hardly inhibited. It is Milgrom's credit to see: "While I do not intend to exonerate the biblical tradition for partaking in the fetishizing of menstruation, one should not pass over Israel's . . . not isolating its menstruants and in imposing nearly the same impurity rules for male genital discharges" (2004, 141). Such flow means the waste of "life" and hence it defiles. While common objects are sanctified by the most holy, which means death for persons, impure things work contamination, viz. a gaseous force or miasma which can only travel within enclosed spaces (Israel sees the demonic as confined, with "clipped wings"). The point is that the sacred has to be protected from impurity, and that is why it is not enough for the individual merely to bathe: (s)he must keep at a distance and make an offering. "From the beginning, Israel eviscerated impurity of its demonic content . . . then . . . airborne impurity was progressively eliminated" (2004, 158).

Leviticus 16

The Preparation of the High Priest (v. 4)

CLEMENT OF ALEXANDRIA (*STROM.* V.2) writes of the priest putting on, "the other tunic—a holy-of-holies one, so to speak—which is to accompany him into the sanctuary; . . . himself distinguishing the objects of the intellect from the things of sense, rising above other priests, hasting to the entrance to the world of ideas, to wash himself from the things here below . . . having become son and friend, he is now replenished with insatiable contemplation face to face. For there is nothing like hearing the Word Himself, who by means of the Scripture inspires fuller intelligence."

Such a theological and abstract interpretation is, of course, the logical expression of a Philonic anthropological-moral approach to the Scriptures. Yet it is very different from the historical and communal ("ecclesiological") concerns of the major Jewish tradition, which views the mention of the priesthood as fairly incidental in this day of ritual to undo the idolatry of the golden calf episode. The Christian approach is in large measure due to the christocentric reading of Leviticus through Hebrews (cf. Backhaus 2009, 62).

"Only when it comes to the Day of Atonement could Origen draw on explicit parallels between the New Testament and Leviticus, namely those found in the Epistle to the Hebrews, particularly chapters 8–10" (Wilken 1995, 87). Wilken's case is overstated, but it has the merit of highlighting what stood out in Leviticus for early Christians—the whole effect of Christ's achievement on the cross. Leviticus 16 was read in the Syriac church—at least by c. 500 AD—during *Easter* week, as notes in the Peshitta manuscripts indicate.

Yet, of course, Origen applies the Leviticus 16 ritual also to the ministry of Jesus and the life of the church within him. Linen clothing denotes Christ's "otherness" from other humans in his sexual behavior and in his thinking (breeches and turban respectively) (cf. Klingbell 2007, 97f). The ecclesiological aspect, however, is what comes to the fore in Origen's reception: the priestly preparation is about putting off the evil desires, because "you have the priesthood because you are a priestly nation" (1 Pet 2:9). The holy linen tunic stands for the nature of earthly body, but Christ's was *pure white* linen. The bands around his thighs signify his chastity, yet the ecclesiological import follows immediately: we should honor members of "the body" (with a literalizing nod to 1 Cor 12:23). The designated person who leads the goat out, then washes his clothing at evening (vv. 21, 26) is the Lord himself who took the clothing of our nature. Further, the two goats are the two thieves on cross. The day of propitiation lasts until the sun sets—i.e., until the end of the world. We stand at the gate waiting for him as he is doing his interceding inside. He does not pray for those who are sent out into desert but for those who are the lot of the Lord. This "lot" does not mean "fate," as men tend to think. Rather, one may become a designated or prepared person by keeping a close eye on God's precepts and though, by dealing with sordid things, one might appear to become soiled, one will eventually become restored having driven out and replaced impure with pure thoughts. This process can be also viewed in Jesus, whom Zechariah 3:4 calls "Jesus [Joshua] the high priest," for a time wearing filthy clothes.

Cyril in his *Glaphyra* observes what became a fairly standard line, close to the spirit of Hebrews: "The Only Begotten came to have mercy and also to be a faithful high priest towards God for the propitiation of sins of the people." Verse 2 presents Aaron as type and image of Christ in that he was not allowed in the Holy of Holies at every time or season; for Christ only went in *once*, to find the eternal redemption. Christ was unlike Aaron inasmuch as the latter offered for his own sins, for he (Aaron) was not free from sin, "being a man." So, on this special day Aaron was not wearing high priestly dress but a simple linen tunic: and the way he was dressed seemed that of the *form* of Christ who knew no sin.

Hesychius, as related by the *Glossa*, holds the priests, or all those who desire to be such, to be required to exercise contemplation of the divine mysteries in which the Holy of Holies dwells. In other words, geographically located holy places (not least in Jerusalem!) are to be ignored. The veil is the flesh of Christ, who became a propitiation by his own blood. The LXX's verb in verse 11 is *exilasētai* ("to make propitious"), which can be explained as God's face becoming less terrible towards them. Later, in verses 23–24, where it mentions an offering for the High Priest himself, this is Christ praying for his humanity, which he received to be saved. That no one should be in the tabernacle except for the High Priest shows how useless all the rest have become, except for one. The dirty clothes of mortality and suffering—which he put on for our sins—are not taken off for good, but through washing immortality and impassibility are put back on, as he enters the camp, the place of angels.

In discussing Christ as High Priest, Ralph emphasizes how his "oneness" has more to do with bringing people together "in himself" (seated in heavenly places) than in any singularity of his person. So in the person of Aaron we understand Christ and the church, the head with the body. There is a mystical identification between the priest and the first goat. Christ had made the first entrance and the believer, like Aaron, will follow and enter therein in the resurrection. Until then, merit and desire, hope and contemplation are symbolized by burnt offerings—some of the present time, others of the future. In the present, someone can be aflame with the fervor of the Spirit and is given over completely to divine service (cf. Augustine on Psalm 65), while in the resurrection to come our death will be absorbed.

Hugh brings it down to earth, or at least church building level. The evangelical High Priest can be viewed in this text as Christ cleansing the basilica, which he dedicated for the consecration of the baptismal fonts and in the immersion of catechumens. Lyra is interested in churchly cleansing, expanding on Hugh he writes: the solemn consummation of the sacrifice (v. 24) resembles the cleansing of the basilica with incense at a dedication, when small linen cloths are used to carry off the sin and even at a baptismal service in the consecration of the font and the immersion of catechumens. Rashi adds that the stripping off of glorious clothing is so to avoid him seeming to represent God as being at home with sin. Christian doctors (especially Peter Comestor) explain the High Priest's disrobing as a mark of humility.

Denys asks: why does he only put on this priestly clothing after making the sin offering, when turning to the burnt-offering? Well, simply that sin is to be treated with humility, and so a whole offering is made with solemnity yet delight. He repeats what Hugh of St. Cher and Comestor have said (see above), then dismisses Lyra's use of Rashi's view that on this occasion the priest could not represent God. For why then do the priests wear their finery when making a sin offering? In any case, by this point the priest has already made atonement for himself and his household, so he would be able to represent God. The disrobing is only after the atoning event.

Calvin agrees with the pre-moderns that the key to the passage is the true identity of the priest. The High Priest in this text is obviously a type: "For whenever the priest stripped himself of his own garments, and assumed those which were holy and separated from common use, it was equivalent to declaring openly that he represented another person," implicitly Christ.

Lorinus comments that the linen clothing clearly refers to the Lord's clothes, for the priest celebrating the sacrifice of the Mass offers the Lord Jesus Christ to the eternal Father for the sins of all the faithful. The clothing manifests purity from all corruption; the priest and the victim united in Christ. Lorinus then speculates in line with Jewish thinking: God created the world for the sake of their Messiah (in *Sanhedrin*, Rab Iohannan). From which it can be gathered that not only Jesus would be pronounced exempt from all future sin but also the most blessed Mary, his most glorious mother. Jesus was not born of a sinful flesh, for the flesh had to be pure, as Mary's was, so that he could purify the unclean world. Where it says, "he washed his own flesh," this figures Christ Jesus who would wash his most holy flesh, exempt from the works of mortality, when he would ornate it with the gifts of glorious immortality, impassibility agility, and subtlety. Priests are to offer up themselves when they offer Christ in the Mass: this is what it means to pray for themselves and the people.

Keil considers the "cloud in which Jehovah appeared above the *capporeth*, between the Cherubim ... not the cloud of the incense, with which Aaron was to cover the *capporeth* on entering (v. 13), as Vitringa, Bähr, and others follow the Sadducees in supposing, but the cloud of the divine glory, in which Jehovah manifested His essential presence." This enables him to read the passage mystically and christologically: in verses 3–5 the High Priest is wearing white, so he is not "penitent"—as "rabbis" and Knobel think—but is shown forth as the Mediator. For MacLaren, Aaron, unlike the Christian, has no right of access but must approach as suppliant; his is religion of anxiety (like all ancient religions).

The Scapegoat (vv. 6–10)

The *Epistle to Barnabas* 7: 9 lambasts the Jews for mistaking the identity of the true Son of God: "[You see] 'one [goat] upon the altar, and the other accursed'; . . . they shall see Him then in that day having a scarlet robe about his body down to his feet; and they shall say, Is not this He whom we once despised, and pierced, and mocked, and crucified? Truly this is He who then declared Himself to be the Son of God. For how like is He to Him!"

Origen remarks: if the people of Israel had been obedient then there would not have been *two* goats offered. This implies understanding the first goat, offered in holocaust, as in no way an offering for sin. It represents spiritual Christians who are fully offered up to God. As for the second goat, the scapegoat, sadly there are some who do not come near the Lord (i.e., mediocre Christians) but who deserve to be sent into the desert, to become like Egypt, Ethiopia, and Cush "given in exchange" (Isa 43:3–4). This is what is required for their purification. So the scapegoat represents not so much those outside the faith, as those within it—for the goat is a "clean" animal—who do not live out the faith.

Augustine had a different view. On the last part of the chapter, he emphasizes that it is not the case that the first of the two goats was offered for any reason other than sin, and its ashes are scattered outside the camp. Between the two goats there was no real difference originally, even though it might be permissible to see them as having different allegorical values. (As to what these are he does not comment.)

Cyril in his *Glaphyra* considers it absurd to think the second goat was offered to evil spirits (Azazel, v. 8): that would be a pagan error. The two goats are exactly the same, however, one is called "the Lord," and the other "the emissary" (and 'the emissary' [LXX *apopompaios*] is the name of the animal, *not* of the one to whom it is sent). Hence the goat that is called "the Lord" is fittingly sacrificed as Christ was, sanctifying the inner tent and the altar of fruits which is on the outside. The other, which is "the emissary," was sent out from those who are with us to the holy city above and now appears before God on our behalf (1 John 2:1–2). He migrated into regions inaccessible to humans (of which the desert is a type) to be our paraclete (advocate). As pioneer he blazed the trail to beyond the veil. In other words, the two goats represent two *offices* of the Savior. Likewise, Hesychius—as preserved in the *Glossa*, and then in more detail in his fuller commentary—is clear that the scapegoat signifies the divinity of Christ, for God alone can take away sins. He was determined to keep his life impassible and uses the humanity as a shield for drawing suffering, while going out to the desert which is a holy place since only God can bear to dwell there, and enemy hosts cannot make their way. This cosmic "monist" vision combined with a Chalcedonian Christology is a novel combination: there is no notion that the desert is where the devil dwells. Procopius too argues that the Law here cannot be teaching superstition, so it cannot mean that demons have to be appeased when law has tried to wean the people off superstition; the sacrifice God ordains is sufficient and nothing else was really needed. So it is better, with Symmachus, just to call it the "going forth goat"; this is just the way of showing Christ's function in removing sins and representing our cause in heaven. It is really an illustration of the effect of the sacrifice, or represents Christ's going into heaven, which is a "desert" in the sense of an "unknown" place, after his resurrection.

Rupert's mood is dark: as a controversial theologian, he identifies the Son of God as one who "becomes" the "son of perdition" like the scapegoat (2 Thess 2:3/ John 17:12). The scapegoat figure has appeared as if from nowhere. It is a big eschatological mystery, but it has to do with the true High Priest at the time when all the Gentiles have been gathered in and the "man of sin" is revealed, the "son of perdition" who truly is the goat made filthy for their sins. Christ plays this role of "man of sin" even though in his innocent self he is the pure Lamb of God. At that point each will receive their fate, either those who are blessed in the name of the Lord and find mercy or those who are cursed in his name and are drowned in the immensity of his wrath. Meanwhile, the goat sent into desert with sins upon it is the antichrist, prefigured by Barabbas, now in the hands of his father the devil.

For Ralph too the attention is given to the Last Judgment. Aaron took two goats: Christ will receive the saintly goats—those who have renounced the desire of this world and have been tested as in a furnace, like a whole offering, lifting them up to equal dignity makes them to judge along with him. The devilish goats, reprobate, as the third class, have only a dark land of shadows to inhabit, with only the devil for company. Everyone else seems to occupy the *space between* the saintly and the devilish goats. Ralph comments that Aaron is commanded to put each hand on the goat and confesses the sins of the children of Israel. Gregory the Great has told us that it means the ungodly will be tormented in eternity, and the righteous, on seeing this, will give thanks to God. They should confess since they too were children of wrath by nature and would have suffered the same if grace had not intervened. The prayer that Christ makes here is not an imprecation so as to curse them, but it simply spells out their doom. Indeed, by rights we all are "to bear our own burden" (Gal 6:5, given an unusual interpretation), yet this passage seems to commend divine grace rather than to show divine justice. Here the mood lifts. For who is this person sent out into desert? It can be no other than "the One in whom the salvation of the elect and the judgments of the damned is located." He is the salvation of God, and ready for those believing to be saved through him and the ungodly to be damned through him (cf. Job 12). If the Apostle (Paul) was ready to punish (2 Cor 10: 6), how much more Christ! So by this goat in the solitude one can discern that great person who was God and man who was ready for whatever God willed. Afterwards he will kill the prince of the evil ones with the spirit of his mouth the others will hear him say, "Away, cursed ones . . . " There is a strong message that Christ in his Second Advent will be both refuge and judge.

Ibn Ezra and Nahmanides sense that God's sovereignty is wide enough for the Accuser to be one who has a role in the mystery. Rashi was even more content to let mystery be and to focus on the *effects* of the ritual. Lyra accordingly has a reading that focuses on the benefits for the community. The scapegoat will be sent into desert to be eaten by wild beasts in a manner fitting for its sins. The goat went far into the desert, to demonstrate that the community was far removed from all occasion of sin, both the acting and circumstances of it. Denys also interprets it "ecclesiologically":

the distancing of vices from the people by the remission of sins (cf. Mic 7 and Ps 103's imagery of "as far as the east is from the west"). It is not to be thought that lots are cast, as Comestor reports, to see which of the two is to be offered to the devil in the desert along with sins and which one is just a whole offering to the Lord. All offerings of whatever sort are made to God alone. The people's confession of sin *then* was not a sacrament in the way that, according to the evangelical law, confession *now* is. As Thomas put it (*ST* Ia–IIae q102) this day was to cover all the mistakes made in offerings over the year. William of Paris asked how could sins be attributed to an innocent goat, but the answer is that the goat did not bear the people's *sins* but rather their *punishment*, and it was able to go out freely and unharmed. If we also ask why after sending the goat out there was any need for another goat to be sacrificed, the answer is that the scapegoat ritual was performed to make the demonic—in which many believed and still do believe—to be repugnant and abominable, and to show that the place of demons is the right place for sins. Here in Denys is a curious attitude to belief in the demonic: it is to be taken seriously enough as to demand its being dealt with in the mind of "weak" believers.

According to Calvin, the scapegoat was a consoling and confirming picture:

> the other was sent away to be an outcast, or offscouring (*katharma* or *peripsēma*) (1 Cor 4:13 echoing Lam 3:45) . . . A more subtle speculation might indeed be advanced, that after the goat was presented, its sending away was a type of the resurrection of Christ; as if the slaying of the one goat testified that the satisfaction for sins was to be sought in the death of Christ; while the preservation and dismissal of the other showed, that after Christ had been offered for sin, and had borne the curse of men, He still remained alive.

The scapegoat was a reassurance that sins had indeed been forgiven. It is "too subtle" to say the scapegoat was "repeller of evils." Spangenberg writes that Christ, on the cross, had a "wilderness experience," as he cried, "Why have you abandoned me?" The Jews today use a cock instead. The contrast of Christian pathos with Jewish bathos is deliberate.

Lorinus comments that tropologically speaking we are to send our sins away, for the Christian life is a continuous sacrifice of the body through penance, and we can't achieve this by learning the theory through study of liberal arts. Calov, considering the right frame of mind (faith) for benefiting from these acts, then asks: But what about all those who do not abstain from sin? For it is not only believers with the gift of Spirit who are able to abstain, since the Israelites were too (Jas 3:2). In a proleptic way they were able to strengthen their faith when they saw the scapegoat sent out. This allows a Lutheran anti-predestinarian conclusion. Willet shows his Reformed credentials by objecting to the notes of the Douai Bible to Hebrews 9:8—that heaven was not open to any before Christ's passion—by citing Augustine's declaration (Epistle 99) that Abraham was in heaven. Yet the Old Testament high priesthood should not be used to elevate the Christian ministry above ordinary believers. Lorinus the Catholic had also argued here that Aaron could only be struck down by God, so the pope is above kingly rule. Yet, counters Willet the Protestant, at 1 Kings 2 we read that King Solomon deposed Abiathar.

Certainly for Reformed exegetes like Willet the "otherness" of the scapegoat does *not* represent Christ's humanity: "

> For these two Goates so like in natures and nothing differing from the other, could not represent two such different persons, as of God and Man, but rather they demonstrate his function as he who is Other in his function of being made sin. Like as the Priest confessed their sinnes over the Scape goat, and so hee was sent away, even so a man must not *precium in se quaerere*, seeke the price of redemption in himselfe, as Master Calvine well observeth, but his sinnes must be put over unto another ... he is partaker of our nature and hath made us partakers of his righteousness.

One finds a scholarly defense of the vicarious nature of the Levitical and of Christ's sacrifice—that the mechanism of the transmission of sins in all sacrifices is most clear in the scapegoat ritual—in the work of William Outram (*De sacrificiis* 1677; ET 1817). He argued, against Socinians and like Johann Crellius (d. 1633), that as animals and Christ are both like and unlike us sinners, the transmission of sins would work and "whatever was even symbolically represented in the one, is really found in the other" (ET 1817, 269). Yet he also maintained the restorative effect of sacrifice against Grotius and the distinction of an imperfect remission (God's forbearance with sin) and a perfect remission (only for those who have repentant faith) (1817, 349ff).

Almost three centuries before Driver (1956), Leclerc on *Lahazazel* (16:8) writes that the Arabic helps us: it means either "a rocky hard earth" or a "narrow place," just as the cognate Hebrew *mahoz* does not mean "fortified place" but a "jutting mountain ridge," as in Judges 6:26. He has some sympathy with the Semitist Samuel Bochartus (*De jure regum* [1650], Bk II c54) who thinks it is like the Arabic inflexion *Hazazil* ("separation"). But John Spencer (*On the Ritual Laws of the Hebrews* [1685], III, VIII) claims that words of Arabic origin are rare in the Pentateuch, yet Leclerc disagrees. It is not, he says, just a tautology here. Spencer opposes those who want to interpret Azazel as a demon, but he guesses to emend it not as "offering" but as "lot for sins" and so the uncleanness of demons is manifest here, to whom the goat laden with sins was sent. But this dualism is not in the text but is just a later invention of Jews. It was actually sent out to wild country. The goat that "(e)scapes" hardly gets off free, argues Leclerc.

Knobel is emphatic that laying hands on the scapegoat was not to atone for *it* (*contra* De Wette and Hengstenberg) for it was already pure. No, by laying on hands the people added their prayers to it, as the Vulgate indicates. Against the LXX idea that *azazel* is descriptive of the goat it is clearly personal and of the recipient of the sacrifice, so as perhaps to be the devil himself (Hengstenberg and De Wette: "*Kakodämon*"). For Azazel is the name of the fallen angel in 1 Enoch (8:1; 10:12; 13:1); so it is more like an evil spirit of the desert, or so the author of Leviticus thought. The Sinai Arabs of "today" fear a similar thing. God has sent sins away with their confession on its head and can thus receive penitent Israel.

Keil raises the stakes higher for theological reasons as much as for reasons to do with the history of religions. "The words, 'one lot for Jehovah and one for Azazel' require unconditionally that Azazel should be understood as a personal being, in opposition to Jehovah." This is not a demon, nor even the fallen angel, as per the Book of Enoch or *Shibe* of the Arabs, but is *the devil himself* as the sole worthy antithesis to Jehovah. Sins were taken out to him "as a proof that his evil influences upon men would be of no avail in the case of those who had received expiation from God, and on the other hand as a proof to the congregation also that those who were laden with sin could not remain in the kingdom of God." Of course, there is not the slightest idea of presenting a *sacrifice* to Azazel.

A generation later Dillmann would contradict his predecessor, Knobel. For a start, in Hebrew thought the devil did not live in the desert. The author, standing in the tradition of Moses, borrowed the idea form outside Israelite circles, but shaped it. Actually any impure spirit is now sent out with the goat and this symbolically to reassure. So the goat represents nobody and is sent to no one. There is some sympathy for Keil's view—that the sins are thus sent back to the one who made them and thus Israel cuts itself off from the evil principle.

René Girard realized that the Levitical scapegoat is not to be simply identified with the later idea of a scapegoat—a figure that is seen to be far from innocent—but he implies that the Levitical idea was a hostage to misfortune. Girard (1998, 62) recalls Guillaume de Machaut's mid-fourteenth-century work, *Le Jugement du Roy de Navarre*, in which Jews are scapegoats for the origin of the plague. Since then the modern world has tried to be progressively ethical but violence has in fact increased as cultic violence has been lost. Girard's conclusion is that the OT presents violence in a positive light, which is not the case in the Gospels. Indeed the violence against Christians in the NT is not mythical, but is simply the very human violence of persecution, when "the Stone" was rejected by the builders. Unfortunately, in Girard's view, the Epistle to the Hebrews takes a retrograde step back to the OT mentality even while claiming how different this new sacrament is from the old sacrifices, for it is still tied up in the conceptuality of sacrifice and takes away the responsibility of humans for Jesus' death, thus legitimating it as divinely willed, just like Second Isaiah. For Girard even self-sacrifice is untrue to the spirit of the gospel, and is a desire to divinize oneself through masochism.

The Sin Offering (vv. 11–19)

The priest is told to take a censer full of burning coals. Aaron like Isaiah (6:6) was purified by this fire; but other people including me, says Origen, will be purified by another fire—not the fire of the altar, which belongs to the Lord, but the fire they make for themselves (Isa 50:11). The same verse here speaks of "incense of composition" because there is not one species of works, but a conglomeration of various kinds of works, which comes from righteousness and piety and continence and prudence and all virtues of that sort. These virtuous works only please God if put together. The phrase "finely crushed" is not superfluous, for these works are to be fine, subtle. We are to look for the particular species or perhaps ingredients of "incense" (e.g., *galbanum* wards off serpents) to hand over to Christ our High Priest, who then presents for us. Origen does not omit to mention the mediation of Christ. Christ considers what each church under heaven offers, and the angels check what each soul brings in terms of works. Likewise today the sanctuary is "double." Externally, priests in the present visible church offer in front of the altar on a fire that Jesus spoke of throwing on the earth (Luke 12:49). Paul, in 1 Corinthians 13:3, shows exactly what it means to make such an offering, as a priest, of oneself—it is to seek martyrdom, to love my brother, or to mortify the flesh. Then one can say, " I have carried the burnt offering to the altar of God and have made myself the priest of the sacrifice."

Too often, thinks Origen, our enthusiasm is from a profane fire, say the passion of anger at the circus. Verse 14 tells us to make all our self-offerings with respect to "the East," that is to Christ, since the mediator's name is "East" (*Oriens*) and as the Sun of Righteousness he will rise from there and give us light to walk in. Now the one who can follow Christ into the inner sanctuary will not be a man (literally "there will be no one," v. 17), but will be like an angel (Ps 81:6), or at least can be called this. Deuteronomy 30:15 reinforces this, that the human soul is neither mortal or immortal, but becomes one or the other depending on what it holds to: if it clings to the earth or death it will die, not in sense of non-existence but of being a stranger to and outside of God, who is the true life.

Hesychius regards the seven virtues as indicated by the sevenfold sprinkling (16:18), or our seven sins are forgiven, as heavenly places receive cleansing by an odor that is the burning up of our vainglory. Ralph insists it was not enough just for sacrifice to be made, but individual's fingers (v. 14) have to be dipped in it, and that means that the church has to be cleansed from its dirtiness by the virtue of faith, then penance and satisfaction. It is wiped by the finger of the priest, that one might understand that forgiveness comes to sinners by the power of Christ. The cloud of penitence defended Aaron from being destroyed, for his heart had been kindled with fervor. Such vapor can work on the mercy seat; that is to say, without much achievement one can find life by imploring and pleading. In this interpretation there is a mixed economy of the piety of the believer and the function of priest.

Lyra is indebted to the Jewish tradition known also to Jerome whereby "mercy seat" (v. 13) should be translated "oracle" because the divine response is heard there. The place of propitiation is thus also the place of prophecy. Hugh of St. Cher had indicated that the turning to the east (16:14) indicated the turning to "bless the Church from the Gentiles." However Lyra is interested in orientation: if the sprinkling of blood was made towards the east, this would mean the Cherubim would be looking west and have their backs to the holiest place. But 2 Chronicles 3 seems to affirm this and, as we know, Solomon's temple was built same way as tabernacle with the cherubim facing east. Our doctors say: "We worship towards the east lest we copy the Jews towards the west." But the priest's acting "towards the mercy seat facing east" does not mean that this "east" is in respect of the whole of the tabernacle, but in respect to the propitiation altar only, "on the east," when the priest was applying blood. The priest was not facing east for he had his back to the east as he was facing the east side of the altar. In other words, the ancient Jews did not do things much differently from how the church operates in its ritual, and their being propitiated is not essentially different from the Christian version.

Denys agrees that this place is well-named "oracle" (LXX) which is where prayers and divine speeches were proffered. By "cloud" is meant that cloud which cared for the children of Israel in the desert and hung frequently above the tabernacle. However, and here he differs from Lyra, the Levitical tabernacle was turned towards the sunset (west), and it does not seem that the cleansing was towards the east but to the west. Lyra stated that the priest as in 2 Chronicles 13 had his back to the east, yet surely the part to which the priest turned was also in the east. But it should be noticed that the faces of the cherubim were not directly set to the east, but rather glanced obliquely at the mercy seat, as in Exodus (25:19f.). (It is as if Exodus trumps Chronicles here.) So the cherubim were turned towards the east, although perhaps not directly. So the Holy Place can still be to the east of them. Moreover, the other place, which could be where the priest was doing the sprinkling, was standing behind the propitiatory altar with his face towards the people who were in the east and who were standing outside. Thus the sprinkling would have been made towards the geographical east, just as both the High Priest and now the priest of the evangelical law, in the midst of his sacrifice turned himself towards the people. The point seems to be, however, that the Jewish way, or direction was different.

There is something of this point in the conclusion which Ratzinger (2000) drew from the "unchangeable" liturgical tradition, that all (not least the priest!) should look to the place of Christ's return, although if that is not possible the cross can serve as the "inner east" of faith and serve as a focal point. In Durandus' *Rationale divinorum officiorum* (c.1285), which became *the* handbook for ritual (Kunzler 2002, 92), the issue of the direction one is facing does not seem a huge concern. Therefore, as he writes (II, 30, 34), "the rite of the synagogue carried over into the religion of the church and the sacrifices of the carnal people were changed in the observance of the spiritual people." Liturgical signs and actions as such are of little interest in themselves and have value only as long as they continue to be explained allegorically, argues Kunzler. This disconnection between the rituals and their meaning reaches "perfection" in nominalism with its incapacity for symbolic thinking, not to mention its incapacity for real-symbolic thinking, making it unable to recognize any longer an inner connection between the exterior, visible, actions and the supersensible-spiritual sphere. One example from this period is Gabriel Biel's (d.1495) *Literalis et mystica canonis expositio*" (Kunzler 2002: 92). However, the clear interest of Lyra and Denys trying to settle a disputed question suggests otherwise: the question of direction did seem to continue to matter well into the later Middle Ages, so long as the meaning of "direction" was kept in view.

Pellikan observes that Christ the Lord in blessed humanity was crucified on the altar outside Jerusalem and spilled his blood seven times for the sins of believers who are members of his body. Christ, as the High Priest of future blessings, in the day of re-propitiation enters into the Holy of Holies as he is given full dispensation to enter heaven and goes into the Father and makes him propitious to the human race and prays for all who believe in him (John 17:9) and at last he will return as judge of living and dead and will make blessed his elect ones who, while they were alive were most devotedly loyal to him in faith, hope, and love.

For Cocceius, "Azazel" refers to that spirit which has not obeyed authority. Ibn Ezra tells us that it is a mystery, and suggests it is a demonic power, which was the kind of thing that made Julian the Apostate deride Moses for offering a sacrifice to a devil. But this was *not a sacrifice* but a "dedication for penance, joined to fasting, which predicts that the elect faithful will have much anguish in the future to endure."

Grotius seems clear that the death of an animal could not move God but was experienced as fair exchange for the punishment for sin. Calov argues that to reason such is to deprive both the Levitical and Christ's work of value; God is moved by sacrifice to see sin as dealt with, and only where sins are expiated is their punishment removed. Those who benefit are those who turn to God in relationship. What was going on here was firstly the remission of *eternal* sins, not just judicial ones, as Grotius thinks (*De Satisfactione* ch. 10, p121): No! The idea that putting a price on misbehavior becomes a way of deterring sin is misguided, as is thinking of the Israelites as receiving only temporal rewards and punishments. Calov concludes that the primary end of these commands (nb. not the *realia*) is to foreshadow the propitiatory sacrifice of Christ; the secondary purposes are (a) the offering of worship, praise, and thanks to God, with ceremonies as like chains to keep the people focused, and (b) the understanding of the varieties of types of blessing from the Messiah which he has achieved on the cross.

The Tabernacle Itself

Augustine finds very little of "difficulty" in chapter 16 to concern him until he gets to verse 16 where he finds the Old Latin translation to be "he shall pray for the sanctuary" (not "expiate" as in the LXX and Vulgate), that is, in the sense of purifying it and the altar through prayer. The Greek verb can only have "*sins*" as its object, but here in the Latin the "*sanctuary*" is the object—or perhaps rather *God* who was behind it— so that the prayer of propitiation could be meant. But what then would it mean in verse 20 to say "and perfect it"? The object *cannot* then be *God* (who is beyond being perfectable) and so it is best to think of a prayer being made for the holy things (the plural is better attested). One should recognize that these holy things need to be kept clean from the uncleanness of the Israelites (or else they would stop doing their job).

Cyril simply observes that the blood of a bull is offered not only for the sanctuary but also for the altar. The *Glossa* explains verse 19 thus: that the powers of heaven do not need to be expiated since they are in a state of perpetual sanctification. But since the smoke of our sins rises up so often—as is said "smoke ascends in his anger" (Ps 17[18]:8) and about Nineveh "its wickedness has come up to me" (Jonah 1:2)—it is fitting that it (Christ's sacrifice) expiate the choir above to take away the awful stench. So it cleanses.

For Hugh of St. Cher, Christ offered the young calf, that is, his flesh, while praying for himself, that is, for his humanity which he had taken to save it, and for his house, that is, for the Jews, from whom he came according to his human nature. The reference to incense is really to its composite nature, so it connotes that his death was for the *totality* of all human beings and their many sins.

Lyra notes that the previous chapter was about "special" purification, and this chapter concerns general purification. Since there are so many ways uncleanness could be picked up, it is a good idea to have this general sacrifice, as a sort of sweeper. He likes what his Jewish sources tell him, that the ceremony was a memorial of the golden calf incident. Therefore, the first offering of the calf is for the Aaronic priestly sin (and has nothing to do with the universal offering of the red cow at Numbers 18, *pace* Peter Comestor), which could include sins of unfit priests serving at the altar. The offering of the ram is more "positive," in memory of that offered for Isaac. As for "and he will cleanse the sanctuary," Lyra takes this to mean not that the sanctuary has its own corruption, but that people and priests corrupt it so it needs to be purified, for it was in the middle of a dirty camp. The confession and atonement is general, in that the priest could not know all the specific sins of the people.

Calvin takes it to be the sacramental action itself that here is cleansed. In the churches, by baptism and the Lord's Supper, God appears to us in his only-begotten Son: these are the pledges of our holiness. Yet such is our corruption that we never cease from profaning these very instruments of the Spirit whereby God sanctifies us. So we pray God will cleanse these defilements. Presumably cleansing prayer is required so that the sacraments keep their efficacy. Calvin thinks the purpose of the Day of Atonement was to ratify all other propitiations made to God during the year and to remind them of the necessity of these.

Calov was far from happy with Grotius' notion, dependent on "recent Jews," who saw verse 24's sacrifice for the sake of the temple altar as about prayer formulas for "good air" or for the keeping of the scepter of Judah. No, it was for the reconciling of the people. For what else was the priest doing in verse 6 other than praying for *people* when praying for "his house"? So also in verse 24 *people not buildings* are meant. Cocceius takes the order that the sanctuary be expiated to signify that the dwelling of God in men cannot be holy without the sacrifice and blood of Christ. According to Hebrews 9:23 the heavens have to be purified not because they need it but that sinners coming there will need it.

For Leclerc it is all about cleansing the temple since it has become polluted through human contact. Nothing could be done for those who had committed capital offences—that is, sins of the mind or intention. God nowhere said that he would remit such through offerings and it is God's judgment that counts. God gives life to men that they follow his laws and if anyone violates those laws through malice or negligence then they deserve to lose that life, if God should wish to use that right. Yet God, with his highest justice, did not want to treat the Hebrews in their sins according to the legal measures, but he relaxed the law and was content with solemn confession of sin and an appropriate punishment.

Penitence as Response (vv. 29–32)

Whereas Ralph's emphasis is on the seventh month as symbolic of grace, Hugh comments that this fasting on the tenth day is to afflict the body, not the soul; just as with Paul in 2 Corinthians 4:16, that the outward man wears away while the inner man is renewed day by day. The Jewish insistence on fasting and rest as a "law for all time" means it continues even after the temple's destruction. Denys takes "all time" (v. 29) to mean that this is not about one special sacrament or calendar observance. Rather, for the *spiritual* understanding of chapter 16, one should only approach *all* the sacraments diligently and only when duly prepared. God's mysteries are not always to be investigated but the heavenly light shines in a weaker way below the clouds of life or even of Christ's humanity. To offer up the calf means the discipline with which we oppose indulgence. To offer up the ram in the whole offering is when the higher part of the soul offers up control along with the lower powers to divine worship. And we offer up the calf when we pray to receive the forgiveness, grace, and salvation made available through Christ's death. And we offer the ram as a burnt-offering when we offer up the most bitter passion of the Son to the Father with thanks. But, fifth, the goat offered up is Christ, in his flesh of sin. He has redeemed the lower sensual part, but that is not enough for salvation for we must add our higher part to God; there needs to be that synergy of merit. Sixth, and last, the goat that is sent out symbolizes that the sins of the people are lamented. The thurible in which incense is burned means the human heart when it is allowed to contemplate ecstatically, within the veil, the vastness of the Trinity. It is notable that it is the intellect that needs to act to complete the reconciliation with God.

The Puritan Willet saw in this ceremony an encouragement to the church to think in terms of general, not particular, confession. And, he said, we should remember that Ezra (Neh 8:4) reformed temple architecture by introducing a pulpit of wood, as if to show that worship is never to serve ostentation. Since the text does not major on whether one faces the east or not, neither should any interpretation. Repentance itself is what, with vice sent away, forgives. As he concludes: "Hierome saith well, . . . what sinne doth not weeping purge?"

For Leclerc, verse 34 shows that sins of the mind and deliberation—such as pride, greed, and drunkenness—were not expiated by these rites, but required instead penitential solemn contemplation, which would engender a hatred of those sins. Leclerc feels confident that such sins can be avoided by the Christian, although this is really made possible by the NT, since the OT makes no provision for help (Heb 11: 27). The "Jewish doctors" teach that here the lighter sins can be redeemed now, with the heavier ones suspended to the Day of Judgment. But the Law here does not have penance as its rationale and there is no mention of any "suspended sentence." What was the use for them of this day if the earlier chapters deal with sin and restitution, well, it could be that sins that would never come to light are dealt with on this special day. Leclerc is unclear whether that includes intentional sins.

Knobel views this chapter as "a restoration of the theocractic community." Such cleansing practice has no corresponding parallels in the ancient world. Against J. K. W. Vatke (d. 1882) there is no need to think it started in exilic times. It was Elohistic, truly ancient. Keil stresses the importance of fasting so it does not become an empty ritual, reflecting a pietistic background where outward discipline matters greatly. The yearly repetition of the general atonement showed that the sacrifices of the Law were not sufficient to make the servant of Good perfect according to his own conscience, and this could not fail to awaken a longing for the perfect sacrifice of the eternal High Priest, viz. Christ. Bonar laments in his concluding thoughts that his era has stifled any consciousness of sin. Therefore "it is only God's authoritative revelation that can ensure the cure, only He can assure us of pardon, and of all the barriers between ourselves and His love."

Contemporary Observations: Christian and Jewish

"One can argue that the Day of Atonement grew out of a theory of a removal of all sinful matter . . . and set up an opposition between God literally placed at the center and the centrifugal wilderness places" (Jürgens 2001, 75). Such polarization needs to be preserved by the priestly action, even while crossing the distance between the two. One could also argue that such things help bring the everyday world into the presence of the holy (Assmann 1991, 13; cf. Janowski and Zenger 2003, 81). Recently a number of NT scholars have argued that Paul did *not* interpret Christ's death as a "sacrifice of atonement" for sins (Lev 4f; 16). "The *huper* formulations do not represent a sacrificial category" (Lampe; but see Frey 2005, 3–50).

On this account, life simply overcomes death by being superimposed on it, rather than going underneath it to deal with sin. The views of Douglas and Milgrom—that life is affirmed to the detriment of death-dealing miasma—give rise to an alternative understanding, one which is positive rather than corrective. In Leviticus 16, when blood is sprinkled to wipe out unwitting sins, in no way is the entire existence of the sinner represented; in fact, there is no representation. Rather, sins that had accumulated at the altar were overcome by this offering of life. As Baruch Schwartz (1995, 3) puts it: Milgrom has realized "that the focus of the priestly *kipper* is the decontamination of the sanctuary from pollution caused by bodily impurities and by Israel's transgressions and penetrating the sphere of the sacred from afar." The giving of life and a healthy respect for mystery is reflected in ecclesial readings too (cf. Kasper 1976, 399). There is also an insistence (e.g., in Baruch Levine's commentary; 1989, 64), with reference to Leviticus 16:33: "The cultic texts understood the verb *kipper* primarily in a functional, or technical sense: 'to perform rites of expiation,' as well as any cleansing of the sanctuary. In such rituals, the physical acts themselves do not forgive, but God does simultaneously." So it is about doing the right thing so that the deity would act. This is not quite *do ut des*, but about God acting through or alongside the ritual.

Yet, on the other hand, interpreters such as Klawans (2007) have wanted to widen defilement to include control of excess of life (especially sex) as well as signs of death. Klawans concludes that defiling transgression undoes the good that the sacrifices outlined in the earlier chapters have accomplished, hence an annual *yom kippur* is needed. In other words, the corrective purpose should not be forgotten—restoration to a pristine state. The institution within Catholicism, since Vatican II, of the annual (Lenten) collective Sacrament of Reconciliation is to be viewed as a biblical-theological attempt to preserve a kind of Day of Atonement, one which turns the church to its Creator in a way analogous to Judaism. The power of the experience as a ritual whose observance has continued into modern times, with startling effects, can be seen in the case of Franz Rosenzweig—the influential Jewish theologian and philosopher—who on Yom Kippur in October 1913 seems to have rediscovered Judaism as a necessary prophetic counterpoint to Christianity, even if the precise significance of Yom Kippur to Rosenzweig is disputed (Horwitz 2006).

Leviticus 17

Irregular Sacrifices (vv. 1–9)

THE CONTEXT IS ONE of unregulated sacrifice made outside the tabernacle, especially to demons (*seʿiyrim*), as Theodoret insists. Hugh of St. Cher writes that these matters are legal and temporal and specify times and places; they are therefore not eternal commands, whatever the force of verse 7. The animals specified were those which pagans used to worship, as Ralph and Augustine affirm. Langton considers "fornication" as the NT equivalent—offering one's body to demons.

Lyra maintains that blood-eating outside the prescribed place was a Gentile practice. Lyra admits that there are places in the Bible, such as Judges 13, where sacrifice is offered by Israel outside the confines of the tabernacle, but this was an exception to the rule, directly commanded by God through an angel, while in 1 Kings 18 Elijah was led by the revealed instruction of God, as the miracle that followed made clear. These things are evil not in themselves but when performed for occult purposes. Denys, following Aquinas (*ST* I-IIae, q102), thinks the "fixed place" mystically prefigures that in the "gospel law" all things would be offered in ecclesial unity, and individual charity would be place on the altar of the one faith, so that all heresies and schisms be avoided.

Brenz comments that 2 Chronicles 33 (Manasseh) shows what goes wrong when God's instructions for worship get ignored, since "all that is not from faith is sin" (Rom 14:23). In the same way, for NT Christians there is to be one "place": Christ alone. Here the Spirit called the godly towards that one sole sacrifice of Christ. As for the prohibition in Leviticus 17, Calvin suggests this is a rule for Israelite believers only and makes sense only in the ancient cultic context, but Lapide writes that this instructs the church concerning the appropriate place for worship. In Christianity we avoid the word "temple," but we do use the term "house of God" (*domus Dei*), which has come to mean the mother church in any one city. Or sometimes it is called "*dominicum*." Lapide is thus able to employ the centralizing principle of vv. 1–9 for the church.

On verse 7 ("to commit fornication with strange gods") Willet gives Abulensis's explanation as "beastly conjunction with spirits, appearing sometime in the shape of men, called *incubi*, sometimes of women, called *succubi*, acting the part of generation, without any carnal delight." Willet ridicules this, since "seldome doe spirits appeare in such beautiful shapes, but for the most part in horrible apparition, and commonly like ugly Negroes, as Oleaster saith, was confessed unto him by certain witches, whom hee delt with in his inquisition." Yet hunting game is allowed when not for ostentation but for refreshing of the mind, confirming of health, or training for war (so it is not for clergymen); and never immoderately, such that the hunting dogs are more cared for than poor servants. Abulensis had noted on verse 13 that they cannot have hunted with dogs or else the food would have been unclean. Leclerc then adds that they did not have any dogs in the desert anyway. Calmet relates Herodotus' report (*Histories* 2.46) concerning "goat demons" (v. 7), that there was a deity in lower Egypt with a goat's face and thighs to symbolize fertility, a bit like Pan. It was not the case that the Israelites believed in this creature, but it was a figure with which they were familiar. The Israelites had learned from their time near this area, "Mendes"—across the branch of the Nile in Tanis.

Henry opposes the seventeenth-century "Cambridge Platonist" Dr. Ralph Cudworth's interpretation, "that while they had their tabernacle so near them in the midst of their camp they ate no flesh but what had first been offered to God, but that when they were entering Canaan this constitution was altered (Deut 12:21) . . . Yet it is hard to construe this as a temporary law, when it is expressly said to be a statute for ever (v. 7); and therefore, 2. It should seem rather to forbid only the killing of beasts *for sacrifice* any where but at God's altar." This is a law that could reasonably be kept. Keil goes further, appealing to Herodotus and Strabo, to establish that it was a Persian custom to spread sacrifices around deities. He thinks that "the expression 'a statute forever' (v. 7) refers to the principle of the law, that sacrifices were to be offered to Jehovah alone, and not to the law that every animal was to be slain before the tabernacle, which was afterwards repealed by Moses, when they were about to enter Canaan, where it could no longer be carried out (Deut xii.15)." This, of course, means that the inspired text of Leviticus is not overruled when Christians stopped *temple* sacrifice, so long as whatever they sacrifice is directed towards God. Dillmann is much more interested in relating how Leviticus 17–25, which he refers to as "holiness laws," is not, as Colenso and Smend thought, the newest part of the book, presupposing Ezekiel, but that some of the most ancient laws are contained probably from two sources, and thinks the thing is hardly Deuteronomic, in light of "the statute given for all generations" (v. 7b).

The Soul and the Blood (vv. 10–14)

Augustine insists that there is no total equivalence of soul and blood, even though the LXX encourages such a reading (*psyche pasés sarkos haima autou estin*), as do the Greek and the Hebrew of Genesis 9:4, where the two stand in mutual apposition. Augustine is aware that the preposition necessitates a translation: "the life of the flesh is in the blood," but gets round the problem by saying there is such identification only in the case of animals. For humans, the soul is *signified by* blood; just like a church, as a people, is signified by the building within which it worships. Theodoret's reason for the prohibition against eating blood is along the same lines, yet more realist: "for you have immortal souls, but the irrational animal has blood instead of a soul . . . to be sacrificed for your immortal and rational soul. If you ate this, you would eat soul which would fill the place of the rational soul."

Procopius develops this further: we have souls, and animals have something that by analogy could be called "soul." So pouring out animal blood on the ground symbolizes how human souls are separated from bodies and in Hades die in a different way. The one who treats the soul like the body and therefore lives according to the flesh will in turn be despised and die. In speaking of wild game (v. 13) those who praise the hunter (devil) are symbolized. Isho'dad comments that Satan, seeing that he could not kill the nature which is the soul, taught his servants to use blood as food.

The *Glossa Ordinaria* cites Augustine's *Locutiones* on verse 10, that the LXX repeats the word "man" (*anthrōpos anthrōpos*) to show that keeping this command applies to "everyman," the uncircumcised as much as to the circumcised. Acts 15:29 is probably in view. The *Glossa*, following Hesychius, then allegorizes "eating blood" to mean hatred of one's brother. The one "eating blood" will be lost from the people, or even the human race. One must be careful or he will send any "lack of mercy and ungodliness along with the evil spirits into the eternal fire which is prepared for the devils and his angels" (Matt 25:41). To show how much in turn we must be merciful, he shows that he shed his blood for our expiation, saying: "I have given it to you." This is followed with a snippet of Hesychius' spiritualizing interpretation of verse 13, that God cares for us by instructing us not to hurt one another, through turning the other cheek. Christ was the sheep that withdrew from all that he was allowed to eat, so violent and greedy men consumed him (cf. Gal 5:15 for this usage). The earth swallows sins once confessed and put to death by mortification.

Ralph first of all tries to be scientific about blood: it has perhaps its source in the depth of the spine from where it feeds us, for to say that it comes from the neck sounds foolish. Yet his foray into the literal sense shudders to a halt when he considers that we can and do eat Christ's blood in the sacrament, and that means that we have to re-think what this command might mean figuratively. The human soul is not to be found in the blood, but only the physical life force that ends with death. In that case, what is the problem with eating it? Well, it symbolizes our consuming what is natural rather than spiritual. Eating blood can also be understood figuratively as symbolizing depravity, since when the higher powers drop their guard, the natural tendency of the soul inclines downwards. Likewise Hugh of St. Cher wonders whether "eating blood" today really results in God's setting his face against a person. What about Matthew 15:11, that it is not the things which go into a man that make him unclean? This command must be taken mystically, and "blood" here means illicit lust that harms the soul. Hugh, with an appeal to Augustine, distinguishes the *soul of the flesh* as some vital force diffused throughout the body's veins from the *soul of the body*, which is not the life, but is the rational soul, which migrates yet ceases with death. Hugh explains the *Gloss* on verse 17 by adding that eating one's sin means fulfilling sin by engaging the will with it, playing to one's lower blood, as it were. Peter Comestor (*Scholastic History*) records that Josephus had said that Moses thought that the soul and spirit were contained in the blood. But we know that the spirit is that which joins the soul to the body and by which the flesh can still operate even when the soul is departed: the spirits and souls of the righteous are in the Lord (Wis 3:1). In other words, not having a soul/spirit distinction made Moses think the spiritual part was in the blood.

In this medieval period "[s]cholastic theologians from Grosesteste and Aquinas to Johannes von Paltz cited Leviticus 17:11 . . . and quoted doctors [*phisicos*] to describe blood as 'the friend of nature and the seat of the soul'" (Bynum 2007, 157, citing Treue 1992, 104). Indeed Grosseteste (*De cessatione legum*, 11) suggests there are two bloods, or rather two types of Christ's blood: one that is from nutriments, and the other blood which is the "friend of nature" and which Moses meant by saying that the seat of the soul is in the blood (Bynum 2007, 143). This was the way that the soul could be present throughout the body and accordingly there were two kinds, bread and wine, in the Eucharist since he assumed both body and soul. The wine represents the blood in which is the seat of the soul. This view is repeated by Biel (*Canonis Missae expositio*, lectio 52, vol. 2, 304): Christ did not die by bleeding, but we live by it, for blood is the only part that can go on living outside the body, and is thus symbolic of Christ himself. Grosseteste was also "symbolic" in his interpretation in another work (*De decem mandatis*): the reason for not eating blood is so manifestly false, it should not be received by Christians with any literal force; "this reason if taken literally is silly, for on that ground we would not be able to eat meat; it can only be meant in a spiritual, moral sense—that we should abstain from delighting in sin" (I, x, 14; 1987, 56f).

Albert the Great maintained the Eucharistic "offering up" to be an oblation of the blood, a lifting up of the blood to heaven where it belongs (Bynum 2007, 217), which presumes the "once for all" (Heb 9:22) death (*Comm in IV Sent*, 4.13, F, art. 23). The logic is that there is an offering of something killed through the priest's acting *in persona Christi*. Unlike at Calvary this is not a passive suffering but the action of Christ who is no longer "victim." However, Aquinas wanted to keep the term "sacrifice" for this oblation. In the *Summa Theologiae*, the term "oblation" is said to be "common to all things in the temple worship of God which ought to become consumed" (IIa–IIae q86, art1 resp); and this is followed by a quotation from Leviticus 2:1: when anyone brings an oblation of a sacrifice to the Lord . . ." Bynum sees two contradictory currents: "On the one hand, both devotional theology and university discourse moved increasingly to stress *sanguis Christi* as drops, bloodshed, as something 'poured out'; on the other, theologians struggled to keep the sacrifice of the Mass 'bloodless,' an image of crucifixion in which the blood is offered up but not spilled anew" (Bynum 2007, 218). In fact, this is not a contradiction if one considers that the devotion to the blood is very much one of looking to the past "sacred head sore wounded." The Eucharistic offering is that—a sort of image to be offered up without involving killing. In that sense the special provisions for blood in Leviticus 17 were echoed in the offering up of the blood without its being "shed anew." The Council of Trent's "bloodless sacrifice" in the Eucharist was a way of following Aquinas where both the Last Supper and the Mass presented or offered the sacrifice of Calvary, such that sins could actually be forgiven in those moments where there was due penitent faith (see McHugh 1991, 175–79). There is in the Mass an offering "for us" of a sacrifice.

Nevertheless, it seems that the majority of later medieval commentators avoided the anthropological and Eucharistic questions in favor of a simple ethical interpretation of that chapter. To eat blood is forbidden, thinks Langton, for it does not mean benefiting from the death of martyrs but rather delighting in their murders or taking pleasure in disrespecting them and the blood of Christ or others whom Christ told us to love. Thomas Aquinas, elsewhere, sees the commandment as driven by "idolatry avoidance" and humanitarianism "because this form of death is very painful to the victim; and the Lord wished to withdraw them from cruelty even in regard to irrational animals, so as to be less inclined to be cruel to other men, through being used to be kind to beasts (*ST* Ia–IIae, q102, art6, ad1). Similarly, Lyra is not particularly interested in the question of blood itself, more in the willful paganism it symbolized. Denys, as a representative of later medieval piety, interprets in a moral way: we do not eat blood, that is we do not condone or share in the evil and carnal works of others, nor inflict cruelty on others, nor profit from their goods and works.

For Brenz, the avoidance of "eating blood" means there is to be no blood-spilling at all. This law intended to restrain humans. For all blood is very special stuff, being for holy use only and thus not for eating. Of course, this is all for the sake of pointing to Christ's blood: and so it is impious to eat it in the Mass. David would not even consume water brought by the three heroes (1 Chr 11). Did Christ himself talk of eating his blood? No, that would have been abominable. He orders us rather to believe that by his blood he has reconciled us and applies to us the merit of his blood by the sacrament of the Lord's Supper, so that our faith be strengthened. Spangenberg affirms that to drink in the way Christ commanded is to believe that by his blood alone he has driven out sins and confirm this faith through the sacrament of the Lord's Supper. Acts 15(:20)'s ruling on not drinking blood was only temporary, for the benefit of Jewish Christians. "Today" drinking blood is not an issue.

Calvin has both a moral and a Eucharistic interpretation. "Although it not be consistent that the blood of a brute should be compensated for by the death of a man, still we must remember that this mode of institution was necessary for a rude people." Further, "we have elsewhere seen in what manner blood atones for souls, i.e., in a sacramental manner, . . . what properly belongs to Christ is thus transferred by *metonymy* to figures and symbols, yet in such a way that the similitude should neither be empty nor inefficacious; for in so far as the fathers apprehended Christ in the external sacrifices, atonement was truly exhibited in them." He adds that the apostolic injunction against blood consumption was a relic of their Jewish origins and not perpetually binding on the church (cf. 1 Cor 10:25).

Lapide, however, thinks one abstains from animal blood for the sake of honoring Christ's blood. Christ wants the same sacrifice of *his* blood (and of his body) to be offered frequently, that "through it and through the sacramental reception, the fruit of his bloody perfect sacrifice made once by him be applied to each person." Hesychius inspires Lapide to think that we are here instructed not to retaliate to any violence, but to correct others through our patience. Willet the Puritan criticizes Lorinus' Catholic interpretation of verse 14 that the prohibition on drinking blood does not apply to Christians living in NT times, so thus one *can* drink Christ's blood. However, writes Willet, "as it was unlawful then to eat the blood of the sacrifices, whereby Christ's blood was represented: so neither now is there any cause of tasting Christ's blood." In other words, the Catholic case for drinking Christ's blood can hardly rely on the OT, which tells its readers *not* to drink blood.

Any Eucharistic reference in these verses is well lost by the early Enlightenment. Calmet reinforces God's method of judgment here where it is not specific (v. 10) with an appeal to a Psalm: if anyone eats blood, fire will come from God's face (Ps 17[18]:9). If the crime was publicly known, the culprit would be sentenced to death, but if kept hidden from view, then God would reserve the right to punish. The reason for this law was to lead the Jews away from cruelty. Now verse 14 reinforces verse 11 to mean he is talking not just about animals but that humans too are included; and it is not unfitting to say this about a human too, that blood carries all that is vital for life. Perhaps "blood" represents the "sensitive" soul. He recalls *Odyssey* 10, where blood was used to conjure up the dead seer Tiresias. Moses would have nothing to do with such things, and even strangled animals are not be eaten, as Acts 15 confirmed.

On not drinking blood, Voltaire notes that the verse makes animals and humans have the same status, with both having life-blood. Bishop Warburton (d. 1779), in playing down the reason for the prohibition to be a belief in human immortality among the ancient Jews, ignores the fact that this belief was common to all legislators of other ancient societies. On Warburton's account, the worst the Jews could do was to threaten death. With irony Voltaire states that the Jewish religion thereby stands out as the most ignorant and superstitious with God speaking to them alone, and that their Christian and Muslim "children" have repeated this bad habit. More modern scholars have tried to universalize their religion, but it is not part of the traditional self-understanding of that faith.

For Leclerc, the cause of the command in verse 10 is the same as that in Genesis 9:4: "restraint." According to *Aeneid* I.118, blood and soul can be confused; see also Servius, quoted by Grotius. The Israelites were wrong to think one could drink any blood not used for expiating sins. Blood of whatever sort, animal or human, consecrated or otherwise, is to be treated with reverence. The blood is to be poured on the ground (v. 13) not in the "snaring" manner of a pagan ritual, but because the blood is the soul of the flesh.

Matthew Henry's approach is nothing if not sensible. Even where there is no prohibition, there can still be reverence:

> The blood of beasts is no longer the ransom, but Christ's blood only; and therefore there is not now that reason for abstaining from blood which there was then, and we cannot suppose it was the will of God that the law should survive the reason of it. Yet . . . God would have his people to regard the life even of their beasts. The blood then made atonement figuratively,

now the blood of Christ makes atonement really and effectually; to this therefore we must have a reverent regard, and not use it as a common thing.

Knobel is careful to emphasize that it is the life, not its vessel, the blood, that counts and which does the work of atonement.

Leviticus 18

Holiness and the Lord's Statutes (vv. 1–5)

WHILE PHILO (*DE CONGRESSU* 28 / *De plantatione* 37) called this passage "the great highway," its reception in the NT was less enthusiastic (cf. Sprinkle 2008). Yet in many ways the Christian tradition's reading is closer to Philo's. Verse 3 inspires Procopius to comment that God shows that his ways are different from the ways in which humans have chosen to walk, and that one must turn back to God's. Sins against nature have the effect of sickness, which causes God and nature to vomit them out. So these are repellent not only to reason, but also to God's mysterious kind of goodness. Our Savior has given a clear picture of what is holy and as we draw near that we can become holy since he is: that familial closeness is our holiness and keeping Sabbath is sign of love in the familiarity/closeness of God.

Hesychius notes that the emphasis in verses 2–3 is on abstaining from certain things, but that verses 4–5 are more about positive righteousness, from which one should recognize that one does not give to God simply by obeying his Law and keeping his judgments and statutes, but rather in giving *oneself*. To paraphrase the text: for you will live in them, giving work to virtues, by which eternal life is kept for men. The *Glossa* is quite clear that there is life only in those who believing in Christ, since the Law does not give life unless the gospel supervenes. To this Peter Cantor adds: it is not enough that we keep the Law in part but it is necessary we observe "every precept and judgment." For they are not to be observed by the Jews alone but by all nations, if they wish to fight for God.

Ralph of Flaix confirms that the former people did not yet know devotion but acted out of fear. Faith is not under the Law, but faith is in Christ, so let us then listen to his precepts, and by walking in his ways, constantly increase in virtue. But Christ's precepts are, or at least include, what we have in the Pentateuch as here. Whereas judgments (*iudicia*) pertain to the punishment of sinners, precepts (*pracepta*) hand down to us the rule for living. Holiness for Ralph is all about keeping "clean" the flow of doctrine that comes through the teachers. Scripture in mentioning the sordid things that follow actually washes them away, so that one does not get contaminated by reading about them. We should not presume to scold the divine Law when it offends us.

Up to this point (Lev 18) the Lord had spoken mysteries, claims Hugh of St. Cher, and not the truth as such. However, now he speaks plainly to instruct and lead them out of evil habits, by first striking fear then speaking love. It is the height of wickedness to live as an example of wickedness, and to refrain from following the nations also includes refraining from their superstitions. The fact that "I am the Lord your God" is repeated reflects the *two*fold testament. Likewise, on verse 23 where it talks about bestiality, Hugh admits that there are many places where people are shocked by Scripture and despise it. Although by a deadly touch (Lev 15:12) the light and the fragile vessels are polluted, yet the springs and cisterns are not (i.e., the doctors who store and give others to drink). So teachers may discuss these delicate subjects but not preach about them. Thus Scripture is not unclean although it might become so in proclamation.

Stephen Langton sounds a practical, pastoral note when he proposes that it is the intention of the whole Law that we abstain from evil things and hold to the good ones. The Father is the name of love, who encourages believers to do mercy in a hidden way. Seeing others punished inspires fear, so that the Son can then inspire love, so that we become doers of the Law. "I am the Lord" is significant here: we are not to ruin our knowledge of him by joining with fleshly things. We are to break our bread with the poor just as he is merciful, where we would expect "because I am just." But it is more fitting to say that we are to be like him in terms of his mercy, and that "blessed are the merciful" is what leads us into the kingdom. "I am the Lord" is the he who does not keep on "showing up" our sins but is ready to delete and cover them when we confess these.

Lyra sums up these medieval "moral" interpretations: first, the Jews who obeyed the laws lived in peace and quiet, but those who did not faced famine and war. As for the life of Old Testament Jews "by grace," although the works of the Law did not justify, still in as much as they were done from obedience to God and by faith in the mediator who was to come, they justified, in that such justification is attributed in Holy Scripture to faith and obedience towards God. Second, in his "moral" explanation, Lyra adds that there is a wider sense to "uncovering nakedness" (v. 6), for the Law uncovers the spiritual nakedness of everyone, except those who manage to be formed by charity so as to avoid sinning. Denys too wants to be cautious: as then, so now: without faith in the coming Savior, these laws cannot give a perfecting form of grace. Brenz highlights the "I am the Lord" (vv. 2, 5): here the Prince God adds his signature to confirm the edict's authority. Prophets were always pushing kings to keep public laws, and even Demosthenes and the Athenians were determined more to keep the old laws than think up new ones. With this note of authority established, he continues: "will live in these"—that is, whoever perfectly fulfills my Law, he merits and gains by his obedience not only the preservation of this bodily life in but also happiness of the future lasting life. Yet since only Jesus has managed this, our righteousness only comes as that of faith when we confess that Jesus is Lord.

Chytraeus takes the content of chapter 18 to be the eternal and unchangeable norms of the divine mind placed in human nature. Because of such illicit relations the Gentiles were vomited out of the land. This is not merely a law of the nations (*ius gentium*) but is by divine law (*iure divino*). This could mean civil morality, but the Christian no longer needs any public laws since his soul is untouched by regulations as much as he is untroubled by life's calamities. For he can believe and having total obedience imputed to him by Christ in turn has the gift to obey the Law of God. Spangenberg strikes a more "communitarian" note: although the Mosaic polity has been abrogated, still the natural law, which is contained in the legislation of Moses, has not been. God knows of a religious and a civil republic. We need to try to follow that perfect righteousness. None can reach eternal life by righteousness of works, but we have to get there by faith through Christ. There are some laws which men can obey externally. But then the inward voluntary obedience means we at least try to reach perfect righteousness by faith in Christ, but what must be on the surface is confession of our sins.

Willet comments on verse 5 that faith in Christ is not commanded in the Law: the Law is "but a way to bring us unto it, and Christ *is the end of the law*: the end, which is faith in Christ and that whereof it is an end cannot be the same." Belief in the triune Creator is required in the Law, but not belief in Christ the Savior. The Law is perfect in theory but imperfect in practice. On Scripture mentioning disgusting things, "but like as the Sunne-beames, shining upon a stinking lake, are not thereby defiled, so the Scriptures, in providing against such unclean sinnes, remained most pure."

Cocceius writes that not all the commands of Moses are contained in the Decalogue. But the "ten words" gave them the reason for doing the others. And the precepts that matter are those in which we live, i.e., precepts of sanctity, in which there is the image of God. And they are immutable since God is. Whereas dogmas about God could be presented differently according to the state of the people, precepts are said more "straight." Cocceius' supersessionist drive to take away any saving power from the former people's Law-keeping means relegating the precepts to laws of nature, written on the heart, yet which, when God and conscience are not revered, will not work (v. 24).

Calmet reports that, according to the Targum's gloss, "live in them" means a long life or eternal life. He approves Lyra's view that this means happiness in this life, as well as the life of grace and lastly the life of glory. The blessing promised is not just avoidance of eternal judgment. Likewise for Henry, with a Puritan's joy in the commandments, the stakes are not just "eternal":

> If we keep God's commandments in sincerity, though we come short of sinless perfection, we shall find that the way of duty is the way of comfort, and will be the way to happiness . . . Yet, it is not so in force in the nature of a covenant such that the least transgression shall for ever exclude us from this life. The alteration which the gospel (Rom 10:5) has made is in the last word ["in them"]: still the man that does them shall live, but not live in them . . . The just shall live, but they shall live by faith, by virtue of their union with Christ, who is their life.

Some in the nineteenth century, not least in the distinguishing of a Holiness Code (H) in Leviticus 17–26 from the rest of Leviticus (see the famous article by Klostermann [1877]), viewed these chapters as concerning "the sanctification of daily life." Mrs. Cornwallis's *Observations* (1820), written as distillation of wisdom for her children, concludes: "How blessed are we to be born in a Christian country, where sin is compelled to hide her hideous head, and where we may live without beholding any dreadful violations of decency." This was not the case in the time Leviticus 18 was written, where preservation from degradation required strong commands.

Incest and Boundaries (vv. 6–23)

Diodore of Tarsus insisted on a purely literal understanding of Leviticus 18:18, that one should not marry a wife's sister while one's wife was alive meant one could marry her after one's wife's death. But Basil of Caesarea (Epistle 199.23 and 217.78) interpreted this more rigorously, writing that, once married, a man's the sister-in-law becomes bound to him through his wife (Lutterbach 1990, 180). The rigorous line was the more influential. In the east, the Synod of Neocaesarea's ruling (355) became an imperial law against such arrangements. In the Western church the ascetic Pope Siricius (*Ep.* 10.10) relayed the canons of a Roman synod to Gallic bishops: one cannot, he said, appeal to the example of Jacob who married two sisters, for that was just a concession. In the Christian Empire the extension of the Roman law of incest to a wider group of family relationships happened under pressure from the Levitical code. Chrysostom in his Homily 34 [6–7] on 1 Corinthians agreed with this sentiment, commenting on Leviticus 18:6: "It is enough for your affection towards them that you were the fruit of the same birth-pangs, and that the others are in a different relation to you. Why would you narrow the breadth of love?" Augustine comments that as for not taking one's wife's sister (v. 18), Jacob did that, although there was not yet a law against it, or one could justify him by saying he was tricked. What *would* be unjust would be to divorce the first sister so as to avoid adultery with the second. The LXX addition ("so as to arouse jealousy") guided Augustine's interpretation. In his *City of God* (XV.16), written around the same time as his *Questions on the Heptateuch*, he systematizes his thinking: "Yet no one doubts that the modern prohibition of marriage between cousins is an advance in civilized standards. And this not only because of the point I have already made, namely that the ties of kinship are thereby multiplied. There is another reason. There is in human conscience a certain mysterious and inherent sense of decency, which is natural and admirable, which ensures that if kinship gives a woman a claim to honor and respect, she is shielded from lust."

The *Glossa* on verse 18, following Hesychius, is aware that the LXX has glossed the Hebrew idiom for sexual relations as "to provoke jealousy." However, the Hebrew idiom "to uncover nakedness" can have a wider meaning than a sexual one, and can also denote "defaming someone" or exaggerating their fault, and that was what Noah's daughters did in Genesis 9. Langton echoes this: "the Lord will not allow a confession of sin to lead to a bad reputation, and we are not to rush to reveal the sins of others in case we incur a curse. For as the *Glossa* [Hesychius in fact] says that is hardly to act in love, which is the fullness of the law." A mixed spiritualizing and literal interpretation follows. The sin of adultery is caused by lust, as in the case of David, and in turn results in murder. The matter of sexual lust overcoming decency—as for instance, if a man insists on sex during menstruation—is also foregrounded.

Comestor thinks that in the beginning the command "to leave father and mother" (Gen 2:24) meant that only two relationships were banned then (i.e., those with one's parents), but that under the Law this grew so that twelve types were disallowed. Hugh St. Cher also observes that this legislation concerns Genesis 2:24, about leaving the family unit. In fact, thirteen relations are excluded, for an increase of humans to worship God is desired. However, in the age of grace a number are excluded from this rule for the sake of continence, and everyone is forbidden to fornicate.

Denys reminds us that Aquinas (*In Sent.* IV, dist. 40) held that incest goes against the law of nature in undermining marriage and is thus not fitting. Affinity (being related through marriage) is no different from consanguinity (being related by blood), since these are people one has to live with. In the new Law the church has ruled that a spiritual closeness (particularly in religious houses) can be an impediment to marriage. The late medieval attitude tends to be restrictive since allowing marriage would have been an incentive to pre-marital sex where cousins lived under the same roof.

Luther mocks the pope for trying to make marriage a matter of coercion and making the jurists have so much work to do. The pope should give counsel without legislating and confusing the issue by saying that secret engagements are not to be entered into, but when they are, they are to be kept. Marriage is for Christian freedom as the only way to a righteousness which excels that of the pagans, so that if a Christian marries his niece on her father's death that should not draw comment. Of course, a forced marriage is no marriage. It is certainly permissible to marry a sister-in-law after a brother's death. Yet these laws were not given to anyone other than the Jews, and Luther is aware of exceptions like Abraham and Sarah. The marriage laws would come back to haunt Luther in the form of Philip of Hesse's bigamy, which Luther preferred as a way of his princely supporter's managing to avoid the charge of adultery.

Brenz writes that in the Law of Moses polygamy was conceded, still it was not allowed to marry two sisters at the same time, lest one torment the other constantly, as happened in the case of Jacob. Not all the possible combinations are mentioned, but natural law insists the list should be expanded. Yet has it not often been shown that through the spread of the gospel into all the world the cult of Leviticus and the commonwealth of Moses have been abolished. Since then this ordering of marriage also has its place among the Levitical law, does it fall with the other Levitical orderings? Not at all! For those things are abrogated which were properly Levitical, which belonged to the Mosaic commonwealth. But these regulations are natural, everlasting, and unchangeable. The Decalogue is to be observed by us with great authority, not because it is from Moses, but because it contains the law *of nature* and indicates the true fruit of faith.

One quickly gets the impression that this was one of the hottest issues in the mid-sixteenth century. "Next to the references to John 17 the most talked-about passage in Melanchthon's correspondence was Leviticus 18—and with good reason" (Wengert 1997, 116). Melanchthon also wrote a treatise on the subject: *De arbore consanguinitatis et affinitatis*. His opponent Osiander had produced in Nurnberg a

Engaging Leviticus

Kirchenordnung for there and for Brandenburg (1533); and then for Pfalz-Neuburg (1543). In the foreword he passed on the general hermeneutical principle of Brenz: "Likewise the Church should have its own rules for order, and one can learn from this set of laws given to the Jews, even if it did lead them to abuse it owing to their own superstition and misunderstanding. We should not ignore something good that has been abused." Osiander adds that in Leviticus 18 Moses is not giving an exhaustive list, but just an indicative one, as was the case in Leviticus 11 where he forbade all animals that don't chew the cud and have cloven hooves. To ignore these moral prohibitions is not just to ignore reason but to ignore Christ who said that no tittle would fall from the Law. Further, in a sermon from 1562 on Psalm 91, as to whether to flee from plague (1975-97, 6; 506-7: Nr 19), he observed: "Moses allowed that a man could wed the daughter of his own brother or sister [although, of course, Leviticus 18 does not mention the niece], so even more so the niece on the dead wife's side is not taboo. However one is not allowed to marry one's aunt because seed is not allowed ever to go back 'up' the line."

Chytraeus points to Roman examples such as Agrippina with Claudius her uncle; what a disaster! Crassus married his brother's widow and that did not end well. He sets out a diagram in the tradition of Melanchthon: one tree of consanguinity and one of affinity, of which there are three degrees: the first type is that a person is given to another through the matrimonial relationship, as Agnes (d. 1143) the daughter of Emperor Henry IV was married to Frederick the duke of Swabia. The second is when there are two persons coming in between, as when Agnes on the death of Frederick married Leopold of Austria, whose father was Otto of Freising, and Leopold was then related to the sister of Frederick the former husband and to all those blood relatives. The third kind is through another person added: as if on Agnes's death, Leopold of Austria married another wife, she would be connected to Frederick and his blood relatives by the third type of affinity. Only after that is marriage allowed. Henry VIII is mentioned, but the case is not discussed.

Lorinus thought it better to say that the patriarchs are excused of marrying a wife's sister because they lived before the Law than to plead with Augustine that they were tricked into doing so. Polygamy *per se* is not contrary to the first law of universal nature, and God accommodated it, as in Deuteronomy 21:15. But Christ brought marriage back to "one to one," as in the beginning (Matt 19:4-9).

Willet reports that for Isidore, Lorinus, and Cajetan consanguinity no longer counts after the fourth degree. "But the other opinion is more probable, that in right line ascending, and descending, the prohibition goeth, in infinitum, infinitely; that if Adam were now alive, hee could not contract matrimony with any." He spots Duns

Scotus and Junius relying on Gaius' *Institutes*. Nature's course is to develop, not stick to its roots. As for affinity, there are three kinds: "the Neere, Middle and Remote; as the brothers Wife is the first kind, the brothers Wives second husband in the second, the second husbands second Wife in the third. Affinity only bindeth in the first case of necessity; in the second for publike honesty: in the third of mere curiosity."

In a work that commented on passages prone to twisting by Protestants, the Jesuit Johannes Paludanus (1620) asserted that once the church used to forbid marriage to the seventh degree of consanguinity, but later to the fourth. Trent denied it could only be those relationships specified in Leviticus that were outlawed. God gave the Law to his particular people in order that the Law could be a common inheritance; but he also gave to his church of the New Testament the care of governing the Scriptures for the sake of all nations.

Bellarmine, in his *De matrimonia* chapter 27, contended that the law of nature only forbids in the first degree of consanguinity whether the relationship is across or down the line and in the first degree of affinity whichever way. He repeats Trent's affirmation that the church may grant dispensations. Lapide writes that the law of nature touches on this and so in individual precepts the word "turpitude" is repeated, since it is vile to marry a relative, since very nature would say that respect is owed to them. Bellarmine judged that many doubtless sinned in individual cases against the law of nature when they had relations with their kin, but does not admit a wider rule.

Willet countered that the pope has no right in "oecomenicall, civill nor ecclesiasticall" law. For the pope is an "enemy of marriage" and forgets that the ecclesiastical right "consisteth chiefly in the preaching of the Gospell and justification by faith in Christ." He then gives examples of shocking dispensations when it suited the pope: "Alexander the sixt dispensed with Ferdinand king of Sicily to marry his father's sister." Simply, since in cases of incestuous marriages God had not actually joined the couple, and thus they can easily be parted.

Lorinus held that not all these commands are fixed laws of nature: for Deuteronomy 25 would not have overruled it in allowing brother to raise up seed and Jacob would not have married two sisters if it were a natural law. And there are diverse punishments, so only some of these were offences against law of nature. But Willet thinks that the God of Deuteronomy 25 is well able to overrule a law of nature, though Leviticus 18 remains such. And so the pope cannot dispense with them despite Trent Session 24, c3: "these Lawes grounded upon the law of Nature, are not to be dispensed with, belonging rather to the Morall, then Judicial law. And that these laws are not abrogated by Christ is evident by Ioan Baptists reprehension of Herod, for having his brothers wife." Penalties may be changed by the church, but moral laws cannot be abrogated.

Many, Calov tells us, have disputed on this verse (v. 11) about a ban on sexual relations with a step-sister; both Reformed, Catholics, "and our own Lutherans" in Rostock, and lastly Grotius who takes it to be a case of adopted step-daughter which is a civil impediment to marriage. Calov doubts this from the Hebrew root, *moldot*. Grotius also argued that the law does not prohibit polygamy, but only where the wives are sisters, and also that the gospel does not forbid what the Law allows, and it must have pleased him that the Socinians and Anabaptists at least agreed with him on this (*lib. II de jure Pacis & Bellis c.V.§9*). Indeed the Law is not clear about polygamy, not even at Deuteronomy 21:15, since although two wives there are mentioned, this is forbidden to the king in Deuteronomy 17:16–17 (although there it is *many* wives, and Grotius would seem to have the better of the argument). Grotius thinks that there might have been some concession from God apart from the case of relations with one's parents. This laxity offends Calov.

Calmet mentions how Justinian had to clamp down on incest, which was rife in the ancient world. The case of Abraham, however, is not a good reason for saying incest was permitted up until the time of Moses. Leclerc remarks that the Persian and Chaldean priests were especially known for incest between parents and children. Not just Justinian but even the Greeks forbade it (despite Jupiter and Juno!), since the whole point of marriage was to link society. The point of verse 18 is not polygamy but marrying two *sisters*, relying on the translation of Serrano the Jew who recently edited the Pentateuch in this city (Amsterdam). Christ and Paul said nothing about polygamy, although it is clear from Deuteronomy 17:1 that that too was outlawed. Now it seems that for the OT monogamy was *preferable*, as Malachi suggests, but Piscator and Junius (as well as many others) are wrong to say that all polygamy is outlawed *here*.

Henry repeats Augustine's point, that it was requisite that it should be made clearly unlawful and detestable for the preventing of sinful familiarities between those that, in the days of their youth, are supposed to live in a house together, and yet cannot intermarry without defeating one of the intentions of marriage, which is the enlargement of friendship and interest. Keil states that for the Egyptians it was lawful to marry sisters and half-sisters but that the licentiousness of the women was very great among them, as Potiphar's wife proved (Gen 39:6ff); Greeks and Arabs were much more strict (Michaelis). Lying with animals was connected in Egypt with the worship of the goat, at Mendes especially, where the women lay down before he-goats (Herodotus 2.46; Strabo 17). Knobel adds that incest laws here are very close to those of present Muslim Arabs, Indian laws, and Romans, though it was the Christians who introduced affinity relations as taboo. Persians and Ethiopians were not so fussy (cf. Selden, *de jure naturali et gentium* 5,11.)

The Dead Brother's Wife (v. 16)

Augustine distinguishes two senses here: the wife of a dead brother or that of a living one. If the former, then Deuteronomy 25:5 encourages such marriage if the deceased was childless (Deut 25:5). Hugh of St. Cher puzzles over this. For if the brother is alive there is a general prohibition on taking another man's wife that would cover it, so it must mean one who is no longer alive, and verse 16 is outlawing this practice. He offers the solution that Deuteronomy 25 only applies when there are no sons to the deceased.

In the famous case of Henry VIII around 1530, the king argued that he must have been a transgressor of the Levitical law, since childlessness was his and Catherine's lot, thus his marriage was dissolvable. Yet the papacy held that, since there had been no consummation between Catherine and Henry's brother, Arthur, there was no basis for Henry to claim he had violated an existing marriage. Furthermore, Deuteronomy 25 implied that Henry was doing his duty to his deceased brother by marrying Catherine. As Bedouelle (1990) relates, four ancient universities were against Henry, and it was only Simon Grynaeus' agreement that Arthur's marriage was immutable and indissoluble that afforded some encouragement to the king. An issue reflected in early modern commentaries (and see the discussion above between Lorinus and Willet) was the "Scotist" view that such prohibitions belonged only to the realm of positive canon, not natural law, and hence were subject to the pope's jurisdiction. That was why Bishop John Fisher thought the only redress was in the papal courts (Scarisbrick 1997).

The Dominican follower of Aquinas, the older Paludanus (d. 1345), in his Leviticus commentary had moved towards the view that the marriage *contract*, not the question of consummation, was what mattered. "[T]he marriage ceremonies as distinct from the marriage act, also set up an impediment to subsequent marriage between either of the parties and the other's relatives—to which the title of 'the impediment of the justice of public honesty,' or simply, 'the impediment of public honesty' was given . . . Like much of marriage law, the impediment of public honesty had its origin in the OT and Civil law" (Scarisbrick 1997, 184). Cardinal Wolsey suggested that Henry would have to argue from "public honesty" that there had in fact been a marriage between Arthur and Catherine *in law*, if not quite in fact, since so many of the Catholic authorities (Vives, Cajetan, and Fisher, relying on Augustine) were against him. Yet Henry was determined to argue that Arthur *had* "known" Catherine, so as to square with the text of Leviticus, and Wolsey's escape route was not taken.

Martin Bucer thought that the prohibition on marrying one's brother's wife was, of course, only intended for while the brother was living. Yet rather than follow the literal sense of Leviticus 18:16 and immediately separate from Catherine, the fact that this marriage had lasted so long should make Henry prepared to live bigamously rather than pretend the first marriage was invalid (*Letter to Grynaeus* 15.8.1531). Christ freed us from the Law in order to hallow marriage (with Catherine) and make it indissoluble. There should be no divorce allowed by the spirit of the NT, which reinforces Moses here. The church has given its consent to Levitical legislation, properly understood; for the spirit of Christ leads us towards all that is fitting (Bucer 2004, 116).

Bucer (2004, 540–42) was asked for advice on two cases brought to him by Herzog Ruprecht of Pfalz-Zweibrücken in August 1541. The first concerned whether a man could marry his dead brother's wife and the second whether a man could marry the daughter of his cousin or a woman the son of her great-uncle. Bucer was convinced that Leviticus 18:16 did not apply in the first case, not least because the biblical law was more flexible than the canon law had become, and love must always be considered in such decisions. The second case was permissible according to biblical example and imperial law. Yet it was clear that some regulation is needed because Deuteronomy 25 was limited to the time of Jewish custom whereas Leviticus 18 was perpetual in its force. However, in that case it was betrothal rather than marriage that the woman and dead brother had, and any impediments according to reason and imperial law can be overcome more than if it were already a marriage relationship. In the second case, surely God would want there to be a happy marriage.

Osiander, writing in 1537 on *Verbotenen Heiraten* (1975–97.6, 414ff), wrote in favor of marrying a sister-in-law: "When someone uncovers the shame of his sister, then that is a 'hesed' which does not mean a thing of shame, but must be translated: 'that is a grace or a favour.' For surely Abraham was able to have Sarah. God does not pay attention to the grades of proximity as jurists do, but intentions of the agents." It is perhaps not surprising that Luther and Melanchthon mocked this rather ridiculous exegesis in a letter to Veit Dietrich (CT 3, 488, Nr 1651).

Lorinus rues that wrong interpretation of chapter 18 has contributed to the evil of a ongoing schismatic defection (the Church of England), whose origin and basis stand on a twisted interpretation of this passage as touching marriage with the wife of dead brother. The treatise by Nicholas Sanders on the Anglican schism should be read, in which particularly sharp contributions are made by Cochlaeus, Gomesius, and Honcada. Wyclif, then Protestants like Luther and Bucer, think this is a human hence civil law, and so the church is not to rule on it. However, the Anglican church had no right to annul the previous marriage to Arthur, because marriage and its law is indeed divine. So, Lorinus.

Willet's response was both Protestant and patriotic: Lorinus, with the rest of his consorts, "bestirred themselves here exceedingly" to argue that the perverse interpretation of this chapter was the foundation of the Anglican schism. "And wanting better arguments, he [Lorinus] with his filthy penne slaundered that famous King, belying him, and saying that Anne Bullen was his own bastard daughter, . . . like as if one should eat the Hen and then the chicken." It would seem that the late medieval church's treating these as positive laws which could be changed played right into the hands of those Protestants who wanted to reserve such matters for civil courts at the time of the Reformation.

Molech and the Nations (vv. 21, 24–30)

Theodoret on verse 21 has: "From your seed you shall not give to worship the *archōn*" (LXX). The Hebrew is *moloch*—the other translators leave this name untranslated, for it was an idol's name (cf. Amos 5:25). The verse forbids children who are temple servants to be sacrificed to idols, or as some say, it forbids the giving of children to foreign rulers, to be their servants or spear-bearers, so that they will not share in their impiety. Augustine translates this verse, "And you shall not give from your seed to serve the prince": this must be the prince who is worshipped in God's place. For the Greek has not *douleuein* but *latreuein*—so it cannot be a man which, after all, Scripture does not condemn serving (*douleuein*), but a *deity*, and so here it is about risking the holiness of the name of God or his people. Procopius is clear that the command not to mix with animals—those without reason (*alogous*)—means that one should not have company with those whose morals are out of place. For Hesychius it means we are not to consecrate even a thought or a doctrine to "Molech," thus keeping away from polluting God's name by the heresy of philosophy.

The *Glossa* interprets the "contaminated nations" (v. 27) as the demons who rejoice in every sin, especially fornication and idolatry, and stain soul and body with these, and the whole man who is called "earth." But God has visited the "earth," that is, the human race. Yet the somber message drawn from verse 29 is that all who do such things after the preaching of the gospel will not find another medicine for evil. And such people will be not be numbered in the list of humans but of demons. On "all the people I threw out before you" (v. 28) the *Glossa* says the amount of punishment indicates the amount of guilt. But the objection comes: this is about either the pains of hell or of purgatory. But it cannot be so understood since each of those is unclear and unseen, so that we are not shown the amount of guilt by the amount of punishment. And moreover God punishes less than people deserve, and one cannot tell from suffering that someone unrighteous (Ps 72, Job, and Tobit 1). The answer is that the Lord strikes for many reasons—to glorify God, to test someone, to humiliate (as in Paul), to begin future punishment now (Herod), and whenever fault is atoned for the guilty as with Mary. Only blows that are for blame can really be called "punishments."

In the modern period, the Protestants take an interest in Moloch and the nations. Luther has some stories to tell about cruelty done by young girls being shut away in monasteries, and Brenz's interpretation attacks Catholic practice. This outlawed worship, opines Brenz, was not unlike what went on under the pope when parents handed over their sons to monasteries in which they were held perpetually to carry out the worship of God. But this parental superstition is not only the ungodliness of idolatry, thinking they are betrothing their children to Christ and being promised eternal happiness for the whole family through their holy rites. Yet this cruelty of perpetual imprisonment goes against natural care (*storge*). Calvin's approach was quite different, remaining with what of the historical sense continues to be relevant in his own time: Moses adverts to adulterous sacrifices, especially to that impure and detestable service of consecrating their children to Moloch, as they called him, the idol of the Gentiles; and then adds a prohibition, that they should give no heed to false revelations. But in these two passages of Leviticus he only enumerates two classes, *viz.*, to use auguries and divinations, and to seek responses from familiar spirits, and to consult magicians or enchanters; yet he includes all the others of which we have previously spoken. And, lest they should think the crime a light one, he says that all they are "defiled" who devote themselves to this kind of curiosity.

Calov reports that on verse 24 Grotius joins with the Catholics such as Lapide to say that some of these things were allowed from the beginning and that it is the business of the universal head of the church to judge which abominations are to be avoided, and which to be allowed. But the Lord says there that *all* such profanities are condemned.

Although "fire" is absent from the text, by association with 2 Kings 23:10 (Targum), Leclerc mentions that it was usual for idolatrous pagans to use fire. However, the mention of fire might be, as Spencer thinks, a reference to illumination, not deadly burning. But on reflection, no, it is a euphemism for burning that the impious priests added! One cannot say that Ahaz's sons survived him and therefore he could not have "made his sons go through fire" since there may have been other sons that did not survive, but we just do not know about them! Dillmann thinks the Molech instruction of verse 21 is very old, and could refer to the deity Baal (cf. Jer 32:35)

What is noticeable is how so many commentators throughout simply skip verse 22 (on homosexual intercourse) as though it were unnecessary to comment, or is just one of a list. Part of the near silence has to do with the discomfort on the theme as something very close to home in certain monastic circles. Extremely significant was the imagery of *immunda pollutio*, as quoted in the Ps-*Theodorean Penitential* 13.1, not as part of Paul's text of Romans 1:25–29 (as Lutterbach thinks it is [2003, 238])—for Paul did not make an association between fornication and cultic pollution, yet Acts 15:20 and hence the Penitentials and preaching up to Alan of Lille (i.e., up to 1200) did. There is a sense of "holding the line" at a higher level of holiness. We shall return to the theme when discussing Leviticus 20:13.

There are a couple of exceptions to this silence over verse 22:

In *Paidagogos* II.10, Clement of Alexandria claims that Plato agreed that only one's own feminine "field" was to be ploughed (Lev 18:22). Do not sow seed where you do not want a crop, since that is only allowed where legitimate progeny is intended. And seed is not to be wasted by those who share in such a divine gift, and is not to be used on hard ground (even as when a woman is menstruating). Clement here weaves a thankful fascination with reproduction and sexual desire as a motor of this with a careful hesitancy about excess.

Cappel writes that Satan is not ashamed to celebrate "this baseness" and gives the example from Aelian (*Varia Historia*, Book 2) that Melanippus was enraged against Phalaridis, and sought conspirators against him, and managed to blackmail Phalaridis' lover, Charito, to strike at him. Charito confessed and Phalaridis spared both their lives and goods. Cappel objects that in this story it wants to praise this love in which both were lost as though it were divine.

Leviticus 19

Holiness, Parents, Idolatry (vv. 1–4)

PROCOPIUS, DEPENDENT ON CYRIL of Alexandria, writes that the time of grace is to be distinguished from the time of the Law, which in turn is to be divided into that of the Law and that of the prophets, which is "the intermediate time." Sacrifice is abominable in the new age of the church however, since, as Paul says (Phil 3:8), it is rubbish compared with knowing Christ. Yet some laws do continue. As Gregory the Great in his *Moralia* (FC 93:392) rather more subtly paraphrased: *Be holy as I am holy*: "If what I [God] order seems difficult, come back to me who ordered it, so that from where the command was given help might be offered. I who furnished the desire will not refuse support."

Ralph takes up a theme already present in the *Glossa*: We are made in God's image and likeness; if we corrupt his work in us, then we need to flee to the repair of his grace. In a sense one honors God by honoring parents, just as the Son towards the Father showed the way of respect which comes with trembling. The rule of keeping the Sabbath rest is actually by grace, but Augustine, on Exodus 20, reminds us that having no fear of punishment is very much what this restful or Sabbath grace means.

Lyra traces the theme of "rational affection" as being well ordered towards "one's superiors" by reverence, towards the poor by mercy, and towards all by innocence and not causing harm. Revering parents should lead one on to revering God who is our spiritual Father. The "deaf person" who should not be cursed means someone who is not present (Augustine, Rashi) and "the blind" can therefore extend to mean the ignorant and stupid. One ought to be careful not to harm them on account of the fear of God who sees and will avenge. So one has to be careful not to slander, and if lawyers are to discuss cases in public, these must be sins that can be proven.

Denys sees here the vast dignity of God who deigns to invite his servants towards likeness to himself. But since no one can acquire holiness without keeping the commands, these are added. The exhortation to godliness, to generosity and fraternal charity shows that the God of the Law is not by nature evil nor even merely "just," but also good and respectful. Denys likes Rabbi Paul (of Burgos)'s idea (*contra* Lyra) that these are new commands, over and above the Decalogue, are founded on it and are not merely repeating it. In the Decalogue it was not made explicit *how* to keep those commandments, or how to cultivate the interior disposition so that they might *will* to fulfill them. The end of the Law, Mosaic as well as evangelical, is true and eternal happiness and is no more than the full reward of divine love (love for God). No amount of observation of laws can produce this end unless these are kept from an interior motion of the will, which wills to obey spontaneously with a decisive mind. The lawgiver intended inner purification to accompany knowledge of commandments. Alexander of Hales and Thomas and Albert think that here Moses instructs an inner love and worship of God and that blame or merit does not lie in the external act except that this happens from an interior mental disposition. But this concern was already there in the first giving of the Decalogue (Exod 20) so that these Levitical laws are not about internalizing the Decalogue but *supplementing* it. Loving one's neighbor as oneself does come from the law of nature as the philosophers agree. Rabbi Paul thinks nature only instructs us to love our friends, but actually friendship is founded on the honest good and is not exclusive.

Brenz agrees that little can be expected from human nature being so weakened by original sin. But the Holy Spirit is given through faith to believers so that they can ensure that *at least* sin does not reign, as Paul says, in their mortal bodies (Rom 6:12). For those who turn against sound teaching there is the magistrate. So it is necessary that the Law is diligently made clear (by proclamation) and that the magistrate watch over it keenly. The Lord encourages the people to obedience by his example: "Be holy *since I am holy*." He demands from them external and political uprightness and obedience to all civil laws. Yet the obedience of "the law in the sight of God" is quite another thing. How can this be achieved? For the Law does not justify in the sight of God but leads us to acknowledgement of sin, that we might try to resort to the true and perfect righteousness through faith in Jesus Christ our Lord. Further, when the Roman Pontiff prohibited priests from marrying he used as an authority of this instruction: "be holy as I am holy." But this is not only to spoil Scripture in prohibiting priests form marrying but it also condemns marriage itself. If it is so unclean then surely it would have been forbidden to everyone! But the sacred letters speak much more honestly about marriage. The apostle says it is honorable, etc. (Heb 13:4). Likewise, while in the Decalogue we are ordered to honor our parents, here we are to fear them, not pay them mere formal respect.

Seeing the repetition of "I am the Lord" in verse 36, Calvin notes: "For whenever God calls himself Jehovah, it should suggest his majesty, before which all ought to be humbled; whilst redemption should of itself produce voluntary submission." Lorinus reminds us that there are those who thought themselves to be holy in their abstaining from female company and all that beguiled the eyes, but who failed to understand that one is only truly holy as God is (v. 2) when thoughts and hearts are. Thomas Aquinas insisted that if the chief intention of human law is to make humans to be friends to each other, then that of divine Law is to make friends between humans and God, and since likeness is the basis of friendship, then if God is best then we ought to be good and holy since he is holy. Lorinus adds that Christ wanted us to imitate the merciful Father and be perfect in mercy. Why the order of mother *then* father in verse 3? Well, really it matters not, but maybe because children spend more time with her at first. The parents have the power to bless or curse—literally. The repetition of the phrase "I am the Lord" is to create fear and love, which is the business of the Law and gospel respectively. Therefore, Christ is said not to have had himself referred to as "Lord" but as "Teacher" by friends and acquaintances, and by gentle names, although, so that he urges humility in the feet-washing of others, he approved that he be called "Master" and "Lord" by the disciples. This accords with Lorinus' distinction between Testaments: the OT does not apply directly to the church, hence the bishop today does not have power of death as the OT priest did, and punishment for greater sins is to be exacted only in the afterlife.

Willet observes that Lorinus mistakenly thinks, from verse 21, that we can become holy by cooperation with grace, as he reads 1 John 3:3. No, that verse "speaketh not of mans natural will, but made free by grace: *every one purgeth himselfe, as he is pure*: he must therefore, first, be pure, before hee can purge himselfe, and it is Faith which purifies not the heart, which faith is the gift of God, not of ourselves."

Patrick asks whether these things are by nature sinful and interestingly answers in the negative. "But the mere force of this word will not warrant such a conclusion; because several things are called in this book an *abomination* which have no moral turpitude in them, but were made so by God's positive laws, as Mr Selden observes (*de Jure Nat & Gent* 5,11, p598). So although lying with one's mother or sister was abominable by nature we cannot say of the rest, that to sleep with a brother's wife is so."

Knobel dwells hardly at all on the details of Leviticus 19 yet singles out verse 13, where the hired worker is not to be oppressed but given his pay at the end of each day, comparing Deuteronomy 24:14f and Matthew 20:8. More significant is the development in late-nineteenth-century thinking with regard to how biblical holiness should be understood. Although Robertson Smith (*Religion of the Semites*, 150) was not sure, Baudissin (1878) established the central meaning of *qdsh* as "separation," from a root meaning "to cut." Milgrom has gone beyond this to a more "positive" sense of holiness (2004, 219f), not least in line with *Sifra Qedoshim* 9.11, that separation *presupposes* rather than makes holiness.

Just Dealings (vv. 9–16)

Ralph observes that verse 9, taken literally, concerns a work of mercy. Yet since it is unclear what this verse actually means when taken literally, a spiritual meaning must be sought. In fact, those who do not allow a spiritual meaning are those who harvest right up to edge! The vagueness of the LXX translation encourages one to look towards the mysterious sense. Brenz interprets otherwise: Divine care for the poor and wandering is clear; and his people should be like him, a father of orphans. Do this that God will bless you in all your works: the political situation will be safe, the crops will do well, and likely your faith will not die but endure. Lorinus adds that when we think of harvesting we should not be distracted by the Latin *segetes*, so that we simply to think in terms of field, but should include fruit of trees, grapes, and honey.

The associated command concerning the poor in verse 15, Denys paraphrases: One should show compassion, but not so as to offend against justice, and nobles are to be shown honor for their superior office (Rom 13). Lorinus takes the expression to mean "to honor": Christ, as human being, paid that to his father, and God can lift his face in the sense of showing benevolence (Num 6:26). Presumably Lorinus thinks it is unnatural to honor one who is poor.

Augustine, in Sermon 38, had said that one curses a deaf person (v. 14) whenever one gives ignorant advice, and one causes a blind person to stumble by wrongly declaring something false instead of true. Gregory the Great's view was that to revile the deaf was to insult someone in their absence, and the deaf person is one who does not have the light of discretion. Dominique Grima warns that at the final judgment God will take seriously those sins that others who are spiritually blind cannot see.

It is stupid, admits Peter Cantor, to insult someone when present, but morally it is much more excusable, for to be ungracious in their presence can be quickly atoned for, but it is very hard to restore when it is a spiritual wrong and the victim lives far away. It is, in fact, the sort of thing Paul accused the Galatians of (5:15), where biting leads to devouring.

Luther was much exercised by verse 16. When there is a dispute we should not tell the world but sort it out, put the past behind us, and not spread calumny abroad. Preachers often think they are above that, but they are the worst and have quite an impact. Worse are those who embellish a story. The "talebearer" (*Verleumbder*) is someone who neither keeps quiet nor reports the person to the authorities but with a poisoned tongue spreads it abroad. Such a person is an eater of dung who rejoices in the quality of such. It is the duty of the emperor to stop this plague with severe means. Churchmen should not speak against anyone accused of adultery or theft, if all one has heard about them came from the poisoned tongue of a neighbor.

Lorinus is careful to mention that verse 12 does not say, "Do not swear by my name," but rather, "Do not swear *falsely* in my name." Ainsworth largely agrees there is such a thing as a lawful oath (Maimonides) but that "the Hebrew doctors" are firm that for needless oaths and all other abuses there is no atonement. "Therefore a man must beware of this iniquity, more than of all transgressions. This is one of the heavy iniquities; although for it there be no cutting off, nor death by the magistrates; yet is there in it a profanation of the holy name, which is greater than all iniquities." According to Calmet, perjury is a great insult to God by asking him to be witness to one's lies, as well as generally destroying reputations of absent people.

Forms of Love (vv. 17–35)

Kugel (1998, 755) summarizes the early Jewish commentary tradition: "Thus, the Bible was understood not to outlaw hatred per se, but hidden hatred, and to indicate that the way to prevent such hatred was through open reproach (if only in the judicial sense)." Targum Ps-Jon Leviticus 19:18 has a sweet reasonableness: "Do not take revenge and do not hold on to hatred, and love your neighbor; for what is hateful to you yourself do not do to him; I am the Lord." R Akiva (*Aboth from R. Nathan*, 26) viewed it as the key to the Decalogue, as did the Syriac *Doctrina Apostolorum*. I.3. The early Christian *Letter of Barnabas* 19:5, encouraged by being part of a small, oppressed movement, has something more ambitious: "You shall love your neighbor even above your own soul [life]." Clement (*Strom*. II, 18) mentions the law of gleaning and Sabbath rest for the land which, he says, show God's benevolence. Humans are expected to reflect this by loving their neighbors. Procopius recognizes that exiles were despised in Greek cultures, except for among the Spartans who obeyed natural law, whereby a man is to be honored on account of his nature, and what there is in common. Origen links Romans 2:14 with Matthew 7:12 in order to identify the Golden Rule with the natural law: the conscience or *synderesis* that told one that the good that must be done (*bonum est faciendum*) was the natural law. Gratian placed the evangelical Golden Rule at the beginning of his *Decretum* as the first principle of natural law (DuRoy 2008).

Ralph, on verse 33, adds that the people were told not to oppress even the alien. Now, the Israelites did not know grace but only fear, yet they were helped by this severity, whereas for us, we are led through divine patience to penitence, since the harsher judgment follows, the more fully kindness can be asked for. God is both: first, righteous; second, merciful. A lot of this chapter is to be taken quite literally. Lyra interprets "Love your friend (*amicum*) as yourself" not to mean equality but similarity of imitation as the relationship between self-love and other-love, since amicable things come to another from amicableness to oneself as Aristotle, *Ethics* 9 has it.

For Denys the Law, when it says they are not to hate their brother in their heart (v. 17), works with a philosophy that every rational creature is made in the image of God and is capable of beatitude and should thus be loved out of charity. For we are all brothers by likeness of nature and the identity of our one heavenly Father and our common origin from the first parents, and this is reinforced by common faith. The Jews are wrong to think one is free to hate one's enemies. If you condone or cover up someone's sin though, that is worse than the sin. One is to love one's friend (*amicum*) as oneself, in God and for the sake of God, that you might both reach salvation together. This does not mean that non-friends/enemies are to be hated, except inasmuch as they have fault in them. However, Jesus in Matthew 5 tells us to love our enemies. So we ought to love enemies for God's sake, who ordered this, and since they are in his image, and inasmuch as he is their Creator and wills their salvation and goads them towards salvation by all sorts of means—by angels, good people, blessings and miracles, warnings and terrors. You shall not seek revenge (v. 18). *Of course*, vindication, which works by the zeal of justice, is part of justice. But in all other things it is better to offer a controlled response.

Calvin, on "not hating one's brother in the heart, but . . ." (v. 17), affirms cultivating "fraternal affection" and comments: "I doubt not but that this part of the verse should be taken separately, nor do I approve of the introduction of the adversative particle *but*, by which translators connect it with what follows," as if to suggest that in rebuking the brother hatred is thereby expressed. On the following command not to take revenge (v. 18), he writes: "under the word *kill* is condensed whatever is opposed to brotherly love . . . In the schools this sentence was grossly corrupted; for, since the rule (as they say) is superior to what is regulated by it, they have invented a preposterous precept, that everyone should love himself first, and then his neighbors." There is a hint of this "scholastic" way of interpreting the commandment as framed by Jesus in Lapide, who spends much time on verse 17. The "as" in "love your neighbor *as* yourself" does not mean *equally* (i.e., love them *as much as* you love yourself) but in a *like* way. Once love is ordered similar signs of love should be shown to the neighbor as to self. In "love one's friend (*amicum*) as oneself," "friend" here is not the one who is kind to us but every neighbor (which is clear from LXX *plēsion* and the Chaldean which translates *chabrach*, that is "your comrade," and that from Hebrew *rea* which means not only "friend," but the transferred sense is "the one who is tied to us by whatever reasons or whom we come across in business"). Every human is a friend to the other as joined in common origin in the first parent and by the image of God, by common redemption, common church and sacraments, common grace, charity, ordination, and the path to eternal life. Various saints, including Ignatius of Loyola and Francis Xavier, are mentioned for their missionary love.

Lorinus reports, rather disapprovingly, that R. David Kimḥi had tried to argue from Psalm 65:18 that God would not hold such an inner hatred accountable, as long as not directed against God and religion. To love neighbor is to love all; for since all are descended from one, so all are neighbors. Abulensia showed that Jews are always obliged to love their neighbors, since this comes from natural law. For, as Aquinas reasons, one ought to love oneself because one is created for the enjoyment of good things. The main reason to love your neighbor is because he is joined to you by society through his capacity for the same beatitude and in seeking beatitude together you are brought towards unity. So when it tells us "not to take revenge" (v. 18), it means that it is peace for our souls that we conform to the righteousness of God rather than our own righteousness. This means letting revenge go or, if one cannot be gentle, at least keeping one's dignity. We should be merciful since we too have faults.

Likewise, for Calov the phrase "not hating in heart" (v. 17) shows that the Socinians are wrong to think that the Old Testament only concerned external religion and not the internal. Verse 18 helps to explain the *lex talionis* in Numbers 35:19 and Deuteronomy 19:12 as not about revenge but about *justice*. Is loving one's neighbor really about giving him justice, as Gregory the Great suggests? For a debt of affection is owed to all people on a ground of communion of nature, though to some more than others since those who are holier deserve more love and such people will have been good influences on us. So it is according to justice to fulfill this command: but *love* can be unequal and according to merits. Moreover, the Vulgate translation at verse 18—"of your citizens" (*civium tuorum*)—perverts "in Jewish manner" a view which Christ chided, that this was about care for fellow citizens and nations whose commerce the Jews used. No, *every* person—common by creation and again by common redemption and grace, as Luke 10:36 ("Good Samaritan") teaches—is our "neighbor." One could add that Alexander of Hales (*Summa* II, IV, tr. 1, q6, 847) wrongly assumes that Leviticus 19:18 included the clause "and hate one's enemies" which the Lord had to correct (Matt 5:44). Calov detects a medieval tendency to make the OT itself seem prone to exclusivism. But, Calov insists, Leviticus itself teaches us that we are all neighbors by condition of earthly birth and heavenly hope. Here Calov shows his anti-predestinarian colors.

Ainsworth thinks verse 17 "teacheth that he who rebuketh not his brother for sin, shall bear sin, that is punishment, for his sake, because he seeketh not to 'save a soul from death' as James 5:20; therefore God will require his blood at his hand, as Ezekiel 3:18." However, one is not to tell the world as a talebearer (19:16). Calmet insists that the text does not need to be translated as "publicly" rebuke. There is indeed an allowance for public confrontation (Matt 18:15-17) but Jesus wants us to go further than that and to refrain from having passion and resentment in the first place. But this religion—here in Leviticus and of Jesus—is to be a voluntary, heart-felt one! If vengeance is allowed in the OT on special occasions it was because the Jews had hard hearts; even pagans have seen how destructive vengeance is—reducing us to beasts—and is far worse than the injury. The love command here was general or universal and Jesus saw the true intention of the meaning of verse 34, although the rabbis narrowed it.

Calmet implicitly accuses the Jews ("many have criticized") of exclusivity in their love. But Bishop Patrick adduces evidence of Jewish inclusivity: "D. Kimchi saith very honestly upon Psalm xv. 3. A Neighbour is every one with whom we have any dealing or conversation." Leclerc notes that the worst hatred is to keep hatred inside—as Seneca said (*De Ira* I, c4), or as was remarked of Tiberius—acting nicely but seething inside (Tacitus IV.21).

If Leviticus has a point to make it is that charity and holiness are *relational* matters. It is not simply about justice conceived of in terms of right and due, but as duties of *care* with the emphasis falling on seeking, like God, consistently to bless, especially those one is committed to by a covenant or contract freely entered into and which raises the status—though not the nature (female, poor, alien)—of the receiver. (One becomes aware of this in the frequent use of the word "caritas" in Gratian's law code.) Just as charity is to go outwards for the sake of the poor and the alien (the particular stress of the last verses of the chapter), so monasteries were not to keep love for themselves—any more than the Father and the Son did in the divine community—and cathedrals would have a list of twelve paupers called *matriculari* or "a cascade of hospitals" overseen by church institutions (Brodman 2009, 14, 66). A certain strictness and discipline accompanied this. The treatise *On Almsgiving* by Innocent III seems to narrow but deepen the church's and individual's obligations in comparison with the oft-cited maxim of Chrysostom that one should give to all indiscriminately; rather one should give *more* to *fewer*. Monasteries in their bi-partite structure mirrored that of Leviticus: dedication to the divine in a charity that sees God as the focal point for common good and the basis of harmony (Aquinas, *De perfectione spiritualis vitae* c. 1269) and distinctive ethical performance that is best when set under a religious accountability. It is worth noting that as Thomas had no Question on "divine holiness," so that this was subsumed under "divine goodness," which expects both reverence and imitation. This was seen in the "win-win" terms of sanctity for the giver and health and even salvation for the receiver. Even after the Reformation the diaconate was established among Protestants from Calvinists to Anabaptists in order to care for the "pious poor, in other words, along communal lines" (Parker 2003, 114). Early modern Catholics too saw certain types of beggars in a positive light.

The fact that Leviticus 19:2 is echoed in the New Testament in two forms—"perfect" (Matt 5:48) and "merciful" (Lk 6:36)—could be viewed not so much as an "effacing of holiness" (for Jesus simply wished to distance holiness from its tired cultic context, Guillet 1990, 190), but rather as a way of showing the range of the ethical dimension of holiness, inspired by one who identified himself with the temple. For the "holiness" Methodist Phoebe Palmer (1837) Matthew 23:19 ("the altar sanctifieth the gift") encouraged entire self-consecration leading to being "on fire for the Lord." This was spelled out in W. E. Boardman's *The Higher Christian Life* of 1849 (Stephens 2010, 266f). In more recent moral theology holiness is rather glossed as "wholeness" with its associated "integration."

Although perhaps more part of the *Wirkungsgeschichte* of Jesus' Samaritan parable (Luke 10:25ff), showing charity to those at one remove from us is already envisaged in verse 34, as Calmet noticed. In the twentieth century one can discern a reaction against cold charity: "Neighbour-love is used on us/we are cobbled together/someone inspires us with trust and puts us in a new place. This place is good/ that we are only in reach of dying, a dumb bunny rabbit, a squashed bug, a blessed heart, no longer in reach of fear, equipped with the poor clothing of neighbour-love" (I. Bachmann, *Nächstenliebe*). Love requires the flame of holiness.

Mixing (v. 19)

Theodoret repeats that through the senses Moses taught the things of the mind. He forbids now the mating of different species, such as the horse and donkey, so that there should be no exchange from the irrational to the rational. For this reason also he calls clothes mixed of wool and linen "adulteration," teaching that actions which are contrary to each other should never be pursued. Procopius thinks that if "not mixing animals in a yoke" seems contrary to reason, then so much the worse for reason: we must bend our reason to God.

The *Glossa* complains that to take what the text says about beasts of burden literally makes no sense, especially since Solomon rode on a mule. The woman of Proverbs 31 was able to tell wool and linen apart and there might be some practical use of discerning animal breeds. But this was originally commanded for Jews not to mix with other races and then offer sacrifices. And Christians are not now to mix with them (the Jews). William of Paris tells us that in the prohibition of "mixing" the order of nature is commended to the people of God, who are to avoid the sin of Sodom and to differ from Canaanites. Modesty and a restraining of lust is more acceptable to God even in the case of our animals so as to observe the boundaries of nature and for the avoidance of monster progeny. Lyra reports that Josephus hinted that maybe the ban on mixed material was meant to set the high priest's "variegated clothing" apart.

Brenz asserts that God created all beasts in their own kind and ordained it that each keep to its own species. To mix them is to twist the general order of creation, which, although no great matter *in itself* or of great moment *in God's sight*, offers occasion to the rash to violate one command, when the keeping off *all* commands is necessary. Moreover, God strongly abominates such promiscuity among humans, so the principle must be observed. Deuteronomy 22 reinforces the rule (and Solon and Plutarch agree) that different types of seed need different agriculture, and they mature at different times. Today one should not try to be *both* papist *and* evangelical—mixing seeds. (This is an allusion to the Philippist "compromisers" who compromised with the emperor during the Interim of 1547–52.)

Mixing is a symbol of hypocrisy, thinks Calov. For the Romans, linen—which is a more subtle cloth—represented the hidden evil. For Ainsworth, to mix kinds is to assert that God did not make things perfect to begin with, but needs help. For Calmet, John Spencer (*On the Ritual Law of Moses* Bk II, c20) over-speculates when he thinks this mixing was done for the sake of pagan gods, as in the cult of Venus and Priapus. There is no evidence for this, he says, except for William of Paris's guessing. As for the two textiles in a coat, well there must be a moral sense to this command. If one takes these words literally they are not worthy of God's grandeur, nor even useful for the common good or economically sound. Pythagoras had riddling instructions and Solomon too (Prov 30:31). Furthermore, it *cannot* be meant literally because the Hebrews *did* use mules.

Engaging Leviticus

Leclerc on these "mixed types" observes that the Easterners liked symbols, although their meaning has often since been forgotten, as when Paul mentions the threshing ox (1 Cor 9:9). Just as abstaining from blood was symbolic, so too those who wish God to condemn the lust for money ought to prove that it is more greed to mix seed than to sow a field with one type of seed only. He quotes Bochartus' three reasons for this law: (1) to counter that which is against nature; (2) to dissuade from promiscuity; (3) to warn Hebrews about mixed marriages. However, Spencer has written that such mixing is against *custom* but hardly against nature, since neither nature gets destroyed. It would have been unnecessary to outlaw, with an obscure law, that which was already forbidden. Leclerc wants to make the point that these regulations, whatever their content, serve to command love for God and neighbor; otherwise they are empty superstition. Spencer makes it sound like Israelites were just as bad as the Canaanites whose land they were about to receive and that they honored demons through cavorting with animals. No, the law is outlawing intercourse of the wrong sort and marriage with idolaters. The animal types are symbolic.

Knobel asserts that this was one example of a discipline that kept the Israelites from various mixings as wrong because things are good enough in creation and should be kept in their own particular types and not adulterated by foreign material. This keeps with Deuteronomy 22's later development of this. Dillmann repeats this verbatim and one feels a chilling whisper of the "to each" (*Jedem das Seine*) slogan of Nazism.

Slave Girl (vv. 20–22)

The *Glossa* had commented that free people (Christians) face death for adultery if betrothed adultery as much as for that of the married, since this symbolizes their freer status compared with the Jews. Yet, following the LXX, the betrothed is ordered to offer sacrifice rather than be killed. More is expected of Christians. Ralph thinks that while a case of sleeping with a slave woman betrothed to someone else meant the death penalty (Deut 22), these verses are more mystical: "free" and "slave" mean the obedient and the disobedient. The maidservant is the noble one who draws her innocence from God himself, as we are since created in his image and likeness. Whereas the one enslaved by sin is not such a handmaid until redeemed by Christ's blood, baptized into his death, and given freedom. But there is death when the soul once liberated from death sins again. So only if not yet free, i.e., not baptized, will the soul not be killed, since much more is expected.

Brenz insists that keeping the "external" Law will not suffice and that one's inner disposition is more important for the sake of eternal salvation. "If a man have sexual relations with a slave woman" (Lev 19:20): well, this is clearly a lesser offence than adultery. But this is only an external level matter. God will judge those who *lust* after women. And there is no other expiation of this wrong in the judgment of God than the death of Christ, if you come to your senses (*resipueris*) and believe in him (or the everlasting fire of hell if you do no come to your senses and do not believe in him). So there are two kingdoms with two laws, as it were: one of natural law for society and one of an inner law of penitence and faith for the eternal kingdom. Lorinus elaborates on this and concludes that baptism after a deliberate wrong does not by itself remove the requirement of penance for the sake of human law, but certainly it does it for God (although see the Council of Trent session 5 *de pecc orig* c5 and session 6, c14.8). Further, there is no real difference to be admitted between praying for oneself and the priest praying.

Irregular Religion (vv. 26–31)

Theodoret warns against running to demons (v. 26) even though they offer immediate aid. Christ put demons in their place even when they acknowledged him. Half-truths are a very dangerous poison. To invoke "Sabbaths" can mean to invoke demons. Then, commenting on verse 31, he notes that the Greeks used to make their children's hair curly and then dedicate them to demons; they would mourn by pulling out their beards and cutting their cheeks in honor of the departed.

Ralph notes that the sanctuary was to be revered (v. 30), hence how much more so the place where we receive the body of Christ. The repeated mention of "I am the LORD" is used as if to say, "Ask me when you need help or revelation!" For only *some* dreams come from God. Lyra observes that bestiality was part of astrological endeavors. Denys writes that even though in divination there is no explicit call on demons, nevertheless they are pleased by the practice. Demonic illusions come from inner motions of dreams. It is fine to use animal behavior to predict the future, such as when dolphins can predict a storm, and one can profit by their presentment. However, to predict in cases where there are no natural causes or signs, this is illicit superstition. Verse 19 alerts us to the abuse by pagan priests of girls when they pretended that God could be worshipped in the idol who loves them and wants to sleep with them. The parents and the victims believed that, and it all happened in the dark. Josephus has a helpful story in *Antiquities* 20: Paulina was deceived by the priests of Isis, and Tiberias killed them. Archbishop Hamilton's catechism of 1552, written at the "dawn" of the Scottish Reformation, interprets (in chapter 8) idolatry not as the use of graven images, but rather: "God almychty expressly in his haly law forbiddis al kindis of withchecraft and siclike devilrie" (Lev 19:26). Borrhaus is not interested in the generalities of verse 26, as Calvin was, but loves the detail. Divination especially offends against the First Commandment. However, it is godly enough to read the signs of the times and diagnose health. Natural things carry portents and Christ did not blame the Pharisees for doing such.

On this theme Brenz says there are two kinds of predictions that the nations observe from birds. One discerned from the birds' call and is known as "augury," another from their flight and is known as "auspices"—Leviticus outlaws both of these. However, this law does not forbid bird-watching so as to find physical reasons for advanced warning of storms, which is only prudent. What is ungodly is attending to the flight or the call of birds to promise something good or bad. So what the discipline of Augury teaches is ungodly. Instead the Christian is to listen to the gospel. He thinks there is a link between the Hebrew word here in v. 26, *theonenu*, and term *onan*, which he claims means "a fixed time." But what kind of observations of times not allowed? Easter festivals are fine or at least indifferent, for as Paul said, "let no-one judge you" (Rom 14:13). But what is to be observed most of all is the Word of the Lord.

Lapide goes into the etymology of *lylm* (v. 31) and renders it as coming from "vanity" or "little god" or a god of night, which is a demon or a thing to be detested from *lah* (Oleaster). By specifying the type as "molten" this does not mean that stone idols were allowed, for it is a case of *synecdoche*. The tropological sense is that the greedy idolize their masses of gold for idols and they run after earthly riches. The gospel tells us to watch idolatry and not to grieve too much for the dead: such marks are just like those that criminals receive, which may not be inappropriate! In attending to the Law we are helped to train our eyes on Christ—to whom it points—and hear his gospel. Lorinus allows that Isaiah 44:5 suggests that writing on palms can be a good thing. This verse has been used to attack the discipline of flagellation, which can be useful but can be abused. "Our [i.e., Jesuit] Gretzer" says that this ruling is not only judicial, as Calvin and Brenz say, but also applies to those who out of the impatience of grief were raising such signs over the dead. Such practices are only bad when they have irreligious ends; hence in the case of Jeremiah 41:5, Calvin admits that this was not done out of affectation and was thus permissible. And the Israelites did seem to mourn in such a way. Certainly one is free to sing when grief turns to joy in memory of Christ's passion and resurrection, but in the OT (for Abraham and David) that did not include physically beating oneself.

On verse 29 Oleaster suggests that "don't prostitute your daughter" refers to a situation that arose after a daughter had a sexual liaison with her father and was told to become a prostitute, with appeal to the case of Lot. Yet Lot should have known better when he thought that the lesser of the two evils was allowed. His case had nothing to do with incest. But we should be certain that he sinned, just as in the case of the Levite and the concubine (Judges 19). Many Greeks were accustomed to prostitute their daughters cultically, in hope of military victory. The law of Valentinian and Theodosius permanently outlawed this as the better Roman legislators had already done. Willlet sees a rule against shaving of beards as against something superstitious or hypocritical "as to imitate Christs thorny crowne in their shaving and leave his holy doctrine, as they do, especially in Iustification by faith onely." In favor of flagellation, Lorinus had appealed to Jeremiah 41:5 and Zechariah 12:10—as if this is to imitate Christ. But, retorts Willet, no one should cut themselves for the dead and one should mourn moderately. The papists do what the Amorites do. Ainsworth agrees that there is to be no "cutting 'for a soul,'" i.e., a dead person (which Virgil also calls "soul" in *Aeneid* III). Paul tells us in 1 Thessalonians 4:13 "not to sorrow as those without hope." There is to be reverence for the sanctuary and neither shoe-wearing nor spitting. And the mourner may not make his house a thoroughfare.

Calmet tells us that the people of Libya still cut their hair in a round style to grieve and Herodotus (*Histories* 3.8) sees this as in imitation of Bacchus/Dionysius. The instruction not to cut one's beard makes him amazed that Moses here goes into such detail, unlike most lawgivers; but it is religiously important that they follow Egyptian fashion of mourning by cutting the ends of beards. Cutting the names of gods in the skin was something early Christians did on their wrists and arms to represent the cross or the name of Jesus Christ.

Leclerc takes these figures mentioned in verse 31 to be the evil spirits themselves—and not just their agents—who were summoned by certain arts so that they could raise up the souls of the dead who would make predictions as requested. Patrick, on verse 28, notes that women in Greenland still pierce themselves and that some pilgrims print a cross on arms after visiting the Holy Sepulcher in Jerusalem and are no better than Jews who wrote the name of God, although circumcision was the only mark allowed. In verse 31, one learns that voices came from the armpits, belly, or both in such cults (cf. Acts 16:16). Maybe these are just old stories. "Yet Oleaster upon Is 24.4 saith he saw such a one at Lisbon, from under whose armholes and other parts of her 'a small voice was heard, which readily answered to whatever was asked.'"

Leviticus 20

"Be Holy as I Am Holy; I Have Separated" (vv. 1–7, 26)

"From Leviticus he [Origen] learned that holiness was not first and foremost a moral or ethical category, but a divine quality" (Wilken 1995, 90). It is "not that Origen makes Leviticus' cultic language moral, but that he makes Christian moral discourse cultic." As with Jewish interpreters, for Origen it was about the transforming power of God's presence in human lives and communities. Indeed, citing verse 7—"be holy as I am holy"—Origen asks: What does "holy" mean in the Scriptures? Origen then replies that in the Scriptures holiness seems to apply not just to people but also to certain animals, such as the first-born, and things like objects of the cult, Aaron's tunic, etc. So there is a negative, external removal from the crowd, followed by a positive setting of one's desire. Origen appears to be implying that holiness is not really about deliberative "ethics," as such, yet is intentional in the sense of letting one's restored innocence express itself, just like the first-born calf. Separation reminds him of Psalm 1:2, whose scene is one of the lover of the Law dwelling in the temple, or rather the Law has become the temple in which he is now enclosed. To be like God is to be far away from all things that are not holy; not commanded by God. This is segregation not in terms of places but of actions; not by regions but by modes of behavior.

Hesychius, commenting on verse 3, opposes the view that "sacrificing to Molech" would not seem to stain the sanctuary if carried on at a great distance from it. Well, he says, the point is that God's name is stained, no matter the distance from the sanctuary. For someone seeing the image of God among the saints is holy in the sight of the one whose image he bears (i.e., God). Idolatry reduces the image of the Lord into slavery and allows the pearl to be polluted by swine. Now the *Glossa* here summarizes that, according to Hesychius, it is bad to let people who are outside fornicate with the devil; but much worse to let it happen *inside* the camp. However, this actually does not appear to have been Hesychius' main concern at all. "I, the *Lord*, have separated": Hesychius continues (on v. 24) that *Christ* has done the separating, through distinguishing who are "Gentiles"—i.e., those who worry about eating, drinking, and clothes. The people thus carried a "principle of separation" at the front of their minds.

Lyra hears in chapter 20 the intention of the legislator, which is to make citizens good and virtuous—to work from love of justice—and to make those who are hardly virtuous fear punishment. It would seem that giving sons to Moloch is a sin that cannot be expiated in this life, even by death. And so some doctors say that he does not incur the pain of death, if all his children are dedicated to Moloch, since he is reserved for a greater punishment—that is, Gehenna. But those who say this contradict the word of the Lord in Ezekiel 19—"If *anyone* repents"—which means that there is nothing in sin which cannot be expiated in this life. But, of course, that includes expiation by the death sentence, which is what is meant here.

Brenz, following a "two kingdoms" approach, argues that the OT Law is for magistrates. The repetition of (some of) these laws is not vain, for now the sanctions are added for the purpose of the administration of the republic. The words are fearful: this has made people think that the OT came not from the God who set his Son, but from a truculent and bloody God. But surely a just God has to coerce the bad as well as watch over good. And the bad cannot be coerced except by punishments. You praise the surgeon for cutting off a rotten limb. And so his terrors should deter. The OT narratives demonstrate this: for serving Molech with his people's connivance God punished Solomon by dividing his kingdom. Manasseh gave his sons over to the fire, and he was captured and taken to Babylon (2 Chr. 33:11). Borrhaus thinks that in the announcing of punishments the civil magistrate is confirmed here in his three tasks: (a) to look after the dignity of the republic; (b) to pass laws through edicts; and (c) to judge, i.e., to protect the innocent and punish the evildoer.

For Brenz, to "commit adultery" means to fail and violate faith in Christ the spouse. The Romans agreed that adultery was a capital offence, yet today we make such people our leaders and elect them to office! The offence of "adultery" has two parts: first, lust (which Moses and Christ warn about), and, second, an external act. So there are correspondingly two punishments: one by God and the other by the magistrate. The point of civil punishment is that *public* morals are upheld in an honest life together, for the flourishing of all virtues and the education of children, etc. The other side to it is in preparation for matrimony with Christ, since the heavenly city is conferred with these gifts.

Calvin continues that the holiness law, according to verse 26, has the rationale of maintaining a separation of God's people from the nations and their pollutions. And so even the distinction of those animals that may be eaten depends on the First Commandment (Exod 20), to which the rule about serving God in a holy and pure way is added, and all infiltration of (pagan) superstitions is stopped so as to maintain the right religion in its wholeness.

Willet finds "I am the Lord which doth sanctify you" (v. 8) to be proof for the deity of the Holy Spirit (relying on Aquinas, *Summa Contra Gentiles* IV, c17, where the case is made that the minister's holiness not important for the efficacy of the Mass). Yet Willet wants to quibble: the "Romans" (i.e., Catholics) are wrong to think that the receiver's faith does not matter, for "the visible sacraments profit not, without the sanctification of the invisible grace."

Matthew Henry has two notes on verse 24 in which sanctification includes separation but exceeds it to mean that word, ordinances, and instruction by the Holy Spirit are also included. "[1.] God's people are, and must be, persons of distinction . . . [2.] God's sanctifying us is a good reason why we should sanctify ourselves, that we may comply with the designs of his grace, and not walk contrary to them. If it be the Lord that sanctifies us, we may hope the work shall be done, though it be difficult." A quite different approach to the question "How are God's people pure and separate from other forms of religion?" can be found in Bonar on verse 26: "The form of church government . . . is not the jewel, but it is the precious case that encloses the more precious jewel . . . If people, on the other hand, are led to mistake the case for the jewel, then the great design is lost. In Popery and Puseyism [i.e., 'High Church' Anglicanism], and whenever the forms of worship are such as they engross the eye and the heart, the truth is lost, out of sight. Our unattractive Presbyterianism is a rough case in the view of many; but it certainly answers the blessed end of preventing any from resting in it as if itself were the jewel."

The tradition works from the principle that judicial law is for evildoers (Rom 13:4). Hence, for it to apply to Christians, judicial command and sanction must be spiritualized. The recent (2005) papal encyclical *Deus caritas est*, s. 31, establishes Marxism as uncharitable because it sees charity as part of the system. This means that "People of the present are sacrificed to the *moloch* of the future—a future whose effective realization is at best doubtful." One does not make the world more human by refusing to act humanely here and now. Yet also the people are to be holy to an extent. They will not serve in the house of the Lord and offend against express commands, particularly against homosexual practice. Benedict XVI's desire that even church cleaners be aware of such basic demands of holiness arguably shows a trust in something akin to the ordered sanctity of Leviticus.

Various Penalties (vv. 9–21)

According to Clement (*Strom.* 2, 23), the gospel adds an interpretation of the laws commanding the stoning of adulterers in verse 10: they should have an opportunity to repent (John 8:1–11). Also, the lawbreakers are already "dead" by the commandments if they live their life by sin. Clement adds from Luke 15:10 and Ezekiel 33:11 that God does not like the death of sinners but rejoices in their life. The emphasis is on being given a second chance to live in God's life.

Origen notes that the precepts of the Decalogue (Exod 20) do not have penalties, since love for God, not fear of punishment, should drive us. Yet if we despise these commands we will very soon lose our status as sons of the Most High (Ps 82:6) and be treated as slaves when punished. The implication is that these penal laws in Leviticus 20 come into force *for those who lose their status as children of Israel*. Now, continues Origen, according to the Law adulterers were put to death and could not seek penance and pardon. Yet Paul in Hebrews 10:28f makes it clear that it is worse than anything to despise the God of the gospel. So the cursing of father and mother means cursing God and Jerusalem. Of course, one is to be good to both kinds of parents—earthly and heavenly—for the spiritual law does not remove the earthly one. In fact, in the Law the offenders are *purged* by death, so that is no crueler than the God of the NT (*pace* heretics). (Since Christ, the punishment is postponed to the future, for some sort of purgatorial cleansing.) Yet the good news is that if someone alerted to sin by word of God flees to gain the help of penitence so that they do not re-offend, then that punishment can be removed. Punishment is measured for quantity as well as quality of sin. Only if sins become spiritual (blasphemy, heresy, pride) do they become unforgiveable.

Hesychius notes that the LXX instead of "his blood shall be on him" is more abstract by rendering "guilty" or "guilty and needing to make satisfaction." He agrees that the command against cursing "mother and father" concerns blasphemy here, and that too is to be ungrateful to nature, since ultimately God is our Father who brought us into life. Or, if the punishment for cursing parents is so severe then how much more that for cursing *Christ* who gives (re)birth to us spiritually. Hugh writes: "And they will bear their sins: or as the *gloss* has it, they will bear the punishment for their iniquities." Then the *Gloss* adds: sin itself will be their punishment. This, of course, is a typically "Augustinian" sentiment. But, counters Hugh, all punishment is from God and no sin is from God, so no sin can be punishment. The solution is that the penalty is double: of sense and of damnation. The punishment of sense is from God and is something, and is not sin since it is an object. The punishment of damnation is the lack of natural good and the loss of grace. One should not accuse the doctor if the potion he gives tastes bitter. Various sicknesses need various remedies yet the salvation of all things is to be found in the word of life. For the righteous person is not *under* the Law but *with* the Law, since he carries it in his will as his guide. But you do not want to remove the medicine from those still languishing. The Spirit knows to whom he should go, to which he should speak, and those he can use to help the sick ones. And one should see as commendable all he writes (in Scripture) and one should not reject or try to amend it. Here Hugh, in "taking on" the *Glossa*, was also challenging Augustine. Such punishment is called sin in one way (i.e., it can be called punishment "improperly"): sin is punishment (i.e., the withdrawal of grace following sin).

Borrhaus thinks "will die without children" (v. 20) means simply that the couple will die before they can reproduce or that they just become infertile, as Gregory the Great asserted in replying to Augustine of England. The point is that their children will not inherit, as Augustine, Ralph, and Cajetan interpret "without succession." Likewise Zanchi comments that in Leviticus 20 and other places God "threatens that he will throw the transgressors of his law from the Holy Land into the land of the Gentiles, that he will send them there to die—what else would he mean but that he would excommunicate them from the church and cause them to die unforgiven in their idolatry and be eternally damned?"

Ainsworth considers the three offences where "cutting off" is the sanction. He is very interested in stoning: "his hands being tied, one of the other witnesses struck him behind upon his loins; if that killed him not, the other witnesses threw a great stone upon his heart; if he died not with it all Israel threw stones upon him" (following Maimonides, and *Sanhedrin* in the Talmud). For Calov "setting face against them" (20:1) means that if judges let things slip through the net then *God* will stop offenders with their early death. He is aware that the Pharisees read ʿ*rrym* (childless) in verse 20 so as to say (strictly) they will die *naked*. This has his sympathy. Some like Osiander have suggested "without divine blessing," but no, it seems to do with the magistrate acting for God to punish severely.

Willet relates that Roman law once allowed a woman to die for adultery but not the man, yet this was changed by Ulpian who said a man had reason to guide him, so he sinned *more*. Now as to whether adultery should these days be punished with death: Well, Calvin thought it shameful that Christians were less moral than pagans (this is a recurrent theme in early modern commentary on morality); and

Julius Clarus, as approved by Lorinus, suggested that the wronged party be allowed to kill both. "Butt his opinion seemeth to be too rigid, that now necessarily in every Christian state adultery should bee vindicated by death: because wee are not simply tied to Moses iudicalls, further than the morall equiry enforceth: and mercy, and clemency better beseemeth the Gospell, than the rigour of the law." "Tempering the law by the cross" (Ambrose, sermon 23) is Willet's motto, but warns: "let it be not more grievous unto us, that our punishment be deferred until the next life." It is *not* the case that the Law was abrogated by Jesus in John 8. The woman was dismissed *not absolved*, as Ambrose (*Ep. 76*) rightly says. There needs to be serious punishment, but maybe death or maybe not. So "the morall law wholly standeth in force, the iudicalls are in part abrogated as they specially concerned the Jewish state, and policy, partly in force, as they are grounded on a moral equity." So there is some discretion for the Christian commonwealth around judicial laws like these, which does not obtain for moral commands.

Calmet is on to *something* when he writes that the method of death, according to the rabbis, was strangling, whereas "his blood upon him" was stoning; yet this is wrong because in verse 2 of this chapter they are said to die the death but then the sentence that follows is stoning. Stoning was the standard or default means of death. The laws that allow the father and the husband to kill the adulterers were received into Christianity as far as having a place in the realm of the civil law's punishment, but *not* so as to make such revenge not sinful. In fact the Christian Emperor Constantine was harsh with his insistence on death for adulterers, and the Theodosian Code instructs burning them in a leather sack. The witnesses would place their hands on their heads to take the pain of death in a case where they were innocent. There would be due process among the Jews such that even if a woman cannot be proved to be untrue, since there was one witness only, the husband should still renounce her.

The Vulgate of verse 10 mentions adultery with a *betrothed* as distinct from with one who is married. Patrick picks on this detail that to make adultery with such to be accounted a greater crime than of one married (stoning rather than strangling done with napkins to one kneeling down in dung with molten lead poured down throats [R. Levi!], which hardly sounds much better!), well "it ought to be considered that the love of those who were newly espoused was commonly more fervent than those who were married, especially among the Jews, who for light causes were wont to be divorced from their wives."

Augustine's approach, by contrast, emphasizes the anatomy of the sin in his Question 73 on verse 10. Where the text has "wife of a man, wife of a neighbor," this either means that if one is not allowed to commit adultery with any man's wife, *how much less* with one's neighbor's wife, or it may just be repetition to show how doubly bad it is.

Gregory the Great answered questions posed to him about family morality, especially unions between those related through marriage (stepmother or sister in law). This was to stop, but in such cases where this had already happened they were not to be barred from communion. Where cousins were permitted to marry they proved incapable of offspring, although the assertion turns out to come simply from Leviticus (20:20f) rather than empirical research into patterns of childbirth (Helmholz 2004, 8).

Something of a "cruel to be kind" penitential system was up and running in Irish Christianity. According to the *Penitential of St. Columbanus* (III, 14–15), adultery with another man's wife meant three years of living on very basic food and paying some monetary "price of chastity" for the wife before guilt could be removed. But if a lay person committed sodomy it would mean seven years of penance, the first three of years with bread and salt and water and dried fruit and the remaining four years to live without wine and meat and finally to be forgiven when the priest prayed for him "at the altar," which gives a very "OT" feel to this envisaged scene. Interestingly in cases of bestiality it is only half a year of bread and water if the culprit is single and a whole year if they are married.

There was the infamous case of Lothar II (c. 858 AD) who, in order to divorce his wife, alleged that she had committed premarital incest with her brother. Hincmar of Reims in his *De divortio Lotharii Regis et Theutbergae reginae* was interested in the salvation of all concerned, hence when a lay court sentenced her to sacramental penance this displeased Hincmar. He ruled that "pollution by sexual misconduct among the married was no cause for separation, while clergy polluted by criminal activity were to be removed from office" (Firey 2009, 15). The wider point was that to make penance public and political very quickly made it false.

Rabanus Maurus liked to back up the penitential canons of the Council of Toledo and others with biblical evidence, especially Leviticus 20–21 on the matter of incest. The focus was on the OT Law. In a few cases this permitted him to diverge from the conciliar decisions, or where none yet had been reached, as in the matter of dealing with killing during wartime. So Scripture was significant even if a relatively small percentage of it was reflected in his two penitential books. This is most apparent in his letter to Heribald (Kottje 1980, 276–78). Also, at the start of Rabanus Maurus' *Penitential* of 841 it states that all vices are outlawed in the Law of the Lord: "Sanctify yourself and be holy" is found in all of Leviticus 20, and this can be paralleled with what Paul says in Galatians 5. For "if according to the historical sense, the lawgiver warned that transgressors of God's commands faced the death of the flesh, and the end of their present life, how much more is the death of the soul to be feared with respect to the command of the Savior and the evangelical doctrine and perpetual punishment than that which has some sort of end. For it will torment without ceasing those who are liable" (PL 110, 467–70). So, mortify members, he suggests, and even though he goes on in the Penitential itself to convey more the rulings of councils and popes, there is no mistaking this strong and solemn scriptural foundation.

Hesychius asserts, on verse 10, that spiritual adultery is even worse than the wickedness of physical adultery (Hosea 7:4 provides the hermeneutical lens here), and in the NT we are warned of those who would inseminate church with the seed of their own teaching, like Hymenaeus and Alexander (1 Tim 1:20). The most he will say on verse 13 is that we have to guard against feminizing and losing strength. The "burn alive" of verse 14 leads to the odd conclusion that lust is the mother of all sin. The *Glossa* picks this out, yet is not happy with much of Hesychius at verses 13–15 and so turns to Origen for help. This sin is an insult to nature. Spiritually understood, the one who is strong in mind is masculine and must by words or actions take care not to become effeminate lest we are dissolved with it and die at the same time. On verse 15 the law of "no sex with beasts" is not superfluous for believers if taken spiritually to mean engaging with depraved earth-bound thoughts. If a man or a woman—not from the natural tiredness (*languore naturae*) but from a deliberate act of will—does so cleave to and indulge evil thoughts, then they are guilty of death. The metaphor is mixed: such people are like animals in their looking earthwards, but to this they add intention.

Hesychius further observes that the burning of v. 14 gets rid of all traces of the culprit, his desire, and his action. Christ spoke about sending a fire, that is, the ministry of the Spirit who takes sinners and their sins out of the midst of the community. It seems as though verses 15–16 (on bestiality) are to be taken literally. From enforced abstinence due to menstruation one is to learn chastity (v. 18). But the spiritual meaning is that one who comes close to Gentile wisdom, with its astrology, is far from God. One should not have that as a bedfellow and delight in it, but rather uncover its wickedness and the origins of such error, like its flow of blood. The "origins" of Gentile wisdom are found in idolatrous practice and are to be "taken out from his people" (LXX)—which means to be shamed as having a false name for wisdom. To lie with such is to expose oneself to it. So such should be disposed of from among his people lest he be reckoned as one who alienated the image of God and himself by ignoring the Creator and so that such behavior is not mistakenly deemed to be wisdom. The connection between the prohibition of sex during menstruation and astrology is apparently "the moon." There is a plain moral instruction against shameful things on which is built an interpretation to guard against spiritual temptation.

In similar vein the *Glossa* asks how a beast can be "guilty" (v. 16) when it is not rational or capable of actively violating law, and his answer is that the text really means a *person* here. Augustine, who did not pause to say much on Leviticus 20, nevertheless did comment (Q74) that the animal can be guilty in the same way as the sea can be angry and that destroying it removes any occasion for unworthy reminder of the deed. But the *Glossa* here seems to have varied his interpretation by saying the beast stands for a person. Ralph comments on chapter 20 as a whole that many of the OT laws were accompanied by examples in OT stories. To take one: "Whoever sleeps with his father's maidservant . . ." Well, that is exactly what Reuben did in Genesis 38. Continuing a two-tier approach founded by Hesychius, for Ralph the commands of the OT Law continue to be medicine to the slower folk in the church and so should not be taken away. However, Ralph chooses an example (19:20) that does not have a corresponding capital sanction in chapter 20, and he does not follow through on the implications of this assertion but implies that hearing the Law is *per se* the medicine. For the NT reinforces an internalizing as one keeps laws, promoting a peaceful conscience into which Jesus leads those who come to him (Matt 11:30). As we fear God he will remake us on the inside, and those who oppose him will be expelled into outer darker places. But almost as a postscript he adds that no one has the power to do these commands unless by grace.

The presupposition of sacramental grace for the fulfillment of ethical codes is clear in Thomas Aquinas' point about the sacrifices, which he liked to call "sacraments." "On the contrary, it is written [Lev 20:8]: 'I am the Lord that sanctify you.' But nothing unreasonable is done by God, for it is written [Ps 103:24]: 'Thou hast made all things in wisdom.' Therefore there was nothing without a reasonable cause in the sacraments of the Old Law, which were ordained to the sanctification of man" (*ST* IaIIae q 102, art 5).

Hugh of St. Cher is aware of the severe penalty here to match serious crimes. Although the gospel does not exact full punishment in this life—since it moderates the harshness of the Law so that people might do penance instead—such a person is still guilty and is thus the same penalty as under the Law. Ralph had also mentioned David and the fact that he was not punished for adultery. Well, the Lord did take his sin away as we learn in 2 Samuel 12. And in such cases we find the form of evangelical gentleness and mercy whenever someone does penance and washes away blame by confession and escapes the sentence of the Law. One should note that all physical adultery implies spiritual adultery, but not vice versa. Does that then mean that physical adultery is the worse of the two? No, since not any sort of mortal sin is spiritual adultery, but only heresy is. The spiritual heretic is the one who corrupts the teaching of the Law, and heresy is a greater sin than physical adultery.

Brenz accuses the papal "impious hypocrites" of pretending that they are not idolatrous. But idolatry must be rightly defined as meaning divine worship not instituted by the word of God but dreamed up by human reason. Also in the case of adultery: both *die*. Although this adultery is indeed worthy of death, our civil laws do not punish it. Execution for adultery is a punishment for political reasons, one that expiates the offence in only an external sense. For in the sight of God sin is expiated by the death of Christ alone, if believed in. Although it seems cruel that anyone should kill another man, yet it is not cruel when it is just. And the "guilt of spilled blood" is not on the magistrate, who kills the man, but on the evildoer himself who deserved and invited such sever punishment by his wickedness and in a sense has killed himself. Brenz thinks the death penalty *should* apply for adultery.

Bucer seemed torn between biblicism and pastoral sensitivity. He writes that it is the sin, not the sinner, that is are to be opposed. True, in such cases as those in verses 10–18 we must attend strictly to the divine word, yet while we are commanded to destroy with all strength such forms of shameful life, with our understanding of human stupidity we should be gracious. Strength should be shown in our *gentle* dealing with divorce cases and such shameful living, not to allow sin to grow worse, but neither to give up on God's help, and to lead such people back into marriage.

Lapide carries out a justification of these severe punishments on the grounds of natural law. Stoning is for Molech worship and for adultery too, yet for one who has mother and daughter together (v. 14), they are to be burned alive. The punishment of burning was established for this incest, since with other more serious crimes only the punishment of stoning was set; the Jews were more inclined to this incest so it was forbidden by a harsher penalty. Sex during menstruation (v. 18) is by the law of nature a grave sin (being bad for procreation), so is to be punished by death. Hence the more weighty theologians teach (although some think differently) that in the new Law this is not mortal sin if a husband commits it (and he lists them as including Abulensia, Soto, Cajetan, and most precisely, Sanchez in book 9 of his *De matrimonii disputatione*, 21). The severity had more to do with ceremonial requirements of holiness that such strictness required. But why then, demands Lapide, is verse 18 included with a number of natural laws if it is a ceremonial one? Well, it would only be a venial sin by nature, but the positive precept makes it a mortal one. A commandment is God's way of singling out certain unnatural things as particularly to be avoided, thus making them mortal sins.

Calmet on "nefarious thing" (v. 17) relates that the Talmuds take it according to this "soft" meaning, as though Moses wanted to insinuate that these sorts of incestuous relations between siblings had been encouraged by the primal cases among the children of Adam (see Selden *de jure natr & gent.* bk 5, c8) yet now had become a crime punishable by the last judgment. But it is more credible that the term *ḥesed* here, which can mean both "mercy" and "goodness" at the same time, really means here the opposite, a godless and shameless action, that the usual terms would not do. Hebrew sometimes uses soft language to designate shameful and hateful things, as when one says "bless" meaning to "curse" (e.g., Job 2:9).

Homosexual Relations

Leviticus 20:13 is even stronger than the parallel verse in 18:22, for it insists on the penalty of death for this practice, with their "blood upon them." In a tour de force argument John Boswell in the 1980s argued that homosexual relationships were actually largely overlooked and sometimes even acknowledged (through a ceremony) in the Western church until the late eleventh-century Gregorian reforms. Boswell drew criticism for failing to pay attention to whether sexuality is constructed or essential, being more concerned to show that Christianity was not always homophobic. He suggests that Leviticus was seen as not binding on early medieval Christians, but to do this he had to argue that Leviticus, as read through Romans 1:26–27, only applied to the special case of heterosexuals engaging in homosexual practice (Boswell 1981, 109). A further argument is that because these verses in Leviticus are couched within a cultic ceremonial discourse, once that context is no longer deemed to be valid, neither can these commandments be. Homosexuality as a punishment for idolatry and polytheism could be widely defined. Peter Cantor's view was that only two sins in the Bible are said to "cry out": "murder and sodomy" (Gen 18:20–21), even while allowing that hermaphrodites be encouraged to be sexually active by choosing one way or the other. As for the reference to Leviticus 20:13: "But how is it that these have fallen into disuse so that what the Lord punished severely the church leaves untouched, and what he treated lightly she punishes harshly? I fear that one may result from avarice and the other from the coldness (*refrigerio:* of charity)" (in *Verbum Abbreviatum*; CCCM 196, 777; Boswell 1981, 377). Cantor's point is surely that the church has been too soft concerning both murder and homosexuality, one which comes from avarice, the other from a lack of charity (love for God and neighbor).

So, perhaps so much the worse for medieval Christianity (e.g., where the Ps-Theodorian *Penitential* 13.1 demands that homosexual practitioners pay with their souls, since they offend against nature, in which sex has to do with childbirth, quoting 1 Corinthians 6:9ff and Leviticus 20:13 together). Around 5–10 percent of delicts in the Penitentials have to do with homosexuality. It was often called "sodomitic rite that is lying with a man in a feminine way," with clear reference to Leviticus 18:23 and 20:13 (as in Columbanian *Penitential* B15) long before Peter Damian coined the term "*sodomia.*" It was the kind of thing God punished by burning the city of Sodom, such that (e.g., in the Ps-Gregorian Penitential of the mid-ninth century) ten years of penance seemed rather light, whereas the Finnian penitential (mid-sixth century) demanded one year's penance if regular activity. It involved contact with excrement. For the Theodorian canons, anal intercourse with a woman was as bad as intercourse with a beast (so *Penitentiale Floriacense* 54; Kottje 1970, 102; Angenendt 2000, 160–74). Paul of Hungary's *Summa of Penance* (1220) was followed by an article by Aquinas in *Summa Theologiae* IIaIIae q 153. According to Jordan (1997, 163), it is a short article and explains that it is a sin against nature in the sense of being against the original constitution of humanity. Incest disrespects parents, but, worse, "sodomy" disrespects "nature" and the Creator. In art 12, ad 3: "Gravity of a sin depends more on the abuse of a thing than on the omission of the right use . . . the most grievous is the sin of bestiality, because use of the due species is not observed . . . After this comes the sin of sodomy, because use of the right sex is not observed. Lastly comes the sin of not observing the right manner of copulation, which is more grievous if the abuse regards the vessel ['vas'] than if it affects the manner of copulation in respect of other circumstances."

These sins in order of gravity reflect the order of being: bestiality (wrong species) then sodomy (wrong genus) then incest (wrong persons). Thomas prepares for these conclusions by mentioning the verses in Leviticus and in Paul. I do not agree with Jordan (1997, 148) that Aquinas misreads Augustine's *Confessions* 3.8.15 here, or that he was threatened by purely unproductive pleasure that transcends animal nature. Rather there is a synthesis of virtue ethics with the spirit of a chain of traditional penitential handbooks such as the list by Raymund of Peñafort (d. 1275).

In Reformation Geneva this crime was not a matter for the church but for the state, although Calvin recommended drowning rather than burning for young recidivists, or at least public binding and beating: "There is the danger that the Savior will inflect a very terrible punishment on the type of men who want to hide this crime and that His wrath will fall on many others." "The assumption was that the accused were given over to an appetite (preference) and that magisterial punishment not ministerial admonition was required" (Naphy 2001, 102). This took the form of execution (in theory) for adults when they seemed knowingly guilty, but the records show some amount of sophistication in distinguishing between causes and crimes. It was a statutory offence in England (1533, 1548) but not in the rest of Europe, even Scotland where Leviticus 20:13 was appealed to directly: the offences of buggery with man or beast seem to have been regarded as very similar (Maxwell-Stewart 2001, 83).

Homosexuality can mean different things through the ages, and is not just a late modern construct (Halperin 1990 fixes on the year 1869 as that of the discovery of the homosexual body, by which he means an entry in the *OED*). "There are places in the Bible where attempts are made to police borders, as in Leviticus, which arguably is one of the Bible's most anxious books . . . Thus the priestly concern with purity became an obsession with the body's porosity" (Loughlin 2006, 116). The Leviticus commentaries by Hartley, Levine, and Wenham are described as "heterosexist and homophobic" and what is prohibited in Leviticus is really homosexual incest (Stewart 2006, 104). The key study of the subject (Lutterbach 2007) observes that Paul Ricoeur, in his *Symbolism of Evil*, encouraged us to distinguish impurity from guilt, yet worries that we often "look down" with our research on the Middle Ages and on other "primitive" cultures.

Leviticus 21

The Priesthood (vv. 1–9)

IN A COMMENT WHICH relates verse 1 to John 11:35, Procopius portrays Christ as a priest lamenting the corruption which underlay death. For Langton, to be polluted by the grief of the dead is to be contaminated by the sins of another and so receive mortal sin. This is when a priest consents to or does not correct sin or repeats sin in the church. And one who carelessly contracts a flaw from an evil source gets contaminated. Too often the church trembles before sin and wants to avoid scandal, so keep quiet about it.

For Borrhaus, in the NT all believers are true priests. The rule against having contact with the dead reminds those who are anointed with the priestly Spirit of Christ that they are called to the hope of life through the profession of resurrection from the dead, since that hope is the one sign of the sacred priesthood of God. The falsehood of the Roman priesthood is shown in that they do nothing but perform funerals, vigils, and commemorative Masses and from these they amass riches that Croesus and Crassus would gawp at. Yet Christ called disciples to leave the dead to bury the dead. Borrhaus condemns the literalist readings of this passage, which supports the scandalous practice that one who wants to be a priest and who had married a widow can then renounce her because she was not a virgin, or generally that marriage is inimical to holiness. Indeed we read here (v. 7) that the lesser priests were allowed widows: this against the *decretum* of the "stupid pastor" (probably the *Liber decretalium Gregorii IX* c. 1231, written by Raymund of Peñafort), which tightened the rules on priestly celibacy. Borhaus insists that only Christ had no defect, when God wanted his glory to appear even in bodily form. For this reason a Latin poet denied that Claudius could be a god since his body was hardly suitable.

Pellican agrees with the idea that to mourn too much is to deny faith in the resurrection, although there is some concession to human weakness, in that they could mourn their wives and near family In a moral application of verse 7, a priest should have a godly wife, and what follows about the High Priest shows how the higher the office, the more holy he must be (cf. Ambrose, *De Officiis* 41). Brenz is keen to distinguish what is said of common priests (vv. 1–9) from that which is addressed to the High Priest. He lists the near kin whom a priest might mourn by attending their funeral *to perform it*, including the unmarried sister (the married sister is in the power of another man). Brenz seems to think the point is not to forbid the priests to pay their respects, and he seems to be thinking here about his fellow ministers of the gospel. But shaven heads in a pagan style (Ezek 44), as Cicero and Herodotus confirmed as Egyptian practice, is forbidden. God's name, Law, and God himself would be profaned if they were dragged into uncleanness. For the crowd would learn from the example of the Levites to despise and loath God himself.

Calvin had written about the abolition of the priesthood in its mediating function, and yet what is fascinating is his own identification, as a widower himself, with the priests who are forbidden to mourn. These priests in turn model something of the perfection of Christ, and so implicitly do Christian leaders. Calvin sees the command coming out of the Nadab and Abihu incident. Abstaining from grief shows the hope of blessed resurrection, and prevents "the bitterness of sorrow from driving out patience and a tranquil state of mind in us." This is not merely the widower Calvin sounding stoic. For in funeral rites the priests were free from grief *so that* the rest of the people could seek consolation from them. This was perfected truly and firmly in Christ who, although he endured not only pain but also the extreme horror of death, was exempt from every fault and triumphed over death itself. So it is that the memory of his cross, with sorrow washed away, makes us glad. On the one hand, the priests are commanded to holiness to reflect on the honor of the worship of God, and, on the other, their lack of holiness necessitated the coming of the one perfect priest—Christ. Notably there is a detail in his treatment of verse 13 that shows how much these principles apply to ministers in Calvin's church—it is perhaps an allusion to the case of Pierre Viret, who in his seventh decade married a teenager, to Calvin's chagrin (see Gordon 2008, ch. 16). The virgin does not mean one much younger, since if "a broken old man lusted after a young girl, that would be vile intemperance."

Lapide, with help from Ralph, interprets tropologically: a tonsure is fine but *total* shaving is not since the thoughts of the flesh about the life of those we are responsible for among family members is not to mean that our mind gets distressed. To cut their skin would be to empty the faith of the resurrection if they do not try to control their grief for the dead. Jerome gives good examples of pagan behavior (in his Epistle 3 to Heliodorus). The priests are called to offer their people to God

(v. 6) since by their teaching them they lead them to belief. It is right that they are also holy who invite others to holiness. Holiness has two parts: it is communicated sacramentally and effected through obedience. God by communicating holiness in ordaining priests also orders them to be holy (v. 8). On account of the dignity of the priest-father, the simple fornication of his daughter is punished by death of fire, just as the Roman vestal virgins were to be buried alive. Calov cites *Aeneid* 11 for the Roman custom of not mixing funeral and offering duties, and *Aeneid* 6, that Roman priests must not even see a corpse, although "the Hebrews," such as Moses de Kotzi, say a priest can bury a corpse in the road. On verse 9 Grotius has tried to argue that the priest's daughter is only to be burned *when married or betrothed*, but, contests Calov, the text makes no such specification.

This law in question is not for all Levites but only the Aaron family, observes Calmet. To associate with the dead would have led them to come too close to the Egyptian religion of Osiris. The priest's daughter must really have been guilty of adultery not mere fornication. On verse 8 Calmet does specify (where the Vulgate is vague) that it means that those who offer bread to the Lord are to be regarded or respected as holy, although it might also mean that they are to be kept an eye on. Matthew Henry writes that ministers are supposed to know more than others of the reasons why we must "not sorrow as those that have no hope" (1 Thess 4:13), and therefore they ought to be eminently calm and composed. Keil thinks Knobel is wrong on verse 4 to think that one is not allowed to mourn for one's wife: she is surely in the group "kin." Knobel has been distracted by the fact that Plutarch says the Romans did not allow this.

The High Priest (vv. 10–14)

For Origen, Jesus is clearly the High Priest and this is the more remarkable for it being his own blood he works with. One who is able to sin cannot be called a Great or High Priest in the way that Jesus can. For his virtuous power excels that of even the great and outstanding. Jesus grew in his soul owing to his great works. It is good to "grow up in soul" as believer, since then one is not so likely to be scandalized as one of the "little ones" (Luke 17:2). The reference in verse 10 to the oil of *gladness* which, when poured on his head, made him "the Anointed," shows his superiority: not even Moses had such "consummated hands" (again relying on the Greek translation). His clothing was light in color, for "the habit" of the High Priest was such that his clothing was marked by the deep light of knowledge and wisdom, and these garments are holy. He will not take the miter off his head, for the head of Christ is God and the Father and the Son are always "in" each other (1 Cor 11:3).

The adjective *christon* qualifying "oil" in verse 12 in the LXX (for the Hebrew *nēzer* qualifying "oil") means that he is more than holy. Aware of the Hebrew term (*nēzer*), the Nazirite idea (Num 6) of one "set apart" is brought to bear (as with Eusebius in *Demonstration* VI.2 [c. 315]). After this intoxicating theological speculation, Origen announced the outworking of this: if the soul is alive, that is, if it does not contain in it mortal sin, then Christ—who is life—will come into that living soul. However, if there is mortal sin and it has not made complete satisfaction, Christ will not come near. That the Israelite High Priest was forbidden to grieve his parents (v. 11) seems objectionable on a literal level. So the text must refer to *Christ*. Given the background principle of Job 14:4–5—that a clean thing cannot be brought out of the unclean—only Jesus could say (through Solomon in Wisdom 8:20) that he had no sin. As for us, we are soiled "in our father" when we do not believe in Christ or when we disobey our mother church. Jesus did not "exit the Holy Place" for he never sinned. And if we meditate on God's law and dwell in the word of God and apply ourselves to his commandments, then we will be among the "holy things." For holy things are not to be found in places, but in deeds and life and patterns of behavior, even if literally speaking we are in the public square, sitting at home or visiting the theatre. (This is very different advice from that of Tertullian in *De spectaculis*.) The High Priest associates only with a virgin of his own race. How can one full of sin who comes into the church be called a "chaste virgin" that she might be worthy to couple with Christ? Well, only in the sense that it is *faith* that matters: "I have betrothed you to me in faith" (Hos 2:20). Philosophical wisdom and the boldness of circumcision do not corrupt this faith, for it remains in the simplicity of confession just as in a virginal state. Why are no widows allowed? Well, with an allusion to Romans 7:1–4, because spiritually a widow will be lacking freedom from the gospel if she thinks she is now free from the Law. Origen is aware that the Hebrew does not have "from his own kind," but adds that this phrase, kept in the LXX, has been lost from the original text Hebrew text because the Jews have lost that special connection. For the soul of Christ from his nature and substance belong to every human soul. The intimacy with God has been taken from the Jews and transferred to the church of Christ.

Augustine sounds a chord very different from Origen and on verse 10 simply mentions, with only a hint of Christology as to Christ's full yet elect humanity, that the High Priest is one who is great among his brothers, on whose head is poured the anointed oil (*oleo christo*!), for Scripture calls that very oil "anointed." This is suggestive of a grace common to Christ (*qua* human) and his ministers. To say "he will not go into a dead soul" is a scriptural idiom "which is quite hard to translate." The body that lacks a soul assumes the name of its director, the soul, just as the building that is called "church," even when the people called "church" have left, is still called "church." Moreover a "dead" soul is one that is "dead to the body." Yet how can anyone enter over a dead soul, which the priest here is forbidden to do, since whoever enters over a dead body cannot step over the soul, since that has now left the body? Well, perhaps only in the sense that it is called that because the soul that gave it its subsistence used to be there. The High Priest will not leave the holy places (v. 12). Obviously this restriction cannot be forever, perhaps only a week. But if they were not forbidden to take wives how could they ever be ritually clean to serve? Did they have a rota? However, the *High* Priest would have to be unmarried, as he has to be in the sanctuary *every day*. And this is what the verse means literally. As for verse 15, it is the Lord who sanctifies. Does Moses not also? The solution is that Moses did so visibly through the sacraments, but the Lord worked and works invisibly, for without this the visible sacraments are futile. It can be learned from examples like John the Baptist and the penitent thief that invisible sanctification was present to them and profited them without visible sacraments, yet these were changed with the age to become altered in form, visible sacraments needing this invisible sanctification to profit. Yet one cannot sanctify without those means: thus Cornelius got baptized (Acts 10).

Jerome replied by letter to Fabiola, who had wanted him to explain the meaning of the vestments of the priests. Yet, wrote Jerome, there are some other important moral lessons here too: verse 10 speaks of the distance and dignity of priest and the following verse teaches that while we respect the affairs of our bodies, if many things drive our affections, then we offend against the Creator of body and soul. Whoever loves father and mother more than Christ is not worthy, and instead we should attend to that Father who never dies or who has died for us in a living way so that he might vivify us who are dead. There is to be no looking back to the "old man" and his ways: only forward. Jerome reminds us (and the *Glossa* will excerpt this) of the unhappy case of Simon who after baptism pined for his former married state, and was not worthy to be the companion of Peter. Not to go outside and pollute the sanctity of God (v. 12) reminds Jerome of that mountain-dweller who went down from Jerusalem to Jericho and got easily wounded, since he was naked [unarmed]. Oil and light medical treatment were tempered with mercy, but since negligence ought to feel pain he was bitten by the sharpness of wine in his wounds, that through the comforting oil he be provoked to penance and by the wine he might sense the sternness of the judge. Through the oil of his anointing we carry him in us, and we ought not to leave the temple (i.e., depart from the Christian confession), nor go out to mix with the unbelief of Gentiles, but always stay inside ministering to the Lord's will.

Severus judges that verse 14 figuratively makes clear that the consecrated man must have a wife who shares his way of life, i.e., one who is religiously instructed and keen for holy things, and attracted to the same causes and actions as her man so that the holy seed remain without alloy. A compromise position was arrived at by Pope Siricius (d. 399), but, as it was soon overtaken by an insistence on clerical celibacy, it was not much appealed to. On verses 13–14 he tells us that priests may marry only once. But the previous verse (12)—about not "going outside the sanctuary for the consecration of the anointing oil is upon him"—that says that priests only have to be active for a year is explained in this context as concerning only the first year of service. "Why indeed were priests ordered to live in the temple far from their homes in the year of their service? Just for this reason: so that they could not engage in physical contact even with their wives, and that shining in integrity of conscience they might offer acceptable service to God. The period of service completed, use of wives was permitted to them for reason of succession alone, because no one from a tribe other than of Levi was directed to be admitted to the ministry of God" (Somerville and Brasington 1998, 41–43). Yet the High Priest's clothing being intact can also, according to *Pauca Problesmata*, figuratively mean that Christ's church is not to be divided and that we can be defiled when we harm Christ and the church with sin. The widow of verse 14 is the synagogue, who is repudiated by Christ, and the harlot is pagan idolatry.

Hugh wonders whether burying the dead is not an act of piety, as we see with Tobias (Tobit 14). But as sin is "death," then touching the dead is sin. It would contaminate the priest in that he would become an accomplice in the crime and could not serve the life of the people. Hence the Lord Pope has no place at funeral Masses. Mystically understood, Christ marries the pure and whole soul, or the church, that she might become one spirit with him. But he took the church from the nations, which had been repudiated and become a harlot for a time in the desert, and afterwards he made her a virgin (cf. Isa 54). Jerome had said about Hosea's wife that the corrupted cannot be made incorrupt. But, says Hugh, that is in the case of physical corruption, and not spiritual which *can* be repaired daily by penance. Hugh objects that on the requirement of marrying within one's kind (v. 13), Ralph was too fussy in objecting that Aaron married outside the tribe—the text merely means that his wife must be Jewish.

For Rashi, the High Priest (and priests in general) should marry a virgin and one from his own people—a Levite. However, there was a concession to this restriction in that he could marry from the royal line (a) due to the nobility of the (Jewish) race; (b) because there should be concord between the temporal (the king) and spiritual (the High Priest) leader; and (c) because it would make the kings more aware of the Law. This is one way of reading that he could marry a non-Levite if she was noble and hence non-"vulgar." Lyra agrees but adds that "widow," taken figuratively, can mean "empty philosophy." Denys is clear that the equivalent of the High Priest is the pope. He should have nothing to do with the "dead." For this reason Rome's parish does not go out into the world. Also, echoing Hugh, the pope rightly stays out of any funeral processions.

Pellican sees the principle as not troubling with one's mother and father when one is doing the will of the Father (Matt 12:48), and, even as a Protestant, he wants to keep the idea that some humans other than Christ are to model sincere chaste living for the church, so that the church as a whole can become such a bride. Therefore, priests always deserve a double honor, i.e., the reverence and obedience of the people. Now for the High Priest, says Brenz, the standards are *even higher*. He will only watch, not perform, a funeral—not even of parents, as is allowed to other priests. And he is not to come out of the sanctuary (which is not to be understood as if the High Priest had always to be in the tabernacle or temple, shut up like in a prison and not allowed to go out; only that he was not allowed to go out for the sake of a funeral). The one Great Priest cannot dirty himself since the crown of the oil of the unction of God is on him. For "crown" the Hebrew has *nēzer* which signifies "separation" but also a crown or diadem. What here is demanded of the High Priest is demanded in Numbers 6 of Nazirites (although not for ever, but only for the time of their separation). While the priests represent all godly Christians, the High Priest foreshadows not the Roman pontiff but *Christ our Lord*. Brenz opposes the Roman practice of "touching" (= praying for) dead folk, and he mocks those who do for being unkind and taking another year to get round to helping a soul out of purgatory. The point is that, for the Reformers, *Christ* was the High Priest, so that the stricter rules about celibacy applied to him only and *not to present priests* who can be holy and married (so, Spangenberg).

Although not one for "easy" identifications of OT figures with Christ, the High Priest has to be given some reference, so Calvin adds: an utmost perfection is rightly required in a priest to be a mediator between God and man; he needs to be exempt from all blame. It follows that a man of angelic purity was to be looked for, who would reconcile God to the world. In his French translation of the *Harmony of the Pentateuch*, Christ's anguish is said to be the Christian's joy.

Lapide, working with Augustine's opinion, argues that priests are to keep from bodily uncleanness and irregularity, first, because their old sanctity and purity was corporeal; second, because priests should be giving the people an example of the heavenly life (and mourning the dead would not do this); third, because the priest is a type of Christ and was called to foreshadow him by his sacrifices. Exceptions are allowed for lesser priests (and where Ithmar and Eleazar are forbidden to mourn their dead brothers Nadab and Abihu [Lev 10:6], that was because they were *recent* priests and God did not want them mourning those who deserved to die).

Lapide then glosses: "he will not take his headdress off for the purposes of lamenting the dead" (v. 10)—allegorically this speaks of the imperturbable, unmovable, and eternal priesthood of Christ, which will never be removed (as Cyril in Book 12 of *De Adoratione* suggests). It was fitting that the wife of the High Priest be pure. So Julius Caesar dismissed his wife Pompeia, since Caesar's wife should be free from all suspicion. The LXX *ekbeblēmenēn kai bebēlōmenēn* sounds like a legal technical phrase, which suggests one who is as divorcee is thus "spoiled." Tertullian in his *De Monogamia* quoted this verse ("my priests will not marry again") thus forbidding a second marriage to them. Perhaps the edition of Theodotion or Symmachus had such an extra phrase, ponders Lapide. But in any case the credibility of Tertullian is doubtful since he wrote this work as a heretic, contending that all second marriages were illicit.

Calmet, commenting on verse 12, writes that "the Jews" say that if the High Priest finds a corpse on road, he can (exceptionally) bury that. Calmet is aware of a concept of graded holiness that requires the High Priest to be more austere, to hold back from going out and grieving, while other priests could and then get purified. Like a pagan first minister, which was the High Priest's role, unction was given on account of purity. For priests today who read this they must ask themselves just what dispositions and qualities God demands to set them apart from the people and from other non-priestly ministers. Augustine thought that the High Priest attained that office immediately after the death of his father, and so he could not go to that funeral; it is probably more likely he was made High Priest before the death of his father. Finally he raises the problem from 2 Chronicles 24:3 that Jehoiada had two wives. Calmet hopes that maybe Jehoiada was not always the High Priest or that he had the wives in succession or that he had two but would have given one up before taking office.

Defects (vv. 16–23)

Jerome and Cyril think that laws that might seem rather harsh and inhumane if taken on the literal level make more sense when universalized to the whole of the priesthood in all ages in a *moral* sense. Theodoret thinks that on account of the Jews' querulous nature, by allowing no one with an outer flaw to approach for service, the sins of the will are also condemned. For the blindness of the eyes signifies a lack of will; the lack of an ear signifies disobedience; the loss of an ear, a lack of discretion; the lack of a hand, laziness. For that reason Leviticus orders that those who present the offerings have all members and the things that are offered teaching those offering that they should have healthy operations of the soul. Also, those castrated are not allowed to serve, for such a one ought to be *fertile in good deeds*, looking after the divine service. Hesychius treats these defects in turn: "blind" means one who cannot see the light of contemplation or wisdom and, pressed down by the darkness of the present life, cannot see where the progress of good work leads. The lame do have this sense of direction, but cannot get there. A small nose is unsuitable as it cannot discern. In the half-blind, whose minds are keen to know the truth, the pupils are clear but with dryness of the eyelids they grow large and with such growth the sharpness is lost.

Severus, understanding these to mean defects of the soul, observes that he must have no passion in the eyes of the mind and in no way be shadowed by this life's fog, but be pure to look on heavenly beauties and thoughts. And making a way through all the commandments (not fulfilling one while limping with another), bearing the opposition to the proclamation of the gospel and the right faith, and strengthened by the coming hope—running without impediment like Paul—he should grow up into the fullness of Christ. And he must not work to an unworthy effect nor offer sterile teaching. The Law is not only concerned with the great passions but also with the lesser ones.

A penitent priest cannot also serve, wrote Gregory the Great (Q.35). Put positively the priest must exercise virtues "in the presence of God" (*Pauca Problemata*). He needs to be wise, righteous, strong, moderate, but must also have right faith, thoughtful hope, and true love. Anyone who presumes will receive punishment like Abihu and Nadab.

Bruno observes that the nose discerns odors—if it is too small it does not get a full impression but if it is too large it exceeds measure (cf. 1 Cor 14:20). The hunchback is the one who is ignorant of heaven and looks only at the ground, whereas the one with scabies is always restless—he works, he grows weary, and he is not healed, since he is a lover of the honor of the world. The following verse (v. 22) offers a nice compromise to the one who is flawed, for he can eat of the bread offered in the sanctuary. It should be understood, reckons Bruno, that although one who has flaws cannot be a bishop, he is still allowed to eat the spiritual food. For none who have a flaw—who have committed a crime—can become a priest, even after penance, although after penance they can partake of the church's sacrament.

In the medieval canon law, "physical defects—the lack of a limb for example—and deficiencies in learning were grounds for refusal to admit to the priesthood. A candidate's lack of proper ordination was another. Illegitimate birth without having secured a valid dispensation was a third, in addition to crimes and sins" (Helmholz 2004, 482, with reference to Duarenus, *De beneficiis* [AD 950] IV.3). *La bible moralisée's* depiction of the hunchback, lame, scurvied man of verse 20 is how usurers who are in the act of taking a child in pawn were often portrayed in the High Middle Ages (Lipton 1999, 35).

Langton thinks that a "small nose" is that which is not suited to taking the measure of what must be learned. A nose must have the subtlety of discretion and a large and twisted nose has too much of that or confuses rightness of action with complexity, especially when one does not wipe such a nose (here he plays on the verb *emungere*, to be shrewd). There is a lot of repetition of the *Glossa* and Ralph here, with only some elaboration of the tradition: the keenness of the pupil also is healthy—for nothing remains when the sword is in the hand of a white-eyed man. To tempt is human but to succumb is diabolical. Skin disease works on the body without inflicting pain and fouls the fairness of the parts of the body—this is like greed where the soul delights and feels no pain. Some are tempted to lie when they think they are being kind to others.

For Lyra, of course, what is at stake was the honor of the worship of God; these things are arranged for the excellence of the priesthood and more so the High Priesthood so as to have the people's reverence for them. That is why none who are "contemptibles" should be priests. A large nose means one is indiscreet, when one needs to have discretion: to be lame means one is poor in advancing in love of virtue; the white-eyed sees obscurely in the things of salvation. There is also something to be learned from this for lay people too. None are to be admitted to the perceiving of the Eucharist, except those who are faithful and clean.

For Lorinus, "blemished" (v. 18) concerns a *fallen* bishop, and any such heretics who return should be received like laymen, as Cyprian instructed in his Epistle 64. Protestants are less interested in discussing defects, but Ainsworth is an exception. Just as the virgin marriages prefigure the marriage of the church and Christ, so to be unblemished is to prefigure the perfections in Christ. The blemishes that disqualify include, following Maimonides, even shaking or being smelly or having halitosis.

On verse 21 Lapide sees a clear reference to the Eucharist, the flesh of Christ under the appearance of bread. So that "this is my body" can be said of the bread (1 Cor 11; John 6). Lapide is fascinated how what we have as bread and the Israelites had as flesh meet in the person of the Lord Jesus Christ. Lapide concludes on the defects (on v. 23) that if this is what was demanded of Israelites, *how much more* is to be expected of Christians offering and eating the body of Christ? For John Moschus (in *The Spiritual Meadow* [c. 600]) relates that the Holy Spirit told Pope Agapito to remove one of the priests who was carrying a fan and to carry out the Eucharist himself. Or in Palladius' *Lausiac History*, chapter 20, we hear that a presbyter in state of fornication was afflicted with cancer, which came out of his head in such a way that his whole mouth appeared in his neck. The blessed Macarius healed him after he promised to sin no more and not minister at altar but become laicized.

Willet likes to take each word of verse 19 and savor it. On properties that prevent being a priest, "the word *qdduk* means slender, when one is as thinne and defective in body, as the crooke-back before spoken of exceedeth." A whole list of pagan parallels follow with remarks about bleary-eyed people and those with pimples on their face. He concludes: In our soul we all have deformities, so we should be modest in our prayers.

The modern commentary, largely under Maimonides' influence, see the physical not as representing the moral, but as demanding a high standard in worship. Calmet simply notes that the rabbis counted 140–42 body flaws that could debar from service. Matthew Henry notes that God made this provision for the preserving of the reputation of his altar, that it might not at any time fall under contempt. Under the gospel, however, "there is many a healthful beautiful soul lodged in a crazy deformed body. Yet, 2. We ought to infer hence how incapable those are to serve God acceptably whose minds are blemished and deformed by any reigning vice." Keil seems to represent a strand of "muscular Christianity," or perhaps an aesthetical one, when he comments that as with the Greeks and Romans, "as the spiritual nature of a man is reflected in his bodily form, only a faithful condition of body could correspond to the holiness of the priest."

Modern liturgists observe that Levitical language was borrowed to shape the ministerial priesthood from as early as the second century and this was, in part, as a reaction against Marcion's denial of the ongoing value of the OT (Tillard 1987, 12). Although "kingdom of priests" (Exod 19:6/Rev 1:6) means something collective (Greshake 1996, 428), apart from Tertullian, nobody would have dreamed of allowing just any baptized persons to preside. In fact, it was probably the bishop's office that was first described in *priestly* language by (pre-schismatic) Tertullian who simply reported the practice of naming bishops as *sacerdotes*, and then Cyprian in Epistle 63.14 and also Origen, while reserving the title "High Priest" for Christ (although the Syrian *Didascalia* II.26.4 would call bishops "levitical high priests"). Augustine perhaps put a brake on this development, although the assumption of Christianity as state religion must have helped to put bishops in their place (cf. Bradshaw 1996, 416f). In any case, an OT model taken rather literally for a wide range of priestly services, including preaching, became more and more centered on the Eucharist and the forgiveness of sins. Meanwhile the NT metaphorical usage allowed concurrently the idea of the people as priests "improperly spoken." Jerome is aware of both types of priesthood (*Dial contra Luciferanos* 4). Lay people by the High Middle Ages, both in East (Nicetas of Ancyra, *Synodes*, c. 1090) and West (Aquinas, *ST* III, q82), bear some form of priesthood.

Now these chapters of Leviticus (21 and 22) deal less with anointing and performance of the cult than with the personal qualities of the mediators and materials. What Greshake does note, after Fransen, is that the word *kleros* was a neologism to describe these ordained people (bishops, priests, and deacons) as inspired by a Levitical background, as a different from the rest of God's people (Greshake 1996, 425). The bishops at Trent made sure that their status was not tied completely to the Eucharist, but to their role as pastors, and yet this was not how it was received. Pius X's *Haerent animo* (1908) in its elevation of priests to heaven while the laity belong to the earth is the apotheosis of clericalism.

Although the real presence and the votive intention of the Mass were unaffected by the moral state of the priest, his accompanying prayers could be (as per the *Interpretacyoun and Sygnyfycacyoun of the Masse [1532]*, which might include the final blessing [Marshall 1994, 57]). There were many sins that could not easily be washed away in the lavabo at the start. Yet the priest was a sinner, unlike Christ, and hence was in some ways more of a representative than Christ was. He was yet meant to be courteous and beyond reproach, but also to look distinctive (Marshall 1994, 133f), i.e., to have dignity.

Leviticus 22

Requirements for Priests Eating the Holy Offerings (vv. 1–9)

FOR CYRIL, IN HIS *De Adoratione*, the Law is eternal; it just needs the right interpretation. Furthermore, a number of these laws make sense only when given a spiritual interpretation applied universally. One such example (v. 4) is when the leprosy of heresy would infect the Christian priesthood, such a person must be barred from it, for such a person would be caught up in works of corruption and passions of the flesh. Unable to be fruitful, they would be contagious by their bad example.

The requirements for Christian priests to be clean because of their regular Eucharistic offering found inspiration in this passage from quite early on, according to texts from Pope Siricius (*Epst. ad Himerium* VII 10) and Ambrosoisater (*Comm. on Timothy*, I.3) (c. 400 AD) that say that the priests should be attentive to being purified at their time of service with regard to sex and alcohol. Any reference to Leviticus 22 and the rest seems a little loose, but one is aware of an argument: *how much more* so should *Christian* priests be clean (Kottje 1971, 225).

Cajetan, saw in the phrase "whatever his uncleanness shall be" (v. 5) an encouragement to universalize and extend Israel's rules on ritual purity. He thus observes that the nations modeled the requirements for their ceremonies "possibly from this chapter": one such was Iamblichus on the mysteries of the Egyptians, responding to Porphyry's horror at mixing the already dead with ritual acts. On verse 9, Cajetan thinks that the Hebrew wording "insinuates" that unclean priests should even be excluded from guarding the temple, i.e., they should be taken off the rota of "duty priests" who perform a solemn duty day and night.

Pellican observes that reverence for the sanctuary is inculcated, for it represents the divine presence and providence for the faithful, and for the things made holy, associated with the action of graces and faith in God. So careless treatment of God's glory leads to injury, even damnation of souls, while a higher level of purity is expected of priests. Today *all* those (lay people included) who set out to worship God the Spirit *in spirit* must purify themselves of all vices. Yet God wanted priests to achieve a purity of body as well as of soul, in order to be good example to the laity. This fastidiousness (reflected in Pellican's humanist aesthetic) meant that before one could lead worship one must be trained in the law, and the corresponding counsel for Pellican's contemporaries is that they be beyond visible occasion for reproach as well as spiritually attuned.

Lapide takes the *corpses* (vv. 4, 8) to speak of sins and *to touch the corpse* means a communication of sins. The priest ought to beware lest he participate in the people's sin and lead a common life, and he should not consent to the principle of sinning, being only contaminated in the sin of the first parents, Adam and Eve. Ainsworth thinks that the demand for spiritual purification especially pertained to the priests and ministers "whom Christ should purify by his grace" as per Malachi 3:2. Corporal cleanliness signifies spiritual cleanliness of Christians. One is to "walk in the light" so as not to be unworthy eaters with a clear reference to preparation of communion as they make a sacrifice of humble and contrite hearts through Christ.

Willet argues that not having uncleanness means undergoing some required preparation of devotion before handling the sacraments, *contra* Lorinus, for whom access to the Eucharist requires no positive preparation, just the removal of any moral obstacle. Willet is pleased that Cajetan affirmed it was a mortal sin not to have actual warm devotion, and that Ambrose (Bk 2, 9 of *De paenitentia*) held it wrong to bind priests to have to give holy things to "dogs." Willet relates that by "unclean until the sunset" (v. 6), some understand "the end of the world," when the Messiah was to come, "by whom we are made cleane; or the end of a man's life, after which there is no forgiveness (Tostatus). But Hesychius better understandeth the time of our repentance: and so by washing is signified our repentance, as John Baptist saith: *I baptise you with water to repentance* (Math. 3.11)." So here baptism is given high value in this Puritan's notion of what makes for purity. He mentions "Jerome's view" that "torn of beasts" could mean "taken by the devil." Where verse 9 has "I the Lord do sanctify them," "Tostatus and Vatable give this sense, 'I command them to be holy,' but more is signified, that the Lord had sanctified them to bee Priests, and so enabled them to the performance of their dutie herein." So there is less excuse for failing.

Outsiders (vv. 10–16, 25)

In the *Epistle to Fabiola*, as repeated in the *Glossa* on verse 15, Jerome states that Christ is of the firstfruits of our gathering, so he rightly lives on our firstfruits, i.e.,

Leviticus 22

the Eucharistic offerings which feed and constitute the faithful people who "see God" (*Isra-el*) through this mystery; and whosoever consecrate themselves to God in the Dominical sacrifice, are the holy of holies, since the body of Christ is made up from these.

Procopius explains that the daughter of the priest (vv. 12–13) is the regenerate soul who has become unbelieving. She is one who after being renewed and freed was then led into the abyss of faithlessness by a wandering demonic seed. She is the Jewish synagogue whom the prophets summoned to repentance. Hesychius too sees an apostate returning to the church here.

For Bruno it is clear that the daughter of the priest is every soul, reborn in the water of baptism, which if she has married anyone from the people—that is, if she has joined with a heretic or unbeliever—immediately becomes a stranger to the spiritual food and to Christ's sacraments. If, however, she rejects the heretics' partnerships and returns to the church, having abandoned her error and all sons of heretical depravity and their works, once again she will be nourished with the food of her heavenly Father who expels none who comes to him. The great mercy of God is proclaimed here and no reason for despair is given (cf. Ezek 33:11.)

Bruno takes "to add an extra fifth part" (v. 14) to mean penitents who humble their *whole self* before the judgment of the priest and also then give some satisfaction in terms of good works to the church. For the "fifth part" is a human—since there are five senses of the body—and to add a fifth means to hand over oneself to the priest, ready to obey his judgment in all things; for he has nothing greater than himself which could be traded to the priest to restitute the loss. This is suggestive that those who want to mix themselves with priestly things should come under ecclesial authority as soon as possible. Langton thinks there is hope for a widowed soul (v. 13) who with the "dead husband" of bad works through meditation on them puts aside her "repudiation"—that is, the will to sin.

For Hugh, "alien" priests refers to heretics or those practicing simony, who ought not to serve the Eucharist. Nothing is to be accepted from the hands of a heretic (even if the Jews themselves did not always keep to this law, as when they received gifts and favors from Hiram and Cyrus). Yet Hugh takes verse 14 to be directed against the clergy who keep back the material inheritance of the Crucified (i.e., riches) rather than help the poor and restore things snatched away from them.

For Cyril, to offer "from the hand of a foreigner" (v. 25) means to try to offer to the Father *without going through Christ*, in whom alone there is access to the Father (Eph 2:18). Langton thinks that foreigners are those impenitents who offer gifts at the altar or those who start penance but do not finish—they are like hirelings (John

10:12) and wish to live for the present time. Priests must not mix their stock with these people and they must preserve the sacraments of their altar, thus not allowing such impenitents the Eucharist, which is the chief and pre-eminent sacrament. Lyra says that Rashi thought that this verse—which is about corruptions in the offerings by Gentiles, who Rashi did think were able to give offerings—has nothing to do with Gentiles, but refers to corrupt offerings from Jews. But surely, Lyra reasons, converts to Judaism would also be allowed, even if not Gentiles. So nothing could be received from Gentiles. So actually our translations understand the Hebrew better than Rashi does. For by faith our hearts are cleansed; by faith our works are sanctified; and whatever is not from faith is sin. In that sense "foreigners" (v. 25) who lack faith may not just simply join in. On the question of foreign involvement invalidating the offering, Lyra and Denys agree that it was another thing to sacrifice *on behalf of* other nations (2 Macc 3; or 1 Esd 6). Even more, there were a number of pious Gentiles, like Job; and he did sacrifice on behalf of his friends. But orthodox "faith" seems to be the criterion.

Borrhaus interprets the "no foreigner" rule to mean "not of the house of Aaron." Yet such a law would yield to necessity, as in the case of David. In the NT Christ is the heavenly Aaron, notwithstanding Hebrews 7:11, even if one were to argue that the order of Melchizedek subsumes rather than replaces that of Aaron. Identifying with Jesus could make one seem foreign in Jewish eyes. Christ did things differently as he invited all who are sick and misshapen. So "foreigners" are allowed to offer, but only if they are "whole." This shows that God has never been foreign to the Gentiles, since he wanted to bless even Pharaoh through Joseph, and Jethro through Moses, and in the figure of Naaman through Elisha. There were many who kept the Ten Commandments through the natural law and observed the Noachic covenant: as Paul would say in Romans 2:14f, the Gentiles have their law. The Jews say that the world is sustained by three things: by the Law as word preached, by true worship, and by works of love.

Lorinus took "ignorance" (v. 14) to mean not recognizing the body and blood of Christ in receiving communion. Willet counters that the elements are but instruments of a mystical feeding: these are being sanctified not changed. For, he contends, even Hesychius adds "one perceives the mysteries, but does not know the power of the mysteries." Hesychius and his contemporaries had no conceit of such transubstantiation; and for Bernard (of Clairvaux) it was not the priest alone who consecrates but the company of people with him. It is part of Willet's argument to suggest that these verses encourage a cultic *and* a moral (everyday) holiness.

Cocceius sees the principle here in verses 10–16: the people were unable to expiate their sins, so they ought not to eat from the holy things, lest it seem that the people become purified by themselves. For the priests point forward to Christ, the only source of true sanctity. On verse 25, the "separatist" principle that gifts not come from the hand of a stranger echoes Ainsworth's treatment of churches refusing state aid. Yet he admits that Darius in Ezra 6:8–10 gave sacrifices for the priests to offer in Jerusalem. In such a case it is only *blemished* as being from their hand and this should be acknowledged, and there is an argument for accepting: "for the heart is towards heaven" (Maimonides, *Maagnasseh Hakorbanoth* 3.3.5). Ainsworth seems tempted, but ultimately not persuaded by this consideration.

Calmet asks, concerning verse 25, does "bread" mean all food? Tostatus and Cajetan answer in the affirmative, that only money could be offered. Or rabbis allowed any offerings without bread to come from Gentiles, which meant all offerings—such as the holocaust and sin offerings—that did not involve bread. So Gentiles may offer these. He quotes Philo (*De legatione ad Gaium*), who says he saw almost all of Augustus's family at the temple, but they were providing non-food things like furnishings and money.

Henry observes how the priests must not "profane the holy things" by permitting the strangers to eat of them, or "suffer them to bear the iniquity of trespass" (vv. 15f): "We must not only be careful that we do not bear iniquity ourselves, but we must do what we can to prevent others bearing it." Yet that does not mean that priests should presume to bear their own sins and those of others rather than casting them on Christ.

The Wholeness of Offerings (vv. 17–24; 26–30)

Cyril (*De adoratione*) is clear that these verses call us to avoid offering anything spiritually weak and flawed. Christ was a victim, yes, but he *chose* to be one and as such really had no weakness. Likewise Christians are not to be blind in not having divine light (that is, illumination through Christ in the Spirit). The *Glossa* is quite clear, that a skin disease (v. 22) signifies a fornicator who stains his own body (1 Cor 6:18). The Irish *Pauca Problesmata* is also clear and specific here (vv. 21–23): "broken" means "is prone to vices"; to have a wen is to burn with carnal lust; a scab is heresy; lacking a tail means lacking perseverance in good works. Most interesting is "without testicles": that means one who wants to sin but cannot. These cannot be offered with the bull; that is, they will not be brought to heaven nor be consorts of the Lord's passion so as to reign with him.

Bruno associates "cleaning up our offering of ourselves" (for that is what is meant) with Luke 20:25—"render unto Caesar"—where Jesus meant that, unlike the grubby image of Caesar on a coin we are to render to God his image, and that means to wash, clean, and not offer ourselves in any way unclean or spotted. On the eighth day (v. 26) offering will be made, for death will mean being handed over to the saints, or perhaps later if some time in purgatory is needed: not all who are saved are immediately welcomed into blessedness.

Ralph's main concern is with the ethical purity of those who claim their offerings are pure: such is the case only when we offer to the Lord without at same time being adulterous, violent, or perjuring. There will be no stain in such a person, especially of mortal sin, which separates from God. As for verse 24, even though Isaiah says that the eunuch is not a dry tree (Isa 56:3), Moses here is praising carnal reproduction because it foreshadows the spiritual fertility—that of which Isaiah speaks—even if, at that point, Moses was not conscious of making parables from these things. To translate into NT realities, the seed that one needs is preaching the Word (cf. Sir 20, which Ralph associates with the NT). A eunuch is a teacher who, since he has no affection towards those who are not his sons, becomes enflamed with fury towards one of his students and too severely punishes the offence, thereby not seeking fruit but satisfying his own anger.

For Hugh the idea was that the calves were castrated in order to make them fatter. Hugh does not see why such a sacrifice should be a problem and concludes by saying that this shows how verse 24 cannot be taken literally but only as a mystery. Langton takes "with a broken hand" (v. 23) to mean teachers who do not know how to preach, just like dogs unable to bark (Isa 56:10). One can see how Isaiah 56 was a rich quarry for the medieval theology of priesthood. Yet the *wholeness* can refer to that of the people whom, in a sense, the priest presents: thus *impetigo* stands for the all too common lay bigamy. The offerings that have flaws in themselves in turn refer to what is lacking in the works of preachers, thinks Langton. These are "the six-sided squared stones" by which sin is figured (e.g., evil thoughts, luxury, omissions), and with these squared stones the devil builds his house. Through negligence, double-mindedness is born and it corrupts and corrodes completely, and is unsuitable for the gaining of the kingdom of heaven where there can be no sin. There is some architectural metaphor superimposed on the language of cultic holiness here. One needs to work in the fear of the Lord and the purity of good intention. The two testicles (v. 23) are Christian life and doctrine: these two produce children for God in holiness.

Where it is a freewill offering (v. 29) Abarbanel spots a difference between Maimonides and Nahmanides here, though Denys thinks there was no real difference between them. The question is: why did Adam and Noah sacrifice? For Maimonides what matters for human perfection is the rational mind (i.e., right persuasions and true and honest opinions) that accompanies any cultic action. It is a meeting of human and divine minds that should take place through the revealed rite. In this spirit of interpretation Pellican takes verse 24 to teach that the sacrifices of the impious and the unfaithful cannot please God: belief is what matters and that is by what the elect are justified. Any superstitious markings or castrations in honor of demons remind him of the excesses of late medieval piety. God does not want offerings from an ingrate (v. 25) and he looks at the person, not the gift. Of course, there needs to be the principle of faith present, and that should include someone who has just converted. God is no respecter of persons but damnatory of superstitions. Therefore to offer mature aged animals (v. 28) means to offer to God a mature and stable faith. The faith of the church is to be fed by milk but only until they are strong to eat the bread and meat of more solid teaching.

Borrhaus notes that God also wants any species to be conserved and is slow to wipe it out. The principle of verse 27 is that God allows us to grow up to be ready for willing self-sacrifice, as he sanctifies us by his word from the world, the flesh, and the devil. Calvin uses this passage to remind his readers of the need to obey God's will for worship. "Neither shall you profane" (v. 32): Let this be carefully observed, that whatever fancies men devise, are so many profanations of God's name. Mark also the mutual relation, when God requires himself to be hallowed, even as he hallows the people. It is as though he commanded them to reflect from whence their superiority proceeded, that they may pay their debt of gratitude to him who is its author." Calov, on verse 27, says that this is not about the Sabbath as being greater than all other things, as Grotius thinks. But it is mystically intended, to show that Christ would not suffer death in his infancy or childhood but in the perfection of manly maturity (following the Reformed Hebraist, Paul Fagius, d. 1549.)

Willet takes the opportunity on vv. 18–23 to argue "against voluntary religion," that "a free offering is so called, not in respect of the thing itselfe, for they had no liberty, or freedome to offer, what they thought good; (onely according to the Law) but in regard of the willingenesse of the mind when one offered them freely, and frankely, not, brought unto it by adversitie." As for the animals' not having ears (as v. 23 LXX suggests): "Touching the tayle, though it be comely in beasts (and yet sometime hunting dogges, and others for speciall use, have their eares and tayles cut off) yet it is a disgrace to a man: as some write of men that have tayles in Java . . . And he [Marco Polo] telleth us a tale out of fabulous Genebrard, how at Dorcester in England, the men had tayles, by the judgement of God, because they derided

Austins preaching." The rule on not offering the very young is not only mystical, as Augustine taught, but plainly teaches humanity about needing to be humane. Yet this does not mean that while they are yet sucking they cannot be *offered*, for Samuel offered such (1 Sam 7:9) for future disposal. So this law is not really about cruelty but rather about the less than fully viable state of the animal. There *could*, he admits, also be a moral reason, i.e., to abstain from cruelty. Or as Ambrose in his Sermon 5.9: "Are thou not pricked in heart, o Christian, when thou seest anothers teares in thy house?"

Leviticus 23

Festivals

IN THE PATRISTIC PERIOD little was made of festivals, which were regarded as "Jewish" (cf. Col 2:16). Methodius of Olympus (d. 310) makes a passing reference to Leviticus 23 when mentioning the Jewish feast of Tabernacles (Succoth) (*Banquet* 9:3):

> Here the Jews, fluttering about the bare letter of Scripture, like drones about the leaves of herbs, but not about flowers and fruits as the bee, fully believe that these words and ordinances were spoken concerning such a tabernacle as they erect; as if God delighted in those trivial adornments, whereas these things, being like air and phantom shadows, foretell the resurrection and the putting up of our tabernacle that had fallen upon the earth, which at length, in the seventh thousand of years, resuming again immortal, we shall celebrate the great feast of true tabernacles in the new and indissoluble creation.

A spiritualizing of "festival" had as much to do with Philo as with the NT and can be seen in Origen's attitude in *Against Celsus* 8.23. The patristic consensus was that the Christian should grasp the spirit of "festival" by living each day in eschatological expectation and wisdom (cf. Ambrose, *Cain and Abel* 2.2.8) (Klauber 1969, 755). But not much later Augustine complained about drunken behavior on Christian feast days intended to honor the martyrs (Epistle 29.9).

However, a bit more than a generation later, Hesychius finds it significant that the LXX text (v. 2) has "holy convocations," emphasizing that aspect of the feasts which is the coming together of people. In observing festivals the church is fulfilling the Law, although not according to the letter. The church now has better festivals to put the Jewish ones in the shade (e.g., with distinctive dates for the spring-time Easter festival). Nevertheless, there is acknowledgement that *real* festivals in *real* time are important, and the church calendar testifies to this. The Middle Ages saw a great increase in Christian feast days until at the Synod of Reims (1408) under Jean

Gerson and at Ratisbon (1524) under Cardinal Campeggio the church stipulated that on all but the high days of the year (twenty-five of them) work should be done after Mass (Villien 1913, 2187). (As of 2011, feast days in a "Catholic country," such as Spain, amount to ten work-free days a year, whereas in laicized France the amount is down to three.)

In medieval Handbooks of Penance there is found some reuse of the instructions of Leviticus 23, e.g., pertaining to fasts, not feasts. "The third fast of the seventh month is prescribed by the Lord through Moses [Lev 23:10, 27, 29 follows]. On this account then, the fast is celebrated in the Church according to ancient custom, or else, because the day shortens and the night is lengthened, for, at the decline of the sun and the increase of the night, our life is shown to decline at the approach of death, which death in God's judgment and in the Resurrection shall be restored to life . . . it is necessary to humble our souls every year in memory and remembrance of so great a mystery" (McNeill and Garner 1990, 242).

Cajetan, reflecting on the Christian liturgy while commenting on Leviticus 23, states that the introduction of the religion of feasts was very necessary, for these are occasions that the unlearned people can be given instruction together and made to look for the Lord's coming. For Cajetan, Passover and Easter come first and the institution of that and other festivals has become a *foundation of polity.* All nations have these types of solemnities but only the people of God have these particular ones, remembrances of divine blessings on which they were to think, like nourishment for their faith, gatherings to hear the word of God, which are like conventions in the tent of meeting. The text of Leviticus 23 calls the feasts "holy," that is, following Cicero's definition (in *pro Cor. Balno*), "fixed, religious, and inviolable." There is a strong early modern flavor of church as a place where one learns things.

Brenz sees festivals as means to remember the miracles God did in creation. Foreseeing some would think the world was eternal, God instituted this "re-creation" through hearing the word and learning true religion. Festivals are primarily intended, however, for the sake of the common "political" good in giving rest to all. These are disciplines to help fulfill one's spiritual offerings of prayer, thanksgiving, obedience, and a contrite heart—and those offerings *are* vital. Brenz here is simplifying, if not quite collapsing, the Annual Calendar. (The Reformed collapsed the calendar completely.) Likewise, Pellican thinks the convocations are for hearing the divine will through the mouths of the prophets and readings of the Mosaic Law. For the Hebrew word *qr'* means "read" as much as "call." These festivals were instituted by God for reconciliation to the Lord and meditation on his benefits.

Lapide asserts that the church calls *all* days holidays by the institution of Pope Sylvester. First, because the Christian is to cease from vice each day and, second, that for ministers, every day Mass is celebrated. The Jewish holidays are twofold: some were instituted by God—such as the Sabbath, Passover, Pentecost, Trumpets, Atonement, and Tabernacles—and others by the Jews—such as that on Adar 15 (as per Esth 9), the purgation of the temple (as in 1 Macc 4:49), or receiving the heavenly fire (2 Macc 1:18; 1 Macc 7:49). Whereas the nations worship with their stomachs, Christians do so with their minds, in spirit and truth. God instituted festivals in order that there be no work, and that offerings and ceremonies be particular to each feast.

Willet in turn enjoys employing Cajetan here. Although by nature there is a universal worship instinct, certain set times are given by God, because if people are left to themselves there would be very few or none celebrated. A festival is not just a rest day but a calling to holy convocation or, as Cajetan has it, for the reminder of Christ's benefits and his second coming. It is lawful for Christians to have special days: Christmas, Easter, Ascension, and the like, and such holy solemnities are not for the sake of our bodies but for God and the soul, as Bernard said. A Catholic view, such as that of Tostatus, is that there are more feasts under the gospel than under the Law because as Christians we must attend more on God's service. However, our "greater" attendance of God is in spirit. We should be sparing in the number of Christian festivals we observe, thinks Willet: "This frequent rejoicing, and number of Festivals, becommeth our countrey in heaven, not this place of banishment."

Matthew Henry viewed festivals as God's ways of not letting much time go past without reminding the people what true worship was, so that they not to incline to heathen superstition. "They were most of them times of joy and rejoicing. The weekly sabbath is so, and all their yearly solemnities, except the day of atonement . . . here were six for holy joy and one only for holy mourning. We are commanded to *rejoice evermore,* but not to be evermore weeping."

Knobel shows awareness that the text of Numbers 28–29 gives substance to the framework of Leviticus 23. The Israelites shared the older festivals with the other ancient cultures; God received special attention at these times, and the festivals helped the religious feeling to be raised into a more lively key, while following the change of nature's seasons. The solar-based festivals, such as harvest, were longer and more important. Greeks tended to have monthly feasts for Apollo; the Romans cleaned hearth and home, as do Hindus today. On the one hand, festivals *divide* God and the world, and yet, on the other, also *unite* them—not for nature's sake but Jehovah's. Thus the *new* moon, not the *full* moon, gained the festival. Moses gave yearly festivals a tight connection to Jehovah, tied them to historical events of the exodus, and gave them national significance. Only the Sabbath was mentioned in the original Decalogue, so Moses here added to the older ones some new, such as Passover and Atonement. The theocratic ideal meant more feasts than usual. Other nations had certain *days* given to God, but Israel went further with a special *month*, the seventh, when, although not total rest was demanded, it had a Sabbath character; then was added then seventh *year*, and a Jubilee over and above that. Knobel believes that the Elohist was permissive in allowing Passover to be celebrated at home but then the Jehovist would makes a pilgrimage custom into a law and a theology of "the Place," although it took till after the exile for it to work as also in the case of Sabbath observance. One cannot observe any trace of the Jubilee year actually being observed at any time in the OT period.

Keil's comment on this is: "Knobel is wrong in identifying the 'holy convocation' with a journey to the sanctuary, whereas appearance at the tabernacle to hold the holy convocations (for worship) was not regarded as necessary either in the law itself or according to the later orthodox custom, but on the contrary, holy meetings for edification were held on the Sabbath in every place in the land, and it was out of this that the synagogue arose." This is a pietistic, almost sectarian vision of worship as provisionally centralized (in the desert) yet for now to be performed in diverse locations.

Sabbath (v. 3)

Augustine, in his Sermon 270, warns: "Take care to carry out what the vacation signifies. A spiritual vacation, I mean, is tranquility of heart; but tranquility of heart issues from the serenity of a good conscience." Here stated is the influential Augustinian view of freedom as "from sin." Hesychius, as reported in the *Glossa*, thinks that the idea is to cease from all servile works, and that the number "seven" is used as well as "one," so that the whole of human life is comprehended, since one day stands for the beginning, the other for the end in which all things can be summed up.

Pellican urges that the seventh day is to contemplate Law and give thanks for blessings, i.e., holy study for the glory of God. Brenz insists that Christ did not rise on the day after the Sabbath in order to consecrate that day (Sunday) as an external and political feast. He rose not to make new politics, but to show us our future resurrection, and freedom from sin and death through him. Willet notes that Bellarmine and Lorinus here teach that sin is no worse when committed on the Sabbath. However, Willet argues, Scripture directly demands abstinence of sin on the Sabbath, of the doing of one's own will. Sin on a Sabbath could be worse, just as sacrilege is worse than common theft. Contrition and repentance are to be looked for on the Lord's Day especially, and Tostatus is right to say that on festival days people are more bound to serve God. As for the observance of the Lord's Day, it is not that Christ left it for his church to decide, for the command comes from *Scripture*. The Sabbath is best kept by the doing of good, as a day of thanks by humble souls in true penitence so that God will rejoice over "you."

Keil considers the Sabbath to be so important that the first day is called Sabbath no matter what day of the week; the word means "rest," not "seven."

Passover and Firstfruits (vv. 5–14)

The key text in Christian Antiquity concerning the Christian Passover is Melito's *On the Pascha* (c. 170 AD), although its texts naturally drawn from Exodus. The very use of the Jewish term is significant, and it has been argued that such Asian Christianity, much of it Quartodeciman (celebrating the Christian feast at the same time as the Jews, that day after 14 Nisan), would rather think of its major (and for the first two centuries *only*) festival as being in connection with Jewish ideas of festival rather than pagan ones. The fact that in the majority Christian calendar it was to be kept on Sunday following the first full moon after the equinox shows some respect for the Jewish roots in still using the moon for computation.

John Chrysostom, in opposing the "syncretistic" Antiochene Christians (who wanted also to follow the synagogue's feasts in 386–87 AD), seems fairly clear that Christ's keeping of the Passover festival did *not* mean that Christians are to continue to keep it. "Why did Christ keep the Passover at that time? The old Passover was a type of the Passover to come, and the reality had to supplant the type. So Christ first showed the foreshadowing and then brought the reality to the banquet table." The Passover celebrations are to be ignored (Col 2:16f). "Our Passover is celebrated three times each week, sometimes even four times, or rather as often as we wish" (*Adversus Judeos* III.4).

For Hesychius, the *land given by God* is the evangelical doctrine and behavior. It is called "land" because of the fruit of virtues that grow from it. It has been given by God and no mediator is needed but he has announced it with his own mouth, that those who enter are to "harvest"; that is, receive the saving word. Christ, the intelligible Priest, offered his body to be raised as the true firstfruits of our harvest. On that day on which we celebrate the resurrection of the Lord and celebrate the spiritual offering (Easter), God wishes us not to forget the Lord's sacrifice, but to offer up the annual immaculate lamb in the burnt-offering to the Lord. Sacrificing the spiritual lamb is, mystically speaking, the handing over of the Lord. Offering a sacrifice of him makes a memorial. And in no other way than through meditation on him and through virtue those things done in the sacrifices are transferred from the sensory to the spiritual. The flour offerings are sprinkled with oil (v. 13), for it is necessary that the perfect humanity and perfect divinity were combined in the oil, i.e., his compassion for us. Thus, in the Eucharist, offering up a symbol of Christ as food of the new barley and oats or fine flour (*chytra*) reconciles us to God, and the food is soft as the commands of Christ are light (as preached in the Gospel, Matt 11:30).

Procopius writes that the time of the resurrection of Jesus transfers those sanctified into the Spirit, that they might bear fruit for God in the new life. The old ferment has gone but this is a new one: the gospel teaching. For we are taught the basics in the Law and as priests in the new era, we cross into newness of life. In practical terms a joyful communion on Easter Sunday is appropriate.

Cajetan's interpretation of the Passover is that, just as the Hebrews went *up* into the Promised Land, so the Savior rising *up* from hell transcended the kingdoms of heaven. Willet insists, however, that the blessed Savior suffered not in the solemn day of Jewish Passover. The Jews made their Passover a Sabbath (i.e., Saturday), so Christ dying on Good Friday was not on the Jewish Sabbath. Lapide describes how the paschal feast was even more celebrated by Christians then by Jews since Christians were freed from the devil. Passover comes, he thinks, from the Hebrew word *phase*, which means "change" or "transcendence." In 417, when they got the date for Easter wrong, this was shown up by a miracle when the water for Easter baptism filled the baptistery on the right night (see Leo, *Epistle* 63). The Passover became a day for the giving of pardons by Christian emperors, as decreed by Valentinian, Valens, and Gratian in 367 AD (see Theodosian Code I.8 *de indulgentibus*.)

Feast of Weeks (vv. 15–21)

Seven weeks after Firstfruits comes the Feast of Weeks (vv. 15–17) in which Jerome (*Ep.* 149) sees *remission* contained in the number fifty ("fifty days"). It was already celebrated by the third century in Rome and Alexandria and given similar status to Easter by Ambrose in the late fourth century, as a fulfilling of the latter, yet given some separate identity by the Cappadocian fathers, with the Feast of Ascension (Rexer 2004, 289f). Jerome writes: There are the five senses given over to the Law of God and the seven-form supervening Spirit of grace in our hearts. (The Spirit takes seven forms—one for each virtue.) These words contain the Decalogue in them (Jerome does not specify which words he has in mind), but also work through love, which covers a multitude of sins (1 Pet 4:8) and "thus we offer a new sacrifice to the Lord from all our dwellings into the use of our priest as we offer our peace offerings.

God takes our weak offerings, made acceptable through Jesus Christ, up with him into heaven and grants us indulgence."

Pellican thinks the ritual described from verse 13 onwards was performed in thanksgiving for the harvest to come. Today, he comments, this is done when Christ is praised even in his poor ones. These Levitical offerings have ceased, but we give thanks for similar works of God's care for us for us. This means there should be no eating of bread or other fruit until God is thanked and the poor shown mercy from our table. Not with drunkenness but with modesty and holy hilarity do we eat. Considering bread and wine to mean "modest fare" diverts from any argument that here the Mass is predicted. The repetition of thanks to be given to the Lord in verse 19 is highlighted. And the blood of the promised Christ, to be shed for the sins of men, is refreshed (a Ciceronian term, often used with "memory") and faith is exercised among the elect and spiritual men of the people of God.

Lapide follows the medieval interpretation: the bundle of sheaves signifies Christ's resurrection since Christ had two days: one of passion and the other of resurrection. He who is a small vessel of myrrh on account of the bitterness of passion is also called a cypress tree on account of his sweetness, as Rupert has it. Our faith and hope in him we offer like these sheaves. Lapide is keen to tie firstfruits and Passover together for the sake of Christian doctrine. Because Christians follow the sun, not the moon, their feasts are moveable, and following Ribera (*De Templo*) we celebrate the following Sunday in memory of Christ, and never on the same day as the Jewish Passover, for Christ died on the first day of Unleavened Bread (i.e., the day *after* Passover). A lot of space gets devoted to the difference of dates, and concludes that Christ wanted to abolish the old Law and put the Christian Law in its place. The feasts of Christians should be celebrated with even more intensity and joy since they have been freed from the devil, by a sort of miraculous deliverance.

Patrick has this to say on verse 16: counting fifty days, we reach the morrow after the seventh Sabbath.

> This day the Samaritans take to have been the first day of the week, after the very Letter of this Law, which is thus made out by the great Primate of Ireland [Ussher]: Our Blessed Lord being slain at the Feast of the Passover, the whole sabbath following (which was the first day of Unleavened Bread) he rested in his grave . . . the matter being ordered so by God that in the observation of the Feast of Weeks, the seventh day of the week (the Jewish Sabbath) was purposely passed over, and that great Solemnity kept upon the first day of the week, no wonder the Christian church hath appropriated that day instead of the seventh.

Engaging Leviticus

Trumpets (vv. 23–25)

Hesychius thinks that the blowing of trumpets serves as a reminder of Christ's resurrection, which in turn is a memorial of the general resurrection to come. The storm of judgment will come in which none can work and the saying will come to mind: "store your treasure in heaven." That time will be a time of absolute quiet with rest from works. Piscator repeats this, but Grotius reads verse 24 as the sign of joy because Isaac had been freed from death and the ram then sacrificed, and in that freeing the future liberation through the Messiah was understood as announced by trumpets, as in Zechariah 9:14. This enlightened approach is an attempt to justify religion and morality, not to do without it. Grotius's view of religion is one that excitedly looks forward rather than taming events by their memorials in calendars. A festival offers a less intense interruption of routine, but it is at least an important interruption and means more than simple remembrance of a past event (Schüle 2003, 370).

Lapide spells out the moral or tropological sense by linking the trumpets to the theme of Jubilee: The number fifty is a sign and symbol of complete penitence and of the remission of sins, as Jerome clearly reaches in the start of the second book of his commentary on Isaiah. Hence Psalm 50 is, more than any other psalm, *the* penitential psalm. This is made clear in the fiftieth or Jubilee year, which is the year of full remission. In that year we offer two breads: that is, the love of God and neighbor. Thomas More honored the feasts with such observance that while he dwelled alone in prison he put on his better clothes which he had brought for him. When some wondered why, since he was alone, he bothered to do this, he said to them: "I dress not for public view but I openly celebrate the honor of God with this feast." And when the sentence of death had been set, but the execution was being delayed, at length he said on the eve of the feast of the translation of St. Thomas of Canterbury: "I strongly desire to travel to God tomorrow; for that day would suit me very well." Since he was hoping for it, God did grant martyrdom to Thomas More that same day on which his patron, whose name he bore, celebrated a like martyrdom (as did the Holy Apostles, for that feast fell on the eighth day of St. Peter and Paul, for whose primacy he spilled his blood).

In addition to this piety, one also notices the Baroque love for the church fathers, and the emphasis that the beginning (and perhaps fulfillment) of the Christian life is penitence. And yet there is an attempt by Lapide to bring into the present the Levitical structures and practices as interpreted in the musical key of the fathers and the saints. "Fifty years" is not spiritualized away, for "we"—that is, the Catholic Church of Lapide's time—do celebrate *literal* jubilees at the Pope's command ever since AD 1300. The Levitical Jubilee is not spiritualized but is transposed into a

Christian Baroque key in which the whole of life is appealed to and tamed. As we have seen, God's providence is seen in his honoring with the same day of martyrdom as that of his patron and English proto-martyr, Thomas of Canterbury (à Beckett). If one honors the festal calendar, God's providence will arrange one's life to become part of that salvation history. Lastly, Lapide observes an anagogical sense: the trumpets linked to the Jubilee feast in Leviticus 23 signifies the universal rest of all the saints in heaven, when they will offer the two breads of firstfruits, that is the glory of the soul and their body.

Day of Atonement (vv. 26–32)

Severus reminds us that *of course* the Day of Atonement is a fast, at least as understood by the Jews in the time of Ezra (Neh 8:1—9:4). Hesychius plays with the theme of afflicting oneself, or one's soul from morning till eve (v. 32). This manifests the propitiation of sins, i.e., liberation in humility to be acquired through afflicting our souls. We must do this from the morning, i.e., from penance, as if as beginners, since even Christ made penance the beginning of his preaching. But we need to build a good life on top of penance, perfect and completed by virtues. Christ completes our works on this day of propitiation. So any bodily delight is to be given up and one must take up a struggle and a right chastening and affliction of the body. And added to this fasting or affliction are certain ceremonial days when a special dark dress is worn to show penance for sins. Instances of fasting can be seen in Mizpah in 1 Samuel 7; the men of Habesh-Gilead before Saul in 1 Samuel 13; and Achab on the death of Naboth.

Pellican, informed by medieval Jewish writers, explains the solemnity in the seventh month as being to atone for the golden calf. As Moses descended with the two tables he brought the gospel of propitiation for the same sin. One does not wait for the last month, but every day we are to recollect out actions and if we let God or neighbor down with word or deed then we are to devote sacrifice—contrite hearts—to expiate. The Jews used these ceremonies to learn things and that is why these lasted several days. For Christians our whole life is to be an affliction for our sins, to the extent that they cannot be cleansed by the blood of Christ our Lord, the Son of God. Curiously for one on the side of the Reformation, Pellican suggests that everyday travails purify, as long as taken together with Christ's blood.

Although Grotius gives also the reason of the golden calf in his note on verse 27, he prioritizes a more naturalistic yet superstitious reason for the Day of Atonement: for averting diseases which were frequent in autumn. It would be odd if anyone had managed to avoid offending against one of all of the numerous commandments all through the year. Matthew Henry, on the placing of the Day of Atonement in the sequence, comments: "Note, The humbling of our souls for sin, and the making of our peace with God, is work that requires the whole man, . . . they must lay aside all their worldly business, that they might the more clearly and the more reverently hear that voice of joy and gladness."

Tabernacles (vv. 32–43)

The *encaenia* of 336 was the first occasion of this new Christian festival, which by rededicating churches celebrated Jesus' purification of the temple, although Egeria's evidence suggests that supersessionism rather than identification with the Jewish Feast of Tabernacles was primary (*Pilgrimage* 48.2; Klauber 1969, 759). For Gregory of Nyssa (*On the day of the Savior's birth*) the Feast of Tabernacles (v. 42) was a prefiguration of Christmas and the New Year, i.e., the Word's human tent. To this he adds, from Psalm 117:26, "blessed is he who comes in the name of the Lord," and insists on the importance of joining in the celebration with heavenly nature, if one is not to lose joy (which has come from heaven). Nyssa anticipated the surge in popularity of feasts in the church from around 450, as individual feasts were given definition and rationale (Drobner 1990). Epiphany would, as recognized first by the Council of Saragossa in 380, come to offer another rationale for celebrating the Nativity.

Hesychius comments on verses 33–36: For whoever uses the present world like a tent and has this festival within them and can rejoice over the hope of the future and who knows that the earthly house of this world will dissolve, such will be taken into the building not made by hands, in the heavens. The LXX has "for a fire offering," which, says Hesychius, encourages one to think of Paul's "to leave this life to go to be with Christ," where we will do no servile work since we will by like angels. The first and eighth day is that of resurrection power, which, as the principle of life in Christ, is also the introduction, the substance, and foundation of the future world. According to the LXX God calls the first day "holy" without addition or qualification, but the eighth is "holy *to you*" (i.e., God's people). For only those who respond to the calling will enjoy happiness; yet the calling is given freely to all (Matt 11:28).

Pellican thinks that the Feast of Tabernacles encouraged the people to think back to the time *before* the exit from Egypt, for some Jews think that God created the world at the exodus! From that same verse (v. 36) Grotius reasons that this Hebrew word (ʿ*tsrt*) is the name given to the last day of the Feast of Tabernacles, for it means "retention" and after that day the people could no longer be retained together. Willet has something similar: "likewise ʿ*atzarah,* or as some pronounce, *gnatzarah,* signifieth a festival day to detain, shut up, because people on that day are held and detained in the service of God." The faithful in spirit always and forever inhabit tents, or memories of their escaping from sins and are now "pilgrims."

Lorinus encourages his readers that the Lord prepares us for strength to do penance, and that this sixth Feast of Tabernacles is one that tells us that our present life is one of pilgrimage (1 Pet 2). For a Christian who on feast days hears of the offering of Christ to the Father in the Mass, as the Mother Church commands, makes a most thankful work to God by offering himself as a whole offering in the fire of the love of God, to be enflamed with the sorrow for sins and subject all ones life to God, whereas the libation is more the works of godliness, mercy, and justice to one's neighbor. Both matter. To bear branches is to do penance, showing our need of God to do any good; the palms signify virtues of the humble and penitent.

Ainsworth observes soberly: rejoicing at Feast of Booths (Tabernacles) was not on the first day but only after sundown, and not on the Sabbath. At a time when they had prosperity this was solemnly to stop them forgetting God and themselves. In booths they were "to remember their miseries past, and to expect a full redemption of their bodies and souls by Christ Jesus our Lord." Patrick points out that since God appointed booths in the seventh month of the year, this was the month we call March when it was cold and rainy. So they were not living in booths for pleasure, but by divine precept (v. 41)!

Maclaren sounds a different, lighter note when he comments: "The feast of tabernacles was the consecration of joy." He sees pagan Bacchanalia as a perversion of the Jewish Psalm-singing. How different the pure gladness of this feast "before the Lord!" He continues by saying that shifting houses helps one to be thankful for settled blessings: "Joy is a duty to God's children . . . The sources of religious joy, open to all Christians, are deeper than the fountains of individual sorrows, deep as life though these sometimes seen."

Keil takes "out of your habitations" (v. 20) to mean not that each house must bring two loaves but that the bread supplied be domestic stuff. His angle is quite different. Dwelling in booths was not intended to bring unsettled wandering to mind, "for the recollection of privation can never be an occasion of joy; but it was to place before the eyes of future generations of Israel a memorial of the grace, care and protection which God afforded to his people in the great and terrible wilderness." So more than mere tents were provided; these booths were better than tents, being more stable, and were future-looking, not past-looking. They "pointed to the glorious inheritance in Canaan," and were real grounds for rejoicing.

Bonar similarly sees Tabernacles as looking ahead and recognizes the seventh month as a kind of Sabbath month, with a note of rejoicing after knowing full atonement. Some think of this as a memorial, with the sons of God shouting for joy at creation. "But I rather think this feast was a memorial in another sense . . . of something taken or done to keep in view that which was lying in sight though not brought forward. In Leviticus the term 'memorial' does not mean the keeping in memory of a thing past . . . [but] something done in order to call attention to something yet remaining; a reminding of something present or something at hand; . . . a calling attention to things coming on and not yet actually arrived."

For some, few things are more important for Christians today than reclaiming the calendar (Hauerwas, *Christian Century* 1/2002, 16), with reference to *The Salt of the Earth Calendar*, printed each year since that date. Yet publications in English and among Protestants on the topic remain few, and on the Catholic side today, perhaps surprisingly, one only infrequently sees scholarly contributions on the theme that combine Bible, tradition, and practice (e.g., Auf der Maur 1983).

Leviticus 24

Lights and Loaves (vv. 2–9)

For Procopius "preparing the light" makes him think of John the Baptist as the light that burned. (John 5:35). Even if the legislator wanted his Law to be eternal, it really only lit the way for those coming to John's baptism. These verses gain their most significant treatment from Bede in his *On the tabernacle*. The "bread" means the church's preachers, which the church never lacks. "Twelve loaves" indicates the twelve apostles whom the Lord chose first to give the food of life to the nations, as he demonstrated in the desert area when Christ told them: "give them something to eat." The copious leftovers of apostolic power show how the crowd does not have the capacity of understanding the mysteries of Scripture. The most "lucid oil" (v. 7), as Bede has it, signifies the power of preaching, for the teachers commend to the Lord their ministry of preaching and the devotion of the heart. Each Sabbath they (i.e., the church's teachers) are arranged and rewarded with rest from their works when the time is completed. The table itself never changes in the temple for Scripture endures through the ages until the Lord returns—only then will we not need it and its interpretations, and then Jeremiah 31:34 ("brother will no longer teach brother") will be fulfilled. There are two ways to understand "they shall be for Aaron and his sons" (v. 9): Christ our High Priest takes the elect out of this life and leads them to increase his body in heaven, or perhaps what is meant is that his body on earth is nourished by the fine examples of those who have gone before.

Pellican takes the twelve pieces of bread (v. 6) to be the articles of faith and all apostolic doctrine by which the Levitical and priestly teaching needs to be recast if it is to be any use for today's church. The placing in two orders signifies the twofold exposition of Scripture: one that was for the hard-necked Jewish people, primed towards faith and fear of God, which was necessary for them; and the other directed towards the same faith but also love, which is given by Christ to the new Christian people. Each people (Jewish and Christian) was meant to complete one church and, before God, to be presented to the Lord on this table. Incense is both devotion and pure grace in the sight of the Lord forever. Chytraeus reasons that if the bread of verses 5–9 symbolizes the Bread of Life, then the table is the evangelical ministry in which bread of life means our Lord with all his benefits and gifts is given to those with faith. Spangenberg condemns "the hypocrites" (Catholics) who re-light lamps in churches and temples because they do not have the light of Christ.

Lorinus explains that the bread being changed each Sabbath day has to do with the fact that after his resurrection the immortal Lord sits at the right hand of the Father in the most holy Mass so that the merits of his most holy death can be applied to the faithful. He finds some support for this in Origen, which then seems to turn him to a more spiritualizing conclusion: that the physical body is remade ("refected") with the physical bread, but the soul is ministered to by the word of God, and hence preaching the word from the Bible to the people is just as crucial. Willet sneers that the Roman Catholics use oil even more than the OT priests did. As for the bread that was kept from Sabbath to Sabbath, some would warrant the reservation of the consecrated host. "To this purpose, Lorinus alledgeth, . . . that it should be kept in a boxe . . . dipped in the blood of Christ and taken to the sick." But, if they admit that the bread needs to be refreshed, is this an admission that it might become moldy? And why, if the doctrine of concomitance is true, need the bread be dipped? We should not look to the Law for precedents. Jesus told them to take and eat not to keep until tomorrow (and he finds Cyril of Alexandria to be on his side here).

In Patrick's account, with his "high church" interests in such things, the number twelve (24:5) matters: "but still twelve Cakes were set before the Lord, because there was a remnant of true Israelites among them and this was a constant testimony against those Apostates." As an Anglican, on matters Eucharistic he seems to want it both ways: "for a memorial" means "for an acknowledgment of God . . . and to represent also that God was ever mindful of his people." So this table where the shew bread stood was really God's altar, and, of course, altars and tables are interchangeable (for this catholic Protestant).

Bonar excels himself in the way he links the peaceful order of the holy things with the disorder of the blasphemer in the later part of the chapter: "Let the priest [Christ] dress the lamp when you feel pride and earthly cares . . . shine calmly; for the light of these lights did not splutter as it burned . . . and a calm light generally shines full . . . Cast your light fair on the world's sins, that they might see them. Point out their ungodliness, their lawlessness, their unbelief. Reprove their acts of Sabbath profanation. Check them when they swear in your presence . . . and speak of a present, immediate, free, full pardon in the Saviour."

Blasphemy (vv. 10–25)

Origen wants to tell us one thing needful: that Moses does not condemn nor acquit in any such life or death case *without referring it to God*. Israelite justice is not carried out simply with reference to law codes. Origen is also concerned that while the action takes place within the camp, the text seems to indicate that the woman's son has come from outside the camp. This uncertainty at the level of the literal sense is no problem if the "going out" is taken figuratively, i.e., out of the way of righteousness or of God's law. It would be this spiritual departure that, once his sin was discovered, would require his physical expulsion and exit from the camp. The Egyptian (paternal) influence seems to have got the better of him. Origen is quick to give this a spiritual sense and show how internal invisible realities are causative of outward states of affairs.

Christians, thinks the Alexandrian, are called to dispute with such heretical and lawless people: those who acknowledges the "maternal" matter of the Scriptures but reject the "paternal" form of their true sense, leading to the blasphemy that God is not the Creator and the Father of Jesus Christ: this is what it means to curse according to the letter and to blaspheme according to the spiritual intelligence. For Origen, the ambiguity in the double crime of "pronouncing the name" and "curse" suggests that the cursing has to do with cursing the neighbor in tandem with pronouncing God's name (cf. Rahner 1983, ch. 8). Paul takes a very dim view of blasphemy, for it is a sin that is mortal in that such people cannot hope to possess the kingdom of God (see 1 Cor 6:9–10). Of course, adds Origen, such a person may yet be saved, even if they will not enter the kingdom of heaven, for in the house of the Father there are many mansions (John 14:2). And if there are more virtues and just the odd vice, then the coming judgment will be more like gold having its impurities removed by the eschatological fire. But even unintentional sins of the lips are sins. As for "exit," well, sometimes it can happen that those who are physically on the inside are in fact spiritually outside and vice versa.

The most difficult phrase to comprehend is, "he will bear the sin": this, for Origen, is something much more severe than being sentenced to death, because in the case of some sins, the sin is dealt with by the death, since God will not demand punishment twice. But to bear it means that death does not remove this type of sin. It is better to suffer for one's sin in this life than in the life to come. Paul, in 1 Corinthians 5:5, seems to have been of that mind: this can apply to human life in general, and one should do penance for the sake of the afterlife. So Origen rejects the death penalty: there might be physical excommunication, but the real penalty is purgatory, which can be lessened if the person is truly penitent in a distraught way with a real mortification of the flesh, and the Lord is gracious to him while outside the church (Rahner 1983, 266–68).

Hesychius had a way of writing a commentary in which textual detail was avoided if it got in the way of making a clear theological point. He allegorizes the story: the Israelite woman is the divine Scripture. The father, however, was Egyptian wisdom and in the shape of this blasphemer the former has been subjected to the latter. The one who is harmed by this external or carnal knowledge—such as the Egyptians have—here "names" Christ (which means to "name in a dishonoring way" or to blaspheme Christ, in that he assigned to Christ some lesser grade of being than to the Father). The plain sense is that such a person had to be expelled and judged by the Law of Moses, which in its own obscure way implies the mystery of the Trinity. There is one rule for all, citizen and sojourner alike. There is allegory in the story, but the punishment was real or literal enough. He who names (*onomazōn*) the name of God "shall be put to death." (The Hebrew, of which Hesychius seems unaware, has "curses," *nokev*—"to denote unfavorably, slander.") It is not naming as such: for does not Isaiah declare, "We know no one but you, we name your name" (Isa 45:5)? The name is not revealed in Scripture but has to be taught through a mediator such as Moses. The distinction is made between those who do the naming without knowledge and those who are guilty of saying it with knowledge given by the Spirit (as in Isaiah). In other words, Christians who know the name of God through the gift of the Holy Spirit are included in this: for us there is no excuse. There are two forms of blasphemy: To curse (*maledicere*) God (ignorantly) is one thing, but to knowingly "name" him in a way that is adverse or detracts from his honor, as here: that is worse. And that is what the son of the Israelite did, even though he had learned from his mother and her traditions.

Procopius in his short note emphasizes the psychological aspect. There is blasphemy in the mind when one venerates false gods. God then punishes by allowing what they delight in to dwell in their consciences, only making sure in his providence—through such laws—that his people do not blaspheme *openly*. Augustine is brief yet unsure in his answer on verses 15–16. It is not the combination of naming God *and* cursing another that makes the offence, since verse 15 ("blasphemes") and verse 16 ("names") are connected by an "and"/"but" (*autem*) and not by "for," as if verse 16 is explaining what blaspheming means. This encourages the Christian tradition to employ a wide definition of the offence, while holding to a basically twofold concept of blasphemy.

In medieval Jewish law the death penalty was only given for speaking God's name. Blasphemy is defined strictly as the Naming. In Leonard Levy's account of the matter, "The Talmud focused on the original injunction from Exodus 22:28, 'You shall not revile God' and defined the crime as tightly as possible" (Levy 1993, 12). However, Christianity allowed for a wider definition, and this may reflect a misreading of Exodus 24:11, due to a misunderstanding of Hebrew parallelism or repetition.

This is reflected in the paraphrase in Peter Comestor's *Scholastic History* where it is the "cursing" of God rather than "naming" that is the issue. By putting two things together or being vague in defining, the range of the concept of "blasphemy" expanded to include public atheism, paths, cursing, and heresy about the Trinity and sacraments. Heresy became *the* charge until the restitution of Justinian's law in the 1100s in the West (in the form of a canon law with a wide jurisdiction). Heresy had "engulfed and superseded" blasphemy, until 1200, when, for theologians like Thomas Aquinas, blasphemy became an aggravated form of unbelief or heresy (*ST* IIaIIae, q13 art 2 & 3). In q14 he moves to consider the meaning of "blasphemy against the Holy Ghost" (Matt 12) as given by Athanasius, that the words of Aaron in the Golden Calf incident—"here are your gods, O Israel" (Exod 34)—was this very blasphemy. But from Augustine Thomas receives the idea that this sin of all sins has more to do with being *obstinately impenitent* rather than simply mocking God. This can be seen received in the Papal encyclical *Dominum et vivificantem* (1986): "blasphemy" does not properly consist in offending against the Holy Spirit in words; it consists rather in the refusal to accept the salvation which God offers to man through the Holy Spirit, working through the power of the cross. If man rejects the "convincing concerning sin" which comes from the Holy Spirit and which has the power to save, he also rejects the "coming" of the Counselor (the Holy Spirit).

On the question of the sanction for blasphemy and who enforces it, Levy helpfully quotes and translates a passage from Aquinas' *Sentences Commentary*: "Heretics," he declared. "by right can be put to death and despoiled of their possessions [by secular authorities], even if they do not corrupt others, for they are blasphemers against God, because they observe a false faith. Thus they can be justly punished [even] more than those accused of high treason" (IV, d13, q2, art3 in Levy 1993, 52). This is a clue, which Levy does not really follow, that the state did have the authority to try people for blasphemy as a crime distinct from the ecclesiastical offence of heresy.

Engaging Leviticus

Levy seems to ignore the fact that since Justinian there had been the civil death penalty for blasphemy. It may be that simply looking at Aquinas, writing for the church, one is not going to find much evidence of this, but in the *Sentences* commentary we see that the state has a right to proceed when the church has tried its best. The church was to *define* it (so Gratian, *Decretum* C.I.2, calls the Arian heresy "blasphemy") but the state was to *enforce*, not least after the reworking of Justinian's civil law in the twelfth century. There was no Roman-style *fas* (divine law) / *ius* (secular law) distinction (i.e., between what is holy and what is lawful: see Piattelli 1998, 53). In the Middle Ages of Christendom, the church had penance and the state had punishment. Most sins by then had become dealt with by private penance supervised by the church, but not the *public* sins of blasphemy and schism in which the *state* was called on to assist.

So, in *La bible moralisée* we find that the form of the crime and the punishment are both clear: the procedure is to present a frame which represents the literal sense of the text and a following one which portrays the application for the present day. In the case of this passage, the emphasis is on the scene of a mocking of the sacraments, possibly by the Albigensians. It is the secular arm that is appealed to since it is clear that blasphemy, unlike heresy, is a *civil* offence.

Lyra, having observed how the lights in the tabernacle shone constantly, contrasts this with the dark story that follows. This man's father was the Egyptian whom Moses killed (Exod 2) and the blasphemer came out of adultery. As for blaspheming, the Hebrews say that he spoke the name of the Lord, which is illicit unless in the blessings of the priest. Some Hebrews say that he would be imprisoned until it was decided whether he would be sentenced to death (i.e., once the judgment of God was known). Others say that the law in Exodus 21:17 is clear enough: cursing one's father is a capital offence, and *how much more so* if it is *God*, who is Father of all by creation, that is blasphemed. God, as the injured party, is not the one who has brought this about but they put hands on him as if to say: "your evil has brought you to death" and he is stoned, to set an example to others.

Denys raises the question: how could there have been a prison for the blasphemer in the desert? Well, he answers, perhaps there was some sort of pit. He quickly moves to the spiritual sense: we see the harshness and imperfection of the Mosaic Law but also the godliness and perfection of the evangelical Law according to which one turns the other cheek and is ordered to love one's enemy and overcome evil with good. Yet heretics, those falsely religious people who have attacked the righteous, must be stopped. We fight more against the spoilings of vices and temptations than against people, and we fight back with every virtue. We do not take out the eye of anyone but lead him to take out the eye of his heart, i.e., ignorance or error. And we should not take out a tooth by which the food of the heart might be eaten, and we shall not break the mental wholeness of our neighbor nor defame him.

Of course, the death penalty was in fact rarely enacted for simple blasphemy, even in the lands where the grip of the civil law was strong. "When asked to explain why the Bible's apparent mandate was not being carried out, commentators were more apt to ascribe this to the lamentable 'want of religion' in their own time than to any disproportion between capital punishment and the just deserts of a blasphemer. They found not fault in the mandate itself. The problem, they said was that if blasphemy were to be punished, as it should have been, too few men would be left" (Helmholz 1996, 262). There was a concern to try to terrorize for the sake of the salvation of the individual soul, which could even at times outweigh any "temporal" concern for the common moral good.

The idea of the state reinforcing the church got eventually introduced to German lands under Charles V, yet the 1532 *Constitutio Criminalis Carolina* did not seem to consider blasphemy to be about oaths or magic, for those things are also mentioned in a separate section. Luther told his students that the later chapters of Leviticus had little to say to them, but that parents and teachers could learn from chapter 24 to watch so that children do not curse with God's name. That name is to be praised not misused, and princes should punish public misuse. This leads him to bemoan the plague of children being too severely punished. In this case the laying on of hands symbolizes that there were a number of witnesses to the crime. Blasphemy also happens when people mistake truth for falsehood and the word of God for lies. But the way to deal with those who are spiritually mistaken is to separate from them, not to kill them. So "spiritual" blasphemy, which is heresy, is to be treated more lightly than the public offence of cursing others in God's name.

Borrhaus considers the example of Phinehas (Num 25) exacting immediate punishment to be exceptional and not to be imitated, except in so far as the magistrate is to be reminded to be *fervent* about his official duties. Due process must be respected but did Phinehas put the public before private and that is what magistrates must do.

For Brenz, the Jews invented a story about the father of this blasphemer in Leviticus 24 as being the one whom Moses killed in the quarrel (Exod 2:11–15). Brenz then asks: "Is the offence just that of naming God as Yahweh or about cursing others in his name?" Brenz seems to prefer the latter. The offence is as much against the first as the second table of the Decalogue. We should note, says Brenz, that they do not kill the offender forthwith, but take him to Moses the magistrate.

But then there is a further deferral: Moses judges this to be a case of blasphemy but for judgment and sentencing refers this on to God; the size of the punishment is not something with which even Moses would trust himself, especially where only one side of the evidence has been heard. And Brenz reminds us that if the accusation is right, then they are refusing the cause of death and putting it on the head of the offender, for he has brought it on himself. However, if they have witnessed falsely they will be guilty of the blood.

What we should learn from this, thinks Brenz, is that we should realize how precious the name of God is and how useful it is, almost as much as God himself. Salomon says so and in Acts 2 "whoever calls on the *name* shall be saved." The name is to be used for freedom, blessing, and all good things, so that it is important that punishment be strict when the good name is abused for *cursing*. Isaiah 34 and Jeremiah 46 are appealed to concerning the killing of the ungodly and concord with Justinian (*In Novellis Constantini* 77). This is a hard but most just law: for God shows himself to be so good that no evil is to be allowed to be associated with his name. Also, in his associating the passage with the Second Commandment the gravity of the offence is reinforced. The passion and wounds of Christ, the sacraments instituted by Christ—since these are salvation, healing, and the means of our heavenly salvation—are no more to be taken in vain. And even should we manage to dodge the magistrate we will not be able to escape the final judgment. A consequence of goodness is opposing evil, including evil within the camp.

Pellican's view is that despising the name of the Lord—which is *shem*, a name blessed above all names—happens when any take the name of the Lord in vain, i.e., swear impiously, deny providence, despise the Law, and mock the word of the Lord. The whole point is that the *community* should show clearly that they are not condoning this blasphemy. Chytraeus sees two sins to consider here: first, the unrighteous anger and desire for vengeance and opposing God's will, but also, second, slandering God by posing as his minister while full of such anger. It is a very serious sin to abuse the name of God, or seek from God to hurt other poor people, or to name the wounds and passion of Christ for the sake of condemning others. This harsh justice should be a deterrent to show how seriously God takes this. Spangenberg notes how the civil law in Justinian's *Novellas* (c. 77) defines blasphemy as including wishing evil things on others, denying the providence of God, swapping true for false worship or human for divine words, or even, as it is popularly believed, expressing the name of God. Note that the blasphemer in the text was put in custody so that nothing was done rashly and without due process.

Lapide first of all quotes Abulensia who ridiculed the standard Jewish interpretation before him, that the cause of the blasphemy could have been drunkenness. No, there was no wine in the desert, not a drop. Lapide observes that the Jews often say "The Name" (*Ha Shem*) rather than name God, yet it would be wrong to think that any sin of naming was involved. For *nāqab* means "perforate," and thus metaphorically to empty of honor, that is, to *blaspheme* and *curse*. Allegorically this blasphemer makes us think of the antichrist, whom the elect will stone on the day of his downfall. Lapide is not quite sure why hands were placed on the head (v. 14). Perhaps it was simply to witness that this is the guilty one, although Nicholas of Lyra might have a point that it is to say: "Evil put you to death, not we." Or maybe this is treating him like a host, an animal sacrifice: that God would put all the punishment of the sin on *him* and not share it out with the people. Just in case we are in any doubt about the horrible nature of blasphemy, Lapide adds that since one cannot kill the Creator, using the tongue against him is as bad as it gets. He concludes by telling us a number of stories about blasphemers. For example, the tongue of the heretic Nestorius was eaten by worms. From more recent times he relates a Dutch case of a man mocking the idea that Mary could cure his blind horse: she did, but blinded him in the process. This indicates that Lapide believed God's own providence would see to God's own judgment of such people in this life.

The point is that in Catholic theology what matters is a malicious cursing of God with heart, soul and voice, but that nothing much is said about any contemporary sanctions. To come (almost) up to date, the *Catechism of the Catholic Church* 1993 (s. 2148) defines blasphemy as:

> directly opposed to the second commandment. It consists in uttering against God—inwardly or outwardly—words of hatred, reproach or defiance, in speaking ill of God or failing in respect towards him in one's speech, in misusing God's name [and Jesus'] . . . The prohibition of blasphemy extends to language against Christ's Church, the saints, and sacred things. It is also blasphemous to make use of God's name to cover up criminal practices, to reduce peoples to servitude, to torture persons or put them to death. The misuse of God's name to commit a crime can provoke others to repudiate religion. Blasphemy is contrary to the respect due to God and his holy name. It is in itself a grave sin.

We can see how wide the definition of "blasphemy" has become.

In their treatment of the subject, late medieval theologians had focused on the OT, especially Leviticus 24, as well as Matthew 25, John 10, and the Apocalypse, but the Reformers also brought in Paul (Loetz 2002, 157). Zwingli and Bullinger, while distinguishing blasphemy and heresy in theory, in practice made heresy and blasphemy overlap.

Yet in the seventeenth century, the "Gutachten" or expert witness reports in Central European blasphemy cases were keen to distinguish heresy and blasphemy, even though at times they confuse the two. They wanted to classify blasphemy theologically and help the civil magistrate. One can account for the increase in blasphemy cases in the early modern Protestant realm on the grounds of biblicism and in Catholic areas on that ground and the efforts of Charles V to make civil law effective in transalpine Europe. In terms of any theology of blasphemy, these early moderns were conservative and followed the late medieval interpretation of Bible. If anything the pastors and theologians who gave evidence were softer in individual cases, while still trying to get the civil magistrate to do God's work. It would seem that the magistrates tended to see heresy as "insulting the divine" under the influence of a third party or sect of erring theologians, a kind of "informed blasphemy." Sometimes it had to do with denying God's almighty power (Loetz 2002, 381–83). In the case of H. R. Werdmüller, in 1659 Zürich, his heresy was so shocking as to be called "blasphemy," since it was not just one heresy but a whole disputatious approach to religion, though in reality he was, thinks Loetz, probably just trying to amuse the elite. Also H. J. Ammann, who, in 1656, had disputed that Christ was conceived by the Holy Spirit and the doctrine of the resurrection of the dead, was accounted a blasphemer because he denied God his due. Blasphemers included those who went their own way of interpreting the Bible, but also—and as often—those more ordinary people who used swear words, while not really intending blasphemy as such.

Loetz insists that what was constant in these cases was *the use of God's name to curse*. Swearing an oath with reference to God or things associated with him went from being acceptable to being punishable, perhaps under the influence of the Corpus Christi devotion, although that seems less likely to have been significant in these Protestant circles. Loetz's conclusion that blasphemy was seen as unrelated to witchcraft, forgets that the overlap of the charges might explain why cases in one era understood as blasphemy could be interpreted as witchcraft in another. (Loetz 2002, 491).

Levy thinks that there was no real distinction made between blasphemy and heresy; that Calvin's opponent Castellio was considered a blasphemer, but just wasn't caught (unlike Servetus who paid for his blasphemous-heretical offence).

> During the seventeenth century, blasphemy increasingly became a secular crime on the continent. It remained, as always, a religious offence, but the state began to supplant the church as the agency mainly responsible

for instigating and conducting persecutions. The association of religious crimes with political ones, such as sedition and treason, had its roots in Exodus 22:28 which declares "You shall not revile God, nor curse a ruler of your people." The intimacy between *laesa religio* and *laesa maiestas*, crimes against religions and crimes against the state, was a feature of Athenian law and then of Roman law, both before and after Christianity became the state religion of Rome.

(Levy 2002, 73)

This connection was revived in the seventeenth century. The Westminster Confession of 1647, which was binding on the Scottish Kirk, in chapter XXIII, section 3, clarified the role of the magistrate in matters of religion: "it is his duty to take order, that unity and peace be preserved in the Church, that the truth of God be kept pure and entire, that all blasphemies and heresies be suppressed."

These emphatic assertions of the magistrate's power were supplemented by a series of prooftexts, which implied that Christian rulers had the same duties as their Jewish counterparts in the Old Testament. To make matters worse (for later Presbyterians), the texts included Leviticus 24:16: "he that blasphemeth the name of the Lord, he shall surely be put to death." The case against Thomas Aikenhead, who was hanged for blasphemy at the Grassmarket in Edinburgh in January 1697, was that he made jokes about hell, described "Trinity" as "a rhapsodie of faigned and ill-invented nonsense" and said the Bible was concocted, Jesus an imposter, and that "God and nature were one" (Spinozan pantheism).

In England Ainsworth made it clear that the Hebrew word *nākab* could be used for naming things in a good way, as in Isaiah 62:2, and hence, despite the inclination of the LXX and Targum, *even naming God without speaking evil of him was meant.* Yet in dialogue with Maimonides Ainsworth simply concludes: "But we know faith and obedience are more important than sounding of syllables." Blasphemy laws could be harmful to nonconformists.

Willet points out that serious cases went to the highest judge, Moses at the first instance, "because it was of great weight, and concerned the glory of God directly" (cf. Exod 18:18, 22). Blasphemy was forbidden by the Third Commandment but no punishment was set there. That "was deferred in the wisedome of God, until it might be by some example of severity established as here [in Leviticus 24]." Moses here was inspired suddenly in this judgment, yet like a good magistrate he delays the judgment by ordering imprisonment as he also did in the case of Numbers 27:1 and 36:1. Such a "cooling off period" (thirty days) was established after Theodosius came to rue the slaughter of the Thessalonians (AD 390). In "laying on hands" the

Israelites showed themselves not guilty of the man's sin, and witnessed against him. God is blasphemed "when his workes are blamed, or if any doe faile in the doctrine."

Calmet relates that rabbis say the story began when this man wanted to pitch his tent among the tribe of Dan and when he was refused he blasphemed in anger. Philo, following the LXX's *onomazein*, thought that the most pure *could* say the name of God, but even they did not, out of respect, as for our parents. Now there seems some superstition here, thinks Calmet, and surely Moses meant something more particular, namely saying *bad* things about the name of God. Calmet asks whether it is believable that God did not want his people to pronounce the name that he had gone to the bother of revealing to them, and that they did not so name him in their prayers sermons and when praising him for his great deeds (Psalms or, e.g., Jeremiah 4:12). It is better to argue that by "the name of God" Scripture can mean *his Majesty*.

Leclerc judged that although these raving imprecations in verse 11 could not harm God, still they were evidence of the impiety of an unhealthy mind, which might lead people away from the worship of God. It is small wonder that a man born in Egypt should break forth in this way (cf. Exod 5:2). He is like the Greek Menelaus, in *Iliad* III, 365, who on breaking his sword on Paris helmet cried out: "Father Jupiter, there is no other God who made you so deadly!" By the rite described in verse 14 it shows that the man deserved the death. And whatever the rabbis say, the name of "Jehova" is not to be understood as the sound of those consonants (as per Maimonides, *De Idolatria* II.10), which is not more holy than any other word. Rather, concludes Leclerc, the crime in question is when ungodly minds denigrate him.

Gerstenberger (2003, 333) emphasizes that the crime is not so much one of cursing as of "hollowing out" (*durchboren*) of God's name. He thinks there is an allusion made to Exodus 21:17 and 22:27, but surely Exodus 20:7 fits better.

Like for Like Punishment (vv. 17-22)

Augustine comments that "to kill a soul" (v. 17) means the same thing as to kill the body, i.e., to take life away. Yet Augustine seems to contradict himself here by then quoting the saying from the Gospel (Matt 10:28) that suggests that killing the soul is *different* and much worse, and then concluding that it means the *same thing* as killing the body, i.e., being killed! The restatement of the *lex talionis* ("law of the tooth") in verses 17-22 is noticed by Lyra who tells us that Rashi says that this is punishment is not given for hitting *any* man but refers to hitting one's *father*, even if death does not follow. Or it should be said (i.e., contra Rashi) that it speaks of hitting any man in cases where death does follow. Pellican asserts that the Jews were quite different from Christians, for they could not grasp that if hit we should turn the other cheek, but by the fear of retribution (the *lex talionis*) they held back from evil. But we Christians are instructed that we overcome evil with good. Ainsworth, on verse 20, holds that compensation should be for five things—damage, pain, healing, resting from affairs, and shame (according to Maimonides in *Chobel* chapter 1, section 103).

Leviticus 25

The Sabbath Year (vv. 1–7, 18–22)

AUGUSTINE SEEMS TO WANT to translate the text of verses 2–4 so that there is not even to be harvesting of the unsown land: it is not the case that what grows of itself might at least be used. What does it mean for the land to have rest? Well, it means that *all* sorts of produce—so everything, not just fields or those things explicitly mentioned—are to be left untouched. Although he permits that people can eat what grows, they must not profit from it. Hesychius allegorizes: the land to be possessed is the Law, which Christians now receive along with the vineyard of the gospel. But the point is that both alike will cease or rest. There is a place in the present life for that which grows of its own accord, namely the natural law and the wisdom that comes from experience.

Ralph is even more "spiritual" in his interpretation: believers are promised the "land of the living" (Isa 53:8) and it is rest without end as the quality of the life to come that is signified by "Sabbath." There are, of course, ages to pass before that arrives: patriarchs, prophets, apostles, martyrs, a time of peace for the church, and the time of Antichrist. A Sunday joins two weeks, being the eighth of one and the first of another, thus symbolizing creation and restoration at the same time.

Brenz takes these verses literally and worries in case a pious creditor be defrauded in this way. Debts cannot be gathered in during the seventh year since there would be no crop to help pay off the debt, so this would have to wait for the following time, as the Hebrew in Deuteronomy 15:1 has it: "at the end of the seventh year you shall pay back." But during the seventh year debts cannot be demanded that year. This is so that people don't get put off helping the poor as the Sabbath year approaches. The idea is that the Lord will bless at all times those who do lend; but if the rich are not generous the Lord will punish, so as to enforce rest on the land and thus the poor and slaves will get away anyway. Moreover, Germany needs each field to rest one in *three* years because it is not as fertile as Canaan. Brenz adds that the ceremonial and spiritual reason for this law is that this time of public rest reminds people about the sin through which they lost the true peace and quiet of paradise—when they gathered fruit effortlessly, and whose happiness the seventh year is a shadow. They are thus being told about the true Sabbath in the kingdom of heaven through Christ.

Lorinus takes the three Sabbaths to designate bodily rest, the rest of individual souls, and that of all souls together. What the reality of that rest exactly is, that is hard to express, but that which seems alluring and often far off is the more recognized and desired. For Lorinus, Cajetan was wrong to take verse 4 so literally that one could go on pruning trees and cutting grass in the seventh year, because these are not specifically mentioned. His fellow Jesuit Ribera took it to signify the rest in heaven in Christ—a transition into his remission; but Oleaster "rightly" prefers the moral reading, that one should not overwork servants. God wants the rich to experience, at least for one day in seven, what the poor experience daily. However, as Aquinas noted, the rest in the seventh year is part of the *ceremonial* law, and Colossians 2:16 tells us that no one should judge others on account of Sabbaths. He reviews various accounts of verse 5 and concludes that whether the prohibition is on cutting or gathering, it does not matter for it all comes to the same thing.

Willett applies a strict literal reading to a strict text. On the question of the seventh year (v. 6), "Augustine thinketh, they might plow, and sow, but the poore were to reape: but the text is plaine, they were not to sow at all. Tostatus thinketh they might plant trees, in their severall and enclosed grounds, and gather the fruits thereof, but the Hebrews hold the contrarie, which is most agreeable to the text." Whatever does grow is for common use.

Matthew Henry thinks the Sabbath year points forward to Acts 2:44, but more obviously the historical Israelites were helped to look "back," since they "were reminded of the easy life man lived in paradise . . . Also, they were taught to consider how the poor lived, that did neither sow nor reap."

The Jubilee (vv. 8–28)

Gregory of Nyssa (*Epistula Canonica* 6) describes the cosmic feast of forgiveness (Easter), but then outlines in canons various sins that require the imposition of penance, in terms redolent of Leviticus, especially where economic oppression and usury are concerned. The church is to exercise good judgment on more subtle forms of idolatry, which go deep into the person. Usury is related to stealing through Ephesians 4:28.

Theodoret writes that the Jubilee year punished Israel's lack of satisfaction by the Law. Interestingly he does not really follow this theological interpretation but prefers the humanity of the literal sense: they continually sowed in order to have more, and the land had no rest in bringing forth fruit. Since in the fields still grew automatically, it is ordered to be reaped and harvested, thus showing humanity to them. For widows and orphans, etc., will get a share of the harvest with them and they rely on it. In that year there was a ransom of debts and freedom for Hebrew slaves. For "ransom" (v. 9) means "freedom."

Augustine sees this Jubilee law as targeting a case of abusive hoarding and so the translation clearly should be "towards profanation" (v. 23) not "towards confirmation"—it is an easy mistake to mix up the Greek terms *bebēlōsis* and *bebaiōsis*. In consequence (v. 24), this happens when some use it for the harm of the Creator of all or things that the buyer might possess it forever. It is important to recognize who the *real* owner is. That is, whenever proselytes come among them—those who are becoming joined to the people and are not in their own country—the Israelites must remember that in God's sight they themselves are also incomers and tenants.

Isidore comments that the reason the Jubilee was never actually practiced was that its fulfillment was always meant to be "eternal" and for humans, in the future. For at the sound of the trumpet, with the raising of all, the possession of humanity will be restored to all. Adam will be returned to the ancient land of his flesh in which he dwelled. Then Abel to his land from which he was ejected by Cain. And then the patriarchs and all souls will receive their bodies, which they left behind, to possess them forever (*Etym.* V, 37,3). But perhaps more significant for the medieval development is what he adds in terms of present-day application to his readers in *Etymologies* VI.18.4–5: as people who are free from every bondage, we receive the coming into us of the grace of the Holy Spirit. This was such that the individual became a place where the fulfillment escaped from being historical into one that took place in the return of all to paradise, a common refrain in the *Glossa* (Quinto 1999, 12). Penance was becoming increasingly a public matter by the thirteenth century, and although Lombard does not mention indulgences, he questioned the need for priestly absolution in completing penance. This in turn was not so far from the reflection by Maimonides on the possibility of avoiding sacrifice when repentance was sincere. The practice was, partly with imagery drawn from Leviticus 14, that in granting indulgences the priest would write off the debt symbolically on the hand: this became very popular as a means of grace.

One can trace a mystical current in Aelred of Rievaulx's (d. 1166) use of "*jubileus*" for the happy mystic, and then Richard of St. Victor (d. 1173) who glossed verse 7 to the effect that the soul reached such a "jubilee" state when the field of the body was quieted from passion (Foreville 1974, 1480). Indulgences in turn would become spiritualized and granted without pilgrimage or Jubilee years (Foreville 1974, 1486) in return for intention to show faithfulness to the gospel and charity to the poor.

Rupert of Deutz takes the term *Jubilaeus* to mean "remit" or "demit," so God, not out of his greatness but from his intent to serve, treats small things as if great in measure. He will give great and eternal rewards to the obedient and everlasting punishments to the disobedient. Now by human reasoning some can assert, as they believe, that God would never deign to communicate through the good things of that land to signify better goods, never using "unsuitable" things of that great land to figure eternal invisible evils. However, we should not think of these land promises *literally*, as if they concerned Israel getting a large empire, like the Romans. No, "our Land" means our *flesh*, and you should give yourself to works of continence after you have borne children, for there should come a time when these motions should stop, and you cease the works of the flesh and *transform* your works of corruption into works of spirit, glory and honor—and people will praise you. The Jubilee means personal forgiveness of those who say "sorry" to us. But fixed festivity ought to encourage such acts of remission. For there are many who, although it is absurd, find it easy to remit the injury to God, but are slow to be gracious when they themselves have been hurt. A selling of a house means the alienation of minds. "The Levite" is the one who although he sins against God and arrogantly despises, yet does not remain in sin for long, waiting for the reek of his sin to make it known, but with God's whispering he is conscience-stricken and makes an effort to confess his sins publicly. Also, as when an adolescent sins *once* with a girl or steals *once*, he should not get the same treatment as a repeat offender.

Whereas Rupert's emphasis was a public one, Ralph's concern was more individualist and heavenly minded. The lost inheritance in Leviticus 25 can be regained by the sacramental penance *and* the satisfaction of temporal pains, which amounts to the ransom price along with contrition. Ralph viewed the prohibition on work as a description of a state of relying on the Lord for feeding, spiritual as well as material. He maintained the distinction between particular and general resurrection, as set out by Rabanus Maurus; also a balance between the literal cycle of feasts as leading to a historical end and the figurative cycle of feasts during the year as a process for the soul (Quinto 2001, 67). Penitence stood as a mere preparation for permanent contrition, which is a price worth more the further away the eschaton is. On verse 10, he said that the possession we lost in Paradise is that which is to be regained in the spiritual Jubilee. The price corresponds to whether one is far from the Jubilee when he sells. One is far when one is borne down by a load of sins and makes himself far from remission and so the price of penance goes up. This is not about any poor

Engaging Leviticus

person who sells his goods out of necessity (we will deal with that below), but is about when talents are used to amass material wealth, endangering our sound mind. In Exodus and Deuteronomy the slave is set free on the seventh year and not the forty-ninth as here. Can the literal sense therefore be saved? Things are not always as contradictory as they seem at first glance. On the question of whether the Jubilee is the seventh, forty-ninth, or fiftieth year, it is better and more secure to go with the mystical sense where it does not matter whether it is seven or seven times seven. So the seventh year signifies the remission given at end of life to the righteous, but the forty-nine is that "universal liberty," to be hoped for at the end of time, and is fuller, for body as well as for soul. We know that some want to have a fiftieth year after counting forty-nine, but it is better just to see there being one year of vacation—to have two would mean even more poverty, which this chapter wants to avoid! Any two literal senses point to the one mystery: it also points to the return of Christ and the general resurrection, as echoed by the Revelation 10 sounding of the trumpet.

Bruno has a much more realized eschatology: his year began, spiritually speaking, when our Lord Jesus Christ redeemed the world from the service of the devil by his own blood and opened the gates of paradise to his faithful, whose blessedness is expected after the seventh seven-year period when the year of Jubilee and praise will begin for the saints. However, God's favoring the poor with his Jubilee legislation needs to be taken seriously, hence literally, so that allegorizing would be superfluous. It is not the land but only its use that gets sold.

Hugh of St. Cher's Dominican *Postilla* and Langton do not see Leviticus 25 as having anything to do with indulgences, but with the furtherance of penance. Hugh in commenting on Luke 16:1–8 does think in terms of help being available from the merits and prayers of saints rather than treasury of merits of Christ. Langton promoted Ralph's idea that the Jubilee must begin in the forty-ninth year. He had to maneuver so as not to advocate a literal Jubilee, or even to encourage such a thought by interpreting, as the *Gloss* had done, that there would be no hierarchies in heaven, even while agreeing there would be no priests nor any need for them. There was to be no application of the literal sense. One might accuse this interpretation of conservatism; Dionysian thinking in an era of Franciscan "liberation theology" as represented by Joachim of Fiore (Buc 1994, 141–46), but there also a sense of a NT hermeneutic, not least from 1 Corinthians 15:24: the present age's dignity and glory would pass.

Yet in 1220, on the fiftieth anniversary of Becket's death (29th Dec 1170), Archbishop Langton solemnly took the saint's corpse from the cathedral crypt into the chapel of Holy Trinity. Indulgence as remission of penance was turned into a fifty-year Jubilee based at Canterbury, granting full indulgence for outstanding penance (Foreville 1958, 38). Body blows of criticisms by Wycliffe, Rome's wish to centralize, and Luther's attack led to its demise after 1520.

Indulgences as a way of negotiating at least some of the spiritual debt go back to the Crusades in 1095 and Pope Urban II's proclamation of full release from sins in return for active support. The canon lawyer Huguccio (c. 1200) spoke vaguely of the theory of "a year to release debts." Two centuries on, the first Jubilee Year was announced with the statement: "For those who will be penitent and confess in this year we have conceded to them not only full and generous, but the fullest pardon of all their sins (Boniface VIII's bull *De centesimo seu iubileo anno* in 1300). Penitent pilgrims also had to travel to Rome and it is reckoned that 20,000 French people made that journey. This was to happen every one hundred years. One can read the reasoning as saying that for the escaping of the diabolical spiritual debts under the new Law, a doubling of the time was appropriate (Lambert 1950). Dante's *Purgatorio* was inspired by and set in the first year of Jubilee (1300). However, the spiritualizing and the lack of clear reference to Leviticus in the literature might be attributable to Pope Boniface's considerable banking interests, and his understandable reluctance to follow the letter of the Law.

Denys teaches that the "land" referred to in the text is the church militant or the monastic life or the humble consideration of one's own weakness. Jubilee is granted by God when someone is incorporated into the church through faith and charity or finds the grace of conversion or true humility. So whenever anyone enters these "lands" then the church herself will glory in the Lord and rest in peace of heart and the monastic life will rejoice in its possessors. By "the field" is meant the lower part of the soul, by "vineyard" the higher portion.

The "six years" are those of one's own life or the present age, and the "seventh year" is either the particular judgment or the final resurrection. Letting the ground grow freely signifies work that is willed by natural reason without any contribution by charity and grace and as such will have no reward, for without charity there is no merit. The Jubilee is the year of the evangelical Law when a full remission of sins is granted to all people who dispose themselves through true contrition and confession. "It will not be sold in perpetuity"—our land is our mortal flesh, which we sell cheaply to the devil when we show the arms of iniquity to sin. A neighbor can rescue someone sold to the devil: for the rest ought to pray for him and seek to lead him back to the state of salvation.

Brenz, in a very long comment, compares Numbers 36 on this rule: one can sell the *usufruct* of the property but not the ownership; and thus the price depends on how long there remains until repossession. The aim was preservation of all tribes, which is what the Holy Spirit was really concerned about, and the final target "our Lord Jesus Christ who alone is our hero to whom all eyes and faces are to be turned." Judah needs to be kept so that Christ could come forth from there, as in Genesis 49, and be recognized. Hence in the Jubilee Christ is proclaimed. The *true* Jubilee starts with Christ's preaching and extends forever: the trumpets are the preaching of the gospel. Thus also in the Christian Jubilee in which we now live Satan has no right to demand what we owe him in terms of death and hell. Also, as in Israel, all was held in common, so there is no distinction between believers. Our task is to maintain this liberty and dignity by thankfulness and the obedience of faith. There is a third Jubilee: the pontifical one, but it is a *fiction*, since it obscures the true Christian Jubilee. The true threshold of the apostles (*Apostolorum limina*) is not where their bones lie but where the gospel received from them is preached, and this in every place and parish. The pope is selective in claiming certain Mosaic legal practices. The political order is established for keeping citizens in peace and honesty, and the ecclesiastical is instituted so that the gospel of Christ might be taught appropriately and its sacraments administered by rite. The church follows Moses on Sabbath days since this makes sense. They could have gathered to hear the gospel every tenth or fourteenth day, and there was freedom to do so. But "seven" seems reasonable. But the worship of God does not serve the end of peace among men but rather placates the wrath of God and is for receiving (*promerendam*) his grace. And in this, even if it seems sensible, if the word is not followed there will be trouble, as when all these nonbiblical things—such as incense, pilgrimages, etc.—are not in Bible. In other words, these laws should be followed as much as is necessary to keep public order, but are otherwise not to be kept. "Keep my precepts" concerns the state. One should obey divine laws in one's law-making not just out of fear of reprisal but out of conscience before God. For the kingdoms and empires of this earth do not belong to magistrates or individual man but to our Lord God, and the magistrates only do the administering of the laws.

Brenz adds that Boniface VII abused the Jubilee by adding to the sixth book of Decretals not only a full and wide pardon but the fullest pardon of all their sins. Especially corrupt was Sextus III who in 1473 made it every twenty-five years, because he needed the money. The accountants of indulgences became poor in each of their provinces since everyone had gone in the Jubilee year to the cathedrals of the apostles to buy them. Luther showed this up fifty years ago! Originally there were outward wrongs which could be punished by fixed rites before they could be absolved so that it could be understood that as the rest were deterred by the example of punishment they should be more careful abut falling. However, later some monks added works of satisfaction, which is horrible idolatry. For it takes the honor for redemption away from God and transfers it to our works. Surely there is a distinction between earthly and eternal punishment. Just as David, though forgiven through Nathan sustained a shocking pile of calamities, such punishments cannot be cancelled by the church but can only be mitigated by sustained godliness and change of life and ardent prayer (Jer 1:8).

Pellican is much simpler: the Jubilee was instituted among the people of God for the consolation of the poor and oppressed in this world. It offers the hope of a better condition whenever men are oppressed in this world through accident or vice, and by the way the path is shown that leads to brotherly communion inasmuch as that can be achieved in this world, along with a prefiguring or life to come. The trumpet proclaims the good news of future remission of sin in the day of propitiation in order that we might learn through penance and faith of the gospel that the Lord God bestows on the faithful remission of sins and hope of future blessedness.

Lorinus sets out to give a history of the Jubilee doctrine. He mentions that Tertullian (*Adversus Marcionem* II.18), like Philo, saw the law as one for the sake of humanity and there is a comment by Eusebius in the catena that also mentions rest for the sake of the fields. But Lorinus denies what John of Salisbury (Epistle 267) claimed, that the Jews never kept this. He also decides to follow the rabbis, as mediated by Paul of Burgos, etc., that it would mean *two* years lost, the fiftieth year coming after a Sabbath year. Buridan held that the Jubilee was to stop the twelve tribes getting mixed up, and thus it concerned only land. Aquinas' theory was that it stopped inequality and unrest. It does not detract from the mystery that the trumpets made a horrible sound. Hugh of St. Cher mentions boys singing so that everyone knew the festival was coming. In Rome today, says Lorinus, at Ascension tide in four places the Jubilee is proclaimed in Latin and Italian, and many are invited from afar. There is a belief that Gregory the Great announced a Jubilee every one hundred years for the remission of wrongs by visiting the basilicas of Peter and Paul along with penance and satisfaction. Sleidanus (the Protestant historian, d. 1556) is wrong to say that the Jubilee was first celebrated every twenty-five years by Sixtus I in AD 125. Some translated "Jubilee" as a movement (*vectio*) which carries us with it and leads us to the death and merits of Christ. Comestor's *Scholastic History* is a bit fanciful in relating it back to the deliverance of Lot. The sense of the (*hiphil*) verb is "to make to arrive at something good." There might be an allusion to Isaac and the ram. Clement VI who made it the fiftieth not forty-ninth year was clear that he was following the OT model more closely than Boniface VIII (one hundred years), who had preferred by having it every century (twice fifty years), so that it might become more precious. Abulensia was the first commentator to really spell this out the connection with Leviticus 25, as well as Cardinal St. George in his treatise *On the Jubilee*, chapter 12: the devil was like the fraudulent buyer. Gratian (*On penance*, d. 1) suggested the idea of a perfect Jubilee remission as a "mopping up" after penance. The number of years to the Jubilee is reckoned by the priest when he fixes the length of penance since full remission from sin takes a period of time. There needs to be confession and no one can impose a time of penance on another if the latter has not clearly taken care of his own sin.

Willet regards the Jubilee as "the restitution of all things" to wholeness, after the general judgment. Such a festival could not have been name after an evildoer like Iobel (Gen 4:21). Cajetan's derivation of the word from germination is a move that Willet finds curious. Simply, the Latin word *iubilare* is derived from the word for "trumpet," according to the Hebraist Junius. It was kept on the fiftieth year according to inclusive counting. There is some evidence from OT that it was kept (2 Kgs 19:29) and it is best to see the passion of Christ as happening in a Jubilee year. Against Lorinus this is not superfluous, "but very usefull, to make the body and type agree together."

To the usual reasons given for the Jubilee, Calov adds his: that this law became the nerve of humanity, kindness, and thriftiness. And Christ came in the thirtieth Mosaic Jubilee. Cocceius adds another reason for the Jubilee: by removing anxiety about poverty that throughout the year they should live as free persons to scrutinize the Law of God and the prophets, which would promote progress in piety and make them look to the fulfillment of divine providence.

Matthew Henry sees the Jubilee as coming after the Day of Atonement in that fiftieth year:

> The wisdom of the Roman commonwealth sometimes provided that no man should be master of over five hundred acres. The Law here holds that no family should be sunk and ruined, and condemned to perpetual poverty. This particular care God took for the support of the honor of that people . . . that it might the better typify that good part which shall *never be taken away* from those that have it. The Jewish writers say that, for ten days before the jubilee-trumpet sounded, the servants that were to be discharged by it did express their great joy by feasting, and wearing garlands on their heads: it is therefore called the *joyful sound,* as in Psalm 89:15. And we are thus to rejoice in the liberty we have by Christ.

Leclerc enters into the big controversy over the numbering of the Jubilee year. Some think it counts from the year after the last one: so if 1600 is a Jubilee, then the next one is 1651, although others think, that like seven Sabbaths, it would be after forty-nine years. There does not have to be a symmetry between calculating the Jubilee and doing that with the days before Pentecost, since Moses did not make that parallel. Leclerc's sense is that Leviticus 25 is a political document in pursuit of the common good. The judgment of Cunaeus (of Leiden, d. 1638) who thinks the Jubilee is the forty-ninth year is to be preferred to that of Petavius (d. 1652) who would make it seem that since every forty-ninth year was a Sabbath year then Jubilee the following year. But if the Jubilee year is the one after the Sabbath year, then three years in seven are barren and useless. God in the Law sets a prohibition, lest those who excel other peoples in no other things except in riches use their freedom and the skills they have to the detriment of the poor. Israel as rich could have cultivated a love of riches leading to inequality, as often happened in Roman Republic. The Jubilee returned to them not only their freedom but their means of support and this would help to stop dissent and revolution, for once people have tasted freedom, they find it hard to lose that spirit. Other legislators like Solon tried to make sure property could not just be sold for any price one wanted (*Politics* II, c4, c7) and one could not sell one's patrimony off. Moses too was trying to restrain greed, as Philo clearly saw. And in agrarian society where there were no mechanical arts, all hinged on the land.

Calmet, on verse 8, discusses whether is it the forty-ninth year or the fiftieth. According to all the doctors and Philo and the rabbis it is the latter. But surely it is the forty-ninth, and to have a fiftieth means having two special years: a Sabbath and then the Jubilee year. Bochartus (*On animal sacrifices* I, l.2.c.42) has observed that a ram's horn would not make a good trumpet. Leclerc thinks that the "jubilee" word means "sound the trumpet" and connects to Jubal from before flood. Calmet prefers to derive it from *hobil*, "to call back," since each thing was recalled to its principle and first master. It seems that the Sabbath year was continued after exile, but not the Jubilee law. Yet the goods that were possessed through succession get to stay where they are and are not to be returned; the same applies where contracts of sale had specified a fixed term of possession. It is just the perpetuity contracts on land that get broken, even if this seems hard to square with Mosaic notion of faithfulness to covenants.

The Hebrew term in verse 23, which the Vulgate translated "in perpetuity" and the LXX "in confirmation," in the Samaritan version is "absolutely." He notes that Leviticus 27:20 is an exception to this rule. The reason is that God did not will that people should alienate their economic substance forever because they are not the owners but merely have the use of it. God has the right to dispose of that which returns to him: the proprietor does not get it back because he was the proprietor before; rather, he buys it back like a stranger.

Maclaren solemnly spells out that what we have in this life is precarious, even if spiritual security is not. That seems to him a fair trade-off. There is to be "no regret, if the Landowner takes back a bit of the land which He [God] has let us occupy. It was the condition of our occupation that He should be at liberty to do so whenever He saw that it would be best for us . . . A landowner stops up a private road one day a year in order to assert his right, and to remind the neighbourhood that he could stop it altogether if he liked." The nature and possessions outstay their possessors who come and go. Christians, like sojourners should "cherish then, constant consciousness of that solemn eternity," as they travel safely through desert with Christ.

Robert North's *The Biblical Jubilee* (2000) reminds us that the most scholarly works of exegesis occupy no neutral space. A literal interpretation of debt cancellation (i.e., monetary not spiritual debts) has become a feature of "ecumenical" exegesis. It is not to be seen as just as an ideal in the minds of Israelites (so German critical scholarship) but as having at least some reality in the life of Israel.

Exceptions for City Dwellings and Levites (vv. 29–34)

Origen comments on verse 32 that there is always the means of getting a house back if it is lost, so if there is some sin which is not a mortal crime or a blasphemy of the faith (which is surrounded by the "wall" of apostolic and ecclesial teaching but consists of a flaw in word or deeds), then this sale and such blame can always be redeemed and no one is to be forbidden for doing penance for such things. For the more serious crimes the place for penance is given only once, but these more common ones that we need more often can be repeated. We should note this is a *moral* fault, not a mortal one, despite the majority reading of Origen's text, as Arnauld (1674, 198–200) had suggested. The Levite is the perfect soul, and the "houses" of the Levites are their faults, which can always be redeemed. One should make sure that one buys back quickly while there is still opportunity, lest we are tricked out of out dwelling in eternity.

Procopius regards the Levites as like Mary in Luke 10 who "has received the better part, from whom it will not be taken away." The promise made the Jews first of all afraid so that they would later return, for it is not the case that all hope is lost for them. The Sabbath of Sabbaths began with John the Baptist. It is a time of forgiveness and penitence as the way of receiving it. Yet the Jews had lost even the grace given to them under Moses by not arriving at Christ, for they only had the benefit for a season and then the Lord returned to claim it. With a quick generalization on the literal sense he writes that property causes wars and disputes. Common use, as it was in paradise, is much more to be praised—as in Acts 2; it was more than nice idea, but a movement that was part of Salvation History.

Bruno is in two minds as to whether to treat this text literally: to sell a house within walls means to be within the church, so that to sell this house means selling one's soul to the devil by sinning as the fortified cities of Israel were lost to Sennacherib (2 Kgs 19). In such a case the Jubilee will not work but he will have to do penance "for one year," which means his whole life. For those outside the walls who are believers but sinful, the Jubilee will be a day of judgment. Unbelievers do not have a Jubilee, for it is only for those delivered from the servitude of sin on the day of baptism. The house that is sold outside the church can return to its owner. But such a Jubilee can only happen once, whereas other Jubilees can happen often through penance. As for what is said about the *Levites'* houses this can be understood literally and simply: "do not let church property be sold." Would that these be observed literally by Christians; that rich people would help the poor apart from heavy interest and the poor could help the rich in service without total ruin. For so often we see a little bit of money lent lead to the devouring of the poor's substance in an instant. One should allow the thing to be returned for the original price without interest.

Ralph thinks the Levites provide an exception to the exception for properties in towns. By "the suburbs that encircle the city" what else is expressed but the divine vision which follows this present speculation to which those setting out will arrive and find pasture, equally spread around and squared. Naboth is presented like a patron saint: defending a just patrimony that was eternal. The exceptions to the rule show there is not a universal freedom. The towns are places where the enemy gets to keep the house where people are too tied to the world and its ways. The city is a fortress and whoever does not have a dwelling therein is exposed to the enemy. It is good to provide for oneself. If, however, he acts badly and loses the field outside the city he will regain possession. So the selling of fields is tolerable and whenever the seller wants it can be recovered, or if it cannot be then it can be recovered through the remission of the Jubilee and the grace of God. The house within the walls can be mystically understood as the observation of virtues. There is a need for virtue without which no one will see God (Heb 12:14). "One year" is the present life—that is all the time one has to redeem in such monastic cases. It is shameful and degrading for one to suffer the loss of a glorious position as a respectable monk; but if he recovers himself within the walls of the city and shows himself to have a level of behavior that is necessary to be kept by all brothers, then he will be allowed to redeem what he has lost when he wants and can find the price.

And even if he cannot afford the price then with divine aid he will recoup it. Build on Christ Jesus and it will last, and for that reason—because the foundation will survive through fire—we need not fear. One will not have what one has tried to cling on to, and such a person who suffers loss when his building is burned and loses the fruit of his own work, he will yet be saved by grace, because he stayed within the walls of the church and hence will regain the health of soul and body.

This passage is particularly suited to Denys's double approach of literal then spiritual interpretation. The literal elucidation starts with his solution to the problem that divides, that we should count forty-nine and then make the following year the Jubilee, rather than seeing it as the forty-ninth year, as some do. The reason behind such legislation given by Aristotle and Aquinas (*ST* IaIIae, q105) is that regulation helps to keep society together. To "eat one's fill" (v. 20) is not meant in the pejorative way, as the Savior meant it in Luke 6, but rather in the sense of "having enough to eat." They should trust in divine providence and not have worldly fears. Just as Christ commands us not to worry about tomorrow, the Law orders us not to worry about the three-year gap between the last harvest and the one to come. Augustine has another reading of verse 23: "the land shall not be sold into profanation," i.e., sold to profane people who will work godlessness into it by serving foreign gods there. Here Denys stretches what he finds in Augustine. Towns were more populous and so could only be redeemed in the first year and Levites had their property to hold on to. Finally there is a literalist parting shot: if Jews were not allowed to be slaves to Jews then how much less Christians to Jews.

Denys's spiritual interpretation then follows: a "property within walls" is the state of salvation or the level of merits or the position which someone has in the church—which is the city of the living God, of which the walls are the angelic guard, the Savior himself, and the presiding of clergy. In that case the person who sells his house by sinning through heresy or schism must redeem it in the first year; but if he perseveres in sin he will be hardened. The house in the town is the existence of merits or the place of virtues surrounded by the wavering and weak. The dwellings of the Levites within the towns can be understood as the virtues and the merits of the religious and perfect, who if they sometime go astray, always have the basis for rising up and are more easily restored and like Paul they strive to live better.

Brenz thinks the law for one "who sells his house" (v. 29) does not fit with the polity of Germany in which we can sell fields and houses in perpetuity. So the Scriptures must have another use for the church. This teaches us, first, that legitimate contracts of buying and selling are divinely ordained and the godly can use them with a good conscience. Next, since the Holy Spirit precisely prescribes the form of civil contracts even in the selling of rural huts, we can see that God does not only establish the principles for the business of principalities and kingdoms, but also for human activities in the most lowly of matters. This admonishes us, that in all our business, however ordinary, we pursue justice and call on God that we might gain his blessing.

Lorinus, on verse 32, thinks that 23,000 Levites could all have fitted into one town, and he wonders why plural "cities" are mentioned! The Jesuit colleague Alcazar tells us that in the blessed eternity there will be no catechumens and there will be none who do not enjoy the security which is prefigured by walls here. Actually, in the city of God any literal walls will be for decorative purposes (cf. Jerome's *Commentary on Ezekiel*, 48).

Willet finds the words evidence that the field of the suburbs is not to be sold. This law held "during the politie of the Jewes: but afterward in the Apostles time, Barnabas being a Levite, sold his field" (Acts 4:36), that he might purchase a better inheritance with the faithful. Calmet reasons that one can buy back in town but not village dwellings, because the former are larger and are the main source of income; whereas in the country they have other resources.

Usury (vv. 35–38)

The ban on loans at interest received an "Ambrosian" exception: Christians *might* lend at interest to each other via a Jew, thought Ambrose (*lib de Tobia* ch. 10; written c. 380). Augustine (on Psalm 128) and Chrysostom had argued against this, on the basis of Luke 6:34, which could be interpreted as suggesting that Christians should not expect repayment of loans. Luke seemed inconsistent, since the parable in Luke 19:27 was at odds with Luke 6:35. Justinian's *Code* (2.33.4) capped interest at 6 percent. "The Paris Synod of 829 shows a wider use of biblical authorities, citing, in addition to Psalm 14:5, Exodus 22:5, Leviticus 25:35–37, Deuteronomy 15:7–10, Amos 8:4–6, and Ezekiel 18:8, and obliquely, the New Testament without specific reference." (Noonan 1957, 15). If originally such morality was only for clerics, then with Jerome's influence, by Charlemagne's decree of 789 it was extended to all. The Council of Lateran II (1139) confirmed that usury was wrong for clerics and this was soon again applied to laity.

Ralph takes Jacob and Esau to recall true brotherly love. Ralph is not really interested in economic questions. It is fine when like Elijah we trade Elisha into service, but bad when we sell him to a foreign master. But in case of a Hebrew master, obedience is shown in order to expiate the disobedience by which our first parents disobeyed God. So one sells oneself when with the vision of eternal retribution he does not flee from humility. Such spontaneous service is liberty. We are all paupers since we have lost those first riches in creation, for we do not have the wisdom to correct our ways, and we need to submit to someone's wisdom in all accountability. We will receive riches as the reward for humility. So the one given to service does not have to be oppressed or threatened but can be treated with mild admonition and with the hope of reward set forth, i.e., treated not as a slave but as a hired hand. There is no force of necessity in love, but the expectation of reward does motivate.

According to Aquinas, trade as unnatural exchange can be checked by the natural order, allowing only moderate profit (*ST* IIaIIae, q77 a4). For Thomas, the new law simply renews the precepts of the old, and both the old and the new simply renew the law of reason. Usury was not to be condemned simply as avaricious, but as a sin against justice it required restitution in a way that a sin against charity, being an internal matter, did not (Franks 2009, 27, 30). Lending money is not like renting a house where money ought to be paid for having it since there is no distinction between the thing and its use, so it should not be paid for twice over, to the threatening of human subsistence. Luther *On Trade and Usury* (1524) agrees with Aquinas (*ST* IIaIIae q78, Art 1), who relies on Aristotle (*Politics* 1.3; 1.10), to argue that a loan might be permissible if it is for a good enough cause. Although Scotus, with religious poverty as a background issue, questioned the Thomistic distinction, the Thomist principle was upheld and stood the test of time, not least through Benedict XV's 1745 *vix pervenit* (Noonan 1959, 361f). Yet, of course, by the time of the Catholic social teaching of the late nineteenth century (such as Leo XIII's *Rerum Novarum* of 1891), usury in practice was a reality, whatever the theory, and so was not directly attacked.

Soto was the first scholastic, around 1540, openly to doubt that Luke 6:35 is a precept. It "has no relevance to the justice of lending at a profit" (Noonan 1959, 346) and the OT laws, as NT commands, are not universally binding unless they can be shown to be part of that natural law. Molina thought the Bible no help at all. Lorinus makes no mention of scholastic arguments, but his sources are all patristic, and the accent is on the greed motive. The devil is a liar for promising all lands. Oleaster thinks the cause of the rule was that just as God gave them the land for nothing there should be no usury, and some think the same reason goes for tithes and firstfruits. He is our God since he possesses us, as if by a right, and works our healing and for that reasons we are given to the One who ought to be worshipped by us.

The attitude of the early moderns to the prohibition of usury (Lev 25:36f) is seen in Calvin's deliberate distancing of modern urban Geneva from ancient agrarian Palestine (Calvin, *CO* XXV, 680–83):

> There is a difference in the political union, for the situation in which God placed the Jews and many other circumstances permitted them to trade conveniently among themselves with out usuries. Our union is entirely different. Therefore, I do not feel that usuries were forbidden to us simply, except in so far as they are opposed to equity or charity . . . Usury is not now unlawful, except in so far as it contravenes equity and brotherly union. Let each one, then, place himself before God's judgment seat, and not do to his neighbor what he would not have done to himself, from whence a sure and infallible decision may be come to. The exercise of the trade of usury, since heathen writers counted it amongst disgraceful and base modes of gain, is much less tolerable among the children of God; but in what cases, and how far it may be lawful to receive usury upon loans, the law of equity will better prescribe than any lengthened discussions.

There is something of the *Realethik* here, one that may have had implications for a Reformation world-affirming spirituality, which nevertheless recognizes the rights of the other under equity. Calvin resisted thinking in terms of a spiritual world to the devaluation of the physical one. His attempt to adapt to a "real world" reminds one of R. Hillel's *prosbul*, in that *if* a debt bond was lodged with the court before the Sabbath year, then the debt was not to be cancelled, but remained enforceable, since people had been refraining from giving loans to each other before the Sabbath year (*Sheviit* 10:5).

On the Protestant side, Calvin's permission is well known, but Willet has perhaps a sharper discussion. Luke 6:35 is not against usury *per se*, for the Lord is telling us to lend to the *poor* without expecting repayment. The Council of Vienne (1311) reinforced this, holding that to take usury is to kill a man. Luke 19:23 gets used to justify usury but that is only a parable; and the idea of getting back spiritual interest for money given is abhorrent. Emperor Anastasius (c. 715) revived it for use in the Byzantine commonwealth after it was outlawed by Leo (c. 500), on the principle that usury was, like divorce, bad and yet permitted because of the hardness of the human heart. Henry VIII outlawed all usury above 10 percent with forfeiture of the treble value. Elizabeth lowered the percentage further.

Willet continues: "The Scripture condemneth not all usury, but onely that which is extorted of the poore." He disagrees with Calvin for seeing this law as "ceremonial." "The fruits of the ground, which one buyeth with an other man's money, the lender may receive, but then they must be accounted toward the making up of the stock."

Usury should not be allowed by the rich who have lands already, nor when directed against the poor (Exod 22:25) and it should be moderate. Also, "we require four virtues in lender and borrower—charity, equity, faithfulness, honesty." These laws tell people to deal justly, not to relinquish business. Lydia in Acts 16 was not diverted from her profession. Yet we are not to swap the gospel with its few precepts for the many legal ones. Is it strange that God annuls the OT law? "No more then for a man to make a model of some curious building, and to bestow some art upon it, which yet afterward he doth breake in pieces, when the house is once erected and finished."

Slavery, Sojourners

Procopius asked in what way one sold into slavery could be redeemed by "one of his brothers" (v. 48). He answered: by acting like those who brought the paralytic to Christ to be healed, and their faith gained the healing for him. And a spiritual bond is stronger than friendship, which comes from mutual benefit. For a blood brother cannot redeem (Ps 48:8). The righteousness of a Josiah could not save Israel. Yet that of Moses did prevail for the people called who were not yet at the time of perfect obedience. Grace was received from Moses' own righteousness for the people through their kinship with him.

A literal obedience of this law was found in Charles the Bald's edict of Pistres in 854, citing verses 39–41 that slaves (prisoners of war) are to be retuned after six years. Yet the "spiritual" interpretation won out during the Middle Ages, which in part reflects the rarity of needing prisoners where a feudal society could provide for services in any case. Ralph claims that one is not yet a servant of sin if it has not yet bent your neck, but it can grow gradually so that whole self gets taken over. The "stranger" or "pilgrim" is one who is not the natural Lord of a human person but has become so through our lack of prudence. Ralph does not say straight out that it is the devil but "the one who came to David so that David took from the flock of another to dine with the stranger." Because of so much coldness of charity and abundant iniquity there are few who show care to neighbors; although such a person sold to evil spirits could be redeemed.

Brenz thinks that where slavery is concerned, the Exodus six-year maximum rule trumps the Jubilee, bearing in mind what Exodus 21:1–11 says. But if non-Hebrews are concerned, then a tough servitude *is* permitted. However, since sin is in the world one cannot really talk about the natural law too much. Slavery is allowed, so long as the conditions are kind. God the Holy Spirit cursed Canaan and approves of servitude; Esau served his younger brother and Paul says we should stay in our calling; he tells slave owners to be kind to slaves, not to free them. The condition of the old slavery, says Brenz, must be observed by us; not that it is to be reinstated under us—by the mercy of God it has been abolished for some time now. The Law helps us understand what it is to be, what Scripture calls "slaves of sin," and teaches us that we have gained freedom through Christ.

Willet, on verse 35, teaches that if humanitarian concern is not to be denied to a stranger *how much more* to a brother: it is not saying, as Cajetan makes it seem, that a poor Israelite is to get treated like a stranger. It is more that money should not thus be leant to the poor, or where the rich use it for pleasure. With a sudden switch to the theology of predestination, any true Israelite or spiritual Hebrew has never sold himself ever out of his inheritance, despite what Bellarmine thinks. Christ is the Kinsman-Redeemer and so there is free manumission to us, violence to the devil, and a ransom to God. Lorinus is wrong to think a man can redeem himself by his own penitence. Moving back to the literal sense, Willet writes that the practice of poverty was only in practiced in the Jerusalem church (Acts 5:4), and things were held in common use but not common dominion, he claims (against the Anabaptists). The Jubilee backs up the principle of family property at the end. It is hard for the owner to enter the kingdom of heaven, but it is not impossible.

Calmet insists that in no way were Hebrews to be slaves. Liberty was a very important principle; except where there was no other means of survival (Maimonides). Lorinus draws a mystical lesson from verse 35f, that one should protect a brother from temptations. Abulensia does not see the connection here with usury. Yet Ambrose calls the promise of riches a great noose. When a fixed sum is given each year or month this, even if not by contract, the one giving the loan seeks something from the other which he is not entitled to, even if voluntarily promised, when the person is poor. Lorinus then reports that Apollinarius "in the Catena" teaches that usury is a deprivation of fear of the Lord and impediment to humanity: we do not it demand if we are all household of Christ. On verses 47–49, Lorinus is angry about the inhumanity of Catholics who sell brothers into the hands of Turks. There has been set up a company for the pious work of redeeming captives, under the name of the Trinity and blessed Mary of Mercedes. Popes Gregory XIII and Sixtus V gave many privileges to this company or confraternity and John VI offered indulgences to those who would rescue captives from there. Peter Serranus has used this verse against women who sell their bodies and men who, with a thousand types of whippings, give themselves over through compulsion. He thinks Vatable and Munster are Judaizing for wanting to have "I AM THE LORD" placed at end of chapter 25.

On verses 49–50 Calmet notes that Athenian slaves could also buy their liberty. Moses here speaks only of the Jubilee year. Could a slave not also get free on

Sabbath year? Yes, plausibly, if the master was a lawful proselyte. But one does not know whether the legislator wanted to accord the same grace to a Hebrew slave sold to a domiciled proselyte. We should not take the silence of Moses to mean that slaves did not get released on Sabbath years. Henry puts his finger on a sore point of Enlightenment society, namely that with the demise of feudalism, taking slaves seemed once more necessary: "Thus in our English plantations the *negroes* only are used as slaves; how much to the credit of Christianity I shall not say."

"They that can give up essential liberty to obtain a little safety deserve neither liberty nor safety." This *bon mot* of Benjamin Franklin was later inscribed on the Statue of Liberty in New York. The Liberty Bell in Philadelphia, rung at the initial reading of the American Declaration of Independence in 1776, is inscribed with *Proclaim liberty throughout all the land unto all the inhabitants thereof Lev. xxv x.* Liberty as almost a spiritual right, asserted by J. S. Mill (1859), has often been a slippery notion. Being so foundational for ethics, "the principle of freedom cannot require that he should be free not to be free" (*On Liberty*, 126).

Bonar concludes with a moral-cum-spiritual interpretation: "An ungodly self-seeking Jew said in his heart 'I might make some gain of this Jubilee. I have a garden in Engedi which I might let at a high price . . .' It is thus that men abuse the doctrines of grace. One uses the Lord's table as a means of establishing his character in the sight of the world."

Coming Up to Date

Whereas Bossuet's *Politique tirée des propres paroles de l'Ecriture sainte* (1700) made no mention of Jubilee, Voltaire saw it standing for economic and political progress. The church continued it: Benedict XIV (Encyclical *Vix pervenit* of 1745, addressed only to the bishops of Italy, and therefore not infallible) wanted to reaffirm it as a spiritual Jubilee in 1750, appealing to an intense religious fervor sweeping through Europe, and even including Protestants. In Catholic circles, it would take the French Revolution and the establishment of other civil codes to establish interest-taking on loans as the norm. The current Roman position is one of permission as the letter of the law but only with the inculcation of a spirit of generosity in the hearts of lenders. John Paul II used the theme to sponsor church ecumenism and mutual forgiveness and pardon. Ricardo Quinto thinks there is no question that the 1950 Jubilee was a time to look back at war and see healing ahead, and that the Assumption of Mary doctrine fitted into that atmosphere. Against A. Gunneweg's rather negative account, that Leviticus was used by Christians to show how corrupt Jews were (see Gunneweg 1988, 5, 21ff, 100ff, 126ff), or E. Otto's presumption against applying OT ethics to today's very different world (Otto 1994), Gerstenberger (2003, 363), as a historian fuelled by curiosity to get inside this world, takes the fulfillment of the Jubilee legislation as largely possible. North's monograph shows how the city-dwelling small farmers and the prevention of large farms are the focus of a chapter that does not really suit grand theories of macroeconomics (which was the cutting edge of the Jubilee 2000 campaign). The chapter calls for secured smallholdings so that the poor can help themselves rather than the cancelling of nations (North 2000, 125), a view echoed touchingly by Milgrom (2004, 311f).

Leviticus 26

Worship and Idolatry (vv. 1–2)

MOST OF THE TRADITION is quick to overlook these verses, which are seen as simply repetition of what is already familiar to readers of the Pentateuch. However, Hesychius teaches that "reverence my sanctuary" means hesitating to approach the sanctuary to receive the Eucharist and judging oneself, not least on sexual innocence, so one has a pure conscience as one partakes.

Brenz thinks the opening verses pertain to the first table of Decalogue about keeping true worship and avoiding idolatry. It does not say "do not erect these things," but rather "do not erect them *in order to worship them*." For if they are merely monuments of deeds—as we see Absalom made, or the twelve tribes in Joshua 22—they are allowed. Lorinus takes the detail here to encourage the outward expression of respect for the altar and hence for the church. Willet hears in these verses that churches are to be held in reverence, however he mocks the idea of revering buildings. Furthermore, one should be careful about giving asylum to those not penitent, as pointed out by Augustine in *On the Harmony of the Gospels* 1.c.12. Willet rages against idolatry: the Jesuit Douai Bible pretends that the prohibition is only of graven *idols* yet that very translation shows that Scripture uses these words interchangeably, despite Bellarmine. Any graphic representation is forbidden. We acknowledge that painting is a gift from God, as with Bezelal (Exod 38:22ff), but no images are for *religious* use! Also, we may adorn churches in decent beauty, but not like a strumpet!

Leclerc takes verse 1 to be not about fancy statues but bare stones, put together in some conical shape (cf. Gen 18:18). The LXX gets the idea with *lithon skopon* or "viewing stones." Such were set up in high places so the could be seen from afar. The Samaritan has *eben mtngdah*, which means they were sources of oracles. And the Egyptians used them, as Strabo tells us, building tumuli of twelve feet in diameter at side of road. Calmet admits that Joshua, Jacob, and Moses did erect monuments, but these were not at all *sacred* or *cultic*. It might be, as the LXX suggests, that a stone was put on the top of the column, or added to a pile of stones in honor of a deity like Mercury, or was painted. It is not what is described in Proverbs 26:8, where it is better to translate: "do not add a stone to a catapult sling." Such amassing among pagans from Indians to the Arabs is attested by Scaliger and maybe from there came the custom of peasants throwing stones at roadside crosses. One should never use the sanctuary as a shortcut; and one should leave it by retreating backwards. Patrick argues they were not so stupid to worship wood or stone, but only once consecrated and then they believed in the presence of their gods therein.

Blessings (vv. 4–13)

Origen speculates that since the rewards are non-corporeal (Eph 1:3) then neither can the punishments be physical. The first reward is rain in its season (v. 4). But surely, reasons Origen, rain falls on the good and bad alike (Matt 5:45) so the reward of rain here cannot be intended literally. Deuteronomy 32:1–2 gives us a clue to the meaning, and Moses himself speaks to that effect: our "earth," that is, our heart, if it frequently receives the rain of the teaching of the Law and has brought forth the fruit of labors then it receives blessings in its season. Also, the promise of blessing on crops cannot be literal, since when God blessed Isaac in Genesis 27:28 Pharaoh prospered just as much. Rather, it is to be understood in terms of the Parable of the Sower (Matt 13:3ff). As for the "trees" within us, these are justice, prudence, courage, and temperance. Above these are the paradisal trees of godliness, wisdom, discipline, and the knowledge of good and evil. And above all is the tree of life. The heavenly Father tends these trees in your soul and sets up plantations in your mind such that each of these trees is somehow a tree of life, for Solomon says in Proverbs 3:18 that wisdom is a tree of life.

Origen continues that animals themselves are neutral things but spiritual beasts (v. 6) are nihilistic spiritual forces (Eph 6:12), like thoughts that seduce us to give up on our faith. We will need to follow such commands to the point of fleeing from ourselves as well as from others who attack. Vice will fail if we have virtue. Spiritual success is guaranteed when believers fight wisely and surely in the words of God, when we expound the Law of the Lord with prudence. Just a few faithful teachers can scatter many demons. What is "new" (v. 10) is that the "new" evangelists have come and so have the apostles. We throw out what is old, from their point of view. We throw the "Law according to the letter" out, so that we might establish the "Law according to the Spirit." Putting off the old man to put on new one sounds to strike an even greater chord of discontinuity, but that seems to be what Origen intends. On verse 11 he asks: what is God's "soul"? Only Christ is God's soul. For just as the Word of God is Christ, and he is also the wisdom and power of God, so also he is the soul of God. "My soul," that is, my Son, "will not abominate you, but I will walk among you" (vv. 12–13). God promises to walk in the hearts of those who are pure.

Hesychius affirms that many Jews have fulfilled the commands of God, though they did not always understand the reason for God's suspension of good things. The best of them, like the prophets, obeyed yet ate the bread of want. For the fullness of reward is, for the Gospel, a goodness that looks beyond circumstances, a bread which lasts (John 6:27). He prefers the LXX reading in verse 4, "trees of the field," which means that even the base emotions of the body can be fruitful towards good. Death will not terrify (v. 6), owing to a peaceful hope in the resurrection. Those who live by the Law cannot be stood up to by bestial demons. God will "look to us," that is, avert death and he will "make fruitful" (v. 9) so as to gather all the commandments into one command of love. His new people will enjoy the old promises (made to the patriarchs) and in doing will make room for new promises. To walk among us (v. 12) means the incarnation by which he became the known God.

Augustine's focus is typically narrower. Although verse 11 seems to say so ("my soul"—*nepheshi*), God does not have a soul any more than he has eyes, etc., so we take these to mean the effects of his operations and powers (e.g., of vision). It is better to think of "soul" as "will" in the case of God. For God is not mutable like soul is but is spirit, without changeability (Jas 1:17). Now the Apollinarians, adds Augustine, (mistakenly) take this to favor their case that the Mediator did not have a human soul, as man, but was only Word and flesh, and his soul was somehow divine. Similarly verse 12 gets linked to 2 Corinthians 6:16 by Aphrahat (d. 345), and Philoxenus of Mabbug (d. 523) reminds his reader that the Word was not changed into flesh: the phrase here is "dwell with them," *not* "dwell in him"(see Brière 1960, 130).

The *Glossa*, on verse 9, adds: "His glance is salvation, for the Lord looked upon Peter who then wept bitterly. If the sun does not look upon the field it will remain unfruitful. God looks on the field of our heart and makes it grow great." For Ralph, the rain spoken of here (v. 3) is the "willing" one of Psalm 68:8, i.e., an outpouring of the Holy Spirit; without which nobody could keep any commands. The land on which it falls is the human mind, as it brings forth a seed (the Word of God) and conceives the will to act well. Maturity of harvest (v. 4f) comes when holy deliberation leads to the execution of the proposed action; while enjoying the fruits is our eventual dwelling in the heavenly city. Wicked beasts are the evil spirits removed form the hearts of believers by the grace of Christ, and although now cast out and unable to get back in, they come close and disturb the peace. The "sword that will not pass over your boundaries" is the divine warning that cuts off sinners (v. 6 and Job 19) and it chastises us in our worldly transitory fixations. It will cease when afterwards the Lord softens his anger towards us. We are to live without fear because we have fear of the Lord only. We acquire the merit of peace by fighting spiritual enemies. Whereas a few verses previously (v. 6) the "sword" meant God's disciplining us, here (v. 8) it means the Spirit, who is the word of God, which Jesus used against the devil. What is "old" is the lust, which makes a person old; most ancient is God's charity, which was the natural food of man before he fell. Now in grace we eat that again. Among those who do not have counsels and precepts a person is left to his own decision what to do or not, and in that case salvation is precarious.

Denys argues that, in fact, the righteous of the OT did not see much of this reward as was promised in Leviticus 26; so that perhaps the literal sense has to be *the promise of* the spiritual. However, the literal explanation could be salvaged if we think not in terms of any given individuals but rather the community. The "rains" here (v. 4) are the communications of the heavenly word, the infusion of grace, the dew of divine consolation, the irrigation of the Holy Spirit. And apple trees will abound, that is people willingly put virtues in action, as the Holy Spirit inspires them. Threshing after reaping (v. 5) is the virtuous exercise of the active life, which achieves its harvest—that is, reaching the actions of the contemplative life. For just as one enters a house by the door, so too through acts of moral virtues one reaches the contemplative life and its intellectual virtues. And you will eat your bread—that is, the body of the Savior in the sacrament—to sufficiency. But there is also a "super-substantial" bread which is tasted through contemplation. Where it has "sleep and nothing will frighten" (v. 26): those who are contemplatives in the Lord and frequently fall asleep in a mystic slumber, which the Lord gave Adam, resting from external things. The "sword" (v. 7) is the Word of God, which does not cross over our boundaries by going away and leaving us, but remains fixed and strong in the church. One eats the oldest grain (v. 10) to be refreshed, by considering and imitating one's fathers who were in the law of nature and Scripture and even the ceremonial laws of the OT (although, for Christians, the new counsels of the NT are to be embraced instead).

Brenz, commenting on the early verses of chapter 26, asks what it means to fulfill the Law so that we might understand to what the promises and blessings of the Law pertain. Well, the fulfilling of the Law is twofold. One is public or political, through the magistrate who is over the common. Of this civil fulfillment Josiah spoke before the Lord (2 Kgs 23). Such political fulfillment of the Law is not perfect in the sight of

Engaging Leviticus

God and it is not of such merit as to reach eternal happiness, no matter how much it pleases God, such that he rewards with many external rewards and blessings. The other kind is the private fulfillment of the Law and the discernment of this is great. Required is not an "Ahab-style" penance, which was hypocritical, but a spiritual one in which no part is violated but all is observed sincerely with full faith, holiness, and truth. Of course, Brenz adds that none except Jesus can do this. Another kind is the fulfillment of the Law by faith where a righteousness that is merited by Christ gets imputed. If anyone from this faith (since faith cannot be lazy) follows the divine calling and does good works as God commands, these (although imperfect) are accepted by God as fulfillment of the Law and we get the blessings Moses promised in these chapters, and hence Christians can gain what was promised to the Israelites. One can be sure that if observers of the Law get bodily curses in this world that there will be in turn heavenly rewards. One will have to take care lest it turn out, as in verse 9 or Isaiah 9:3, "you have multiplied the nation but you have not increased joy." For you will not always please the Lord in large numbers.

Large numbers (v. 9) are not necessarily a sign of blessing, agrees Pellican. In the covenant it is for God to provide as he did in not sparing his Son, and for us to be careful in worship, and to be forgiving and humble. Chytraeus speaks concerning these early verses of a distinction between (a) the promise proper to the gospel, which is free, and (b) the promises of the Law, which have a condition attached, that of fulfilling the Law. There is also a contrast between the promise of *material* benefits for Christians, which are conditional, and that of *eternal* goods, granted without exception because of Christ.

There are two things which keep the commonwealth secure, asserts Lorinus: the hope of reward and the fear of punishments. God wants us to understand eternal versions of the things promised here, for as Denys (with Hesychius) notes, punishment is not enough nor is reward what is fitting unless everlasting—one in hell, the other in heaven. God had to deal with the Hebrews like children, i.e., in terms of material things. Now, of course, a number of them knew the spiritual goods, but this Law of Moses did not by itself guarantee such. The observer of the Law was able to gain justifying grace towards the heavenly kingdom, but not by looking to the Law in itself without Christ, from whom all grace comes.

MacLaren takes the image of verse 10 to demand: "Accept cheerfully the law of constant change under which God's love has set us"; welcome the new as well as treasure the old. God changeth all things. "God hath more light yet to break forth from His holy word."

Curses (vv. 14–39)

Theodoret explains: "and you will be in the land of your enemy" (v. 39). For they were slaves in Babylon for seventy years, and from the time of Saul until the imprisonment for 490 years. This says that for seventy years the land will be unsown, since they will be living elsewhere. Hesychius criticizes those who pay less attention to the intention of the lawgiver than to the traditions of the elders, and miss the spirit of the Law among external details and when the gospel was announced made it seem extremely difficult (v. 15). It was not the case that the Jewish teachers taught wrong doctrines, more that their own interests made them reject Christ's words and dispersed God's covenant or took it into error. The punishment, continues Theodoret, will be a sevenfold one of full and total corruption; a hardening, with God wearing away that hardness by their trials among the nations, although Scripture will seem opaque (v. 19). The sword is the Word of God, which, in the tongues of the church's teachers, vindicates the covenant of the gospel and convicts those who can neither keep the Law nor welcome the gospel: but if one neglects the spiritual sword one will die from spiritual plague, far from the safety of truly holy people (vv. 23ff). Hesychius blames the Jews for being over-literal with the non-moral law, so as to distract from keeping the Decalogue (v. 26). He has a problem with the Sabbath commandment, which although inserted into the Decalogue is not of them: this must reflect accusations that Christians were breaking the moral law by not celebrating the Sabbath. Hesychius retorts that they understand the Sabbath "negatively" as simply an empty day ("vacation").

Hesychius sees the Jews as rightly punished by God through the Romans, as described by Josephus. What seems really to annoy him, to the point of an unambiguous declaration against the Jewish people, is that they misrepresented Christ and what he stood for. Their dispersion would be intellectual as well as physical, to the point where they can find nothing in common with the saints. The land of their enemies is interpreted as the New Testament and they will find it hard to live in Christian society. The *Gloss* will sum up Hesychius: The Jews have not understood the spiritual lesson of the laws and so these verses were literally fulfilled. He picks up the Pauline themes of emulation in Romans 10:19, echoing Deuteronomy 32:21.

Ralph, commenting on "vainly sow seed" (v. 16) in the light of the Parable of the Sower, writes: "When someone falls, it takes a while to lose the feeling of righteousness, and spurred by the word of another he tries to rise, yet enslaved as he is he cannot do it without God." Yet when one becomes used to sinning then gradually one neglects oneself and loses the feeling of pain. The seed cannot do its work but is devoured by enemies. There is no security without God, but with God turning his face against him the despiser comes to realize there is no hope except in the precepts. The metallic heavens (v. 19) are the Scriptures and the earth the human mind. When hardened sinners cannot get anything useful from preaching to convict them, when the prophets of the Law are read and the gospel recited and God's dew comes down on the earth and a lethal sleep comes over them, they become bestial, losing reason to the senses. What is this sword (v. 25), except the mild and seductive praise of empty words as it praises our perverse acts? David longed to be free from this "sword" when he prayed to God in Psalm 143: save me from "the sword" and those with empty talk. In other words, God will send in this lying spirit: they flee to the multitudes of the reprobate as they try to defend themselves. The pestilence (v. 25) means a general shared mutual consideration of evildoing; sickness comes from such bad examples and pretenses. Being afflicted in cities is worse and follows from being defeated in battle. Matthew 5 tells us we must settle with our adversary (the word of God) such that we turn from our sins while we are on the road, i.e., while still alive. On "ten women with one pan" (v. 26), Ralph comments that even the Jews do not accept the literal sense here: why would a besieged city be short of pans, after all? It means, mystically, the doctors of the Law falling out as they try to understand literally, or the Pharisees of which Jesus spoke in Matthew 15. They never find satisfaction for hunger.

Lyra notes that cannibalism (v. 19) occurred at the siege of Samaria (2 Kgs 6) and also at the siege of Jerusalem by the Romans under Titus. God here threatens the withdrawal of his aid and dispersion among the nations. Judges 7 tells of people killed by their own in a rout, who fell even when nobody was following (v. 17). Denys repeats what Comestor noted: there are more warnings than there are promises, which perhaps shows that there is more sin around, or it is more complicated and its range included eating one's own children, which Lamentations 4 tells us happened in Israel's history. Willet adds to this theme: more terrors than rewards are announced, since the former have more effect on the wicked and stubborn. God is, however, most angry when he delays wrath as he allows people like the Amorites to continue in their sins.

For Cajetan, the "statutes" in verse 15—as distinct from "commandments"—mean the ceremonial ones, which do not have a reason except that God decreed them, such as "do not plant with two, different seeds." This is a clear definition of the Hebrew word *ḥuqqim* as meaning "arbitrary" ceremonial laws. Some think "the enemy land will consume you" refers to the ten tribes gathered by Shalmanzar, never to return from captivity and of all those Jews exiled from Judah; but Cajetan thinks not, for the Jews *did* return, as Ezra 6, Nehemiah, and Esther make clear.

The eating of sons (v. 29) writes Pellican, is the worst extreme. The wrath of God drove them to this through their minds being hardened, and since their "souls will be abominable," judgment carries on beyond death. Willet contends that Maldonatus (d. 1583) on Lamentations 2 accuses Calvinist women at the siege of Sancerre of doing just that. "But let him blame withal the salvage cruelty if his Catholicks who enforced them to do that."

Brenz notes that it is to be thought that there are the deserts of all curses and calamities where there is ungodliness and sin. For one it to reckon that curses come from ungodliness, not ungodliness from curses. Chytraeus more systematically classifies suffering in four principles: (1) the punishments of the ungodly who violate the Law; (2) the cross of the godly; (3) God is not bound to one way for settling matters; (4) God is not bound to respond immediately to our prayers.

For English Puritans, England's covenant with God was at least analogous to that which Israel had. One was John Preston who in the late 1620s preached to Charles I on verse 25's "sword which would avenge the quarrel of my covenant" with ominous language, also to be found in the rhetoric of Samuel Bachiler's *Miles Christianus* of 1629 (Vallance 2005, 35, 42). To "flee when none pursue you" (26:17) reminds the Puritan Willet of Cain, whose mark was "a continuall shaking and trembling of his body and a ghastly countenance." Even when cauterized such men are never insensible, even when in mirth. In 1631 Richard Turuin, a merchant of Tickhill, Yorkshire owed £70.9s3d to Edward Wright Alderman of London; he pretended he had paid via George Hadley, a dealer for the Alderman, but his conspirator buckled due to conscience and "he cryeth out that he saw the devil stand by him threatening to teare him in pieces."

Calmet writes that "you oppose or march against me, so I will march against you" (v. 28), refers back to verse 21 about walking in their set ways. He adds that verse 34 speaks of seventy years of exile to make up for those Sabbath years ignored during the four hundred and ninety years of the monarchy. Scripture here represents the earth as something animated and capable for feeling. He finds it curious that some rabbis give the sense of this verse—"each will corrupt their brothers"—to mean that each carries the punishment of brothers if he does not speak out against them. They will dry up in their iniquities (v. 39), either by the remorse of their consciences or in punishment of their ungodly deeds: "iniquities" can include their own punishment.

Willet relates that Lorinus says on verse 30 that these idols (*ḥammim*) were "certaine faire buildings, or galleries to walke in, for pleasure in the Sun-shine; which are threatened to be demolished and throwne downe." Whereas in the Bible translations of Munster and Vatable they are called *solaria*, Tostatus is probably right to think they were images for worship of the sun, set high above altars. Grotius sees the origins of idolatry in sun worship. So fire was allowed to the Jews at first in gratitude for the sun, but later abuse led to it being banned. Against this Calov argued that it was not the case that sun worship was ever permitted, or that it all began soundly enough: but we know, as Strabo and Scaliger tell us, that *ḥammim* is the same as the Egyptian god Ammon, and fire was worshipped as divine.

Luther had written in more than on place of the Law serving "to make guilty those who are smug and at peace, so that they may see that they are in danger of sin, wrath, and death, so that they may be terrified and despairing, blanching, and quaking at the rustling of a leaf" (v. 6; e.g., *Lectures on Galatians*, 1535; LW 26:148). So later in his career verse 36's "the sound of a leaf shall terrify them" became a stock figure to depict the terrified conscience (Pauck 1961, xli). Likewise Patrick comments: "And so they are noted at this day to be mean-spirited and faint-hearted: it scarce ever heard that a Jew listed himself for a soldier, or engaged in the defence of his Country where he lives." Patrick observes more examples from other histories of such calamities (v. 22): "one Monument of which continues still in the Church. For the Solemn prayers in Rogation Week were first instituted (as Sidonius relates) by Mamertus Bishop of Vienne in France, for this reason among others, that wolves and other wild beasts did very great mischief in those parts."

Matthew Henry sums up these verses as to do with breaking the covenant. Although every breach of the commandment does not amount to a breach of the covenant (we would be undone if it did), yet, when men have come to such a pitch of impiety as to despise and abhor the commandment, the next step will be to disown God, and all relation to him. Keil, on verse 16, comments that the Goths called this fever *brinno*, from the word "to burn," and *heito* ("heat") and this refers to the droughts that happened in the Judges period and in, for instance, 1 Kings 17:1, when it was very common in Palestine. War is even worse when it is between allies that have fallen out, when revenge makes it sharper. And the plague has a way of getting in behind walls. Knobel seems insistent that the Sabbath years were not kept, in line with 2 Chronicles 36:21.

Restoration (vv. 40–45)

For Theodoret, God gives the reason in verses 42–45 as to why he shows so much philanthropy: "for through the promises to fathers I will forgive their transgressions and all nations will acknowledge through amazing wonders, for I will care for them differently and they will be called my people." For in the first place it mentions Jacob, for he was ancestor to them alone, unlike Abraham and Isaac. Hesychius traces the theme of salvation history to the end of the chapter. He likes the LXX reading of verse 41 "*eudokésousin*" ("find pardon") through the punishment they have carried for their sins, rather than prayer being the means, which is what Hosea 4:8 means by "they consume the sins of my people": that is to suffer the right amount for their own sins and then confess them, even what they did to Christ. In verse 42 Jacob gets first mention because he is closest to the Gospel in order. A remnant of Jews will be saved (v. 44), as Paul tells us, concurring with Moses. And as it says in verse 46, the OT laws are to be carried into the evangelical grace in order to inculcate wisdom and right behavior, and the Jews too will then be able to interpret and use these laws in a better way.

Ralph takes the rest of chapter to be as prophesy of Jewish history from the exile onwards. Due to the patriarchs God will remember his covenant: and, like Cain after murdering Abel, the Jews will be given some guarantee of life. For the church, speaking in the Psalms, says that she will not kill them, lest the memory of the former people be lost (Ps 59:11). The Lord promises a memory of them also in Daniel 10. Yet if we turn to the last captivity of the Jews, then the land which is deserted by them is actually the church which although founded in the root of that olive tree, whose branches the Jews were, yet they have been broken off from the tree to make room. This is the earth that opened its mouth and confessed and received the blood of the brother, one who spoke more eloquently than Abel (Heb 11:4). This earth rejoices in its multitude but grieves that it does not have its fellows in faith and what remains after they were ejected by their exacting sins. The Lord will remember this land when he will take up their prayers and will admit that unbelieving people to the grace of faith to the paternal land of their origin (*tanquam ad paternum solum*). Their partial merits will help, and the land (i.e., the prayers of the holy church) will help them but they will also pray from themselves, as soon as they have recognized their sin.

Brenz sees the conclusion of the chapter as having been fulfilled in return from exile in Babylon, and so is not going to be fulfilled for them again. Manasseh serves as a case of a penitent king whose sufferings got his kingdom restored (2 Chr 33). Where the Vulgate has "pray for their acts of ungodliness" (v. 43) the Hebrew has *yirzueth avonîm*. As some translate: they will bring a punishment of their wrongdoing. Often the crime and the punishment are called the same thing in Scripture. Others translate: they will expiate their wicked deeds, as in Isaiah 22 with the term *raza*. The parts of penitence are described: the first part is shame and confession. Then faith must be produced from the promise, which was spoken to Abraham. It is as with captives praying towards the temple and remembering the promises at the time of Solomon's dedication of it. The penitent must not think that it is his prayers or works that please God, but must rather believe that he has a propitious God because of Jesus Christ. True penance acts to please God by the merits of Christ as faith embraces them.

Pellican reckons that "*until* they confess their iniquities" (v. 40) carries no implication of things necessarily improving. Then they will do penance uselessly by confessing the sins of their fathers but will not be heard. When their works were clearly given to evil, although they were warned yet so often they persevered and were hardened and persevered that way until the end. On verse 42 he is precise about the fate of the Jews. There is a denial of any proto-Christian Zionist thinking. The "remembrance of covenant" is that point when God is mindful to expel the Jews and then follow up with the gospel. It is hopeless for the Jews as a people, although verse 44 has hope for those individual faithful among them to be kept for God's glory. There is no hope that they will return to Canaan, for the place of his glory will be eternal. In this covenant the most glorious Jerusalem will have "Rome and the Patriarchates" as its suburbs. For if the throne and crown are in Jerusalem, then the whole earth is that Jerusalem, and for those Jews who recognize this there will be no more misery. But those who do not receive it and who cling to temporal glory, they will, as in a lasting tiring sickness, most unhappily dream that Jerusalem the Golden will be in Palestine, which they will never see.

On verse 42 and "covenant" Willet reckons that Jacob gets mentioned first because he received blessing given to Abraham and also that given to his own family. Tostatus thinks there is no precedence meant, but Lorinus here "falleth foul upon his great master, saying, that he cannot think anything in Scripture is spoken casually, or by chance but that 'every iod or tittle hath its virtue.'" Lorinus thinks it is because Israel is named after Jacob. Theodoret and Denys were right to say that the sequence is by way of ascent. Though one could argue that Jacob had the clearest revelation of the gospel of all of them.

For Cocceius, in stark contrast to Pellican, God expelled the Jews from the land so they would take time to pay close attention to their sins. God does not want to alienate them from the inheritance. If therefore their uncircumcised hard hearts will be humbled, and they subject themselves to the righteousness of God and the preaching of the gospel, they will be snatched away from their own wickedness and will lay down their conscience of sinning, and the threats to exile them will no longer apply, for they will not be in the land of nations but in their own fatherland.

Patrick refers God remembering the covenant in verse 42 to the restoration of Ezra 1. He finds the following verse (v. 43, "the Land also shall be left of them [again] and shall enjoy her Sabbaths") to be very obscure unless we take it to speak of a new expulsion out of their Land. These last verses must be referring to recent history up to the present day and in line with verse 44 as we see today they are not destroyed utterly, "as if their misery were almost expired and their day of redemption drawing nigh." However in order to qualify for redemption, insists Patrick, they must confess sin of fathers not least in crucifying Christ.

Leclerc translates verse 40: "They will *expiate* their sin." Even though *ratsah* means "test," here "expiate" is clearly meant. But this sin cannot be dealt with by sacrifice; however God's peace can be sought by confession and begging for divine mercy and a change of ways. He adds that verse 43 places an emphasis through repetition. The legislator saw what would happen to people who denied divine providence, like those Philistines in 1 Samuel 6:9 who, struck by plague, blamed Israel for spreading it. Keil observes in marginal notes on verse 43, in the spirit of Luther: "Pleasure, i.e., just as they had pleasure in their sins and felt disgust at my laws, so they would now take pleasure in their punishment and say 'We have just what we deserve.' This pleases God, so that He becomes gracious once more."

Walk in My Precepts (v. 3) / I Will Walk among You (v. 12)

The archbishop of St. Andrews, John Hamilton's *Catechism* (1552: chapter 3) asserts that God promises temporal prosperity to the people who keep his commandments, and Christ confirms this by saying that all things will be added to those who seek first the kingdom of God; but also that the disobedient people will be punished first with worldly loss, then spiritual judgment. Not quite a century later (in the 1620s) William Struther in his *Scotland's Warning* (1628) was to observe that the warning had not been heeded: "Doubtless this tyme of the reformed Churches, is the tyme of punishment, we have had long Prosperitie, the cleare light of the Gospel, and offer of Salvation, but have abused it, and now God is revenging on us the quarrell of his Covenant" (quoted in Mullan 1998, 198).

In the additional comments made to Lyra's *Postilla* on chapter 26 much is made that the verse "I will walk among you and will be your God" (26:12) is to be taken in a positive sense (not about God's visitation to judge) as a prediction of the incarnation. Christ was recognized as the Messiah by the Hebrew boys on Palm Sunday (Matt 21). 1956 in Basel saw Karl Barth (Barth 2003, 56–60) expounding: "Just as the milkman, postman or meter inspector goes up and down our streets among our houses so too God already strolls around in our midst (*wandelt*), even if he is at the edge of 'our spirituality,' saying: 'Yes, I want to be your God.'" Of course, a covenant works both ways and includes the sense of the vassals or "junior partners" allowing the Sovereign to work his will through them. Covenant ideology was no softening of the doctrine of predetermining grace in Reformed Christians, *pace* Perry Miller (Miller 1956).

Leviticus 27

The Value of Vows for Humans (vv. 2–8)

LEVITICUS 27 IS NOT clear on whether the vow is to thank for past help or to secure present help. There was a reaction in Judaism to the idea of humans being able to bind God and possibly the LXX translation of *ndr* by *euche* evidences this. For all that Jesus denounced *abuses* of vowing (Mark 7:9–13) he did not reject vows, nor did Paul with his Nazirite vow (Acts 18:18) and his counsel on celibacy. Cyprian in his *Testimonies* 3.30 seems to have re-employed Old Testament language, but only from Psalm 76:12.

Early church material on vows and Leviticus 27 is scarce. One has to look at Origen's *Homily* 24 on Numbers 30 (*Sources Chrétiennes* 29, 405): "if we offer our justice we will receive God's in return; our chastity, then the chastity of the Spirit which excludes spiritual fornication; our thought, then the thoughts of Christ." The content of the vow as sacrifice receives most attention. A higher good is chosen that excludes a morally permissible good by renouncing it. What is noticeable in the Christian history of the idea is that vows concerned the dedication of *oneself*. Augustine, in *City of God* 17.4, lay the accent on divine grace, maintaining that Hannah who vowed (1 Sam 1:11) was too weak to have fulfilled it. Yet a monastic vow once taken *has* to be kept even when found to be hard (Augustine, *Epistle* 127.8 in Lohse 1963, 82).

The monetary equivalents for human beings to be vowed (vv. 3–8) and for the redeeming of unclean animals and other property already indicates a readiness to be flexible, and illustrates that already in this law there is a humane tendency. An exception to this non-literal and non-monetary concept of the vow appears in the *Canones Hibernienses* (Bieler 1963, 166) where verse 28 is quoted to forbid offering something a second time as a tithe, except for the same bit of ground, which can be offered each year since it will have new produce on it.

Hesychius is more interested in the moral than the specifically religious interpretation. Concerning an unclean animal (v. 11) he writes: it is one thing to be sanctified, another to be holy; one thing to offer to God, another thing to be of God. What then is offered and sanctified begins to be holy, which it was not before and gradually becomes. But what is holy of God does not need to grow since it is perfect. For it is good to be sanctified by the teaching and help of another but better it is to be able to sanctify others and this is the property of only a few. In the ritualized atmosphere there was a strong sense of consecration making the person (or their service) holy *in himself* (or *itself*) (Iogna-Prat 2006, 262). The Benedictine Rule did not speak of "vow" but "promise"; yet the idea of vow comes to express what the inner calling is (Frank 1984, 307). The *Glossa* added to Gratian's *Decretum* the key principle: "To make a vow is a matter of the will; to fulfill one is a matter of necessity" (Helmholz 1996, 233). So it is fine to swear an oath as long as not in vain (Exod 20:7). In the Decretal of Gregory IX (1230) (C22, q1, c13), Augustine is employed: oaths "come from evil but are not evil per se." One should be careful and not rash. David did not fulfill his oath to kill Nabal, but otherwise one should fulfil oaths even when inconvenient (C22, q4,c23; cf. Josh 9:15–20).

And yet papal power would come to be seen as the means of dispensation to escape from religious vows. Yet ideally, since Bernard of Clairvaux (d. 1153), the vow is a second baptism since the first one has faded. Hence by the High Middle Ages the vow was being more associated with penance. A synthesis of both is found in Aquinas' conception of vow as an active road to perfection (Lohse 1963, 159): in any case, the goal is God's honor (*ST* IIaIIae q.38, art 5). It is an intensification of life understood as penance, setting out towards a goal not a receiving of a change in state (Frank 1984, 308). Franciscans would argue that a vow removed guilt as well as punishment.

Ralph encourages his monks. God delights in the death of his sons when they have given of themselves against their enemies. Literal martyrdom is exceptional. The obedience of Abraham, not the death of Isaac as such is what God wanted. God does not demand what we cannot give.

Not all will receive this word of monastic renunciation, but some, when told "go and sell all you have," go away sad. Yet "the field" is to by bought by spiritual exercises so that we possess our souls in eternity and we are to consider what measure of precepts our souls are sustaining. The cases of Samuel and Samson illustrate vows lasting until death. Mystically, one can be redeemed when there is congruent satisfaction for a vow. Priests sell holy things when they accept temporal reward, and go easy on the souls of those people whom the devil then devours. All that is consecrated to God must thoroughly die, which—through the filter of Galatians

5:24—speak of mortification. Nobody knows the hour of death, so our "one-fifth" is a prepared disposition of one's life to God's mercy. Whoever faces death with a good mind converts his necessity into a reward. One cannot choose one's death but it is in God's hands whether it will be hard or soft. One should not be terrified so much as to become changeable. Jesus was so tempted but said "your will be done."

Bruno is quick to quote Psalm 75:12 ("return your vows to the Lord") and relates that penance for not keeping a vow will change according to sex, age, and situation to be determined by the "priest," just as in verses 2–8. A woman will give less because she is weaker, although the redemption gains her just as much. Priests in judging these cases will use their discretion and part of this is perhaps employing these basic principles. The Savior was baptised to sanctify the waters and the baptismal foundation of penance leads one back to Christ's work. There is an allusion to Jesus being sold for thirty shekels with the idea that his soul is what redeems, although a variety of penances are still required.

The canon law gathered in Gratian's *Decretum* (c. 1200) makes much of Chrysosotom in his *Homily* 40 on Matthew: "Whenever one sees a cleric suddenly doing penance and humbles himself he [i.e., the one seeing] should not grieve since he has sinned but be confounded that he has lost his glory." The *Decretum* then comments: "The daughter in the Matthew 9 story is the secret sin which the parents have confessed in the presence of apostles. In Leviticus we are taught that whoever offers the house of his conscience or the field of his lifestyle to God through penance and wishes to redeem his life from vain living through good works he cannot do that unless he brings the sanctuary shekel that is works of penance and the amount should differ according to the size of sin, as to whether penance is short or long and that is for the priest to judge, with full remission in the Jubilee only" (*Decretum* II, Causa XXXIII Q III; *De penitentia* Dist I, c87). According to Gratian, Hesychius is wrong to think that immediately after the penance has been decreed someone is fully healed from sin.

Denys regards the legal vows to be an imperfect type of vows which are now perfected in the church, especially when Christians promise to enter a monastery (of either sex), or rather take solemn vows beyond the novitiate and commit themselves by a vow to the three matters (poverty, chastity, and obedience) with all religion, like offering a tree with its fruit to God. The vow is an act of virtue that excels others and can be viewed as worship. Just as in the OT some vows could be redeemed, so too in the church some vows are dispensable while others are not. As for how to absolve them, well, by "forty shekels" we should understand exercitations of virtue with a special peacefulness and abundant grace of the Holy Spirit; by "thirty" it means conjugal continence or simply keeping the Ten Commandments. Women are not so suited to contemplation, except by a special grace. Just as one is not to redeem a "clean animal" (v. 9) so too one cannot get someone else to say your offices, while by "impure animal" is meant any bad deed under appearance of good one, and a "first born" is a perfect disciple in intimate union with God and requiring no further human sanctification. Some say that the Lord Pope cannot dispense a solemn vow of continence, which Albert also affirms. So too Thomas in *Summa Theologiae* (IIaIIae q88); but in his *Commentary on the Sentences* IV he says the opposite. Reference is made to the story of the Evangelist Matthew's niece remaining true to a vow of virginity rather than marry the Ethiopian king, even though he promised to become a Christian. Thomas teaches (*ST* IIaIIae q189, a2) that good works done under a vow are more meritorious, since a vow is act of worship.

Cajetan on verse 6 makes the nice comment that in giving of the firstborn, the idea is that the whole family gets lifted up to God with the firstborn, and is thus sanctified. He is still operating in a medieval world, but his Reforming contemporaries would make vowing seem more problematic. Luther was released from a vow taken while fearing for his life in a thunderstorm some fifteen years earlier, although there are grounds in Gratian (*Causa* 17) for concluding that a vow taken in such circumstances to be valid but not fully obligatory (Helmholz 1996, 231f). Melanchthon in his *Augsburg Confession* (1530) 27.20 attacked the idea that a monastic vow was a "second baptism." Also the notion that performance of a vow achieves pardon besmirches the gospel, in his opinion. Luther, maintains Melanchthon, was not the first to call for reform here. The vow in the OT was an outward form of religion that then suited the apostolic life, but is not the concern of the NT for other Christians (1 Tim 5) and today is neutral (adiaphoric). Lutherans rejected the medieval "evangelical counsels"—which were extensions or intensifications of the baptismal promise—as superfluous, since the good should be kept without them, and freedom became bondage (see Lohse 1963, 370). Yet Calvin had some place for these where there was willingness and an awareness of grace. His *Institutes* (IV, 13) speaks of three considerations: to whom is the vow sworn, knowing one's limits, and right intention—e.g., to thank, to escape punishment, to avoid temptation. In all this there is no mention of Leviticus 27, which makes Calvin's exegetical work on this chapter all the more interesting (see below).

Pellikan, on verse 6, argues that he who receives much from the Lord is much obligated to him. The reason as to why the Lord deals with each differently is to be humbly accepted. Brenz attacks the Roman Catholic "hypocrites" for using these texts to promote the idea that vows can only be redeemed at a heavy price. For such Levitical laws are now abrogated, so the pope has no such right to demand vows, and there are duties of charity which we should simply attend to. These vows have no place in Christianity. We should not be making up new duties but getting on with what God has commanded. The papal theologians teach that auricular confession is necessary from this chapter and humanly invent the length of time for penance when all it needs is an instant of true repentance and faith in Christ, and from that point onwards to do the works that God commands. The task of the priest today is about administering gospel forgiveness to those who confess, and not to say that all sins must be spat out if they are to be saved, and not to be scrutinizing for hidden sins.

Lorinus comments on verses 1–9: no one will receive grace in return for anything they offer, unless they also offer themselves. There is another reason for vows according to the *New* Testament: a vow of a holy order transfers a person to God wholly and in a fixed manner unless there is a dispensation (which requires a serious cause), whereas in the OT redeeming the vow is more ordinary. Abulensia is a safe guide on this. A human soul cannot be given a value; but a selling of the self was possible as in Leviticus 25. And God was content to allow that a certain price be paid instead of the death that he who vows himself like a sacrificial animal should have suffered.

The Puritan Willet insists that a purpose to do a thing is not sufficient to make a vow, which is a "kinde of Contract betwixt God and man, obliedging a man to the performance of something." The religious vow is something strictly interior, "a private Law, done out of a religious affection towards God," and dependent upon God's grace to attain fulfillment. In the London-held discussions surrounding the *National League and Covenant* (1643) it was realized that while an oath was made with men before God, with a covenant it was the other way around, with God before humans (Vallance 2005, 84). The term "vow" was dropped for the term "covenant," yet the oath was reinforced as this commitment had public implications. Such covenanting can be seen as analogous to a vow to enter a religious order, including the idea that obedience to God trumped any other political affiliation.

Redeeming Animals and Things (vv. 9–24)

Hesychius holds that the instruction for redeeming a house (v. 14) once consecrated to the Lord is clearly about that baptism and penance, having added to it "supererogatory" works of a holy person, which can make up the shortfall of righteousness.

Bruno writes that to vow one's house can also have a spiritual meaning, where one has to give oneself over to God in baptism and faith and the priest will tell one what to do to get the house back. This legislation that allows redeeming oneself helps to stop greedy priests fixing any price they like for freeing from a vow. The offering of a clean animal (v. 9) equals a work free from all malice that must be carried out. However, there might be vows that are impure and are not to be carried out; instead the priest will ask the one who vows to pay with penance. The "fifth part" in verse 19 represents one's own understanding. For we are first governed by the priest's teaching and instruction but later we progress and we ought to add our understanding, while the proper priest, after verse 23, is he who leads his brother to penance. Ralph takes the extra fifth (vv. 13, 15, 19) to be a type of confession, when we bring what is hidden in us up to surface and acknowledge this as well as the act we are confessing, which the animal represents. Is it the case that property cannot be touched by Jubilee laws once vowed? Well, this Jubilee consideration brings the price down, yet with a fine, and is a sign of divine mercy, which is also austere. It is not contradictory to divine goodness to show toughness to people, along with a severe threat so that they will not fail again. Redemption consists not in penance alone, as in the case of the unclean offering and the vow of the house, but in the compensation of righteousness; in other words, through godly actions, not just the sacrament. We will be judged according to the measure of the Word of God.

Borrhaus holds that the new consecration in the new covenant does correspond to the legal consecrations in one way, that we who have been initiated in Christ through baptism are now freely consecrated to God. Baptized into death and resurrection through penance and walking in new life, the end of this consecration is a glorious transformation. As in the vows of the Law, those who had vowed to God, redeemed at a price, announced their thankful vow, so also in the Gospels holy people in Christ made a consecration to him of themselves. So in these external things there is a foreshadowing; but the truth has nothing to do with clothing, food, and times. Vows of such a sort are made today are not only not salvific but are also *blameworthy*.

Calvin states the general principle about redeeming a vow. God permitted that what was promised might be redeemed at a certain price, in order that their offerings might be voluntary. "By the imposition of this ransom, which was of the nature of a fine, rashness was punished, and future inconsideration prevented, so that they might consider well what they were about before the made their vow, and that it might not be disagreeable to them to stand by their promises."

It would appear that Calvin saw religious use in the practice of vowing. However, on verse 14 he comments that God put up with much abuse while not liking the idea that one could "bargain with God," for he appreciated it could help people to do good things. In the heat of Reformation controversy Calvin is less generous than he was in the *Institutes*. There is an example from Gregory IX's *Decretals* III, 24 on pilgrimages and crusades, where the Suffragan bishop of Sens was allowed by Innocent III to put off the crusade now that Count of Champagne was dead, but to send money equal to the expenses of the undertaking. Calvin concludes by arguing that John 4:21 is a text against pilgrimages, and that "men act wickedly when they wrest to themselves what God has reserved for his own discretion." The priests of old followed fixed rules, and there was no license, as the Catholic Church gives itself, to make a profit.

Lorinus reports that some of his fellow Jesuits (e.g., Lessius) have questioned the text at verse 10. Yet this idea of commuting vows makes sense because God is more pleased with a better good. Oleaster, in the tradition of Suarez, warns that this is a *ceremonial* law and hence does not obligate but Thomas insists that this law can be used not because of any force of the Mosaic Law, but of the natural law (*ST* IIaIIae q88 a10ad1). And since the force of vows comes not from the vow itself but from the consecration one needs a priest to absolve, and not any ordinary one, since this is not just a case of penance; the authority of the church in the eternal court is needed to commute one's offering. In offerings of a thing, which are used like bread, something else can be given of like value, but in cases of religion the value of the other thing has to be greater. As for any dispensation of solemn vows this is difficult and this passage cannot be used for that, despite Hugh of St. Cher's opinion: it cannot apply when making a vow about a higher thing. Admittedly it is not the case that one *always* has to have the authority of a superior to commute or vary a penance, say when away on pilgrimage.

Calmet interprets to "offer the Lord a soul" as to offer an *animal*, so it can be human or non-human. If there is no redeeming then the persons will remain in the service of the temple, or the animals will be offered or sold. On verse 14 he mentions that the rabbis saw such sales as employed for the repair to the temple. Moses is saying nothing in verse 16 about the fertility of the land; it just means the measurement according to the span of a throwing of seed.

Willet, on verse 11–13, asks how something unclean can be accepted for a vow when not as a sacrifice? He approves of Calvin's explanation that it is the *price* of the unclean beast that is offered not the beast itself. Perpetual tithes do not include ceremonial ones; only votive ones out of pure devotion are perpetual, as per Aquinas (*ST* IIaIIae q87 art1).

To prevent the superstitious vow there is to be no liturgy for a vow and no saints should be invoked, "yet we confess, that to vow a thing commanded of God is *actus cultus divini*, an act of divine worship, and well pleasing unto God." Willet here shows the ongoing Puritan fascination with vows (see Hardman Moore 1991). The principle here is also to be found in Psalm 76:11: "return your vows to God." Yes, but persons must be at liberty, and the content of the vow must not be a sin, a worthless act, or an impossible work. God is no hard master (Matt 25:24). Willet likes Erasmus'

Engaging Leviticus

story of the Englishman on board a ship who vowed in a storm that for divine deliverance he would deliver "golden mountains" to Our Lady of Walsingham, or a waxen candle as big as himself to St. Christopher in Paris. When asked by a crewmate to confirm this, "he replyed softely (lest St. Christopher should hear him) 'Hold thye peace foole; doest thou thinke I ever meant to doe it. If ever I recover shoare, he gets not so much a tallow candle of me'" (Erasmus, *Colloquy on Shipwreck*).

Keil concludes that vows are no part of covenantal laws, but were added on at the end, almost a freely willed expression of piety in response to the instructions in previous chapters. Yet vows too needed regulated. So, for instance, on verses 16–25: "The reason for selling the field at the time when he had vowed it to the sanctuary, need not be sought for in caprice and dishonesty, as it is by Knobel. The field was vowed in this sense, that it was not handed over to the sanctuary (the priesthood) to be cultivated, but remained in the hands of the proprietor, so that every year he paid to the sanctuary simply the valuation price."

The Ban

On this chapter Lyra gives by far the most space to the tricky question of verse 29, where a human being cannot be bought back but has to be killed. The ban (*ḥerem*) can mean either "sanctification" or "destruction," depending on the context, e.g., the *ḥerem* (destruction) for God's glory when Jericho deserved it for its sins. The goods captured in a city are *ḥerem* in the other sense (set apart for God) and cannot be used for anything else. Yet this verse gives him problems: a person surely *should* not be killed, and a field *cannot* be. For a Hebrew such dedication can mean ministry in the temple. This did not apply to Gentiles, although those from other tribes, such as Samson and Jepthah, could be permitted (in certain conditions), and a Gentile maidservant could be allowed to bring wood and water to the temple, like the Gibeonites in Joshua 9. The second sense of *ḥerem* is destructive, as when Saul was criticized by the Lord for sparing the Amalekite fatted animals out of greed (1 Sam 15). So it could be that what is meant is that there will be no redemption of one guilty of bloodshed. What it might mean for us now is metaphorical: that one consecrated to Levite-style service is "dead" to divine service, just as a city can be said to be " killed" when no rebuilding is possible.

Cajetan remarks that the ban or *anathema* does not mean "destruction," as in Joshua, but that the field would be thoroughly God's and would be "banned" in the sense of not being for sale but belonging to the priests by everlasting right. However, a sold field cannot be this but will come back to him under the law of Jubilee. Even according to the literal sense, a ban does not mean *literal* destruction: Jephthah's daughter might have involved a real destruction, but the law here is to vow someone or something "in the mode of destruction." In her case the vow was not licit, since it is licit to vow the destruction only of an enemy of God's people (evildoer or blasphemer). There are some who say that Jephthah's daughter was not killed as an offering. This is because she did not say she mourned her life but only her virginity, and that the worst thing that happened that she was secluded from the world of men and was only allowed out for four days a year. Drawing on the Hebraist Sebastian Munster (d. 1552) and logic, he mentions those who say that Jephthah had vowed distinctively, namely, "*What* (not whom) I meet first from my household will belong to the Lord and I will offer it."

Calov relates that Junius, swayed by the LXX on verse 29, tries to get round the problem by translating this as being about consecrations by men, presumably of animals. But there is no mention of animals in the verse, which clearly means consecrations *of* men, which must be fulfilled through their death. Some like Cappel think this means that God was allowing human offerings, as he would with Jephthah and Christ. Calov reckons it is best to see it as a function that would be taken over by civil magistrates and is really talking about deserving *criminals*. Leclerc notes that some rabbis thought that those condemned to death for a crime could be redeemed, yet this verse treats only *enemies*, such as those in city of Hormah (cf. Num 21:2f), but not so as to allow innocent *Hebrews* to be traded over to death for the glory of God.

On verse 26, one cannot vow (sanctify) the first born, insists Calmet, since they already belong to the Lord (Exod 13:2), but that would seem to apply to animals only, since for children like Samuel there was an offering. He argues that verse 28 in Hebrew means something different from the Vulgate, with the sense of someone "anathematizing" something to the Lord such that it cannot be sold. It meant having power over family/household, remarks Calmet. Voltaire was offended by the idea that all that was offered could not be redeemed. It seems to him pretty clear in the cases of Jepthah and Achan that children did die under the ban—the Bible is just like that. For Knobel there was no doubt, from the temple terminology used, that the Elohist wrote this last chapter. Prisoners were often dedicated to holy temple service; and could be redeemed. But verse 28 shows that humans could be offered in the cases of captives. It was hard to get out of these vows, yet usually one could; only in cases where people had been idolatrous or resisted (Jos 6:17; 1 Sam 15:3) was it harder. Jephthah was the only case where this "ban" was not on God's enemies; we hear of such things in Caesar *Gallic Wars* (6.17). The only reported time that this law ever worked in Israel was under Hiskia (2 Chr 31:5ff).

Dillmann argues that the ban was common in the ancient Near East and was a way of dealing with whatever was of itself offensive to God (as per Deut 7:25

[Dillmann likes to be led by Deuteronomy]). Here it is more than merely that which was meant by Micah 4:13 but was a consecrated destruction for the sake of honoring or placating God (cf. Deut 13:17; 1 Sam 15:33). The case of Jephthah's daughter is better understood as an offering and not a ban like here, which is meant to be of enemies only, and done publicly, not by individuals.

Tithes

What also mattered was that all that had been said about the cult required the maintenance of the priesthood: in the medieval church tithes were held to be due as by divine right, not just positive law of the church on grounds of necessity (Helmholz 2004, 436). Vicars took the small personal tithes, i.e., the profit made from the produce of the land, even though there was usually a landowner (often ecclesiastical) between the priest and the One with ultimate dominion. Perhaps for this reason in medieval Christian practice vows did not serve the same function of monetary upkeep, but were a way of ensuring serious commitment to the numbers of Christian "Levites."

Brenz, like other Reformers, thought that vows should decrease and tithes increase. What we are called to offer up as tithes is spiritual and we tithe with the authority of public consensus for the upkeep of the legitimate ministry. This means the amount demanded can be varied according to need. Paul said about food: no one may judge you in tenths and twelfths; yet the papists are greedy and want to be the pig-herds of Epicurus, not the flock of the Lord. There was clearly a present danger for not paying taxes to church during the precarious times of the interim of 1547–52 when Protestant freedom to worship was in great danger.

Borrhaus insists that the idea of tithes goes back to Abraham, but is found also in the profane stories of Hercules. The aim of tithes was to keep God's goodness in mind, that he gave the earth; and that was what Abraham was doing in giving to Melchizedek when he received blessing from the greater (Gen 14:17–24). The other reason they tithed was for the maintenance of sacral order, and thirdly, for the shadowing of the spiritual tithes. A tenth, of course, denotes perfection, that God is also the end as well as the beginning of life, so that we know to refer all things to his glory, whether gifts of the body (beauty), external benefits, or spiritual gifts. It keeps one humble unlike Pharaoh or those kings who like to extort tithes from others not in order to serve God better. Tithes are not to be kept on the basis of abrogated Mosaic law, as our opponents wish, but as of ancient custom for the care of civil functions and for the maintenance of the lawful functions of the church, such as the ministry of the word and the teachers of scholars, and for the sustenance of widows and orphans. No fixed amount is set in the NT for ministers but, although we cannot use the ceremonial law, we can use what Paul says about civil powers. So although the principle is no longer valid on the grounds of the *ceremonial* law, on the grounds of *the law of the nations* it is still in force and tithes should be paid, just as to kings.

Verse 30 tells us, thinks Pellican, that God is to be thanked by all and all tithes are thus to be turned to pious use. People should be reminded that both divine command and natural law require payment for his good pleasure. If today tenths do not suffice, the ministers should have ninths or eighths, for the law of charity and the very best and irreproachable ordaining of God demand it. For love is stronger in the gospel than law, just as love is greater than fear.

Willet remarks that ministers of the gospel should have at least a tenth. Since they are more glorious than Levites a tithe should be a minimum (cf. Gal 6:6). Tithes in these days of the gospel (*o tempora! o mores!*) are getting changed such that "Haire is given in place of wool or glass for diamonds." This was a trend that began under popery, he claims. Tithes are entailed upon ministers (see Num 18:21) and cannot be cut off by the pope or King Henry. Willet ends with an uncharacteristic approval of his Jesuit adversary: "It is a good admonition which is given by Lorinus: Let those lay-men take heed, who have a graunt of tithes, upon this condition, that hereafter they must make restitution. For if clergy are barely maintained with a poor endowment, then the scholar will lack books and the people will go famished spiritually."

Calov views tithes as for the ministry's maintenance and showing gratitude for remembered benefits. In his annotations Leclerc seems to agree to a large part with Selden (*The History of Tithes*, 1619) regarding Abraham's giving tithes to Melchizedek, but tithes did not begin with a revelation to Abraham, but were part of the religious sense of humankind which he had observed among the Canaanites. If Jesus is to have come from a good tradition going back to Adam, then those people between Adam and Abraham must have been religious. In matters that were neutral (adiaphoric) then there was no reason why Israel should not have copied its neighbors.

Coda (27:34)

For Knobel, the commands are negative, specific, and simple to remember, but not constructively inducive to joyful piety. That negativity is typical of the Law given at Sinai. Contrast this with the pre-modern Calov, who takes it that these are the precepts for carrying out the divine cult, by which the propitiating sacrifice of Christ was graphically depicted and our Eucharistic offerings foreshadowed, that with due thanksgiving we would show ourselves grateful to God for his immense blessing by the preaching of the gospel, sincere godly living, patience, and help to neighbors. Contrast this further with the fact that the mention of Mount Sinai leads Lorinus to long to escape from the red thorny life, which "Sinai" indicates, to the holy mountain of lection and purity, on Mount Tabor where we will live forever in eternal tents.

It has to be said that there is something about the technicality of this closing chapter that makes one think that these laws were intended for practice and not some literary-theological fiction or some pious fraud. Schwartz (2004, 277) gives a simple but convincing account of the placement of chapter 27 at the end of the book, i.e, on the grounds that this last chapter presupposes the legislation of chapter 25, but that theologically speaking there is a "thematic unity" between chapters 25 and 26. More than this, chapter 27 suggests that the due response to judgment, exile, and the offer of deliverance is renewed dedication in joyous service.

Bibliography

Non-Commentary Primary Literature:

Adamnan. 1958. *De Locis Sanctis*. Edited by Denis Meehan. Dublin: Dublin Institute for Advanced Studies, School of Celtic Studies.

Arnauld, A. 1674. *De frequenti communione liber*. Paris: Pierre le Petit.

Bachmann, Ingeborg. 1983. *Sämtliche Gedichte*. München: Piper.

Biblia Latina cum Glossa ordinaria. 1992. Edited by M. T. Gibson and K. Froehlich. Turnhout, Belgium: Brepols.

Bischoff, B. and M. Lapidge, eds. 1994. *Biblical Commentaries from the Canterbury School*. Cambridge: Cambridge University Press.

Brenz, Johannes. 1970. *Werke; eine Studienausgabe im Auftrag des Vereins für württembergische Kirchengeschichte*. Edited by Martin Brecht and Gerhard Schäfer. Tübingen: Mohr.

Bucer, Martin. 2004. *Schriften zu Ehe und Eherecht: Deutsche Schriften*. Book X. Edited by Stephen E. Buckwalter, Hans Schulz, and Thomas Wilhelmi. Gütersloh: Mohn.

Calvin, Jean. 1863–1900. *Ioannis Calvini Opera quae supersunt omnia*. Vol XXIV. Brunsvigae: Schwetschke. (= CO)

Cornwallis, Mrs. 1820. *Observations, Critical, Explanatory and Practical on the Canonical Scriptures*. London: Baldwin, Cradock & Joy.

Ephraim. 2001. *Armenian Commentaries on Exodus-Deuteronomy Attributed to Ephrem the Syrian*. 2 vols. Corpus Scriptorum Christianorum Orientalium, 587–588: Scriptores Armeniaci, 25–26. Louvain: Peeters.

Eusebius of Emesa. 1957. *Eusèbe d'Émèse, Discours conservés en latin*. SSL 26–27. Edited by É. M. Buytaert. Louvain.

Grosseteste, Robert. 1987. *De Decem Mandatis*. Edited by R. Dales and E. B. King. London: British Academy.

Guillelmi Duranti Rationale divinorum officiorum. 1995. Edited by A. Davril and T. M. Thibodeau. Turnholti, Belgium: Brepols.

Hildegard of Bingen. 2010. *Physica. Liber subtilitatum diversarum naturarum creaturarum*. Edited by Reiner Hildebrandt and Thomass Gloning. Berlin: De Gruyter.

Hugh of St. Victor. 2007. *Hugh of Saint Victor on the Sacraments of the Christian Faith*. Translated by Roy Deferrari. Eugene, OR: Wipf & Stock.

Isidore of Seville. 2006. *The Etymologies*. Edited by Stephen A. Barney. Cambridge, New York: Cambridge University Press.

Selden, John. 1695. *De jure naturali et gentium*. Leipzig: Schrey.

Bibliography

Kant, Immanuel. 1949. *Critique of Practical Reason and Other Writings in Moral Philosophy.* Chicago: University of Chicago Press.
Novatian. 1972. *De cibis iudaicis.* Edited by G. F. Diercks. CCSL 4. Vienna: Österreichischen Akademie der Wissenschaften.
Osiander, Andreas. 1975–97. *Gesamtausgabe.* Edited by Gerhard Müller and Gottfried Seebass. Gütersloh: Gütersloher Verlagshaus Mohn.
Outram, W. 1770. *De sacrificiis.* Translated by John Allen as *Two Dissertations on Sacrifices: The First on All the Sacrifices of the Jews.* London. Holdsworth and Ball.
Paludanus, Johannes. 1620. *Vindiciae theologicae aduersus verbi dei corruptelas* Antwerp: Aertssius.
Robertson Smith, William. 1894. *Religion of the Semites.* London: Black.
Voltaire. 2010. *La Bible Enfin Expliquée* V1 (1777). Whitefish, MT: Kessinger.

Secondary Literature

Affolter-Nydegger, Ruth. 2000. "Hugo, Richard und Andreas von St. Viktor als Exegeten." In *Sinnvermittlung: Studien zur Geschichte von Exegese und Hermeneutik,* I, edited by Paul Michel and Hans Weder, 173–206. Zürich: Pano.
Ages, Arnold. 1965. "Calmet and the Rabbis." *Jewish Quarterly Review* 55.4: 340–49.
Albarello, Carlo. 2003. "Walafrid Strabo commente l'Exode: tradition textuelle et grammaire exégétique." *Recherches Augustiniennes* 33: 179–207.
Angenendt, Arnold. 1993. "Mit reinen Händen: Das Motiv der kultischen Reinheit in der abendländischen Askese." In *Herrschaft, Kirche, Kultur,* edited by G. Jenal, 297–316. Stuttgart: Hiersemann.
———. 1994. *Heilige und Reliquien: Die Geschichte ihres Kultes vom frühen Christentum bis zur Gegenwart.* Munich: Beck.
———. 2000. *Geschichte der Religiosität im Mittelalter.* Darmstadt: Primus.
———. 2003. *Grundformen der Frömmigkeit im Mittelalter.* Munich: Oldenbourg.
———. 2008. "Sacrifices, Gifts and Prayers in Latin Christianity." In *Cambridge History of Christianity c. 600–c.1100,* edited by Thomas F. X. Noble, Julia M. H. Smith, 453–71. Cambridge: Cambridge University Press.
Arduini, Maria Lodovica. 1979. *Ruperto di Deutz e la controversia tra Cristiani ed Ebrei nel secolo XII: Contesto critico dell' Annulus seu dialogus inter Christianum et Iudaeum.* Edited by Rhabanus Haacke. Rome: Istituto storico italiano per il medioevo.
Armogathe, Jean-Robert. 1989. "Epilogue." In *Le grand siècle et la bible.* Paris: Beauchesne.
———. 2001a. "Les deux livres." *Revue de théologie et de philosophie* 133: 211–25.
———. 2001b. "Per annos mille: Cornelius a Lapide et l'interprétation d'Apocalypse XX." In *Formes du millénarisme en Europe à l'aube des temps modernes,* edited by Jean-Raymond Fanlo and Andre Tournon, 97–108. Paris: Champion.
Assmann, Jan. 1991. "Der zweidimensionale Mensch: Das Fest als Medium des kollektiven Gedächtnisses." In *Das Fest und das Heilige,* edited by Jan Assmann and Theo Sundermeier, 13–30. Gütersloh: Mohn.
Auf der Maur, Hansjörg. 1983. *Feiern im Rhythmus der Zeit I. Herrenfeste in Woche und Jahr.* Regensburg: Pustet.
Aumann, Jordan. 1980. *Spiritual Theology.* London: Sheed and Ward, 1980.
Backhaus, Knut. 2009. *Der Hebräerbrief.* Regensburg: Pustet.

Bailey, Joanne. 2003. *Unquiet Lives: Marriage and Marriage Breakdown in England, 1660-1800.* Cambridge: Cambridge University Press.

Balthasar, Hans Urs von. 1993. *Explorations in Theology: Creator Spirit.* San Francisco: Ignatius.

Barth, Karl. 2003. *Gesamtausgabe I. Predigten 1954-1967.* 3 vols. Zürich: TVZ.

Bataillon, Louis Jacques. 1986. "De la lectio à la praedicatio. Commentaires bibliques et sermons au XIIIème siècle." In *Revue des sciences philosophiques et théologiques* 70: 559-74.

Bataillon, L.-J., G. Dahan, and P.-M. Gy, eds. 2004. *Hugues de Saint-Cher († 1263), bibliste et théologien.* Brepols, Belgium: Turnhout.

Baudissin, W. H. Graf. 1878. *Der Begriff der Heiligkeit im Alten Testament.* Heidelberg: Grunow.

Beatrice, Pier Franco. 1978. *Tradux Peccati: Alle fonti della dottrina agostiniana del peccato orignale.* Milan: Vita e Pensiero.

Bedouelle, Guy. 1990. "The Consultations of the Universities and Scholars concerning the 'Great Matter' of King Henry VIII." In *The Bible in the Sixteenth Century*, edited by David C. Steinmetz, 21-36. Durham, NC: Duke University Press.

Bedouelle, Guy and Le Gal, Patrick. 1987. *Le "divorce" du roi Henry VIII: études et documents.* Geneva: Droz.

Benrath, Gustav Adolf. 1985. "Die theologische Fakultät der Hohen Schule Herborn im Zeitalter der reformierten Orthodoxie (1584-1634)." *Jahrbuch der Hessischen Kirchengeschichtlichen Vereinigung* 36: 1-17.

Bergen, Wesley J. 2005. *Reading Ritual: Leviticus in Postmodern Culture.* London: T. & T. Clark International.

Bériac, Françoise. 1988. *Histoire des lépreux au moyen âge. Une société d'exclus.* Paris: Imago.

Bériou, Nicole, and Touati, François-Olivier. 1991. *Voluntate Dei Leprosus: Les Lépreux entr conversion et exclusion aux XIIeme et XIIIeme siècles.* Spoleto: Centro italiano di studi sull'alto Medioevo.

Berkowitz, Beth A. 2007. *Execution and Invention: Death Penalty Discourse in Early Rabbinic and Christian Cultures.* New York: Oxford University Press.

Bertholet, Alfred. 1901. *Leviticus.* Tübingen: Mohr Siebeck.

Bieler, Ludwig. 1963. *The Irish Penitentials.* Dublin: Four Courts.

Blacketer, Raymond A. 2006a. "Calvin as Commentator on the Mosaic Harmony and Joshua." In *Calvin and the Bible*, edited by Donald McKim, 30-52. Cambridge: Cambridge University Press.

———. 2006b. *The School of God: Pedagogy and Rhetoric in Calvin's Interpretation of Deuteronomy.* Dordrecht: Springer Netherlands.

Boda, Mark. 2007. *A Severe Mercy: Sin and Its Remedy in the Old Testament.* Winona Lake, IN: Eisenbrauns, 2009.

Bonar, Andrew A. 1984. *Andrew A. Bonar: Diary and Life.* Edited by Marjory Bonar. Edinburgh: Banner of Truth.

Bori, Pier Cesare. 1987. *L'Interpretazione Infinita: L'ermeneutica cristiana antica e le sue transformazioni.* Bologna, Italy: Il Mulino.

Bos, Frans L. 1932. *Johannes Piscator; ein Beitrag zur Geschichte der reformierten Lehre.* Kampen: Kok.

Boss, Gerhard. 1962. *Die Rechtfertigungslehre in den Bibelkommentaren des Kornelius a Lapide.* Münster: Aschendorff.

Bibliography

Boswell, John. 1981. *Christianity, Social Tolerance and Homosexuality: Gay People in Western Europe from the Beginning of the Christian Era to the Fourteenth Century*. Chicago: University of Chicago Press.

Boulhol, Pascal. 2002. *Claude de Turin: Un Évêque iconoclaste dans l'occident carolingien*. Paris: Augustiniennes.

Brade, Lutz. 1975. *Untersuchungen zum Scholienbuch des Theodoros Bar Konai: Die Ubernahme des Erbes von Theodoros von Mopsuestia in der nestorian Kirche*. Wiesbaden, Germany: Harrassowitz.

Bradshaw, Paul. 1996. "Priester/Priestertum, III/1." *Theologische Realenzyklopädie* 27: 414–21.

Brandy, Hans Christian. 1991. *Die späte Christologie des Johannes Brenz*. Tübingen: Mohr Siebeck.

Brecht, Martin. 2000. "Brentii Ecclesia. Der Prediger von Schwäbisch Hall und seine Kirche." *Blätter für württembergische Kirchengeschichte. Im Auftrag des Vereins für württembergische Kirchengeschichte* 100: 186–214.

Breuer, Edward. 2001. "Naphtali Herz Wessely and the Cultural Dislocations of an Eighteenth Century Maskil." In *New Perspectives on the Haskalah*, edited by S. Feiner and D. Sorkin, 27–47. London: Littman Library.

———. 2008. "Jewish Study of the Bible Before and During the Jewish Enlightenment." In *Hebrew Bible/Old Testament, II*, edited by M. Saebø, 1006–230. Göttingen: Vandenhoeck & Rupprecht.

Breytenbach, Cilliers. 1989. *Versöhnung*. Neukirchen: Neukirchener Verlag.

Brière, Maurice. 1960. *Les Homiliae Cathedrales de Sévère d'Antioche*. Syriac translation by Jacques d'Édesse. Patrologia Orientalis 29. Turnhout, Belgium: Brepols.

———. 1978. "Sancti Philoxeni Episcopi Mabbugensis Dissertationes decem de uno e sancta Trinitate incorporato et passo (Memre contre Habib). III, Dissertationes 6a, 7a, 8a." Translated by M. Brière and F. Graffin. Patrologia Orientalis 39. Turnhout, Belgium: Brepols.

Brodman, James William. 2009. *James Charity and Religion in Medieval Europe*. Washington, DC: Catholic University of America Press.

Browe, Peter. 1967. *Die Verehrung der Eucharistie im Mittelalter*. Munich: Hüber.

———. 2007. *Die Eucharistie im Mittelalter*. 2 vols. Berlin: LIT.

Brundage, James A. 1995. *Medieval Canon Law*. London: Longman.

Buchinger, Harald. 2005. *Pascha bei Origenes*. Innsbruck: Tyrolia.

Burkert, W. 1984. *Anthropologie des religiösen Opfers. Die Sakralisierung der Gewalt*. Munich: Fink.

Buytaert, Eloi Marie. 1949. *L'héritage littéraire d'Eusèbe d'Émèse: Etude Critique et Historique*. Louvain: Bibliothèque du Muséon 24.

Bynum, Caroline Walker. 2007. *Wonderful Blood: Theology and Practice in Late Medieval Northern Germany and Beyond*. Philadelphia: University of Pennsylvania Press.

Camelot, Pierre Thomas. 1988. "Procope de Gaza." *Catholicisme* 53: 1117.

The Canons of Hippolytus. 1987. Edited by Paul Bradshaw. Bramcote, UK: Grove.

Carlson, Eric Josef. 1994. *Marriage and the English Reformation*. Cambridge, MA: Blackwell.

Carmichael, Calum. 2006. *Illuminating Leviticus: A Study of Its Laws and Institutions in the Light of Biblical Narratives*. Baltimore: Johns Hopkins.

Casel, O. 1960. *Das christliche Kultmysterium*. Regensburg: Pustet.

Cazeaux, Jacques. 2007. *La contre-épopée du desert: Essai sur Exode-Lévitique-Nombres.* Paris: Cerf.

Chadwick, R. 2004 "Alexander Mclaren." *Dictionary of National Biography.* Online edition. http://www.oxforddnb.com/

Châtillon, J. 1955. "Isidore et Origène. Recherches sur les sources et l'influence des Questiones." In *Vetus Testamentum d'Isidore de Séville: Melanges bibliques rédigés en honneur de André Robert,* 337–547. Paris: Bloud et Gay.

———. 1992. *Le Mouvement Canonial a Moyen Âge: Réforme sde l'église spiritualité et culture,* études réeunies par Patrice Sicard. Paris: Brepols.

Chydenius, Johan. 1965. *Medieval Institutions and the Old Testament.* Helsinki: Helsingfors.

Clarke, E. G. 1962. *The Selected Questions of Isho bar Nun on the Pentateuch.* Leiden: Brill.

Cooper, Alan. 2004. "A Medieval Jewish Version of Original Sin: Ephraim of Luntshits on Leviticus 12." *Harvard Theological Review* 97: 445–59.

Coppens, J. 1971. "Le Sacerdoce Chrétien: Ses orgines et son développement." In *Sacerdoce et Célibat: Études Historiques et Théologiques,* edited by J. Coppens, 49–101. Louvain: Peeters.

Coster, Will. 1990. "Purity, Profanity and Puritanism: The Churching of Women 1500–1700." In *Women in the Church,* edited by W. Sheils and D. Wood, 377–87. Oxford: Blackwell.

———. 2000. "Tokens of Innocence: Infant Baptism, Death and Burial in Early Modern England." In *The Place of the Dead: Death and Remembrance in Late Medieval and Early Modern Europe,* edited by Bruce Gordon and Peter Marshall, 266–87. Cambridge: Cambridge University Press.

Cottret, Bernard. 2003. "Calvin, entre la Loi et la Parole." In *Bible et literature,* edited by O. Millet, 53–70. Paris: Champion.

Countryman, William. 1988. *Dirt, Greed and Sex.* Philadelphia: Fortress.

Courtenay, William. 1985. "The Bible in the Fourteenth Century." *Church History* 54: 176–87.

Crawford, Patricia. 2004. *Blood, Bodies and Families in Early Modern England.* Harlow: Pearson Education.

Cressy, David. 1993. "Purification, Thanksgiving and the Churching of Women in Post-Reformation England." *Past and Present* 141: 106–46.

Crossan, John Dominic. 1982. "Difference and Divinity." *Semeia* 23: 29–40.

Dahan, Gilbert. 1985. "Les interprétations juives dans les commentaires du pentateuque de Pierre le Chantre." In *The Bible in the Medieval World: Essays in Memory of Beryl Smalley,* edited by Catherine Walsh, 131–55. Oxford: Blackwell.

———. 1999. *L'exégèse chrétienne de la Bible en Occident médiéval, XIIe–XIVe siècle.* Paris: Cerf.

———. 2002. "Le Commentaire medieval de la bible. Le passage au sens spirituel." In *Le commentaire entre tradition et innovation,* edited by M.-O. Goulet-Cazé, 213–32. Paris: Vrin.

———. 2004. "L'Exegese de Hugues. Méthode et hérmeneutique." In *La méthode critique au moyen âge,* edited by M. Chazan and G. Dahan, 65–100. Turnhout, Belgium: Brepols.

———. 2005. "L'exégèse de la bible chez Guillaume d'Auvergne." In *Autour de Guillaume d'Auvergne,* edited by F. Morenzoni and J.-Y. Tilliette, 237–70. Turnhout: Brepols.

Dalferth, Ingolf. 1994. *Der auferweckte Gekreuzigte. Zur Grammatik der Christologie.* Tübingen: Mohr Siebeck.

Danieli, M. I. 2000. "Levitico." In *Dizionario Origene: La cultura, il pensiero, le opere,* edited by A. M. Castagno, 236–37. Rome: Città Nuova.

Bibliography

Davidowitz, K. S. 2006. "Schoah." *Lexikon für Theologie und Kirche* 3. Aufl., 9: 195. Freiburg: Herder.

de Boer, Erik A. 2003. *John Calvin on the Visions of Ezekiel: Historical and Hermeneutical Studies in John Calvin's "Sermons Inedits," Especially on Ezek. 36–48.* Leiden: Brill.

———. 2007. "*Harmonia Legis*: Conception and Concept of John Calvin's Expository Project on Exodus-Deuteronomy (1559–63)." *Church History and Religious Culture* 87: 173–201.

Demaître, Luke. 2007. *Leprosy in Premodern Medicine: A Malady of the Whole Body*. Baltimore, MD: Johns Hopkins University Press.

Demarest, Bruce. 1976. *A History of Interpretation of Hebrews 7,1–10 from the Reformation to the Present*. Tübingen: Mohr Siebeck.

Demmer, Klaus. 1995. "Gelübde III: Theologisch-ethisch." *Lexikon für Theologie und Kirche* 3. Aufl., 4: 415–16.

d'Esneval, Amaury. 1978. "La division de la Vulgate latine en chapitres dans l'édition parisienne du XIIIe siècle." *Revue des Sciences Philosophique et Théologique* 62: 559–68.

de Jong, Mayke. 1976. *L'inspiration biblique d'Etienne Langton d'après le commentaire sur Ruth et les Interpretationes nominum hebraicorum*. PhD diss., University of Caen.

———. 1995. "Old Law and New-Found Power." In *Centers of Learning*, edited by J. Drijvers, 161–76. Leiden: Brill.

de Lubac, Henri. 1959. *Exégèse médiévale: les quatre sens de l'Écriture*. Paris: Aubier.

Deuschle, Matthias. 2006. *Brenz als Kontroverstheologe: Die Apologie der Confessio Virtembergica und die Auseinandersetzung zwischen Johannes Brenz und Pedro de Soto*. Tübingen: Mohr Siebeck.

Dillmann, August. 1897. *Die Bücher Exodus und Leviticus*. Edited by Victor Ryssel. 3rd ed. Leipzig: Hirzel.

Dittmann, Wolfgang. 1966. *Hartmanns Gregorius. Untersuchungen zur Überlieferung, zum Aufbau und Gehalt*. Berlin: Schmidt.

Donnelly, John Patrick. 1976. "Calvinist Thomism." *Viator* 7: 441–55.

Donovan, Daniel. 1970. *The Levitical Priesthood and the Ministry of the New Testament*. Münster: Privately Published.

Douglas, Mary. 1966. *Purity and Danger: An Analysis of the Concepts of Pollution and Taboo*. London: Routledge.

———. 1975. *Implicit Meanings: Essays in Anthropology*. London: Routledge.

———. 2001. *Leviticus as Literature*. New York: Oxford University Press.

Driver, G. R. 1956. "Three Technical Terms in the Pentateuch." *Journal of Semitic Studies* 1: 97–98

Drobner, Hubertus R. 1990. "Die Himmelfahrtspredigt Gregors von Nyssa." In *ERMHNEUMATA: Festschrift für Hadwig Hörner zum sechzigsten Geburtstag*, edited by Herbert Eisenberger, 95–115. Heidelberg: Carl Winter Universitätsverlag.

du Roy, Olivier. 2008. "The Golden Rule as the Law of Nature, from Origen to Martin Luther." In *The Golden Rule: The Ethics of Reciprocity in World Religions*, edited by Jacob Neusner and Bruce Chilton, 88–98. New York: Continuum.

Duval, Yvette. 1988. *Auprès des Saints. Corps et âme*. Paris: Desclée.

Eberhart, Christian. 2002. *Studien zur Bedeutung der Opfer im Alten Testament. Die Signifikanz von Blut- und Verbrennungsriten im kultischen Rahmen*. Neukirchen: Neukirchener.

Ebner, Martin, ed. 2003. *Das Fest: Jenseits des Alltags*. Neukirchen-Vluyn: Neukirchener.

Eco, Umberto. 2007. *On Ugliness*. Rizzoli, NY: Rizzoli.

Ego, Beate, Armin Lange, and Peter Pilhofer, eds. 1999. *Gemeinde ohne Tempel: Zur Substituierung und Transformation des Jerusalemer Tempels und seines Kults im Alten Testament, antiken Judentum und frühen Christentum.* Tübingen: Mohr.

Edwards, Burton van Name. 2003. "Deuteronomy in the Ninth Century." In *The Study of the Bible in the Carolingian Era*, edited by Celia Chazelle and Burton Van Name Edwards, 97–113. Turnholt, Belgium: Brepols.

Elliger, Karl. 1966. *Leviticus.* Tübingen: Mohr Siebeck.

Elliott. Mark W. 2008. "Leviticus in the Low Countries: Lapide and Grotius." In T. Römer, *Leviticus and Numbers*, 677–84. Leuven: Peeters.

———. 2009. "Four Types of Early Modern Reading of Leviticus 16." In W. François and A. van Hollander (eds.), *Infant Milk or Hardy Nourishment? The Bible for Lay People and Theologians in the Early Modern Period*, 451–65. Leuven: Peeters.

———. 2010. "Leviticus between Fifth-Century Jerusalem and Ninth-Century Merv." In Vahan S. Hovhanessian, *The Old Testament as Authoritative Scripture in the Early Churches of the East*, 35–42. New York: Peter Lang.

Emery, Kent. 1988. "Twofold Wisdom and Contemplation in Denys of Ryckel (Dionysius Carthusiensis, 1402–1471)." *Journal of Medieval and Renaissance Studies* 18: 99–134.

Esneval, A. d'. 1981. "Le perfectionnement d'un instrument de travail au début du XIIIe siècle: les trois glossaires bibliques d'Etienne Langton (1976)." In *Culture et travail intellectuel dans l'Occident médiéval. Bilan des 'Colloques d'humanisme médiéval' (1960-1980)*, edited by G. Hasenohr and J. Longère, 163–75. Paris: Centre national de la recherche scientifique.

Euler, Carrie. 2003. "Heinrich Bullinger, Marriage, and the English Reformation: 'The Christen State of Matrimonye' in England, 1540–53." *Sixteenth Century Journal* 34: 367–93.

Evans, G. R. 1986. *The Thought of Gregory the Great.* New York: Cambridge University. Press.

———. 2004. "Gloss or Analysis? A Crisis of Exegetical Method in the Thirteenth Century." In *La Bibbia del XIII secolo: Storia del testo, storia dell'esegesi*, edited by G. Cremascoli and F. Santi, 93–112. Firenze: SISMEL.

Fabry, Heinz-Josef, and Hans-Winfried Jüngling, eds. 1999. *Levitikus als Buch.* Berlin: Philo.

Felici, Lucia 1995. *Tra Riforma Ed Eresia: La Giovinezza Di Martin Borrhaus (1499–1528).* Firenze: Olschki.

Felmberg, Bernhard. 1998. *Die Ablaßtheologie Kardinal Cajetans (1469–1534).* Leiden: Brill.

Field, Teresa. 1991 "Biblical Influences on the Medieval and Early Modern English Law of Sanctuary." *Ecclesiastical Law Journal* 2: 222–25.

Firey, Abigail. 2009. *A Contrite Heart: Prosecution and Redemption in the Carolingian Empire.* Leiden: Brill.

Fitschen, K. "'Die Transformation der christlichen Festkultur. Von der Aufklärung zur Konfessionalisierung im 19. Jahrhundert." In *Das Fest: Jenseits des Alltags*, edited by Irmtraud Fischer and Christoph Markschies, 307–37. Neukirchen-Vluyn: Neukirchner.

Fitzpatrick, P. J. 1991. "On Eucharistic Sacrifice in the Middle Ages." In *Sacrifice and Redemption: Durham Essays in Theology*, edited by Stephen W. Sykes, 129–56. Cambridge: Cambridge University Press.

Fletcher, Anthony. 1994. "The Protestant Idea of Marriage in Early Modern England." In *Religion, Culture, and Society in Early Modern Britain: Essays in Honour of Patrick Collinson*, edited by A. Fletcher and Peter Roberts, 161–81. Cambridge: Cambridge University Press.

Bibliography

Fonrobert, Charlotte Elisheva. 2000. *Menstrual Purity: Rabbinic and Christian Reconstructions of Biblical Gender.* Stanford, CA: Stanford University Press.

Foreville, Raymonde. 1958. *Le Jubilé de saint Thomas Becket du XIIIe au XVe siècle (1220–1470).* Paris: S.E.V.P.E.N.

———. 1974. "Jubilé." *Dictionnaire de Spiritualité* 8, 1478–87. Paris: Beauchesne.

Frank, K. S. 1984. "Gelübde IV. Katholische Überlieferung und Lehre." *Theologische Realenzyklopädie* 12: 305–9.

Franks, Christopher A. 2009. *He Became Poor: The Poverty of Christians in Aquinas's Economic Teachings.* Grand Rapids, MI: Eerdmans.

Franz, Adolph. 1909. *Die Kirchlichen Benediktionen im Mittelalter.* Freiburg: Herder.

Frey, Jörg. 2005. "Probleme der Deutung des Todes Jesu in der neutestamentlichen Wissenschaft. Streiflichter zur exegetischen Diskussion." In *Deutungen des Todes Jesu im Neuen Testament*, edited by J. Frey and J. Schröter, 3–50. Tübingen: Mohr Siebeck.

Gane, Roy. 2005. *Cult and Character: Purification Offerings, Day of Atonement, and Theodicy.* Winona Lake, IN: Eisenbrauns.

Gaon, Solomon. 1993. *The Influence of the Catholic Theologian Alfonso Tostado on the Pentateuch Commentary of Issac Abravanel.* Hoboken: KTAV.

Garber, Zev, and Bruce Zuckerman. 1989. "Why Do We Call the Holocaust 'The Holocaust'? An Inquiry into the Psychology of Labels." *Modern Judaism* 9.2: 197–211.

Gaudemet, Jean. 1984. "Quellen des gratianischen Dekrets" *Ius commune* 11: 1–29.

Gerstenberger, Erhard. 1993. *Das Dritte Buch Moses.* Göttingen: Vandenhoeck and Ruprecht.

de Ghellinck, Joseph. 1939. *Littérature latin du moyen âge.* Paris: Bloud & Gay.

Gibaut, John. 1989. "Amalarius of Metz and the Laying on of Hands in the Ordination of a Deacon." *Harvard Theological Review* 82.2: 233–40.

Girard, René. 1987. *Things Hidden Since the Foundation of the World.* London: Athlone.

———. 1989. *The Scapegoat.* Baltimore: Johns Hopkins.

Glaser, Karl-Heinz, and Steffen Stuth, eds. 2000. *David Chytraeus (1530–1600): Norddeutscher Humanismus in Europa. Beiträge zum Wirken des Kraichgauer Gelehrten.* Ubstadt-Weiher, Germany: Regionalkultur.

Godden, M. R. 2001. "Gregory the Great and the Anglo-Saxons on the Dangers of Dreaming." In *Rome and the North: The Early Reception of Gregory the Great in Germanic Europe*, edited by R. H. Bremner, Kees Dekker, and David F. Johnson, 93–113. Paris: Peeters.

Goering J. 2008. "The Scholastic Turn (1100–1500): Penitential Theology and Law in the Schools." In *A New History of Penance*, edited by Abigail Firey, 219–37. Leiden: Brill.

Gordon, Bruce. 2008. *Calvin.* New Haven: Yale University Press.

Gorg, M. 1998. "Gelübde II. Altes Testament." *Religion in Geschichte und Gegenwart* 4. Aufl. Edited by Hans Dieter Betz et al., 3: 605–6. Tübingen: Mohr Siebeck.

Gorman, Michael. 1997. "The Commentary on Genesis of Claudius of Turin and Biblical Studies under Louis the Pious." *Speculum* 72: 279–329.

———. 1996. "The Commentary on the Pentateuch attributed to Bede in PL 91:189–394." *Revue Benedictine* 106: 61–108; 255–307.

Grabbe, Lester L. 1993. *Leviticus.* Society for Old Testament Study Old Testament Guides. Sheffield, UK: Sheffield Academic Press.

———. 2004. "Review of Mary Douglas, *Leviticus as Literature.*" *Journal of Ritual Studies* 18: 157–61.

Grabill, Stephen J. 2007. *Rediscovering the Natural Law in Reformed Theological Ethics.* Atlanta: Emory.

Grässer, E. 1993. *An die Hebräer 2*. Zürich: Benziger.
Graf, Friedrich Wilhelm. 1987. *Theonomie: Fallstudien zu Integrationsanspruch neuzeitlicher Theologie*. Gütersloh: Mohn.
Grégoire, Réginald. 1965. *Bruno de Segni, exégète médiéval et théologien monastique*. Spoleto, Italy: Centro italiano di studi sull'Alto Medioevo.
———. 1995. "Le interpretazioni altomedievali dei testi veterotestamenti sulla giustizia." In *La giustizia nell'alto medioevo (secoli V-VIII)*, 423-40. Spoleto, Italy: Centro italiano di studi sull'Alto Medioevo.
Greshake, Gisbert. 1998. *The Meaning of Christian Priesthood*. Dublin: Four Courts.
Griffiths, Richard, ed. 2001. *The Bible in the Renaissance: Essays on Biblical Commentary and Translation in the Fifteenth and Sixteenth Centuries*. Aldershot, UK: Ashgate.
Gruenwald, Ithmar. 2003. *Rituals and Ritual*. Leiden: Brill.
Guillet, Jacques. 1990. "Sainteté de Dieu- Sainteté de l'homme." *Dictionnaire de Spiritualité* 14: 184-92. Paris: Beauchesne.
Guinot, Jean-Noel. 1995. *L'Exégèse de Theodoret de Cyrrhus*. Paris: Beauchesne.
Gunneweg, A. H. J. 1988. *Vom Verstehen des Alten Testaments*. Göttingen: Vandenhoeck and Ruprecht.
Hagen, Kenneth. 1974. *A Theology of Testament in the Young Luther: The Lectures on Hebrews*. Leiden: Brill.
———. 1981. *Hebrews Commenting from Erasmus to Bèze 1516-1598*. Tübingen: Mohr.
Hailperin, Hermann. 1963. *Rashi and the Christian Scholars*. Pittsburgh: University of Pittsburgh Press.
Hallensleben, Barbara. 1985. *Communicatio: Anthropologie und Gnadenlehre bei Thomas de Vio Cajetan*. Münster: Aschendorff.
Halperin, M. 1990. *One Hundred Years of Homosexuality and Other Essays on Greek Love*. New York; London: Routledge.
Hardman Moore, Susan. 1991. "Sacrifice in Puritan Typology." In *Sacrifice and Redemption: Durham Essays in Theology*, edited by Stephen W. Sykes, 182-202. Cambridge: Cambridge University Press.
Harlé, Paul. 1986. *Le Lévitique: Bible d'Alexandrie*. Paris: Cerf.
Harrington, Hanna. 1996. "Interpreting Leviticus in the Second Temple Period: Struggling with Ambiguity." In *Reading Leviticus: A Conversation with Mary Douglas*, JSOT 227, edited by John Sawyer, 214-43. Sheffield, UK: Sheffield Academic Press.
Hartley, John E. 1992. *Leviticus*. Dallas: Word.
Hartmann, Wilfried, and Kenneth Pennington. 2008. *The History of Canon Law in the Classical Period, 1140-1234: From Gratian to the Decretals of Pope Gregory IX*. Washington, DC: Catholic University of America Press.
Hartwich, W. D. 1997. *Die Sendung Moses*. Munich: Fink.
Hausherr, Reiner. 1988. "Über die Auswahl der Bibeltextes in der Bible moralisée." *Zeitschrift für Kunstgeschichte* 51: 126-46.
Helmholz, R. H. 1974. *Marriage Litigation in Medieval England*. Cambridge: Cambridge University Press.
———. 1995. "The Bible in the Service of the Canon Law." *Chicago-Kent Law Review* 70: 1557-81.
———. 1996. *The Spirit of Classical Canon Law*. Athens: University of Georgia Press.
———. 2004. *The Oxford History of the Laws of England*. Vol. 1, *The Canon Law and Ecclesiastical Jurisdiction from 597 to the 1640s*. Oxford: Oxford University Press.

Bibliography

Heschel, Abraham. 1937. *Don Jizchak Abravanel*. Berlin: Reiss.

Hill, Robert C. 2001. "Old Testament Questions of Theodoret of Cyrus" *Greek Orthodox Theological Review* 46: 57–78.

Hirshman, Marc G. 2005. "Origen and the Rabbis on Leviticus." *Adamantius* 11: 93–100.

Hoffmann, Georg. 1973. "Lutherische Schriftauslegung im 17. Jahrhundert, dargestellt am Beispiel Abraham Calovs." In *Das Wort und die Wörter*, edited by H. Balz, S. Schulz, 127–42. Stuttgart: Kohlhammer.

Horvitz, R. 2006 "From Hegelianism to a Revolutionary Understanding of Judaism: Franz Rosenzweig's Attitude toward Kabbala and Myth." *Modern Judaism* 26: 31–54.

Hotson, Howard. 2007. *Commonplace Learning: Ramism and Its German Ramifications, 1543–1630*. Oxford: Oxford University Press.

Houlbrooke, Ralph A. 1998. *Death, Religion, and the Family in England, 1480–1750*. Oxford: Clarendon.

Houtman, Cornelius. 1994. *Der Pentateuch. Die Geschichte seiner Erforschung neben einer Auswertung*. Kampen, Germany: Pharos.

Ilich, Ivan. 1987. "Hospitality and Pain." Paper presented in Chicago. http://www.davidtinapple.com/illich/1987_hospitality_and_pain.PDF.

Iogna-Prat, Dominique. 2006. *La Maison Dieu*. Paris: Seuil.

Jagersma, Hendrik. 1972. *Leviticus 19: Identiteit, Bevrijding, Gemeenschap*. Assen, the Netherlands: Van Gorcum.

Janowski, Bernd. 1980. "Erwägungen zur Vorgeschichte des israelitischen selamîm-Opfers." *Ugarit-Forschungen* 12: 231–59.

———. 1982. *Sühne als Heilsgeschehen: Studien zur Sühnetheologie der Priesterschrift und zur Wurzel KPR im Alten Orient und im Alten Testament*. Neukirchen-Vluyn: Neukirchener.

Janowski, Bernd, and Erich Zenger. 2003. "Jenseits des Alltags: Fest und Opfer als religiöse Kontrapunkte zur Alltagswelt im alten Israel." In *Das Fest: Jenseits des Alltags*, edited by Irmtraud Fischer and Christoph Markschies, 63–102. Neukirchen-Vluyn: Neukirchener.

Jordan, Mark D. 1997. *The Invention of Sodomy in Christian Theology*. Chicago: University of Chicago Press.

Jung, Volker. 1999. *Das Ganze der Heiligen Schrift: Hermeneutik und Schriftauslegung bei A Calov*. Stuttgart: Calwer.

Jungmann, J. A. 1952. *Missarum sollemnia; eine genetische Erklärung der römischen Messe*. Vienna: Herder.

Jürgens, Benedikt. 2001. *Heiligkeit und Versöhnung: Leviticus 16 in seinem literarischen Kontext*. Freiburg: Herder.

Jüssen, Klaudius. 1931. *Die dogmatischen Anschauungen des Hesychius von Jerusalem, Tl. 1: Theologische Erkenntnislehre und Christologie*. Münster: Münsterische Beiträge zur Theologie.

———. 1957. "Die Mariologie des Hesychius von Jerusalem." In *Theologie in Geschichte und Gegenwart: M. Schmaus zum 60. Geburtstag*, edited by Johannes Auer and Hermann Volk, 651–70. München: Fink.

Kahles, Willhelm. 1960. *Die Geschichte als Liturgie: Die Geschichtstheologie des Rupertus von Deutz*. Münster: Aschendorff.

Karpp, Heinrich. 1969. *Die Busse. Quellen zur Entstehung des altkirchlichen Busswesens*. Zürich: EVZ.

Kasper, Walter. 1976. *Jésus le Christ*. Paris: Cerf.

Kaswalder, Enzo Cortese-Pietro. 1996. *Il Fascino del Sacro: Alla riscoperta del libro del Levitico*. Milan: San Paolo.

Kehl, Medard. 2006. "Priestertum. II Systematische-theologisch." *Lexikon für Theologie und Kirche* 8: 584–86.

Klauber, Martin I. 1993. "Between Protestant Orthodoxy and Rationalism: Fundamental Article in the Early Career of Jean LeClerc." *Journal of the History of Ideas* 54: 611–36.

Klauber, Thomas. 1969. "Fest." *Reallexikon für Antike und Christentum* 7: 747–66.

Klawans, Jonathan. 2000. *Impurity and Sin in Ancient Judaism*. Oxford: Oxford University Press.

Klepper, Deeana. 2007. *The Insight of Unbelievers: Nicholas of Lyra and Christian Reading of Jewish Text in the Later Middle Ages*. Philadelphia: University of Pennsylvania Press.

Klingbell, Gerald. 2007. *Bridging the Gap: Ritual and Ritual Texts in the Bible*. Winona Lake, IN: Eisenbrauns.

Geerlings, Wilhelm, and Christian Schulze, eds. 2002. *Der Kommentar in Antike und Mittelalater: Beiträge zu seiner Erforschung*. Clavis Commentariorum Antiquitatis et Medii Aevi 2. Leiden, Brill.

Klostermann, August. 1877. "Ezechiel und das Heiligkeitsgesetz." *Zeitschrift für Lutherische Theologie und Kirche* 38: 401–45.

Knipp, David. 1998. *"Christus Medicus" in der frühchristlicher Sarkophagskulptur* Leiden: Brill.

Knöppler, Thomas. 2001. *Sühne im Neuen Testament: Studien zum urchristlichen Verständnis der Heilsbedeutung des Todes Jesu*. Neukirchen: Neukirchener.

Kottje, Raymund. 1970. *Studien zum Einfluss des Alten Testaments auf Recht und Liturgie des frühen Mittelalters (6-8 Jahrhundert)*. Bonn: Röhrscheid.

———. 1980. *Die Bussbücher Halitgars von Cambrai und des Hrabanus Maurus*. Berlin: De Gruyter.

Kramer, Hans. 1974. *Unwiderrufliche Entscheidungen im Leben des Christen*. Munich: Schöningh.

Kraus, Hans-Joachim. 1982. *Geschichte der historisch-kritischen Erforschung des Alten Testaments*. 3rd ed. Neukirchen-Vluyn: Neukirchener.

Kremer, Jacob. 1985. *Lazarus, die Geschichte einer Auferstehung: Text, Wirkungsgeschichte und Botschaft von Joh. 11,1-46*. Stuttgart: Katholisches Bibelwerk.

Kristeva, Julia. 1982. *Powers of Horror: An Essay on Abjection*. Translated by L. S. Roudiez. Columbia: Columbia University Press.

Krochmalnik, Daniel. 2003. *Die Bücher Levitikus, Numeri, Deuteronomium im Judentum*. Neue Stuttgarter Kommentar Altes Testament 33/5. Stuttgart: Katholisches Bibelwerk.

Kuefler, Mathew. 2001. *The Manly Eunuch: Masculinity, Gender Ambiguity, and Christian Ideology in Late Antiquity*. Chicago: University of Chicago Press.

Kugel, James. 1998. *Traditions of the Bible*. Cambridge: Harvard University Press.

Kunzler, Michael. 2002. *The Church's Liturgy*. New York: Continuum.

Lacombe, G., and Beryl Smalley. 1930. "Studies on the Commentaries of Cardinal Stephen Langton." *Archives d'histoire doctrinale et littéraire du Moyen Age* 5: 5–266.

Lambert, G. 1950. "Jubilé hebreu et Jubilé chrétien." *Nouvelle Revue Theologique* 82: 234–51.

Landgraf, Artur. 1954. *Dogmengeschichte der Frühscholastik*, III.1. Regensburg: Pustet.

Lane, D. J. 2003. "The Reception of Leviticus: Peshitta Version." In *The Book of Leviticus: Composition and Reception*, edited by Rolf Rendtorff and Robert A. Kugler, 299–322. Leiden: Brill.

Bibliography

Laplanche, François. 1989. "Entre mythe et raison: l'exégèse biblique des protestants français au XVIIe siècle." *Foi et vie* 88: 3–20.

———. 1994. *La Bible en France entre mythe et critique*. Paris: Albin Michel.

———. 2006. *La crise de l'origine: la science catholique des Évangiles et l'histoire au XXe siècle*. Paris, Albin Michel.

Lares, Micheline Maurice. 1974. *Bible et civilisation anglaise: naissance d'une tradition*. Paris: Didier.

LeBoulluec, Alain. 2005. "La foi ('pistis') entre croyance et savoir selon Origène dans le 'Contre Celse.'" *Théologiques* 13: 59–78.

le Bras, Gabriel. 1938. "Les Écritures dans le Décret de Gratien." *Zeitschrift der Savigny-Stiftung für Rechtsgeschichte* 27: 47–80.

Leichtfried, Anton. 2002. *Trinitätstheologie als Geschichtstheologie: "De sancta Trinitate et operibus eius" Ruperts von Deutz*. Würzburg, Germany: Echter.

Leloir, Louis. 1971. "Valeurs permanents du sacerdoce Lévitique." In *Sacerdoce et Célibat. Études Historiques et Théologiques*, edited by J. Coppens, 23–47. Louvain: Peeters.

Leonhard, Clemens. 2000. "Tradition und Exegese bei Ishodad von Merv (9Jh.) am Beispiel der Opfer von Kain und Abel (Gen 4,2–5a)." In *Zu Geschichte, Theologie, Liturgie und Gegenwartslage der syrischen Kirchen Ausgewählte Vorträge des deutschen Syrologen-Symposiums vom 2.–4. Oktober 1998 in Hermannsburg*, edited by Martin Tamcke and Andreas Heinz, 139–79. Münster: LIT.

———. 2001. *Ishodad of Merv's Exegesis of the Psalms 119 and 139–147*. Leuven: Peeters.

Lépin, Marius. 1926. *L'idée du sacrifice de la messe d'après les théologiens depuis l'origine jusqu'à nos jours*. Paris: Beauchesne.

Leppin, Volker. 2004. "Einleitung." In *Historiographie und Theologie*, edited by W. Kinzig, Volker Leppin, and G. Wartenberg, 11–18. Leipzig: Evangelische.

Levene, Abraham. 1957. "Pentateuchal Exegesis in Early Syriac and Rabbinic sources." *Texte und Untersuchung* 63: 484–91.

Levine, Baruch. 1989. *Leviticus*. New York: JPTS.

Levinson, Wilhelm. 1943. *England and the Continent in the 8th Century*. Oxford: Oxford University Press.

Levy, Leonard W. 1993. *Blasphemy: Verbal Offence against the Sacred*. Chapel Hill, NC: University of North Carolina Press.

Lienhard, Joseph T. 2001. *Exodus, Leviticus, Numbers, Deuteronomy*. ACCS OT 3. Downers Grove, IL: InterVarsity.

———. 2002. "The Christian Reception of the Pentateuch: Patristic Commentaries on the Books of Moses." *Journal of Early Christian Studies* 10.3: 373–88.

Lipton, Sara. 1999. *Images of Intolerance: The Representation of Jews and Judaism in the Bible Moralisée*. Berkeley: University of California Press.

Lloyd, Gareth. 2007. *Charles Wesley and the Struggle for Methodist Identity*. Oxford: Oxford University Press.

Loetz, Francesca. 2002. *Mit Gott handeln*. Göttingen: Vandenhoeck and Ruprecht.

Lohse, Bernhard. 2003. *Mönchtum und Reformation: Luthers Auseinandersetzung mit dem Mönchsideal des Mittelalter*. Göttingen: Vandenhoeck and Ruprecht.

Lottin, Odon. 1942–1960. *Psychologie et morale aux XIIe et XIIIe siècles*. 6 Vols. Louvain: Abbaye du Mont César.

Loughlin, Gerard. 2006. "Omphalos." In *Queer Theology*, edited by G. Loughlin, 115–28. Oxford: Blackwell.

Luciani, Didier. 2005. *Le Lévitique Éthique et Esthétique* Bruxelles: Lumen Vitae.
Lutterbach, Hubertus. 1998. "Die Speisegesetzgebung in den mittelalterlichen Bußbüchern (600–1200). Religionsgeschichtliche Perspektiven." *Archiv für Kulturgeschichte* 80: 1–37.
———. 1999. *Sexualität im Mittelalter. Eine Kulturstudie anhand von Bußbüchern des 6. bis 12. Jahrhunderts.* Köln: Böhlau.
———. 2000. "Sexualität, IV. Historisch-theologisch." *Lexikon für Theologie und Kirche* (3. Aufl.) 9: 516–18.
———. 2003. "Die mittelalterlichen Bußbücher—Trägermedien von Einfachreligiosität?" *Zeitschrift für Kirchengeschichte* 115: 227–44.
———. 2007. "Sexualität macht unrein?" *Stimmen Der Zeit* 225: 31–43.
Macfarlane, Alan. 1986. *Marriage and Love in England.* Oxford: Blackwell.
MacLaren, Alexander. 1906. *The Books of Exodus, Leviticus, and Numbers.* London: Hodder & Stoughton.
Maier, Christel. 2006. "Rupert von Deutz: Befreiung von den Vätern. Schrifthermeneutik zwischen Autoritäten und intellektueller Kreativität." *La Revue de théologie et de philosophie* 73: 257–89.
Marshall, Peter. 1994. *The Catholic Priesthood and the Protestant Reformation.* Oxford: Clarendon.
Martyn, J. Louis. 1997. *Galatians.* New Haven: Yale University Press.
Martyn, John R. C. 2004. *The Letters of Gregory the Great.* Toronto: Pontifical Institute of Medieval Studies.
Massmann, Ludwig. 2003. *Der Ruf in die Entscheidung: Studien zur Komposition, zur Entstehung und Vorgeschichte, zum Wirklichkeitsverständnis und zur kanonischen Stellung von Lev 20.* Berlin: de Gruyter.
Maxwell-Stuart, P. G. 2002. "Bestiality in Early Modern Scotland." In *Sodomy in Early Modern Europe*, edited by Tom Betteridge, 82–93. Manchester; New York: Manchester University Press.
McHugh, J. P. 1991. "The Sacrifice of the Mass at the Council of Trent." In *Sacrifice and Redemption: Durham Essays in Theology*, edited by Stephen W. Sykes, 157–81. Cambridge: Cambridge University Press.
McNeill, J. T., H. M. Gamer, eds. 1990. *Medieval Handbooks on Penance.* New York: Columbia University Press.
Menk, Gerhard. 1980. "Das Restitutionsedikt und die kalvinistische Wissenschaft." In *Jahrbuch der Hessischen Kirchengeschichtlichen Vereinigung* 31: 29–63.
Michalski, J. A. 1915. "Raschis Einfluß auf Nicolaus von Lyra in der Auslegung von Lev. Num. Deut." *Die Zeitschrift für die Alttestamentliche Wissenschaft* 36: 29–63.
Milgrom, Jacob. 1971. "Leviticus, Book of." In *Encyclopedia Judaica*, vol. 11, edited by Cecil Roth, 147. Jerusalem: Keter.
———. 1998–2003. *Leviticus.* 3 vols. New York: Doubleday.
———. 2004. *Leviticus: A Continental Commentary.* Minneapolis: Augsburg Fortress.
Miller, Perry. 1956. *Errand into the Wilderness.* Cambridge: Harvard University Press.
Molenberg, Cornelia. 1990. *The Interpreter Interpreted: Iso Bar Nun's Selected Questions on the Old Testament.* PhD diss., Groningen University.
Moll, Helmut. 1975. *Die Lehre von der Eucharistie als Opfer. Eine dogmengeschichtliche. Untersuchung vom Neuen Testament bis Irenäus von Lyon.* Bonn: Hanstein.

Bibliography

Montecchio, Luca. 2000. "I Precedenti del Giubileo nell'Anno Mille?" In *Dante e il giubileo: atti del Convegno, Roma, 29–30 Novembre 1999*, edited by Enzo Esposito, 43–54. Firenze, Italy: Olschki.

Moody, Michael. 1987. "The Apostasy of Henry Ainsworth: A Case-Study in Early Separatist Historiography." *Proceedings of the American Philosophical Society* 131: 15–31.

Morey, James H. 1993. "Peter Comestor, Biblical Paraphrase and the Medieval Popular Bible." *Speculum* 68: 6–35.

Morin, M. 2000. "Dominique Grima, un exégète thomiste à Toulouse au début du xive siècle." In *Eglise et culture en France méridionale (xiie–xive siècle)*. Cahiers de Fanjeaux, 35: 325–74. Toulouse, France: privately published.

Mougel, D. A. 1896. *Denys le Chartreux, 1402–1471. Sa vie son role*. Montreuil-sur-Mer, France: Imprimerie de la Chartreuse de N.-D. des Près.

Mühling, Andreas. 2009. "Arminius und die Herborner Theologen: am Beispiel von Johannes Piscator." In *Arminius, Arminianism, and Europe: Jacobus Arminius (1559/60–1609)*, edited by Marius van Leeuwen, Keith D. Stanglin, and Marijke Tolsma, 115–34. Leiden: Brill.

Mullan, D. 2000. *Scottish Puritanism, 1590–1698*. Oxford: Oxford University Press.

Muller, Richard. 2003. "Henry Ainsworth and the Development of Protestant Exegesis in the Early Seventeenth Century." In *After Calvin: Studies in the Development of a Theological Tradition*, 156–74. New York: Oxford University Press.

Naphy, William. 2002. "Sodomy in Early Modern Geneva: Various Definitions, Diverse Verdicts." In *Sodomy in Early Modern Europe*, edited by Tom Betteridge, 94–111. Manchester: Manchester University Press.

Nasimiyu-Wasike, Anne. 1992. "Christianity and African Rituals of Birthing and Naming." In *The Will to Arise: Women, Tradition and the Church in* Africa, edited by M. A. Odoyoye and M. R. A. Kanyoro, 40–53. Marynoll, NY: Orbis.

Nautin, Pierre. 1977. *Origene: Sa vie et son oeuvre*. Paris: Beauchesne.

Nieden, Marcel. 1997. *Organum Deitatis: Die Christologie des Thomas de Vio Cajetan*. Leiden: Brill.

Nelson, Janet. 1977. "Inauguration rituals." In *Early Medieval Kingship*, edited by P. Sawyer and I. N. Wood, 50–71. Leeds, UK: University of Leeds.

Noonan, John T. 1957. *The Scholastic Analysis of Usury*. Cambridge: Harvard University Press.

North, Robert Grady. 2000. *The Biblical Jubilee . . . after Fifty Years*. Rome: Pontificio Istituto Biblico.

Noth, Martin. 1962. *Das dritte Buch Mose*. Göttingen: Vandenhoeck & Ruprecht. [= ET. 1965. *Leviticus: A Commentary*. London: SCM.]

Nüssel, F. 2005. "Die Sühnevorstellung in der klassischen Dogmatik und ihre neuzeitliche Problematisierung." In *Deutung des Todes Jesu im Neuen Testament*, WUNT 181, edited by J. Frey und J. Schröter, 73–94. Tübingen: Mohr Siebeck.

O'Connor, Michael. 2007. "Rhetoric and the Literary Sense: The Sacred Author's Performance in Cajetan's Exegesis of Scripture." In *Faithful Performances: Enacting Christian Tradition*, edited by Trevor A. Hart, Steven R. Guthrie, 109–21. Aldershot: Ashgate.

Ocker, Christopher. 2002. *Biblical Poetics Before Humanism and Reformation*. Cambridge: Cambridge University Press.

Ohst M. 1995. *Pflichtbeichte: Untersuchingen zum Busswesen im höhen und späten Mittelalter*. Tübingen: Mohr.

Oleaster, Jerome. 1556–58. Hieronymus. Commentaria in Pentateuchum Moysi. Lisbon.
Opitz, Peter. 1994. *Calvins theologische Hermeneutik*. Neukirchen-Vluyn: Neukirchener.
Otto, Eckart. 1994. *Theologische Ethik des Alten Testaments*. Stuttgart: Kohlhammer.
Padilla, C. R. 1996. "The Relevance of the Jubilee in Today's World (Leviticus 25)." *Mission Studies* 13: 12–31.
Parker, Charles H. 2003. "Calvinism and Poor Relief in Reformation Holland." In *The Reformation of Charity: The Secular and the Religious in Early Modern Poor Relief*, edited by Thomas Max Safley, 107–20. Leiden: Brill.
Pauck, W. 1961. *Introduction to Martin Luther, Lectures on Romans*. Louisville: Westminster.
Perrone, Lorenzo 1980. *La Chiesa di Palestina e le controversie cristologiche*. Brescia: Paideia.
Piattelli, D. 1998. "Religionsvergehen: II Altes Testament und Judentum." *Theologische Realenzyklopädie* 29: 51–54.
Poorthuis, M. J. H. M., and J. Schwartz. 2000. *Purity and Holiness: The Heritage of Leviticus*. Leiden: Brill.
Poschmann, Bernhard. 1928. *Die abendländische Kirchenbuße im Ausgang des christlichen Altertums*. Munich: Kösel.
Pralon, Didier. 1995. "L'allégorie au travail: Interprétation de Lévitique X par Philon d'Alexandrie." In *ΚΑΤΑ ΤΟΥΣ Ο': Selon les Septante*, edited by M. Harl, 483–97. Paris: Cerf.
Probst, Manfred. 1976. *Gottesdienst in Geist und Wahrheit: Die liturgischen Ansichten und Bestrebungen Johann Michael Sailers*. Regensburg: Pustet.
Quinto, Riccardo. 1994. *"Doctor Nominatissimus": Stefano Langton e la tradizione delle sue opera*. Münster: Aschendorff.
———. 1999. "L'idea del giubileo in alcuni commenti medievali al Levitico e nella letteratura teologica sino al 1250." *Studia Patavina* 46: 317–35.
———. 2001. "Giubileo e attesa escatologica." *Medioevo* 26: 25–109.
———. 2004. "La parabola del Levitico, in La Bibbia del XIII secolo: storia del testo, storia dell'esegesi." In *Convegno della Società Internazionale per lo Studio del Medioevo Latino, 1–2 Giugno 2001*, edited by G. Cremascoli and F. Santi, 187–267. Firenze, Italy: SISMEL.
Rahner, Karl. 1983. *Theological Investigations*, Vol. 15. London: Darton, Longman and Todd.
Ratzinger, Joseph. 1999. *Many Religions, One Covenant: Israel, the Church, and the World*. San Francisco: Ignatius.
———. 2000. *Der Geist der Liturgie*. Freiburg: Herder. [= ET 2000. *The Spirit of the Liturgy*. Translated by J. Saward. San Francisco: Ignatius.]
Rawcliffe, Carole. 2006. *Leprosy im Medieval England*. Woodbridge: Boydell.
Rendtorff, Rolf. 2004. *Levitikus 1–11*. Neukirchner-Vluyn: Neukirchener.
Rendtorff, Rolf, and Robert A. Kugler, eds. 2003. *The Book of Leviticus: Composition and Reception*. Leiden: Brill.
Ruether, Rosemary Radford. 1985. *Women-Church: Theology and Practice of Feminist Liturgical Communities*. San Fransisco: Harper & Row.
Reventlow, Henning-Graf. 1988a. "Bibelexegese als Aufklärung. Die Bibel im Denken des Johannes Clericus (1657–1736)." In *Historische Kritik und biblischer Kanon in der deutschen Aufklärung*, edited by H.-G. Reventlow, W. Sparn, and J. Woodbridge, 1–19. Wiesbaden: Harrassowitz.
———. 1988b. "Humanistic Exegesis: The Famous Hugo Grotius." In *Creative Exegesis and the Bible*, edited by H.-G. Reventlow and B. Uffenheimer, 175–191. Sheffield, UK: Sheffield Academic Press.

Bibliography

———. 1997. *Epochen der Bibelauslegung*, III. Munich: Beck.

Rexer, J. 2003. "Die Entwicklung des liturgischen Jahres in altkirchlicher Zeit." In *Das Fest: Jenseits des Alltags*, edited by Irmtraud Fischer and Christoph Markschies, 279–306. Neukirchen-Vluyn: Neukirchner.

Riché, P.- Lobrichon G., eds. 1984. *Le Moyen-Âge et la Bible*. Bible de tous les temps 4. Paris: Beauchesne.

Riess, R. 1995. *Abschied von der Schuld?* Stuttgart: Kohlhammer.

Rodrigues, Manuel Augusto. 1990. "Le Commentaire sur le Pentateuque de Fr. Jerónimo de Azambuja (Oleastro)." In *Théorie et pratique de l'exégèse*, edited by I. Backus, F. Higman, 231–41. Geneva: Droz.

Roll, Susan. 2003. "The Churching of Women after Childbirth." In *Wholly Women, Holy Blood*, edited by Kristin De Troyer, Judith A. Herbert, Judith Ann Johnson, and Anne-Marie Korte, 117–41. Harrisburg: Trinity.

Rose, Martin. 1977. "Konrad Pellikans Wirken in Zürich 1526–1556. Bemerkungen zur Einschätzung eines Lebenswerkes." *Zwingliana* 14: 380–38.

Ross, Allen P. 2002. *Holiness to the Lord: A Guide to the Exposition of the Book of Leviticus*. Grand Rapids, MI: Baker Academic.

Runia, David T. 1993. *Philo in Early Christian Literature: A Survey*. Philadelphia: Fortress.

Rüting, W. 1916. *Untersuchungen über Augustins Quaestiones et Locutiones in Heptateuchum*. Paderborn, Germany: Schöningh.

Ryan, L. 1962. "Patristic Teaching on the Priesthood of the Faithful." *Irish Theological Quarterly* 29: 25–51.

Sawyer, John F. A. 1976. "A Note on the Etymology of *Sara'at*." *Vetus Testamentum* 26: 241–45.

———. ed. 1996. *Reading Leviticus: A Conversation with Mary Douglas*. Sheffield, UK: Sheffield Academic Press.

Scarisbrick, J. J. 1997. *Henry VIII*. New Haven: Yale University Press.

Schachten, Winifried H. J. 1980. *Ordo Salutis: Das Gesetz als Weise der Heilsvermittlung; zur Kritik des Hl. Thomas von Aquin an Joachim von Fiore*. Münster: Aschendorff.

Schockenhoff, Eberhard. 1990. *Zum Fest der Freiheit. Theologie des christlichen Handelns bei Origenes*. Mainz: Grünewald.

Schenker, Adrian. 1989. "Gelübde im Alten Testament: unbeachtete Aspekte." *Vetus Testamentum* 39: 87–91.

———. 1993. "Die Rolle der Religion bei Maimonides und Thomas von Aquin. Bedeutung der rituellen und liturgischen Teile der Tora nach dem Führer der Unschlüssigen und der Theologischen Summa." In *Ordo sapientiae et amoris: Image et message de saint Thomas d'Aquin à travers les récentes études historiques, herméneutiques et doctrinales: Hommage au professeur Jean-Pierre Torrell*, edited by C.-J. Pinto de Oliveira, 169–93. Fribourg: Éditions Universitaires.

Schöllgen, Georg, and Frank L. Hoßfeld. 1994. "Hoherpriester." *Reallexikon für Antike und Christentum* 16: 4–58.

Schüle, A. 2003. "Ereignis versus Erinnerung. Gibt es eine moderne Festkultur?" In *Das Fest: Jenseits des Alltags*, edited by Martin Ebner, 353–78. Neukirchen-Vluyn: Neukirchner.

Schulte, Raphael. 1958. *Die Messe als Opfer der Kirche*. Münster: Aschendorff.

Schwager, R. 1978, *Brauchen wir einen Sündenbock? Gewalt und Erlösung in den biblischen Schriften*. Munich: Kösel.

Schwartz, Baruch J. 2003. "Leviticus." In *The Jewish Study Bible*, edited by A. Berlin, M. Fishbane, and M. Z. Brettler, 203–80. New York: Oxford University Press.

Seidl, Theodor. 1982. *Tora für den Aussatz-Fall*. St. Ottilien, Germany: EOS.

Seifert, Arno. 1986. "Reformation und Chiliasmus. Die Rolle des Martin-Cellarius-Borrhaus." *Archiv für Reformationsgeschichte* 77: 226–64.

Selement, George. 1973. "The Covenant Theology of English Separatism and the Separation of Church and State." *Journal of the American Academy of Religion* 41: 66–74.

Sheridan, Mark. 2003. "The Influence of Origen on Coptic Exegesis in the Sixth Century." In *Origeniana Octava: Origen and the Alexandrian Tradition*, BETL 164, edited by L. Perrone, 1023–32. Leuven: Peeters.

Siemens, Peter. 1994. *Carl Friedrich Keil (1807–1888)*. Giessen: Brunnen.

Siquans, Agnethe. 2002. *Der Deuteronomiumkommentar des Theodoret von Kyros*. Frankfurt am Main: Lang.

Smalley, Beryl. 1968. "Ralph of Flaix on Leviticus." *Recherches de théologie ancienne et médiévale* 34: 35–82.

———. 1974. "William of Auvergne, John of La Rochelle and Thomas Aquinas on the Old Law." In *St. Thomas Aquinas, 1274–1974: Commemorative Studies*, edited by A. Maurer, vol. 2, 11–71. Toronto: PIMS.

———. 1981. "An Early Twelfth-Century Commentator on Leviticus." In *Studies in Medieval Thought and Learning*, 27–48. London: Hambledon.

———. 1984. "Glossa Ordinaria." *Theologische Realenzyklopädie* 13: 452–56.

Smith, Lesley. 2007. "Nicholas of Lyra and Old Testament Interpretation." In *Hebrew Bible/Old Testament: The History of its Interpretation*, vol. 2, edited by M. Saebø, 48–64. Göttingen: Vandenhoeck & Ruprecht.

Somerville, R. and B. C. Brasington, eds. 1998. *Prefaces to Canon Law Books in Latin Christianity: Selected Translations, 500–1245*. New Haven, CT: Yale University Press.

Southern, R. W. 2001. *Scholastic Humanism and the Unification of Europe*. Vol. 2. Oxford: Blackwell.

Spicq, Ceslas. 1944. *Esquisse d'une Histoire de l'Exégèse Latine au Moyen Age*. Paris: Librairie Philosophique J. Vrin.

Sprinkle, Preston. 2008. *Law and Life: The Interpretation of Leviticus 18:5 in Early Judaism and in Paul*. Tübingen: Mohr Siebeck.

Staley, Vernon. 1910. *The Seasons, Fasts and Festivals of the Christian Year*. Oxford: Mowbray.

Staubli, Thomas. 1996. *Die Bücher Levitikus, Numeri*. Stuttgart: Katholisches Bibelwerk.

Stefaneschi, Iacopo. 2001. *De centesimo seu iubileo anno*. Milan: Sismel Edizioni del Galluzzo.

Steck, Wolfgang, ed. 2000. *Der Liturgiker Amalarius: eine quellenkritische Untersuchung zu Leben und Werk eines Theologen der Karolingerzeit*. St. Ottilien, Germany: EOS.

Steiger, J. A., and U. Heinen, eds. 2006. *Isaaks Opferung (Gen 22) in den Konfessionen und Medien der Frühen Neuzeit*. Berlin: De Gruyter.

Stephens, Randall J. 2010. "The Holiness/Pentecostal/Charismatic Extension of the Wesleyan Tradition." In *The Cambridge Companion to John Wesley*, edited by R. L. Maddox and J. E. Vickers, 262–81. Cambridge: Cambridge University Press.

Stevenson, Jane. 1998. "Ephraim the Syrian in Anglo-Saxon England." *Hugoye: Journal of Syriac Studies* 1. Online: http://syrcom.cua.edu/Hugoye/vol1No2/HV1N2Stevenson.html.

Stewart, Columba. 1998. *Cassian the Monk*. Oxford: Oxford University Press.

Bibliography

Stewart, David Tabb. 2006. "Leviticus." In *The Queer Bible Commentary*, edited by D. Guest, R. E. Goss, M. West, and T. Bohache, 77–104. London: SCM.

Stoelen, A. 1953. "De Chronologie van de Werken van Dionysius de Kartuizer. De erste Werken en de Schriftkommentaren." *Sacris Eruditi* 5: 361–401.

Stoellger, P. 2005. "Deutung der Passion als Passion der Deutung. Zur Dialektik und Rhetorik des Todes Jesu." In *Deutung des Todes Jesu im Neuen Testament*, WUNT 181, edited by J. Frey and J. Schröter, 577–607. Tübingen: Mohr Siebeck.

Stone, Lawrence. 1990. *Road to Divorce: England 1530–1987*. Oxford: Clarendon.

Straw, Carole. 1989. *Gregory the Great: Perfection in Imperfection*. Berkeley: University of California Press.

Stroumsa, Guy G. 2009. *The End of Sacrifice: Religious Transformations in Late Antiquity*. Chicago: University of Chicago Press.

Swanson, R. N. 2007. *Indulgences in Late Medieval England: Passports to Paradise?* Cambridge: Cambridge University Press.

Tampellini, Stefano. 1996. "L'esegesi del Levitico di Esichio di Gerusalemme." *Annali di Storia dell'Esegesi* 13.1: 201–9.

———. 1999. "Aspetti di polemica antigiudaica nell'opera di Esichio di Gerusalemme (con particolare attenzione al 'Commentario al Levitico')." *Annali di Storia dell'Esegesi* 16.2: 353–58.

———. 2003 "Influssi alessandrini sul 'Commentario al Levitico' di Esichio di Gerusalemme: Confroti con Origene e con Cirillo di Alessandria." In *Origeniana Octava*, edited by L. Perrone, 1023–32. Leuven: Peeters.

Tillard, Jean-Marie Roger. 1987. "Sacerdoce." *Dictionnaire de Spiritualité* 14: 1–37.

Timmer, David E. 1989. "Biblical Exegesis and the Jewish-Christian Controversy in the Early Twelfth Century." *Church History* 58: 309–21.

Tischler, Matthias Martin. 2005. *Die Christus und Engel-weihe im Mittelalter*. Berlin: Akademie.

Torjesen, Karen Jo. 1986. *Hermeneutical Procedure and Theological Method in Origen's Exegesis*. Berlin: de Gruyter.

Track, Joachim. 1996. "Das Opfer am Ende. Eine kritische Analyse zum Opferverständnis in der christlichen Theologie." In *Abschied von der Schuld*, edited by Richard Riess, 140–67. Stuttgart: Kohlhammer.

Treue, Wolfgang. 1992. "Schlechte und gute Christen. Zur Rolle von Christen in antijüdischen Ritualmord- und Hostienschändungslegenden." *Aschkenas: Zeitschrift für Geschichte und Kultur der Juden* 2: 95–116.

Utzschneider, H. 1996 "Vergebung im Ritual. Zur Deutung des Hattat't Ritual (Sundopfer) in Lev 4,1–5,13." In *Abschied von der Schuld*, edited by Richard Riess, 96–119. Stuttgart: Kohlhammer.

Vaccarri, Alberto. 1918. "Esichio de Gerusalemme e il suo 'Commentarius in Leviticum.'" *Bessarione* 22: 8–46. [Reprinted in 1952. *Scritti erudizione e di filologia* 1: 165–206.]

Vallance, Edward. 2005. *Revolutionary England and the National Covenant: State Oaths, Protestantism and the Political Nation, 1553–1682*. Woodbridge, UK: Boydell.

van Engen, John. 1983. *Rupert of Deutz*. Berkeley: University of California Press.

———. 2001. "Ralph of Flaix: The Book of Leviticus Interpreted as Christian Community." In *Jews and Christians in Twelfth-Century Europe*, edited by Michael A. Signer and John Van Engen, 150–70. Notre Dame: Notre Dame Press.

van der Wall, Ernestine. 1993. "Between Grotius and Cocceius: The 'Theologia Prophetica' of Campegius Vitringa (1659–1722)." In *Hugo Grotius, Theologian: Essays in Honour of G. H. M. Posthumus Meyjes*, edited by Henk J. M. Nellen and Edwin Rabbie, 195–215. Studies in the History of Christian Thought 55. Leiden: Brill.

van Asselt, Willem J. 2001. *The Federal Theology of Johannes Cocceius: (1603–1669)*. Leiden: Brill.

Verger, Jacques. "L'exégèse de l'Université." In *Bible de tous les temps: Le Moyen Âge et la bible*, edited by P. Riché, G. Lobrichon, 199–232. Paris: Beauchesne.

Villien, Abbé. 1913. "Fêtes." *Dictionnaire de Théologie Catholique*, 5: 2183–91. Paris: Letouzey & Ané.

Vitali, Dario. 2006. "L'eucaristia in Bruno di Segni." *Rivista di Teologia* 47: 219–40.

Vizotsky, Burton L. 1998. *Fathers of the World*. Tübingen: Mohr Siebeck.

von Campenhausen, Hans F. 1963. *Kirchliches Amt und geistliche Vollmacht in den ersten drei Jahrhunderten*. Göttingen: Vandenhoeck & Ruprecht.

———. 1964. *Die Idee des Martyriums*. Gottingen: Vandenhoeck & Ruprecht.

Walker, P. W. L. 1990. *Holy City, Holy Places?: Christian Attitudes to Jerusalem and the Holy Land in the Fourth Century*. Oxford: Clarendon.

Wasselynck, René 1965. "L'influence de l'exégèse de Saint Grégoire le Grand sur les commentaires bibliques médiévaux." *Recherches de théologie ancienne et médiévale* 32: 165–92.

Wassermann, Dirk. 1996. *Dionysius der Kartäuser: Einführung in Werk und Gedankenwelt*. Salzburg: Institut für Anglistik und Amerikanistik, Universität Salzburg.

Watson, Francis. 2004. *Paul and the Hermeneutics of Faith*. Edinburgh: T. & T. Clark.

Watts, James. 2007. *Ritual and Rhetoric in Leviticus: From Sacrifice to Scripture*. Cambridge: Cambridge University Press.

Weinberg, Joanna. 2009. "A Rabbinic Disquisition of Lev 26:3–13." In *Scriptural Exegesis*, edited by D. A. Green and Laura S. Lieber, 121–34. Oxford: Oxford University Press.

Wendebourg, Dorothea 1984. "Die alttestamentliche Reinheit Gesetze in der frühen Kirche." *Zeitschrift für Kirchengeschichte* 95: 149–70.

Wenger, Antoine. 1956. "Hésychius de Jérusalem. Notes sur les sermons inédits et sur le texte grec du 'Commentaire sur le Lévitique.'" *Revue des études augustiniennes* 2: 457–70.

Wengert, Timothy. 1997. "The Biblical Commentaries." In *Philip Melanchthon (1497–1560) and the Commentary*, edited by T. Wengert and M. P. Graham, 106–48. Sheffield, UK: Sheffield Academic Press.

———. 2005. "The Priesthood of All Believers and Other Pious Myths." *Sessions of the Institute of Liturgical Studies* 2005. Online: http://www.valpo.edu/ils/publications.php.

Wenham, Gordon. 1992. *Leviticus*. NICOT. Grand Rapids: Eerdmans.

Wicks, Jared. 2008. "Catholic Old Testament Interpretation." In *Hebrew Bible/Old Testament: The History of Its Interpretation*, vol. 2: *From the Renaissance to the Enlightenment*, edited by Magne Sæbø, 617–48. Göttingen: Vandenhoeck & Ruprecht.

Wilken, Robert. 1995. "Origen's Homilies on Leviticus and Vayikra Rabbah." *Origeniana Sexta* 118: 81–91.

Witte, Jr., John. 1986. "The Reformation of Marriage Law in Martin Luther's Germany: Its Significance Then and Now." *Journal of Law and Religion* 4.2: 293–351.

Woodbridge, John. 1989. "German Responses to the Biblical Critic Richard Simon: from Leibniz to J. S. Semler." *Wolfenbüttler Forschungen: Historische Kritik und biblischer Kanon in der deutschen Aufklärung* 41: 65–80.

Bibliography

Wright, David F. 1983. "The Ethical Use of the Old Testament in Luther and Calvin: A Comparison." *Scottish Journal of Theology* 36: 463–85.

———. 1986. "Calvin's Pentateuchal Criticism: Equity, Hardness of Heart and Divine Accommodation in the Mosaic Harmony Commentary." *Calvin Theological Journal* 21: 33–50.

Zachman, Randall. 2007. *Image and Word in the Theology of John Calvin*. Notre Dame, IN: University of Notre Dame Press.

Zemler-Cizewski, Wanda. 2008. "Rupert of Deutz and the Law of the Stray Wife: Anti-Jewish Allegory in 'De sancta trinitate et operibus eius.'" *Recherches de Théologie et Philosophie Médiévales* 75: 257–69.

Zimmermann, A. 1931. "Bruno von Segni." *Lexikon für Theologie und Kirche*. 2: 596.

Zocca, Elena. 1996. "La lebbra e la sua purificazione nel 'Commentario al Levitico' di Esichio: Un tentativo di confronto con la tradizione esegetica precedente e contemporanea." *Annali di Storia dell'Esegesi* 13.1: 179–99.

Zürcher, Christoph. 1975. *Konrad Pellikans Wirken in Zürich, 1526–1556*. Zürich: Theologischer.

Zürcher, Josef. 1956–1960. *Die Gelübde im Ordensleben*. 3 vols. Einsiedeln, Switzerland: Benziger.

www.ingramcontent.com/pod-product-compliance
Lightning Source LLC
Chambersburg PA
CBHW080756300426
44114CB00020B/2736